ALEXANDER HAMILTON

'And in regions far,
  Such heroes bring ye forth
  As those from whom we came;
  And plant our name
  Under that star
Not known unto our North.'
        To the Virginian Voyage.
                —DRAYTON.

ALEXANDER HAMILTON

An Essay on American Union

BY

FREDERICK SCOTT OLIVER

NEW EDITION

WITH FRONTISPIECE AND A MAP

G. P. PUTNAM'S SONS

NEW YORK

1925

Printed in Great Britain by T. and A. CONSTABLE LTD.
at the University Press, Edinburgh

TO

THE MEMORY OF

CHARLES WELLINGTON FURSE

WHOSE FRIENDSHIP ENCOURAGED ME

TO UNDERTAKE THIS WORK.

PREFACE

I WISH to acknowledge the debt I owe to various friends who have done me the honour to read the proofs of this essay. I have not ceased to marvel at their kindness and their patience. Their advice has helped me at many points, and, although their frankness has occasionally been somewhat disconcerting, it has been mingled with encouragement. As a result I have completed a task which less biased critics may well consider to have been presumptuously undertaken.

In particular I have to thank Miss Mary Stubbert for her valuable assistance; but at the same time it is necessary to make it clear that she is not to be held responsible for the opinions I have ventured to express on men and events. I am well aware that in several instances she is in disagreement with my conclusions. I wish also to thank Mr. William Wallace, who has read and corrected all the proofs for the press, and has compiled the chronological table which will be found on pages 490-4.

The references need a few words of explanation. *The Works of Alexander Hamilton*, in twelve volumes, edited by Senator H. C. Lodge (2nd Federal Edition, 1904), and *The History of the Republic of the United States of America, as traced in the Writings of Alexander Hamilton and of his Co-temporaries*, in seven volumes, by his son John C.

Hamilton (1857), are mentioned in the footnotes for the sake of brevity as *Works* and *History* respectively. The *Life* which is quoted is *The Life of Alexander Hamilton*, in one volume, also by his son (1834). There are several modern lives and studies of Alexander Hamilton—by Mr. John T. Morse, jr., in two volumes (1882); by Senator H. C. Lodge (1886, 'American Statesmen' series); by Dr. W. G. Sumner (1890, 'Makers of America' series); *Hamilton and his Contemporaries*, by Mr. C. J. Riethmüller (1864); *Alexander Hamilton: a Historical Study* (1877), and *The Life and Epoch of Alexander Hamilton* (1879), by Mr. G. Shea. A comprehensive bibliography of the period will be found in the *Cambridge Modern History*, vol. vii. pp. 780-810.

The *History* by John C. Hamilton is open to all the objections that may be alleged against a life written by a son. It is the work of a vehement partisan. Nothing that Alexander Hamilton did is wrong, and all the deeds of his opponents are as black as ink. But, notwithstanding, it is a book of great value. Of the subject as a man it does not afford a single glimpse; but it abounds in evidence with regard to his career. It is full of quotations from the letters of friends and enemies, and the abstracts of debates are illuminating. Dr. Sumner's volume, on the other hand, has a considerable interest because it is written from the point of view of the American free-trader, and although the author generously acknowledges the great qualities of Hamilton, he boldly challenges his economic conclusions. Mr. Riethmüller's book was written during the War of Secession. It is full of sympathy, but arrives at a strange conclusion. Hamilton, in his opinion, would have acquiesced in the dismemberment of the Union.

It must be frankly admitted that no adequate life of Hamilton has yet been written. His achievements have been chronicled, praised and condemned; but in the case of such a character it is impossible to rest content with an account of his public deeds. Hamilton awaits a true interpreter, and it is hardly necessary to say that the present volume does not aim at supplying the deficiency.

The only vivid account of 'the man' with which I am acquainted is to be found in the historical romance by Mrs. Atherton, entitled *The Conqueror*. If the writer of a dusty, historical essay may speak without impertinence of the merits of such a work, I should venture to express my admiration for the insight of the authoress. Her presentment of Hamilton, in my humble judgment, is not merely a masterly work of art, but a most serious and truthful portrait.

Mrs. Atherton has led us to expect that one day she will give us an authentic life of her hero. I could have wished that she had accomplished her task before I had engaged on mine. At any rate I venture to express the hope, which many others must entertain, that her promise will not remain for long unfulfilled.

F. S. O.

CHECKENDON COURT, OXFORDSHIRE,
22nd January 1906.

CONTENTS

xi

BOOK III

THE FEDERALISTS (A.D. 1789-1791)

BOOK IV

THE DEMOCRATS (A.D. 1791-1794)

BOOK V

THE POLITICIANS (A.D. 1795-1804)

BOOK VI

CONCLUSION

INTRODUCTION

But be the worke-men what they may be, let us speake of the Worke; that is; the true greatnesse of kingdoms and estates; and the meanes thereof.—BACON.

ALEXANDER HAMILTON

INTRODUCTION

ENGLISHMEN for the most part are not learned in American history. Possibly at the bottom of their neglect lies an opinion that the study would prove more profitable than entertaining, richer in useful lessons and estimable characters than in stirring events and figures of a romantic interest. It is necessary to admit that the whole narrative has fallen under the suspicion of being somewhat akin to a moral tale, in which persons of Radical and Tory proclivities play the parts respectively of Sandford and Merton, in order that, in the end, democracy and business methods may be glorified in the eyes of men.

The wars of Independence and Secession are the only events with which, as a rule, an Englishman pretends to an acquaintance, and when he has stated it as his opinion that the former was a wise resistance to an intolerable oppression, and the latter a humane and heroic enterprise to put an end to slavery, he has usually come to the end of his conversation. It is not the purpose of this essay to question either of these judgments, but to consider a struggle entirely different in its character, which had its origin in the war with Britain and its sequel in the war between North and South.

When peace was signed in 1783 the States had indeed secured their independence, but union seemed even more remote and difficult of attainment than nine years earlier when the war began. The United States are to-day so firm a political fact that it is not unusual to overlook the critical and dangerous period during which they were disunited. We are apt to imagine that the war was waged against an enemy as compact as ourselves, not against thirteen jealous allies whose only serviceable bonds of union were an aspiration towards independence and a common enemy.

Another view of the matter has been put forward upon high authority. We have been told that, in the passionate heat of victory, a unanimous and patriotic impulse, working in half-molten metal, wrought and fashioned a noble constitution. This statement is dramatic, but untrue. No travesty of the facts could indeed be more complete. The metal was stone-cold, full of cracks and flaws and fissures, when the Convention of Philadelphia, six years later, welded it together. After more than four months of angry debate, the Union was in the end confirmed, but only by a narrow majority, and amid indignant protests. Upon its first announcement, it had many more enemies than friends throughout the continent. For every state claimed a separate sovereignty, and was reluctant to part with any shred of its authority. Only after a long and difficult assault were they persuaded that there would be a greater benefit in the surrender.

When the Constitution was at last acknowledged there remained a still more arduous undertaking; for it was necessary to set Government to work, to defend it against the open and covert attacks of the party of disintegration, and to devise a policy which should have sufficient strength and dignity, and hold upon the hearts of men to support the fabric of the Union.

In dramatic quality the history of the war is inferior to the course of events after the war had ended. The whole situation becomes more tense. The clash of personal forces is fiercer, the action swifter; motives, principles and tendencies are easier to comprehend. War is always a confusion, filled with irrelevant and distracting excitement. The hero, indeed, is visible, but his subordinates are a part of the spectacle, not actors in a drama. Private character is smothered by discipline or overwhelmed in a single patriotic purpose. On the signing of peace men begin to regain their humanity. Their tongues are loosened. Ideas and counter ideas spring up as soon as the frost-bound repression is relaxed. The interest shifts from the opposition of masses to the visions and beliefs, the rivalries and hatreds, of individual men.

In the Revolution, Alexander Hamilton played no prominent part. He was a boy at college when discontent drew to a head, and at the date of the skirmish of Lexington was only eighteen years of age. In the War of Independence his share was subordinate, though it was brilliant and effective. But when the war had ended, he became the master spirit of America.

In the great rebellion Washington was the master spirit. In the great struggle to prevent the breaking of the Union, Lincoln was the master spirit. In his fitness for the particular crisis Hamilton was the equal of these men, and it would be hard to find higher praise. In character he was their equal; in force of will; in efficiency; in practical wisdom; in courage and in virtue. But in a certain sense his greatness surpasses theirs, for it is more universal and touches the interest of the whole world in a wider circle. He was great in action which is for the moment, and in thought which is for all time; and he was great, not merely as a minister of state, but as a man of letters. In constancy it is customary to compare him with the younger Pitt, who was his contemporary. In political foresight and penetration it is no extravagance to place him by the side of Burke. He shares with Fox his astounding genius for friendship.

The end of the eighteenth century was a fertile period. Great men abounded in it. Talleyrand had known them all, and had contended with most of them. He was himself one of the greatest; certainly one of the coolest observers. He cherished few illusions, and it has never been said of him, even by his bitterest enemy, that he suffered his judgment to be duped by his affections. In statecraft he had a wide horizon, and his experience enabled him to make just comparisons. He mentions Hamilton with the greatest of his contemporaries, even with Napoleon, and mentions him with them in order to place him above them. Hamilton's portrait hung in his study till he died, and on it was an inscription in his own hand, ' that he had loved Hamilton and that Hamilton had loved him.'

To subjects of King Edward the history of the Union of the States should be of profound interest at the present time. Under many aspects the problems in America at the end of the eighteenth century and in the British Empire at the beginning of the twentieth bear a startling likeness to each other. In the memoirs of the chief actors we find a frequent echo of our own phrases. The attitudes of men, according to their various temperaments, are the same. There are the same enthusiasms and the same suspicions; the same vehement desires, indignant against all the race of sceptics; the same pleas of insuperable obstacles and the imprudence of a rash initiative. A slightly formal and old-fashioned speech enhances rather than conceals the likeness, as the portrait of an ancestor in prim cap or flowing periwig startles the beholder by its resemblance to some familiar youthful face.

This romantic influence is not without its danger, and is

apt to work in our minds with an excessive vivacity, luring us too readily to the conclusion that history is about to repeat itself. It is well to remember that when the gods arrange the pieces upon their broad chessboard in situations which surprise us by their similarity to the order of some previous game, it is commonly with the whimsical intention of solving the problem in an altogether different manner. Viewed with less excitement, the things themselves lose not a little of their likeness, and important differences appear. We are therefore well advised if we are wary and do not assume too much.

To say, at the present crisis, that the study of American history may prove useful and suggestive, is so obvious a reflection that it can only be excused by the almost universal omission to undertake the labour; but to conclude that the Union of the States is a precedent governing our own case would be idle talk. For it is the business of the British people to-day, as it has been for four centuries past, not to follow precedents, but to make them. If it were possible to find among the lives of the nations any parallel to the British Empire, it might be different; but no parallel exists in any records for so diverse and marvellous a growth.

One of the chief merits of the Americans when they framed their constitution was their earnest determination to consider the facts of their own case before all else, and their firm refusal to be led blindfold either by history or logic; and these, perhaps, are the only rules which can be recommended absolutely for every quandary, the only examples which it is safe to follow to the letter. Our eternal warning should be the Chinese tailor who copies a coat even to its patches. When we begin to grope and rummage for precedents, our decadence cannot be long delayed. The situation must be viewed by each race and generation boldly through its own eyes, not timorously with a forefinger in the guide-book of history. For though we turn over pages never so industriously to discover how foreigners or our own kinsmen have acted in circumstances somewhat alike, we shall never arrive at any ready-made solution of our difficulty.

Nor, on the other hand, is it the highest wisdom to entertain an undue reverence for our own institutions, for though these are an elastic garment, there may come a time when they will no longer serve. It is a vain hope that by cheerfully ignoring danger we shall avoid it. It is rash to assume that a constitution must always grow, and that it can never be made; or that, by spiriting and conjuring over the respectable antiquity of the Privy Council, we shall be able to convert the loose confederation of our Empire into a firm union.

BOOK I

THE INDEPENDENCE OF THE STATES

A.D. 1757–1783

*Character is of a stellar and undiminishable greatness. What others effect by talents or by eloquence, this man accomplishes by some magnetism. 'Half his strength he put not forth.' His victories are by demonstration of superiority, and not by crossing of bayonets. He conquers, because his arrival alters the face of affairs. 'O Iole! how did you know that Hercules was a God?' 'Because,' answered Iole, 'I was content the moment my eyes fell on him. When I beheld 'Theseus, I desired that I might see him offer battle, or at least guide 'his horses in the chariot race; but Hercules did not wait for a contest; 'he conquered whether he stood, or walked, or sat, or whatever thing he 'did.' Man ordinarily a pendant to events, only half attached, and that awkwardly, to the world he lives in, in these examples appears to share the life of things, and to be an expression of the same laws which control the tides and the sun, numbers and quantities.—*EMERSON.

BOOK I

THE INDEPENDENCE OF THE STATES

CHAPTER I

Boyhood

THE childhood of Alexander Hamilton ended when he A.D. 1757 was eleven years of age. For four years he was a storekeeper's clerk at St. Croix, in the Leeward Islands; for three he was a college student at New York; for six he was a soldier in the War of Independence. After these experiences, at the age of twenty-five, he was admitted to the bar. His professional career covered a period of twenty-two years; but during five of these he was Secretary of the Treasury in General Washington's cabinet, and withdrew entirely from practice during the term of his office. He was killed in a duel at the age of forty-seven, when his fame as a lawyer stood at its highest.

These are the main divisions of his life; but the bare catalogue gives an incomplete idea of his activity. While he was a student he wrote and spoke so as to produce a considerable influence upon the whole State of New York. While he was a soldier he was also an organiser, a diplomatist and a writer of despatches that have a world-wide celebrity. From the time he left the army and joined the bar until he became head of the most arduous department of government, his energies were more deeply engaged in promoting the Union of the States than in the practice of

11

A.D. 1757 the law. From the date of his retirement from the cabinet until his death he was at the same time leader of the bar and the acknowledged chief of a powerful political party. He was a boy for eleven years only. Perhaps it would be truer to say of him that he was a boy throughout the whole of his marvellous career.

For youth was the distinguishing note of his career. His triumph was the triumph of youth: his failure the failure of youth. His personal charm and exuberant confidence did not follow the normal course, mellowing in middle life into a genial tolerance, a quieter wisdom, a less vehement but more masterful efficiency. The change was in a contrary direction. He beheld mankind hobbling and hurrying after impossible compromises, striving timidly to keep the peace among their ideas by smiling with an equal favour upon the most irreconcilable and deadly enemies. It is true that under this disappointment his courage never flagged. His efforts were as heroic at the end as at the beginning. But his heart was filled with a fierce impatience and an anger which broke away at times from his control. Like a boy who has dreamed a dream, but cannot prevail with men to accept it in all its glorious symmetry, he came to despair of the consequences to a world containing so much obstruction and so many fools.

It is a rare occurrence under popular government for a young statesman to hold the predominant power, for the policy of a nation to be moulded by the thoughts of a fresh and eager mind, and executed by the vigour of a spirit not yet tamed to an immoderate reverence for obstacles. For where the people hold the ultimate control, a patient dexterity, with which no man was ever born, has in the long game of politics an undue advantage. Youth, with a wise instinct, abstains as a rule from conspicuous activity in serious matters until it has acquired the craft which is the necessary complement of its force, and when it bursts at A.D. 1757 last upon the admiration of its fellow-citizens, has entered into the shadowless and dusty realm of middle age.

This unfortunate exclusion of youth is to be lamented, for age is too considerate of rubbish. Like a housewife in her lumber-room, it shrinks from the wise sacrifice of useless possessions, pleading ever that at some future day they may recover a portion of their former value. The destructiveness and extravagance of youth are in many cases the best economy and the wisest defence of a nation. The perfect government would maintain the balance of youth and age, of confidence and experience, no less carefully than the balance of poor and rich, of force and breeding, of honesty and honour. The embargo on youth impoverishes the quality of statesmanship; but how to remedy the evil is a problem which still seeks an answer. All that is most excellent in popular government, the wide interest in public affairs, the sense of duty, the pursuit of a worthy ambition, tend to swell the ranks of old age; while each fresh complexity of the conditions and growth of the great machine entrenches the veterans more firmly in their advantage.

Hamilton was not merely a good soldier, a great lawyer, a statesman of rare and exceptional splendour, but also a figure of deep romantic interest. Such an endowment is uncommon, especially in Anglo-Saxon communities, where a wise absorption in a single activity is approved by public opinion, and any variety of talents is viewed askance. But the explanation of his character is not to be found in the dramatic temperament. Had he been a better actor he must assuredly have been a more successful politician. He was as heedless of all matters of style and deportment as of his popularity, or even of his life. Ever intent on objects, he followed them in and out through the crowd of rapidly changing events, caring infinitely less for the opinion people

A.D. 1757 formed upon his personal merits than for the ultimate success of his pursuit. Few men, filling so large a space in history, have been less concerned with their own particular appearance or fame in the pageant of affairs. He became a soldier upon a generous impulse, a lawyer for a living, a statesman because it was the strongest passion of his nature to promote union, order and progress. The circumstances of his birth and of his death, his private adventures and the publicity that political malice has caused them to assume, cannot by any ingenuity be traced to a disposition for the picturesque.

To pretend that he had no joy in battle, no exultation in victory, would be absurd, for his nature was frank and vehement. He was never detached and seldom reticent. To endure human folly in patient and hopeful expectation of the inevitable reaction was contrary to his character. He had no hatred of limelight nor horror of applause, but both with him were secondary matters. Throughout his whole life the paramount motive was to get things done, not to make himself a great fame by doing things. So unusual an ambition has caused him to be suspected of an inordinate subtlety. To the common politician whose main sincerity is his determination to ride into popular notice on the back of a grievance or a fit of hysterics, such an attitude is wholly incredible. He cannot fathom the depths of a spirit that loves union, and order, and progress for their own sakes, and seeks power, not as an end in itself, but as a means to the accomplishment of a vision. And yet, to the candid reader of Hamilton's life and writings, nothing is clearer at every turn than that he came to enact his high and notable part in public affairs chiefly because it seemed to be the only way open to him of getting the work done which he considered essential for the salvation of his adopted country.

Alexander Hamilton was born a British subject in the A.D. 1757
island of Nevis, in the Leeward Group, on the 11th of January
1757. On both sides he was of gentle descent.[1] His father
was one James Hamilton, a younger son of Hamilton of
Grange, in Lanarkshire; his mother, Rachel[2] Faucette, the
daughter of a Huguenot emigrant. Rachel Faucette had
been previously married to a Dane, but finding her life
insupportable had left him.[3] Gossip asserts that, divorce
having proved to be impracticable, she took the law into
her own hands and accepted James Hamilton as her second
husband, but without the blessing of the Church. While
we cannot accept Alexander Hamilton's illegitimacy[4] to be
a matter of certainty, there can be no doubt that it was
believed in by his contemporaries, and was made the subject
of sneering references in the correspondence of his political
enemies.[5] His father was a merchant; an amiable man,
but feckless and unfortunate, so that almost from infancy
the boy owed his support to relatives of his mother.

In the small and leisured society of a sugar island the
circumstances of a family can hardly have been a close
secret from its neighbours. Even if no stain attached to
Hamilton's birth, his poverty and dependence were obvious
to all men. He was a boy of strange precocity and a
remarkable intelligence, sensitive, affectionate and deeply
attached to his mother—a brilliant and beautiful woman
who died while he was still a child. In temper he was
fiery and passionate, but delicate in frame and puny of
stature. With such a constitution of mind and body, and
in such circumstances of poverty and dependence, it needed
something greater than an ordinary hero to emerge unhurt.

The most remarkable fact about his boyhood is the

---

[1] Appendix I.   [2] The Christian name is given by Mrs. Atherton.
[3] *History*, i. pp. 40-43.   [4] Lodge's *Hamilton*, Appendix, pp. 285-297.
[5] Sumner's *Hamilton*, p. 1.

early development of his character. Before he was sixteen he had served an apprenticeship to practical affairs in the warehouse, or store, of Nicholas Cruger, a substantial merchant of St. Croix, by whom he was sent to other islands on important business, and left in complete control of the staff, correspondence and undertaking, during the prolonged absence of his master in the Northern colonies. There is a letter[1] of this period to the firm's agent in New York in reference to the cargo and return cargo of the sloop *Thunderbolt*, which shows more than a mere facility in business forms and phrases. What most impresses us in the document is the careful foresight and arrangements of which it forms the record. It is the letter of one who feels his responsibilities, but is not overburdened by their weight.

Another letter of an even earlier date has a wider celebrity, but in spite of its precocity of language is of less value as illuminating his character. It is addressed to his school-fellow Stevens.[2] "To confess my weakness, Ned, my ' ambition is prevalent, so that I contemn the grovelling ' condition of a clerk or the like, to which my fortune, etc., ' condemns me, and would willingly risk my life, though ' not my character, to exalt my station. I am confident, ' Ned, that my youth excludes me from any hopes of ' immediate preferment; nor do I desire it; but I mean ' to preface the way for futurity. I'm no philosopher, you ' see, and may justly be said to build castles in the air; my ' folly makes me ashamed, and I beg you'll conceal it; yet, ' Neddy, we have seen such schemes successful when the ' projector is constant. I shall conclude saying, I wish there ' was a war."

Here indeed is the accustomed language of the infant prodigy. Both words and sentiments are striking, but they

---

[1] *Works*, ix. pp. 38-39.   [2] *Ibid.* ix. pp. 37-38.

are the convention of youthful genius. They reflect a glin
of the dramatic from the great light of subsequent events;
but are really less remarkable than the quiet, executive
letter on freight and accounts, staves, hogsheads, mules,
and the armament which is desirable in view of the ' Guarda
Costas which are said to swarm upon the coast.'

We may believe him to have been sincere in his contempt
for ' the grovelling condition of a clerk,' but he soon had
reason to bless the results of his service. For a boy loving
books and conscious of an extraordinary facility in the use
of language, there is a constant danger that his intelligence
may be brought under the domination of words. At the
most impressionable period of his life Hamilton learned the
hard lesson that the finest phrases, though they may temporarily sway the dispositions of men, will never alter a
single fact of their existence; that the most fluent explanation will never wipe out the ill results of a bad bargain,
a want of foresight or a misplaced confidence. Throughout the whole of his writings we are conscious of this
quality—that he was ever striving to express in language
which admitted of no misunderstanding, ideas which he had
already brought to the test of things. It is a rare quality
in any man, but more than usually rare in lawyers and
politicians, never to allow words a part in completing the
fabric of an imperfect thought. The experience gained
in Nicholas Cruger's store was of great value in itself;
but the habit which it imposed upon his mind of going
always to the facts was immeasurably beyond all other
benefits.

With so much knowledge of his temperament and
circumstances it is natural to picture an austere youth :
courageous certainly, but somewhat bitter and sardonic,
narrow in his sympathies, chary of his confidence. But
early responsibility failed to give him even a grave face.

B

The imaginary portrait is wholly at fault. The real picture
shows a boy of a gay and affectionate disposition, bubbling
over with hope, naïvely exulting in the consciousness of his
powers, winning friends wherever he goes and keeping them
without an effort or a calculation, merely by the charm and
sincerity of his spirit.

His 'grovelling' clerkship ended and he became a student,
as the result of a hurricane.[1] Shortly after midsummer
1772 the Leeward Islands were devastated by a tempest
of remarkable violence. Hamilton wrote a description
which was published anonymously in the adjacent island
of St. Kitts. The principal personages were impressed by
its vigorous merits, and the authorship was soon discovered.
It was felt that a boy of so great talent deserved to have a
chance given him in the world. His proud relatives were
not hard to persuade. Their kindness supplied the funds
necessary for a college education, and, armed with intro-
ductions from his friend Dr. Knox, a Presbyterian minister
he set out for New York a few weeks later. The vessel
caught fire on the voyage, but the flames being got under
she landed her passengers in safety at Boston Harbour
sometime in the month of October.

Hamilton appears to have directed his course of studies
without the aid of any guardian. His first step was to
enter himself at a grammar school where he remained
for a year. He then presented himself to the head of
Princeton College and underwent a private examination.
We may presume it was entirely satisfactory, seeing that
he thereupon proposed to the principal, and the principal
gravely recommended to the trustees, that he should not be
fettered by the usual regulations as to years, but should
be allowed to pass through the curriculum as rapidly as his
progress justified.[2] The trustees not being amenable he

[1] *Life*, pp. 6 and 7.   [2] *Ibid.* p. 9.

entered at King's College (Columbia), which was ready to
take him upon his own terms.   Here he remained for two
years, working with an extraordinary swiftness and industry, but finding time notwithstanding for college debates,
political pamphlets, the writing of verses and for general
society.   He appears also to have given much of his time
and thought to religion, and, by the testimony of his friend
Robert Troup, was an earnest believer in the doctrines of
Christianity.

The plan of his education was therefore a curious inver-
sion.   After a training in affairs he submitted himself to an
academic course, and the unusual order of events had at
least this advantage, that he knew with greater clearness
than most students what he wished to learn, and why he
wished to learn it.

CHAPTER II

The Quarrel with Great Britain

IN the autumn of 1773, within a few months of Hamilton's
enrolment as a student at King's College, Boston Harbour
was black with tea.   He visited friends in that town in the
following spring, and returned to New York a convert to
the policy of resistance.[1]

The true importance of Hamilton is not in the events
which led to the great rebellion, but in those which flowed
from it.   It would therefore be out of place to enter upon
an elaborate discussion of the causes of the war; but in
attempting even the briefest summary of the situation, we
are met at once by the difficulty which arises when popular
opinion has accepted and embalmed an explanation which is
not in accordance with the facts.

[1] *Life*, p. 25.

A.D. 1773
Æt. 16
'The Revolution,' it has been said, 'was merely an episode in British history, but it is the American epic.' The early chroniclers of the Republic abounded in pious panegyric. They chanted pæans, and pointed morals, and delivered philippics against tyranny and oppression without check or contradiction; for in England the minds of men were turned away from a distasteful subject to matters of more immediate and absorbing interest. A war which has failed is a dreary topic, and in the events which crowded upon Europe at the end of the eighteenth century, achievements of a contrasting glory were not far to seek.

In these propitious circumstances, the crude theory that right lay wholly upon one side, and wrong upon the other, was boldly put forward. So careless were our ancestors in the matter, that the growth of this heroic legend has had a free course until, in popular discussions upon both sides of the Atlantic, it is now usually assumed to be outside the region of criticism. The world is required to believe that in 1776 the majority of Americans were good men, and the majority of Britons bad ones; that the former were liberal and intelligent, the latter dull and furious; that the leaders in the one case were disinterested patriots, in the other the corrupt sycophants of a tyrannical madman, and that, in Washington's vigorous words, all loyalists and Tories were merely 'abominable pests of society.' This opinion in time came to be accepted, like a quack medicine, mainly because it was well advertised. The plain man was captivated by the simplicity of a statement which his intelligence could grasp almost without an effort. Fluent moralists among us, writing with no more serious motive than to celebrate the triumph of their own party principles, found the explanation admirably suited to their purpose, and gave their solemn blessing and approval to the myth which our kinsmen had invented, as Romans before them had devised the legend of

Romulus, Remus and the she-wolf to adorn the illustrious foundation of the city.

The balance of legal right was almost as plainly in favour of the British contentions as the balance of common-sense was against them. The Supreme Courts of Appeal in this country and the States, sitting in banc for a new trial of the issues involved, would probably be forced to decide, as a matter of law, that upon most of the essential points our ancestors were technically in the right. On the other hand, a jury of men of the world would almost as certainly conclude that imprudence rarely steered a more perilous course or followed it in a spirit less likely to escape ship-wreck. It is difficult to believe that legal right really mattered a great deal to any one. The fundamental, para-mount, determining cause of the war with Britain was the need of getting free from restraint, and this need was realised rather by a kind of instinct than by any reasoning. It drew its main force much more from a vague fear of what might happen in the future than from any material damage or political injury that had actually occurred.

As things then stood, the simplest and most obvious way of dealing with the difficulty seemed to the one side to be coercion, to the other side revolt. On the one hand there was a new country, vigorous and remote, possessing enormous resources of which it was at least dimly conscious, eager, hopeful and impatient in pursuit of its destiny; on the other an old, dignified, slow-moving, sceptical people, lack-ing certainly in sympathy, but lacking most of all in knowledge of any circumstances but its own. By the constitution, imperial sovereignty was in the hands of the second, and the real danger of the situation lay in the mixture of sense of duty, selfish interest and ignorance which the British cabinet brought into its attempt to rule over an impetuous subject at such a distance in time and miles. But, granting so much, we may dismiss without ceremony all the bogeys with corked eyebrows which the patriotism of early American historians has constructed. The evil was hindrance, not tyranny; vexatious, but not ill-meant, delays; a tendency to strangle colonial ambitions and to impede action by processes and references, ceremonies and forms, by disparaging criticisms and buckets of elder-brotherly cold water. But a settled policy, even serious isolated acts, of tyranny, as tyranny has generally been understood, never did happen and never could have happened.

It is impossible to conduct successfully the infinitely less complex affairs of an ordinary business from a centre separated by great distances from its branches, unless the manager be given so free a hand that he becomes in fact the predominant partner within his own sphere. The British king and people failed to realise this essential limitation of their sovereignty. It was no wonder, for no country in the world had ever realised it before them. The essence of the difficulty was never clearly stated by either side, so little was it grasped by reason, so much was it a matter of mere instinct. Americans felt that a free hand was a necessity, and that under existing circumstances they would never obtain it. It seemed to them that they were not understood, which was true, and that they could never hope to be understood, which was probable; for it was impossible at that date to foresee ocean greyhounds and Marconi installations, and a system of news—truthful, rapid and cheap—which at the present time seems not beyond reasonable hope. When it is a question of preserving or accomplishing a political union, it is time, not distance, that is the great obstacle. The swift interchange of thought and the simultaneous impulses which spring therefrom are even greater forces for binding nations together than are safety and speed of travel to and fro.

A.D. 1773
ÆT. 16

The two nations, therefore, came in the end to a desperate struggle, the one side for its independence, the other for its dignity, and being for the most part of the Anglo-Saxon stock, they brought up their batteries and engaged in a solemn and interminable argument on the principles of constitutional law. Beyond sharpening the wits of the disputants and improving the education of their readers, this long-range duel of claims and counter-claims served no important purpose and has needlessly obscured the issue for future generations. In great events it is always well to look for the idea, and the idea in this case was neither legal right nor private rights, was not even freedom, but only independence.

The American loyalists or Tories suffered greater evils and showed a finer judgment than either Parliament or Congress; but as loyalty, like treachery, bears a certain relation to the issue of any struggle, the virtues of these men have rarely received a fit acknowledgment. They failed in their endeavour. The great Washington denounced them in the harsh terms which have been already quoted. The epic required that they should be painted black. Consequently they have been set down for the most part as sordid schemers, and for the rest as unreasoning fanatics moved by a spirit of impossible loyalty. But the motive of the Americans who stood out against their fellow-colonists was neither a private advantage nor a sentimental attachment. Their aim was the security of an inheritance, and they judged any attempt to sever or divide it to be the greatest of all political crimes. The Empire had been built up with painful effort, and, in their opinion, a people that was worthy of it would have endured, in order to maintain it, much greater sufferings than had ever been inflicted by British statesmen. Oppression and injustice were evils which time would surely abate. The Tories had a settled belief in their countrymen on both sides of the ocean, and foresaw what is obviously the truth, that when the temper of the disputants should have cooled, the wrongs and grievances would gradually disappear. They were people of the old school, who considered patience to be the final test of national greatness. They had a sound instinct of statesmanship, a memory of the slow movement and ultimate triumph of England under the Tudors; and they were content, as their ancestors had been content, who lived, and fought, and grumbled under the two Henrys and Elizabeth, to endure obstruction and delay, regarding these things even with a measure of gratitude as a precaution imposed by Providence in order that the mortar might have time to set. They abhorred the idea of a jerry-built nation. The desire of their hearts was a British North America; the chief of their fears was a foreign conquest, settlement, or intrusion.

Foreign interference, as their terrors painted it, has been successfully withstood, but it must be remembered that within a few years of the foundation of the new republic the attempt was made and reached the height of a serious danger. The great majority of the citizens were ready to welcome it. The leaders of the popular party even invited it, and it was prevented only by the efforts of Washington, Hamilton and a few others who were covered with opprobrium as their reward. But if in one form the disaster of foreign influence has been avoided, almost by a miracle, it is worth considering whether in another the fears of the loyalists have not been to some extent realised. A cosmopolitan America, though they did not foresee the possibility, would certainly have been distasteful to their principles. They did not desire a huge immigration of strange people, and would hardly have accepted the mere predominance of the English tongue throughout the union as a proof that their aim of a British North America had been realised.

A.D. 1773
ÆT. 16

The central idea of these Tories was the preservation at all costs of an existing union, and their failure to achieve it was due no less to the raw impatience of their fellow-colonists, than to the blundering management of the British Cabinet, which always pushed things to extremes at the wrong moment.   Between these headstrong opponents there was no possibility of accommodation.   Every act of either party, after disagreement first arose, appeared to the other in lurid colours.   The Canadian War had left a legacy of ill-feeling and distrust.   The British considered, with some reason, that the colonials had often shirked their fair share of danger and hardship; that their governments had been niggardly, cheese-paring and ungenerous in the matter of supplies; that they had created difficulties and sought a profit at a time of national crisis.   They argued further that the taking of Quebec and the total expulsion of the French from the north and west of the continent were of much greater benefit and moment to Americans than to Englishmen.   The colonies had been preserved from the imminent danger of a French envelopment, their borders had been placed in a position of comparative security from the instigated raids of ferocious savages, mainly by British arms and treasure. As a consequence, the indignant Briton viewed the American as a creature of the blackest ingratitude, canting about his rights, like a fraudulent bankrupt, in order to escape the payment of his just debts.

The colonial opinion of the mother country was equally unflattering, and probably equally just.   The colonists despised the home Government for its lack of foresight, knowledge of conditions and estimate of difficulties.   The British officer, who is apt upon occasions to be wanting in tact, had not brought any exceptional qualities of efficiency or resource to reduce the balance of his social imperfections.   In consequence, the colonial picture of his patronising

1773
Æt. 16 kinsman represented him as a swaggering bully, bloated
with a fatuous and misplaced self-confidence, who misunderstood everything and everybody, and by reason of his
natural endowment of stupidity, was destined in the nature
of things to continue to misunderstand until the end of
time.

The old country was wounded in its feelings, the new
country in its pride, and both doubtless with much reason;
but if all the evil that each thought of the other had been
true, it was still entirely unimportant. There are moments
in the happiest history of the best husbands and the most
perfect wives when the estimate is equally black; but
circumstances being favourable, charity, laughter and a
true sense of proportion enter in to set the matter right.
But in this unfortunate union the circumstances were
unfavourable, and time only widened the cleavage. The
difficulty was that Britain would not consent to a partner-
ship, which was the only solution, but insisted upon a
dependency. The American colonists therefore hardened
their hearts and would accept nothing short of independence.

Raw feelings alone will never make a great revolution.
They are but light and trivial breezes. Blowing with the
current they would hardly have raised a ripple, but blowing
against it they covered the surface with a thousand white
and angry waves, which overwhelmed all the light craft of
conciliation and drowned every peacemaker, lay and official.
Lord Rockingham, with Burke to find him brains, was as
helpless as Lord North. Every act, word and proposal of
every negotiation was suspect by the other side. Little
things not worth a second thought, the small blunders of
obscure officials, old wives' grievances, and the absurd and
unintended wrongs done by pompous men, elevated themselves into national questions, and became the food and

nourishment of disputants upon constitutional and legal A.D. 1773
right.   ÆT. 16

We may dismiss the theory of malign intriguers who perverted the judgment and poisoned the affections of the American people. The misrepresentations of Samuel Adams, the craftiness of Franklin, the heroics of Henry, and the phrases of Jefferson, were no more the cause of the rebellion than the obstinacy of George the Third, the pedantry of Grenville, the flippancy of Townshend, the indecency of Wedderburn, or the easy, good-natured facing-both-ways of Lord North. We have been inclined to dwell too much upon the defects of individual men and to attribute too great a power to minor influences, which, although they exasperated the combatants, could never have caused the combat and in many instances were merely the external phenomena of a great struggle.

CHAPTER III

Early Writings

By his own account Hamilton started as a loyalist, and was converted to the popular side by his visit to Boston.[1] His sympathies were always aristocratic, and he was born with a reverence for tradition; but his strongest instinct was for the orderly achievement of a practical end. He was ever quick to make up his mind, and having come to a decision, to take all the steps needful for attaining the objects of his policy.

In the month of July (1774) following his matriculation, a great meeting was held 'in the fields' with the purpose of influencing the vote of New York in the election of

[1] *Life*, p. 25.

delegates to the first Continental Congress. It was a popular convocation, and had the advantage of a political martyr as its president.[1] The speeches were hearty enough, but, as might have been expected, ignored the most essential points of the argument. Hamilton, instigated thereto by his friends, mounted upon the platform, and supplied the deficiencies. He was a young-looking boy of seventeen, and began with hesitation; but being desperately in earnest, and having a natural gift of expression, he held his audience, gaining confidence as he proceeded. "His mind ' warmed with the theme, his energies were recovered; ' and, after a discussion clear, cogent, and novel, of the ' great principles involved in the controversy, he depicted ' in glowing colours the long-continued and long-endured ' oppressions of the mother country; he insisted on the ' duty of resistance, pointed to the means and certainty of ' success, and described the waves of rebellion sparkling ' with fire, and washing back on the shores of England the ' wrecks of her power, her wealth, and her glory." [2]

This incident has a great celebrity, and we can well believe it all. But here again we are face to face with the infant prodigy, the same who wrote in his twelfth year to Ned Stevens that ' his ambition was prevalent.' Our astonishment is less that he should have made such a gifted speech, than that having made it he was ever heard of again.

Of a different character altogether from this incident are his pamphlets, which were printed in quick succession between the end of the same year and the midsummer following. Before Christmas he had undertaken the defence of the first Continental Congress against the attack of Dr. Seabury, a clergyman (afterwards a bishop) who wrote under the signature of a ' West Chester farmer.' Hamilton's

---

[1] Captain Alexander M'Dougal, imprisoned 1770 for seditious libel.
[2] *Life*, pp. 22-23.

Full Vindication[1] provoked a reply, and in February there A.D. 1775
came a rejoinder, *The Farmer Refuted.*[2] He continued to Æt. 18
write upon similar themes in Holt's *Journal,* and in June
he published another pamphlet under the title of *Remarks
upon the Quebec Bill.*[3]

These works, although enjoying a considerable fame (they
were generally attributed to the experienced pen of Mr. Jay),[4]
are not of great importance either as history or literature.
But they speak a different language from the infant prodigy,
and bear a nearer family resemblance to the letter that dealt
with staves and hogsheads and Guarda Costas. There is, of
course, a considerable number of words expended upon the
texts of slavery and tyranny. The future bishop is well
bethumped. The premises are not reasoned but accepted,
as we should expect in the case of a boy of eighteen;
but nevertheless, rhetorical exaggeration and turgid general-
ities play but a small part. In the first pamphlet the most
telling argument is a sober and practical analysis directed
to disprove the assertion that Britain had but little, the
colonies everything, to lose by such a stoppage of trade as
was advocated by Congress. It concludes with a vigorous
epistle to the farmers of the New York colony, somewhat in
the manner of the *Drapier Letters*; as simple and direct,
almost as hearty in its intolerance, but a few degrees more
just in its foundation.

In the second pamphlet Hamilton pursued his victim
with an ardour whetted on applause. It abounds in bad
law, bad history and bad philosophy, but is more than
redeemed by an exuberance of common-sense. The central argument admits the allegiance due by the American
colonists to a common sovereign, but repudiates the authority
of the British Parliament. A democracy attempting to rule

---

[1] *Works,* i. p. 4.   [2] *Ibid.* i. p. 55.
[3] *Ibid.* i. p. 181.   [4] *Life,* p. 37.

over another democracy he holds to be a worse tyrant than any autocrat.[1] He deals with the pretensions of the home Government in the first place on the theory of the British constitution, and having established their absurdity by this examination, he next overwhelms them by an appeal to the Natural Rights of Man. Satisfied with his victory in this empty game of battledore and shuttlecock, he proceeds to a technical argument drawn from the charters of the colonies, and concludes triumphantly by denying the rights of Britain to tax her colonists or to legislate for them. He justifies, however, upon the ground of an implied concession, her claim to regulate their trade for the advantage of the empire, and even for her own particular advantage as a return for the protection afforded by her navy.

The alternative to a slavish submission is civil war, and accordingly to sustain the confidence of his country-men in such a struggle he describes in a hopeful spirit the boundless resources of the colonies, their indepen-dence of external commerce, their fitness for the peculiar warfare that is likely to be pursued, and paints in the gloomiest colours the difficulties and embarrassments against which their oppressors will be forced to contend. No hope remains in patience and loyalty, in petitions and remon-strances, but only in arms. The discipline of Britain will in the end prove powerless against the patriotism of America, and a favourable neutrality, if not an active interference, on the part of France and Holland, will sustain them in their struggle for freedom. "I earnestly lament 'the unnatural quarrel between the parent state and the ' colonies, and most ardently wish for a speedy reconciliation '—a perpetual and *mutually* beneficial union"; and he protests that he is 'a warm advocate for limited monarchy, and an unfeigned wellwisher to the present Royal Family.'[2]

¹ *Works*, i. p. 81.   ² *Ibid.* i. p. 176.

This pamphlet was published early in February. In the A.D. 1775
third week of April the British troops were routed as they ÆT. 18
withdrew from Lexington, and before the middle of May
the strong posts of Ticonderoga and Crown Point had fallen
into the hands of rebel raiders under Allen and Benedict
Arnold. In June the American militia was defeated
at Bunker Hill after a gallant resistance, and George
Washington was appointed by the Second Congress to the
office of commander-in-chief. Henceforth for many years to
come the written word was to exercise less influence than the
loaded musket. The *Remarks on the Quebec Bill*, a short
and acrimonious document, whose chief object appears to
have been to excite religious prejudice against the British
Government for their toleration, or, as Hamilton preferred
to allege, their establishment of Roman Catholicism in
Canada, marks the ending of his youthful fertility. It was
published in the same month that saw the battle of Bunker
Hill.

The pamphlets ceased, and by degrees the speeches ceased
also. Hamilton joined a volunteer corps called the Hearts
of Oak, drilled early in the morning, and wore a uniform of
green, with brown leather facings, and the appropriate motto,
Freedom or Death. He turned from constitutional law to
the study of strategy and tactics, and had the honour, with
his comrades in arms, to draw the first fire of his Britannic
Majesty in the colony of New York while engaged in removing the guns from the harbour battery. The chronicler,
searching for evidence to support his favourite idea of the
infant prodigy, has recorded that when H.M.S. *Asia*, lying
at anchor, let off a broadside at her godsons of the Hearts
of Oak, " Hamilton, who was aiding in the removal of the
' cannon, exhibited the greatest unconcern, although one of
' his companions was killed by his side." [1] We may believe

[1] *Life*, p. 48.

it or not as we choose, but such events are at any rate unfavourable to the composition of pamphlets.

We hear of him again on three occasions during these
months, playing a part which is noteworthy and highly
characteristic. For all his love of freedom, his hatred of
lawlessness was the stronger passion. Both indeed had
their origin in his detestation of injustice and oppression.
His fame stood high with the revolutionary party, whose
enthusiasm had christened him 'the oracle';[1] but he did
not hesitate to risk his popularity by withstanding the
violence of the mob against private individuals suspected of
Tory proclivities. There is an element of comedy in the
student of King's delivering a lengthy harangue from the
College steps in order to give his principal the opportunity
of escape to a British ship of war; while, from an upper
window, this worthy gentleman, mistaking the object of the
address, besought the people who had come to tar and
feather him not to listen to his defender because he was
'crazy.' With less success he attempted to prevent the
destruction of Rivington's press.[2]

It is not without importance that upon the appearance
of the first pamphlet Hamilton was approached by the
loyalist party with flattering offers of employment if he
would transfer his services to the other side. Such proposals
must have been attractive not only on account of his youth
and poverty, but for the further reason that so many of his
sympathies were bound up with the ideas of monarchy and
a settled constitution. His prompt rejection of the offer
is all the more remarkable, when we remember that it has
been the ignorant habit of Democrat historians to write of
him as if he had been a pure adventurer, and that even
in recent times apologies for his career and appreciations of
his character, with equal ignorance and less excuse, have

---

[1] *Life*, p. 37.   [2] *Ibid.* pp. 48, 49.

tacitly assumed the justice of the charge.   Only in the most
romantic sense can Hamilton be termed an adventurer:
only because he was a young man from a strange land
seeking adventures; never because he sold his sword. A
character less mercenary, and less concerned in any personal
advancement, save as a means of rendering better service
to the state, has never played a part upon the public stage.
To the Dugald Dalgettys of history he bore no resemblance
save in his courage; and if we are in search of an analogy
we shall find it rather among the knights of the Round
Table than among the soldiers of fortune.

We cannot deplore the interruption of his pamphleteering;
but, on the contrary, and in spite of the merits of his work
in this direction, must judge it to have been most fortunate.
Such extraordinary facility, such dangerous precocity,
needed the sternest antidotes. In the moulding of Hamilton's great character, the counting-house of Nicholas Cruger
and the campaigns of Washington were the severest and the
best influences, for both called upon him in harsh tones to
be certain that his words corresponded with some fact, and
were not merely words. The questioning of such experiences
will take no denial; and the man who, possessing high gifts
of thought and eloquence, finds himself forced by circumstances to endure their relentless catechism, may hope to
enjoy his reward by escaping for ever from the bondage of
phrases.

CHAPTER IV

The Beginning of the War

THE War of Independence covered a period little short of
nine years, if we reckon it to have begun at the skirmish of

Lexington[1] and to have ended when General Washington bade farewell to his officers at Fraunces' Tavern.[2] During the whole of this time there was a military organisation and an army in being. The issue indeed was decided at Yorktown[3] more than two years earlier. After that event Britain gave up the hope of regaining her colonies and undertook no further enterprises.

The maxim which insists upon strategy as a deciding factor in a long and dreary struggle never found a more conspicuous illustration. With bad strategy victories brought no profit, while with good, defeats were matters of but little moment. Strategy may be defined as a wise alliance with circumstances which, in case of success, will follow up the pursuit, and in case of failure will screen the retreat. The strong sense of Washington was incapable of distraction from this consideration either under adversity, of which he had a wide experience, or in good fortune, which occasionally rewarded his devotion.

It has been assumed that in the case of the colonists strategy was an easy matter; that it was obvious, and from the beginning had determined the course of their efforts and the ultimate issue of the war. The Americans had a base of operations in every village, an army in the whole population. Before a British advance the waves parted, as the Red Sea before the army of Pharaoh, only to engulf and overwhelm them. Our own countrymen, on the other hand, had but one base—the sea. Yet when we consider the matter, the contest was not so unequal as our apologists have alleged. A population of some two and a half millions sprinkled upon a coastline of twelve hundred miles as the crow flies, or, if we count the great bays and indentations and the extent of navigable rivers, more than twice as much again, must in the end fall a victim to any

[1] 19th April 1775. [2] 4th December 1783. [3] 19th October 1781.

great power holding command of the sea. Nothing appears
more certain than that, had our ancestors maintained their
maritime supremacy, the rebellion must have perished of
sheer exhaustion.

At the critical moment, when the resources of Congress
were at their last extremity, naval superiority upon the
coasts of North America passed into other hands. What
it is also easy to forget is that Britain, as happens from
time to time, was at war with the world. France and
Spain and Holland were at open war with her. The
Baltic States—Russia, Denmark and Sweden—had allied
themselves in an armed neutrality. At all points throughout our dispersed empire we were outnumbered and on
the defensive. "The Marquis de Lafayette," Washington
wrote in July 1780, "will be pleased to communicate
' the following general ideas to Count de Rochambeau and
' the Chevalier de Ternay as the sentiments of the under-
' written:—In any operation, and under all circumstances, a
' decisive naval superiority is to be considered as a funda-
' mental principle, and the basis upon which every hope of
' success must ultimately depend."[1] On land the great
captain had done his utmost. Circumstances of hill and
river, swamp and forest, farm and desert, had been bound in
alliance to his victorious arms; but for the supreme victory
there was need of a general strategy in which the blue
ocean played a part. Failing that confederate, the only choice
for his wearied veterans and a devastated people was submission to the British Parliament, or some great trek into the
prairies of the West. It is not the least of the glories of
an imperishable fame that one who was so hot and eager a
soldier should have grasped thus coolly and considerately
the essential, unalterable condition of final success.

[1] Sparks's *Washington*, vii. p. 509.

At the beginning of the war (1775) the King's army under General Gage held Boston, in Massachusetts. The distinguishing note of this period was a fear on the part of the British to strike hard while conditions were still favourable to their arms. This fear arose from an ill-grounded hope that the mere display of military strength in a defensive attitude might be sufficient to overawe and suppress the rebellion without recourse to sterner measures which would, it was thought, add to the difficulties already existing the further obstacle of bitter memories.

The centre of disaffection was in the northern states of New England, and the object of King George's Government was to overawe the rebels by pressure on the heart. General Washington received from Congress his commission as commander-in-chief shortly before midsummer. In July he settled down to the siege of Boston. His army, though full of spirit, lacked both organisation and discipline. When he had to some extent remedied these defects, it was discovered that there was no gunpowder. His opponent, on the other hand, commanded a body of troops, as well-trained and courageous as Europe could produce. He was superior in numbers and well supplied with ammunition. He was not a brilliant man, but had he merely consulted the drill-book and moved his pieces in a mechanical fashion, he must have destroyed the beleaguering army of militiamen.

Dulness in a general officer is in itself a serious obstacle; but when one of that quality is bound by the careless pedantry of instructions, his unfortunate army becomes mere food for bullets. The idea of reconciliation was in the air. The tone of despatches from one of the most incompetent ministers for war that ever sat in a British cabinet filled the slow mind of Gage with a fear of winning a bloody but decisive battle. From the beginning it was an ill-conducted war. Mediocrity appointed mediocrity;

lectured it to be dilatory; dwelt with a kind of drunken wisdom upon the advantage of building golden bridges; paralysed it with a fear to strike; failed to send it reinforce-ments; from time to time forgot even that it existed; and only under the cold douche of disaster roused itself to deal out solemn blame. So during the whole of that summer, autumn and winter General Gage sat in Boston, growing more and more uncomfortable, doing nothing, and allowing Washington to drill his men, find gunpowder, and hem him in.

As the days began to shorten, an American expedition under Montgomery departed up the Hudson by the lakes George and Champlain to invade Canada. Early in November St. John surrendered to him after a siege of fifty days, and before the middle of the month Montreal was also taken. In September a second column under Arnold set out through the woods of Maine, and after incredible hardships arrived before the Heights of Abraham. Carleton, with a thousand men, held Quebec for the King.

Contrary to colonial expectations, the country did not rise at their coming in any enthusiasm for freedom. Possibly there was some lurking suspicion that King Stork would prove a worse tyrant than King Log. Hamilton's eloquent pamphlet against the establishment of Papacy and the applause which greeted it may well have disturbed Canadian minds. The invaders received but scant help. Their two columns joined forces before Quebec, but on the last day of the year Carleton drove back the assault. Mont-gomery, a gallant and noble figure, was killed in the attempt; and Arnold, no less brave, was forced to retreat with great loss and hardship, having gained nothing by the attempt.

Meanwhile, Washington was engaged in a great struggle

to make his army effective. Patriotism was prevalent, but by no means universal. Corruption, stock-jobbing, and an eagerness to make a profit out of army supplies were matters which stirred his indignation even in the early days of the contest. Congress was inclined to argue, and to make long speeches, and to invoke general principles of considerable grandeur but no practical utility. It was invested with high duties but meagre powers. All affairs, military and diplomatic, were in its hands; but as funds, without which duties have little chance of getting themselves performed, depended entirely upon the voluntary contributions of the various States, Congress lacked the right to enforce its will, and had to rely upon moral influence for its supplies.

In spite of the danger that menaced them, the states, from memory of British oppression, were deeply concerned with a pedantic idea of liberty, and never abandoned an unreasonable suspicion of a strong central government. Their jealous refusal to delegate power or to part with any of their individual rights, even to a congress elected by their own citizens, was the cause of more disasters to their arms and more embarrassment to their leaders than all the assaults of the enemy. Their prejudice against a regular army was ineradicable. They sought to preserve the superiority of the civil power over the military by a system of short enlistments that regarded four months as the proper term of service, and a year as justifiable only in circumstances of extreme emergency. To make the task of the commander-in-chief quite beyond the wit of man, Congress, in its anxiety to conform to this general idea of political liberty, decreed that a want of discipline should not be punished without the consent of the state to which the delinquent had the honour to belong.

The Second Year of the war (1776), despite the failure of
the Canadian invasion, opened gloomily for the British. Their stolid occupation of Boston had entirely failed to win over colonial opinion, or to daunt the rebellious spirit of the New England states. Sir William Howe had succeeded General Gage. Easy, indolent and good-humoured, he was entirely lacking in the quality of swift decision. Like his elder brother, the distinguished admiral, he was a friend of Benjamin Franklin's. He had much sympathy with the colonial grievance, and was appointed partly on his merits as a soldier, partly with a vague idea of conciliation. It is always dangerous to attempt a combination of these functions while victory hangs in the balance.

Early in March Washington, having organised and increased his army, occupied Dorchester Heights and commanded the British position. A fortnight later Sir William, finding his lines untenable, embarked the troops and sailed to Halifax, where, until June, he waited for reinforcements which had been promised but never came. Washington, foreseeing that the next move of the British must be against New York, marched southwards, arriving in that city towards the middle of April.

The British general, holding the absolute command of the sea, determined, as had been foreseen, to occupy New York and to make it the base of operations for his main army. Between Boston and New York, as strategical positions, no hesitation was possible; for the latter city, commanding the mouth of the navigable waterway of the Hudson, was immensely superior. Moreover, it was to a large extent a friendly city, full of rich and respectable Tories. But although from a purely military point of view the exchange was profitable, the loss of Boston was in the political aspect a damaging blow to British prestige. It filled the raw colonial troops with confidence in themselves and in their leader, and relaxed that pressure upon the heart of the rebellion which had been rightly judged of high importance by the King's Government.

For the moment Britain was at peace with the rest of the world, and providing she could have kept the flames under and conserved her authority among the colonists, there was no immediate menace of foreign attack. Holding an absolute command of the sea, it seems as if her right strategy would have been to strain every nerve for the provision of enough troops to seize and hold the great towns along the coast—Boston in the north, Charleston in the south, New York commanding the mouth of the Hudson, Philadelphia the estuary of the Delaware; from these strong positions upon a common base, the sea, to have pressed and strangled the revolution by a grinding occupation, to have discouraged its forces by frequent expeditions, and to have worn down resistance by sheer exhaustion of funds. When we remember how nearly the revolt came to failure from lack of money on more than one occasion, and even when in a military view affairs wore a fortunate appearance for the colonists, we can hardly resist the conclusion that had the war been directed at its beginning in the grand manner of Pitt instead of by the diffidence of Lord North, if the advantage of sea-power and of the long purse had been fully realised and used with intelligence and without mercy, neither the genius of Washington nor the devotion of his troops could have secured independence for the allied states.

But no nerves were strained. Energy and intelligence did not exist. Sir William Howe, disappointed of reinforcements and paralysed by dilatory instructions, sailed towards midsummer for New York and established himself at Sandy Hook and Staten Island. On the 4th of July an eloquent document, drafted by one Thomas Jefferson of Virginia—a ready penman but a shrinking antagonist—was issued to the world. The *Declaration of Independence* was a useful assertion, for it had a dramatic quality which stirred men's hearts.

A few days later Admiral Lord Howe arrived with an addition to the fleet and reinforcements for the army, bringing powers to offer pardon and amnesty, which unfortunately the evacuation of Boston and the enthusiasm excited by the famous *Declaration* had shorn of all hopes of success. The failure of an expedition against Charleston brought the forces who had been engaged in it back from the south. Sir William Howe accordingly found himself in command of some twenty-five thousand men with a fleet in support excellent in itself and admirably officered. Against him were thirty thousand American levies.

Washington held New York. A part of his army, five thousand strong, was in August entrenched at Brooklyn, in Long Island, separated from the city by a sea channel a mile in width. On the 27th the British general attacked and inflicted a severe defeat upon his opponents, who lost two thousand men. But, fearing great bloodshed and a crowning victory, he failed to storm the trenches. His delay allowed, or tempted, Washington to bring up more troops, making his effective total nine thousand combatants. It was a mistaken policy, which with a swifter antagonist must have resulted in ruin. But Sir William, though a sound man, was leisurely, and by the time he had matured his plans, the prompt action of the American general had rendered them fruitless. The obvious measure was to make use of the fleet and cut the nine thousand off from the mainland. While Sir William was considering this excellent method Washington realised his danger. A fog fell opportunely, as in some Homeric contest, and under the protection of the gods the colonial troops withdrew in good order, and unmolested, across the dividing arm of the sea. It was a masterly performance, and atoned for the bad judgment which had incurred the risk.

Washington realised that New York could no longer be held. On military grounds he desired to burn it, but political considerations rendered this course impracticable. About the middle of September Admiral Howe forced his way up the Hudson, threatening to cut off the American army who found themselves obliged to evacuate the city and to retreat up the east bank of the river. But General Howe was dilatory and made no effective pursuit. A month went by, during which the colonial army dwindled to twelve thousand men. In the middle of October the fleet forced its way still further, past forts and obstructions, causing Washington to retreat to White Plains, where he took up a strong position. Sir William, without undue haste, attacked him towards the end of the month and drove him, but in good order, out of his entrenchments. Again there was delay, and afterwards a spell of unpropitious weather which induced the British commander to withdraw. A few days later he successfully attacked the American forts on both sides of the river, capturing two thousand men and a large store of munitions. Under this heavy blow Washington withdrew to the west bank of the river, and, during November, with a rapidly shrinking army, was pursued by Cornwallis southwards across New Jersey; but always without disorder or defeat. In the early days of December he arrived at Princeton with barely three thousand ragged men, and the British troops at his heels. Finding his position impossible, he crossed the Delaware river, destroying behind him all the boats for many miles along its course. The population wavered, and many of them came in seeking the royal pardon. Congress was helpless, though still loquacious. Considering Philadelphia, where they sat, to be in serious danger of capture, they departed to Baltimore. Their fears, however, were groundless, for to a commander like Sir William Howe the difficulties of transport through an unfriendly country, in the depth of winter, presented too great an obstacle.

It was the fate of the British general to nourish himself upon text-book probabilities and the phrases of war. He appears to have concluded, upon the best possible grounds, that the American army had dissolved. Accordingly, withdrawing a great portion of his troops to comfortable winter quarters in New York, he left a long, straggling line of posts parallel to the Delaware.

Washington may have harboured illusions contrary to the teaching of the Pundits, but he had the great gift of turning them into realities. With small thanks to Congress he brought his ragged and bootless army up to the strength of six thousand men, and planned an elaborate attack at different points upon the extended British line. But he reckoned without his generals, and to a certain extent without natural obstacles. Gates, Ewing, Griffin, Putnam, Cadwalader, some for good reasons and others for bad, all failed him, and he went with his lonely column across the Delaware on a bitter night. With less than twenty-five hundred men he marched, after the arduous crossing, nine miles through darkness, with a sleet-storm driving in his face. As he approached the village of Trenton, held by Hessians, word reached him that the arms of his right flank were wet. He sent them word 'to use the bayonet, for the town must be taken.' At Christmas daybreak he stormed, took two thousand prisoners, and returned whence he came.

The alarm reached New York, and Cornwallis, the ever-vigorous, sallied out to inflict punishment. Leaving three regiments at Princeton he pushed on against the enemy, who had again crossed to the east bank of the river.

But Washington, evading the rush, slipped past him, and cut to pieces the three regiments left behind at Princeton. Upon this unlooked-for event Sir William judged it wiser to leave the line of the Delaware and concentrate his main army for the winter in New York. The colonists, dispirited by the autumn reverses, were now filled with new courage, and the task of withdrawing the British posts was none too easy.

It was a gallant campaign, and from the political standpoint something even greater. In the severest weather, with starved and ill-clad troops, absurdly inferior in numbers, and depressed by the memory of many months of defeat, Washington twice within a few days succeeded by the force of his great will in concentrating his small column in superior strength and destroying his enemy unawares. The mobility of footsore men in wintry weather is a contingency that text-books dealing with average conditions are justified in ignoring. But as Britons we must concede that there is a contrast not wholly in our favour between Sir William Howe, comfortably eating his Christmas dinner by a warm fire in New York city, and this calm American, undeluded and undismayed, deaf equally to false hopes and to despair, who, realising that the thing most necessary to his country at the moment was victory, lifted his weary militia through the snow and won it.

CHAPTER V

The Course of the War

In January (1777), at the beginning of the Third Year of the war, Washington took his troops into winter quarters at Morristown, keeping close watch upon New York, where all the British regiments lay huddled together, after their evacuation of New Jersey.

By March his five thousand men had again dwindled to three thousand under the hardships of famine and an ill-equipped camp. Congress did little to support his arms beyond passing resolutions that victories ought to occur. It intermeddled, making unfit military appointments, and giving commissions to foreigners flown with European tactics and personal complacency.[1] Boots and stockings, food and great-coats, even muskets and gunpowder, were sadly wanting.

In May, having collected seven thousand men with much difficulty, and mainly by his personal exertions, Washington broke up his cantonments. Sir William Howe's plan of campaign was re-formed partly upon his own experience and partly by help of the valuable suggestions which packet boats brought him from the War Office. His main army was to take Philadelphia for its objective, and he formed the intention of marching upon that city through New Jersey.

From Canada an expedition under General Burgoyne (a gifted and fashionable soldier with a reputation for wit, who had passed over the head of Carleton, in spite of the merit which attached to that officer's defence of Quebec) was to force its way south by Lake Champlain and the Hudson river. A junction was to be made with Sir Henry Clinton, who, according to the arrangement, was to sally out from New York. The objective of this combination was the isolation of the disaffected New England states. This part of the plan was arranged between Burgoyne and Lord George Germaine, the Secretary of State for War, and was not even communicated to the British commander-in-chief until he was committed to his southern movement.

Two figures in this war occupy a unique position: Washington, because it has never been possible to praise

[1] Hamilton to Duer, *History*, i. p. 431.

him beyond his merits; Germaine, for the reason that no blame has ever done justice to his incompetency. A nation can only expect humiliation when, regardless of its interest and its honour, it entrusts its War Office to a soldier of battered reputation, incapable of transacting the simplest business with industry and despatch. If a layman may presume to offer an opinion upon such high matters, it would be that the Canadian expedition was singularly futile in its design, and was based upon a misapprehension of books rather than upon any understanding of the facts. For Burgoyne's column was, as the saying is, 'in the air.' It was obliged to carry its supplies, and could never have hoped to hold any lines of communication. When it had passed on its way, except for a certain devastation, it might as well never have been there. It is only dream-strategy which attempts to cut off a province by drawing a line which is immediately rubbed out behind the pencil.

The Hudson river was a different matter. There was a possibility of holding that waterway, and thereby making a division that it would have been difficult for the colonists to obliterate. But to such an end, concentration of the whole British army was necessary. For this purpose Burgoyne was wanted at New York, not at Ticonderoga; and Sir William Howe, having regard to the smallness of his total force, had no business to be thinking of Philadelphia. But the strategy was arranged from home. That in itself was an evil of the first magnitude; but having been so arranged, it was essential that it should have been firmly imposed upon the generals who were to carry out the campaign. This was omitted, although Germaine appears at one time to have realised the necessity of clear orders and afterwards to have forgotten. A letter directing the British commander-in-chief to operate upon the Hudson so as to

support Burgoyne was actually written; but the Secretary for War refused to sign it because no copy had been
taken, and being committed to a holiday in Kent, he would
not wait until this omission had been rectified. The letter
was never sent, and Sir William Howe, who, with many
merits, lacked a swift intelligence, was left to guess at the
meaning of a plan made by other people.

In the third week of July, General Howe, judging
it impracticable to march south upon Philadelphia with
Washington hovering upon his right flank, put his troops
into transports and rounded Cape May into the estuary
of the Delaware. But finding himself confronted with
forts and other difficulties, he put about and sailed away
to the south, round the Capes of Delaware, up the long
Chesapeake Bay to the Head of Elk, where he finally
disembarked. His expedition had occupied more than a
month, and it was now near the end of August. As the
result of much seafaring the indefatigable traveller was
nearly as far from Philadelphia as when he started, and the
army of Washington was hovering on his left flank instead of
on his right. He was separated from his base at New York
by a hundred and forty miles or thereabouts of hostile
country (measuring as the crow flies); or, if it were a
question of returning as he came, by some four hundred and
fifty miles of sea. Washington on the easy interior lines
had moved his army south to Germantown with the idea of
defending Philadelphia.

On the 11th of September the British army in superior
numbers defeated Washington at the Forks of the Brandywine and opened the way north to Philadelphia, which
they occupied towards the end of the month, after fighting
another, but smaller, engagement, in which they were also
victorious.

Sir William then divided his army. One portion held

Germantown, while the other attempted to reduce the American forts which surrounded the mouth of the Delaware. Washington, undismayed by his ill-luck, brought up his army, now diminished to eight thousand men, to the attack of Germantown. It is probable that with seasoned troops and favourable weather he would have been successful. Fortune favoured him to begin with, but a mist fell (not opportunely, as at Brooklyn) which confused and misled his officers. A panic ensued, and he suffered a severe defeat. What is remarkable about the performance is the tenacity it displays. With a raw army he had suffered two defeats and lost the city which it had been his object to cover; but a little more than a fortnight later he had inspired sufficient spirit in his men to attack his victorious enemy in its lines. Beaten once more, he withdrew undismayed to prepare for further operations. Partly, no doubt, it was the personal qualities of the man, but partly also the wise alliance with circumstances which the British had disdained, but which Washington had priced at its true value. In spite of victories Sir William Howe was ever unable to pursue.

Burgoyne had moved from Canada shortly after midsummer with three thousand regular troops and five hundred Indians, and had recaptured Ticonderoga with stores and guns during the first week of July.

But Clinton at New York had found himself too weak to venture within striking distance to support the expedition, which was slowly struggling south through swamps and forests with a heavy train of artillery, baggage, and supplies; harassed by a multitude of invisible foes in camp and upon the march.

In the middle of October all Washington's anxieties for the safety of the New England states were brought to an end by the surrender of Burgoyne with between three and

four thousand men to a force five times his number at
Saratoga, thirty miles to the north of Albany, and about a
hundred and eighty from New York.

The full consequences of the surrender at Saratoga can
hardly have been clear at once even to the sagacious mind
of the American commander-in-chief. It was one of those
small battles which are remarkable in history for having
changed the whole face of a situation. It secured the
northern states from any serious attack; raised the confidence of the American army, Government, and citizens;
depressed in equal proportion the spirits of their enemy;
dislocated his plan of campaign, and endangered the position of his main army at Philadelphia by releasing large
reinforcements. These were the obvious results, but also
the least important.

Up to this time Britain had not only held command of the sea, but had enjoyed complete immunity.
She could carry her troops to and fro along the coasts where
and when she liked. A few frigates were sufficient protection against American privateers. The immediate effect
of Saratoga was to menace this invaluable security. The
ultimate effect was to destroy her naval superiority in those
waters, and by this means to bring the war to a disastrous
ending. An alliance with a great sea power was, from
the point of view of the states, the most important object
of diplomacy, and Saratoga is a memorable battle chiefly
because it was the direct cause of such an alliance.

The neutrality of France had no tinge of benevolence for
Britain. The ministers of Louis XVI. were watchful and
jealous. The loss of Canada and the triumphant administration of Pitt were memories which still rankled. Under a
thin veil of private adventure France had sought from the
beginning to furnish the rebellious colonists with the sinews
of war. She had regarded with a favourable eye the enlist-

ment of her subjects as volunteers. But the prestige of her ancient rival was as yet unshaken. France was willing to comfort the enemies of the King of England, but her policy stopped short of open war. For this step more was requisite than the Bourbon alliance. The revolutionary states must first give some signal proof of their superiority. In the surrender of Saratoga she found a justification for bolder measures. Britain thenceforth was no longer engaged in a purely domestic warfare with her rebellious children, but had to defend herself also against two great European powers—France and Spain.

Towards the end of November, Sir William Howe had taken the forts upon the Delaware, and his supporting fleet had safe access to the estuary. In the beginning of December he made preparations for a forward movement against the American army, but nothing came of it, and Washington retired unmolested into winter quarters at Valley Forge.

If the results of a campaign could be measured by the comfort of the adversaries when it has ended, or even if it bore any fixed relation to the number of victories won in the field, the British general would have had good reason for complacency. But the hard order of facts ignores these minor considerations. It was probably clear even to Sir William Howe, amiable, courteous, liberal, but a frank hater of all arduous affairs, that the starved and shivering regiments in the hills fifteen miles away were the real victors, although he lay pleasantly at Philadelphia with his fleet anchored in the Delaware under silenced forts.

At the beginning of May (1778), in the Fourth Year of the war, the French alliance became known and was eagerly welcomed in America. A fortnight earlier, Admiral d'Estaing had set sail with twelve ships of the line, his total force both

in numbers and weight of armament being greatly superior
to the fleet serving under Lord Howe. But his voyage was
performed with all the deliberation that had marked British
enterprises on land. He had no luck with the elements, nor
much skill. It took him twelve weeks to arrive.

Meanwhile it had been arranged that the Howes, upon
their own request, were to be relieved. They heartily disliked the job, and they disliked even more the ministry
under which they had the honour to serve. Sir William
was superseded by Sir Henry Clinton before the middle of
May. The stout old admiral should shortly have followed his
brother home, but as he was on the point of handing over his
command, news reached him of d'Estaing and his superior
fleet. In such circumstances he let his resignation wait over.

Also in the month of May (though for all the effect that came
of it 'tis hardly worth mentioning) commissioners arrived,
appointed under the Conciliatory Bills—Lord Carlisle, Eden,
and Johnstone—to offer concessions and accommodations.
But as the Americans, bound by the terms of their alliance
with France, demanded the recognition of their independence, or the withdrawal of King George's troops as a
preliminary to all negotiations, nothing but some delay was
the result — delay hurtful to Britain, having regard to
d'Estaing, who was approaching with his superior fleet.

A few days before midsummer, Clinton evacuated
Philadelphia, and started to march northward, through New
Jersey, to his base at New York—none too early, for d'Estaing
was already much overdue. Lord Howe, in his cool,
workmanlike manner, unperturbed by the British Government's neglect to reinforce him, or even to send him word
of the sailing of the French admiral (such oversights he
appears to have taken with resignation, as he did gales,
shoals, and tides, and the other natural hazards and conditions of his service), got on board his transports all the

stores and supplies and sailed for New York, arriving there without misadventure.

Clinton was less fortunate. He had been compelled to return north with his army by land, for the reason that his ships afforded barely sufficient accommodation for the large numbers of loyalist refugees whom it was considered unsafe to leave to the tender mercies of Congress. His force numbered ten thousand. Against him were thirteen thousand colonials, who hung upon his left flank and threatened to envelop his rear.

On June 28 Washington sent orders to General Lee, who commanded the advanced division, to attack the British at Monmouth Court-house. But Lee was a thoroughly incompetent soldier, and evidence has come to light in recent years which raises the suspicion that he was also a traitor.[1] He hesitated, expressed grave doubts and found delay wiser than action. Cornwallis, realising the danger, pushed forward his baggage, and came to the aid of the rearguard. Being met by no attack, he proceeded with his usual prompt valour to deliver one. Lee thereupon ordered a general retreat.

It was a day of excessive heat, when the astonished Washington, riding forward at the head of his main army, encountered a string of fugitives. They were ignorant of any reason for their flight except that it was by order. With the aid of his staff, the rout was checked and the battle re-formed. Cornwallis was driven back, the lost ground recovered, and the exhausted troops bivouacked on the field. The British had lost a rearguard action, but the Americans had lost the opportunity of a crowning victory. By the following morning Cornwallis had withdrawn, and Clinton's army was safe, if not from effective pursuit, at least from annihilation.

A grateful tradition has so recklessly transformed the

[1] Fiske's *American Revolution*, i. pp. 300-306.

character of Washington that he has become a kind of
mechanical monster stuffed with incredible copy-book
headings, strangely unlike the altogether human and
passionate hero that he was in fact. At Monmouth Court-
house on that blazing, winking, dusty afternoon, the commander-in-chief received the report of his subordinate.
A blast of pale anger, a terrific eloquence of unprintable
scorn, and General Lee vanished from all part and prominence in the war. After a feeble recovery of the spirits,
a few months of inglorious notoriety, some bursts of impu-
dence and muttering discontent, he faded utterly out of
the knowledge of men.

Sir Henry Clinton's retreat had cost him fifteen hundred
men by the time he reached the southern shore opposite
Staten Island. Here he put his army on board Lord Howe's
transports, which having disembarked their passengers in
safety had now returned across the bay to his assistance.
By the end of the first week in July he was safe in New
York, but only in the nick of time.

The British admiral, unlike his adversary, had been
fortunate as well as skilful. Having secured the army,
he prepared to encounter d'Estaing, who commanded a
fleet of double his numbers and more than double his
armament. The episode of which this gallant and good-
tempered gentleman was the hero is one of the few in the
history of the American War to which the British nation
can look back with unmingled satisfaction. He disposed
his small fleet in so masterly a fashion across the entrance
to New York harbour that d'Estaing judged him, after a
careful reconnaissance, to be unassailable, and towards the
end of July moved to Rhode Island, a hundred and fifty miles
to the north, where a colonial force under General Sullivan
was endeavouring to drive the British out of Newport.[1]

[1] Mahan, *Types of Naval Officers*, pp. 276-284.

But on the 9th of August, to the bewilderment of the allies, the British fleet appeared off the entrance to Narragansett Bay. Lord Howe had received reinforcements, which brought his strength in numbers up to about two-thirds of the French. The adverse balance, in his opinion, might be redressed by seamanship, and in this he rightly believed himself to hold an easy superiority. The British had lost command of the sea, and so long as he should lie at anchor in New York harbour, the allies had gained that inestimable advantage. The best he could hope for with so inferior a force was to produce a deadlock in which neither party held a clear predominance.

His unforeseen arrival and daring menace drew the French admiral in pursuit. After two days during which Lord Howe skilfully manœuvred in the open sea, a gale sprang up which separated the two fleets and inflicted so great damage upon d'Estaing that he considered it imperative to retire to Boston, fifty miles further north, to refit. Upon this General Sullivan was obliged to withdraw, which he did in high dudgeon, relieving his wounded feelings in indiscreet and bitter criticism of his faint-hearted ally. Colonial opinion echoed these hot opinions, so that it needed all the cool tactfulness of Washington to prevent the prophecy of Chatham coming true, and the 'unnatural alliance which had been welcomed with such fervid enthusiasm from falling hopelessly to pieces.

D'Estaing sailed for the West Indies early in November, and his departure gave back the command of the sea to Lord Howe's successor. Under favour of this condition the British pressed an attack in the southern states, capturing and holding the town and harbour of Savannah.

The Fifth Year of the war (1779) lacked the excitement of great events. The want of French co-operation until the

late autumn produced a deadlock.   In the chief seat of
the war, the state of New York, Washington did not feel
himself strong enough to attack the British lines, while
Clinton was too weak to push his army into the open and
risk a pitched battle in a hostile country.

For the first time since the beginning of the war, winter
had passed without famine or excessive privation among
the colonial troops.   But Congress had less credit for this
result than the increased authority of the commander-in-
chief and the disastrous experience of previous years, which
even the state governments who held the purse-strings
were driven to respect.

Congress was in fact as bankrupt as ever of executive
powers, and still more bankrupt in the matter of capable
men.   For the need of officers had drawn many away, while
foreign missions had found more congenial employment for
others.   The finances of the country were in a most
melancholy state of exhaustion ; while profit-making and
corruption took a heavy toll upon the meagre funds.
'Speculation and peculation,' in Washington's phrase, were
deadlier enemies than the fleets and armies of King George.
In such circumstances a campaign of passive resistance,
upon which Washington had determined, placed a severe
strain upon the spirits of his dwindling army.

In the spring the British operations were confined to a
series of raids which have raised the usual cloud of charges
and countercharges of barbarity which are incidental to the
nature of such a plan of campaign.   Where the devastation
of homesteads is the deliberate policy of a commander, the
argument of expediency will not wipe out bitter memories,
whether the general be British or American—Clinton in
New Jersey or Sherman in Georgia.

In June the British showed an inclination to extend
their posts along the Hudson.   Forts were captured

and recaptured, occupied and demolished, but no events happened which gave a decided advantage to either side. Washington turned a deaf ear to all heroic advice, and steadily pursued his weary strategy of squeezing Clinton back into his lines as often as he showed a disposition to move out of them. He turned an equally deaf ear to the cries of Congress for a more ferocious retaliation in the matter of the raids. He knew his own business and the nature of war. Considering he was but a plain country gentleman and a soldier, he also understood with marvellous insight those orators and journalists, drunk with the rumours of outrage and atrocity, ignorant of warfare and by temperament averse from it. He rated the value of their counsel at a price that was unflattering, and the opinion of the army supported him in his clemency.

As was but natural, there were strong murmurs against the French. For ten months the alliance had lain dormant. The sea-power of Britain was as absolute as it had been in the early years of the war. On the 1st of September, however, d'Estaing reappeared off Savannah, which was still in British hands. In co-operation with the American besiegers he delivered an attack which was repulsed. During October he sailed away with the greater part of his ships for France, so that even the menace of a superior hostile fleet in the West Indies was withdrawn, and Britain resumed her command of the sea.

CHAPTER VI

The End of the War

IN the early days of the Sixth Year of the war (1780) the outlook of the American States seemed as hopeless as in the black autumn of '76.   Men suffered less, or at any rate felt their sufferings with a duller ache, but no excitement would have been so dangerous as the weariness that was hanging on their shoulders.   It seemed to them as if, in spite of all their valour and devotion, in spite of the capacity of their leader and the success of his strategy, in spite even of their superior numbers, more earnest spirit, and the advantage of a well-known and friendly country, they were after all about to be crushed by the sheer weight of an enemy who, possessing boundless resources, would neither budge nor yield.   Their treasury was as dry as a summer sandbank, and foreign loans were hard to come by.

Congress was sometimes hysterical, often absurd, and always impotent.   It passed resolutions, gave much advice to the commander-in-chief, and sat for ever whistling for a wind.   The state governments were filled with jealousy, spleen and suspicions, by no means groundless, one of another.   They were incapable equally of effective co-operation and of delegation of their petty sovereignties to the hands of a federal power.   The Army, under ill treatment and neglect, was dwindling, and had even become mutinous. The people had comforted their sad hearts with a splendid alliance, but the nuptials were barely concluded when, like the citizen's fashionable wife, the partner proved gadding and unprofitable.   The British enemy remained in stolid occupation of the chief commercial city; and in this commanding position, which enabled them always to menace injury, and often to inflict it, they remained unassailable so long as they held command of the sea.   In the early weeks of the year the royalist army in the south, reinforced by sympathisers among the American citizens, and led by Sir Henry Clinton himself, was vigorously pushing on the siege of Charleston with good prospects of success.

The feeling of discouragement was not only excusable as a

weakness of human nature, but was grounded in the very facts of the situation. Had the British government been willing to risk some bold stroke of magnanimity, had it acted with more astuteness and greater energy, or had there arisen some statesman of the mettle of the elder Pitt, suddenly awakening the slumbering spirit of patriotism among the people, we feel that, even at the eleventh hour, our ancestors might still have turned the tables on their adversaries and prevented the disruption of the empire. The faults of King George the Third have been conceded with a liberal hand, and are written large in every schoolbook of history. It is but due, however, to his memory to recognise that, although the beginnings of the quarrel may have been owing in great measure to his defects of judgment and of temper, he stood alone among his ministers, and all but alone among his subjects, in the possession of that spirit and pride of duty that made the strength of Washington and his ragged army.

In April Lafayette returned from France bringing news of a French fleet and army to sail without delay. Washington thereupon turned his mind to plans for a joint attack upon New York, and to the alternative scheme for a combination against the enemy in the south. But on May 12 Charleston, hitherto deemed impregnable, was stormed and captured by Clinton, an achievement which deserves high praise for its skill and daring. His losses were but two hundred and fifty men, and with this small sacrifice he secured the town and harbour, and took six thousand prisoners and four hundred guns. Having secured his conquest, he left Cornwallis in command in the south, which now lay open to invasion, and returned to New York. Washington held grimly to the Hudson river, and awaited the coming of the French forces.

Towards the middle of July an army of five thousand

men under Rochambeau, and a small fleet with seven ships
of the line under de Ternay, arrived once more off Rhode Island, bringing intelligence of a larger fleet that was to follow. Their arrival was welcome; but the orders of the French Government that no important enterprises were to be undertaken until the promised reinforcements should appear produced much heartburning. Weeks went by, and then word came that the second fleet lay in Brest Harbour blocked by a British admiral.

Under this disappointment the heads even of good soldiers and citizens began to swim, and the mouths of men were full of contradictory reasons for resting from the struggle. Some drew attention to the empty treasury; others to the fact that the French had now come; others, again, demonstrated convincingly that the British were worn out, and as good as beaten already. August saw the army on the verge of dissolution. But Washington, as ever, was calm, industrious and determined; writing with suppressed passion to Congress; inspiriting his troops; reasoning with men by letter and speech, and succeeding somehow in keeping things together.

September was a black month for the Americans. Cornwallis in the south with two thousand men utterly defeated their army, over three thousand strong, at Camden, under Gates, the conqueror of Burgoyne. Washington returning from a meeting with Rochambeau learned of the treachery and flight of General Arnold commanding at West Point. Meanwhile the army watching New York starved and became more mutinous. Admiral Rodney with a portion of his fleet visited the city, but unfortunately he did not see his duty in the same light as it had appeared to Lord Howe. The French were left undisturbed at Newport, and he sailed back to the West Indies.

A.D. 1781
Æt. 24 When the Seventh Year of the war (1781) opened, Greene, the best of Washington's generals, took command against Cornwallis in the south. He had succeeded Gates, whose vanity and incompetence were at length manifest even to Congress despite his flattery and intrigues. A column under Arnold, now in the British service, ravaged Virginia. Washington's hands were full of disciplinary matters. There was a mutiny of the Pennsylvania regiments, due to the misery of their conditions, and when that was settled, another broke out among their comrades of New Jersey. Some hanging was necessary, from which the commander-in-chief did not shrink.

Greene, opposed to the main army under Cornwallis, made a successful retreat, drawing the British two hundred miles from their base, but leaving both the Carolinas at their mercy. On March 15, Greene with four thousand five hundred men judged himself to be in sufficient strength to turn and risk a battle with his redoubtable antagonist, who had less than half his numbers. But he was heavily defeated at Guilford Court-house; though, like many of the British victories, this one also was barren of good results for the conquerors. Cornwallis found himself obliged to retreat to Wilmington, and the Americans re-entered South Carolina. Again at Hobkirk Hill on April 25 Greene was beaten by a small force of nine hundred men under Lord Rawdon, but being too weak to pursue, the British troops were forced to retire on Charleston.

At the end of March de Grasse sailed from Brest with an overwhelming fleet of twenty-six ships of the line and a large convoy, arriving at Martinique in the last days of April.[1]

Cornwallis at Wilmington debated whether he should rejoin Rawdon at Charleston or push on to Arnold in the

[1] Mahan, *The Influence of Sea Power in History*, chap. x.

north. At the end of April he determined on the latter
course, and the fate of the war was decided.

On May 20 Cornwallis met Arnold at Petersburg, when
their united armies amounted to five thousand men. Taking
command, he sent Arnold back to New York. Clinton when
he heard of this movement condemned it, and with good
reason. The position of an army resting on the Chesapeake
depended for its safety on command of the sea, and this upon
his information was unlikely to be retained for many weeks
longer.

Washington, having full knowledge of the intentions of de
Grasse, discussed with Rochambeau the alternatives—a
combined attack upon Clinton's army in New York, or upon
that of Cornwallis in the south. Having decided upon the
latter course, the allies determined to alarm Clinton by the
feint of an attack, which succeeded so well that he applied
to Cornwallis for reinforcements.

Towards the middle of August a frigate brought word that
de Grasse might shortly be expected in the Chesapeake.
Washington wrote immediately in reply that he would join
him with as many troops as could be spared from the
investment of the main army of the British.

In Virginia, Lafayette with light troops had for some time
been watching and harassing Cornwallis, who had gradually
withdrawn to the coast, and was established with his principal force at Yorktown, on the south shore of the estuary
of the York river.

On the 21st of August Washington began to move his
army southwards. On the 23rd and 24th he crossed from
the east to the west bank of the Hudson river. On the
27th de Barras, the French admiral at Newport, sailed with
his fleet of eight ships of the line, and eighteen transports
carrying troops and a siege-train, to join de Grasse in the
south.

Rodney in the West Indies, at the news of the French departure from these waters, had detached Hood with fourteen ships to follow them.[1] Making a quicker passage, the British arrived in Chesapeake Bay three days before the enemy, and finding no trace of him sailed on to New York. Admiral Graves at that station had five ships of the line, and was Hood's senior officer. He took command of the united fleet, and having word of de Barras's departure from Newport, weighed anchor on the 31st in the hopes of delivering a crushing blow. But the French had good luck in their sluggishness, and Graves went past without sighting them. When he arrived in Chesapeake Bay he found only the fleet of de Grasse, which outnumbered him by five ships of the line. He engaged gallantly, but without discretion, and allowed de Grasse to manœuvre him gradually out of the bay, declining action for five consecutive days. Meanwhile de Barras arrived with his contingent, and Graves, hopelessly outnumbered, withdrew to New York. It was a good scheme on the part of the British, and miscarried partly through ill-fortune, but mainly through a lack of wits.

September opened hopefully for the allies. On the 2nd Washington, having taken every ingenious precaution to conceal his departure, reached Philadelphia with his army. About the same time Clinton appears to have first realised that he was seriously bent on a southern movement. In the south Greene engaged Colonel Stewart at Eutaw Springs, and fought an indecisive battle, but the result was to force the British commander to fall back upon Charleston, thereby cutting off Cornwallis's retreat towards the south. On the 22nd French transports carried Washington's army down the Chesapeake and up the James river to Williamsburg. On the 28th he marched on Yorktown. The meshes were

---

[1] Mahan, *The Influence of Sea Power in History*, chap. x.

being drawn very tight round the best soldier who had
fought in America for King George.

The French fleet held the river mouth against escape or succour.   To the south, the estuary of the James, four hundred miles of hostile country, and the army of Greene, cut off all hope of a retreat on Charleston.   To the north the York river, over a mile broad, separated Cornwallis from his outpost at Gloucester.   To transport his little army, numbering somewhat more than seven thousand men, in open boats across such an obstacle, exposed during the process to attack from the fleet at anchor in the bay, having transported it in safety, to traverse Maryland and Pennsylvania and New Jersey to New York, four hundred miles away, with an elated enemy on his heels and lining every wood and river bank upon the march, was an opportunity so slender that only desperation could have thought of clutching at it. Across the peninsula to the west, cutting him off entirely from the mainland, lay the army of Washington, eighteen thousand strong—eleven thousand Americans and seven thousand Frenchmen—with a heavy and well-appointed siege-train.   The allies were full of fresh hope and ardour, and their great leader was calmly confident of a crowning victory at last.   Discouragement and disease among the British and their Hessian mercenaries increased the odds against Cornwallis.   So matters stood on the 1st of October 1781.

On the 5th the Americans opened their trenches. On the 14th two commanding redoubts were captured —the first by a light corps led by Colonel Alexander Hamilton with great judgment and gallantry, the second more deliberately by the French.   The game was hopeless from the beginning, and now it was all but played out. Still the intrepid defender remained obdurate to all talk of a surrender.   If he could not avert the inevitable, he could at all events add another example of courage and resource to the great tradition of the British arms. His ammunition was giving out, and many of his soldiers were sick. He made a night attack, spiked guns, destroyed some earthworks, but to no purpose. Then he formed an audacious scheme of escape to the north. One contingent crossed successfully to the northern shore; but even the elements were against him. A gale sprang up in which no open boat, weighted to the gunwale with men and stores, could ever hope to live.

So upon the 19th of October, there being no other course available, he surrendered. In a war which was the grave of most men's reputations who had in it any prominent part, military or civil, Cornwallis almost alone added to his fame. For not only was he a soldier of stainless courage, but he had a bold and steady judgment, and in his actions a promptness that was lacking in all the others.

Yorktown was the end of the war. Charleston and Savannah were evacuated in the succeeding year, and only New York remained in possession of the King's troops.

Washington was not less admirable in success than under defeat. He had no thought of taking his ease until not only victory, but the fruits of victory, had been secured. The general conviction that the war was over seemed to him to be fraught with dangerous possibilities. Negotiation must follow, supposing both parties to be inclined to peace. Having regard to the alliance with France and Spain, who as yet had tasted little of the sweets of conquest, had settled but few of their old accounts, and had enjoyed revenge only, as it were, vicariously, in the profit

taken by a third party at the expense of their ancient foe, A.D. 1781
it was probable that such negotiations would extend over a ÆT. 24
long period.

Washington was still too weak to turn Clinton out of
New York without French aid, and the French had other
more urgent uses for their ships and men. But it was a
clear necessity that Clinton should be kept fast under lock
and key, otherwise, when it came to a treaty, the British
Government might have some solid advantage to throw
into the scales. At all costs the colonial army must be kept
in being, an effective force, capable not only of defence but
of aggression. In this attempt it was necessary to reckon
with Congress and the state governments, and the temper of
the civil population and the army itself, who were, one and
all, weary of the war, and only too much inclined to a
complacent admiration of their past valour. At no period
of his career had the commander-in-chief to encounter
difficulties that were harder to contend with, and his credit
stands as high in these irksome labours as it did at Princeton,
Valley Forge, or Yorktown.

In March, in the Eighth Year of the war (1782), the A.D. 1782
British House of Commons voted for the discontinuance of ÆT. 25
hostilities, and Lord George Germaine resigned. There is a
touch of irony in the event; for his retention of office would
now no longer have been of any conspicuous injury to his
country.

In May Washington was imploring the states for men,
and for money to pay the troops and to provide them with
supplies.[1] The question of arrears and pensions was very
urgent. In October we find him writing to the Secretary

---

[1] Sparks's *Washington*, viii. pp. 284-88.

of War on these matters, pressing immediate consideration of the just claims of his soldiers, "after having spent the ' flower of their days, and many of them their patrimonies, ' in establishing the freedom and independence of their ' country."[1]

But in Congress, and not only in Congress, but also in the people, there was an exaggerated standard of political morality founded upon stock phrases regarding the subordination of the military to the civil power. In times of war this excessive virtue had yielded with a sigh to the importunate violence of events, but with the return of peace it sought to stifle the memory of its lapse under a prudish, circumspect, precise and jealous behaviour. The army was at last told in plain words that it placed too high an estimate both upon its importance and its claims. It was exhorted to practise the virtue of patience. By and by, when the civil power should decide in its wisdom that the time was ripe, something would probably be done. As a matter of grace, relief would then be doled out, of such a kind as prudent citizens, without losing sight of first principles, could allow to thoughtless fellows who had risked nothing but their fortunes and their reputations for the common good. Addressed in terms of so cool a gratitude, the army began to murmur mutinously, and to consider whether after all it was not master of the situation. There was talk of a dictator,[2] which threw Washington into a rage and Hamilton into a fit of laughter.

In the following year things became graver. There was open sedition, of which the heroic Gates was the secret instigator.[3] The army, urged in anonymous broadsheets to use force for securing its well-earned provision of half-pay, gave an attentive ear. Gates in former years, with the aid

---

[1] Sparks's *Washington*, viii. p. 354. [2] *History*, ii. p. 111.
[3] *Ibid.* ii. pp. 393-94.

A.D. 1782
Æт. 25

of Congress, had endeavoured to supplant Washington in the chief command. He now turned upon his former ally, and made it the object of his mean intrigues to destroy the affection of the army for its great leader by forcing him to act as the protector of Congress.

There was only one man in America capable of quelling the mutinous spirit, and he, by the irony of fate, was in full sympathy with the grievance. His enemies counted safely that to Washington disorder and civil war would appear even greater evils than the suffering of his soldiers. They judged rightly that he would not hesitate in his course of action. A meeting of the discontented assembled upon an appointed day, and Gates was called on to preside. Washington attended with a set speech in writing in his pocket. "He, who had never been greeted but with affec-
' tion, was received with cold and calm respect. It appeared
' as though sedition had felt it necessary to commence her
' secret work by engendering suspicions against the Father
' of his country. He arose: he felt the estrangement—
' he paused, and he doubted of the issue. As he uncovered
' his venerated head, and was about to address them from
' a written paper in his hand, his eye grew dim, and he
' uttered this pathetic unpremeditated remark: ' Fellow
' soldiers, you perceive I have not only grown grey, but
' blind in your service.' " [1] He then proceeded to read his speech, which was an indignant condemnation of the conspiracy; but the phrase of his opening had been enough. "Awed by the majesty of his virtue, and touched with
' his interest in their sufferings, every soldier's eye was
' filled with a generous tear; they reproved themselves
' for having doubted him who had never deceived them:
' they forgot their wrongs, in the love of their country
' and of their chief." [2]

[1] *History*, ii. p. 391.   [2] *Ibid.* p. 393.

A.D. 1783   By the autumn of 1782 the allies of the states were in a
Æt. 26   more accommodating humour for discussing terms of peace.
In April, Rodney in the West Indies had broken the line
of de Grasse.   In September, Elliot at Gibraltar, after a
three years' siege, had burned de Crillon's famous batteries
to the water's edge.   The preliminary articles of peace were
signed on January the 20th, 1783, and the welcome news
reached Washington in March.   In November the British
army left New York, and before Christmas Day the American
commander-in-chief had bidden his officers good-bye and
laid down his commission in Congress.

CHAPTER VII

The Military Secretary

A.D. 1776   IN March '76, a few days before Washington drove Sir
Æt. 19   William Howe out of Boston, Hamilton was appointed to
the captaincy of the company of artillery which had been
raised by New York state.   In January of the same year
he had celebrated his nineteenth birthday.   Murmurs on
the score of his youth were quieted by testimonials from
the military instructors, and at the earliest opportunity by
his conduct in the field.   It is notable that he laboured at
the science of his profession during the twelve months that
intervened between his enrolment in the Hearts of Oak
and the battle of Brooklyn, with the same zeal which he
had previously given to philosophy and the classics.   In
drills and gun-practice he was equally industrious, and
valued the smart appearance of his company to the extent
of giving the larger portion of his allowance from the West
Indies to their external embellishment.[1]

[1] *Life*, p. 52.

In the famous passage from Brooklyn he brought up the rear, comported himself in such a manner as to win considerable credit, and lost his baggage and a gun. He attracted the favourable notice of Greene, the best general who served under Washington, and afterwards, during the retreat from New York, of the commander-in-chief himself, who was impressed by his earthworks at Harlem, and engaged him in conversation.[1] At White Plains he again won admiration for the coolness and courage with which he used his battery to check the British attack.[2] In October, after the fall of the posts on the Hudson river, he volunteered to retake Fort Washington, but the offer did not commend itself at headquarters.[3] In the late autumn, when the American army was falling back through New Jersey, dwindling in numbers and hope, he again earned high praise by the bold and sagacious handling of his battery for the protection of the rearguard in its crossing of the Raritan.[4] By the end of the year he had won as great a fame for his soldierly qualities as a few months earlier for his pamphlets and speeches. A contemporary record is quoted by his biographer:—"I noticed a youth, a mere stripling, 'small, slender, almost delicate in frame, marching beside 'a piece of artillery with a cocked hat pulled down over 'his eyes, apparently lost in thought, with his hand resting 'on the cannon, and every now and then patting it as 'he mused, as if it were a favourite horse or a pet play-'thing."[5]

On the 1st of March 1777 he was appointed aide-de-camp to General Washington with the rank of lieutenant-colonel, and entered into close relations with that great man which lasted for the whole period of their joint lives. It is fair to assume that he owed this appointment as much

[1] *Life*, p. 56.   [2] *Ibid.* p. 56.   [3] *Ibid.* p. 56.
[4] *Ibid.* p. 57.   [5] *History*, i. pp. 137-8.

to his reputation with the pen as to the handling of his battery. The combination of qualities made him invaluable. Washington was overwhelmed with correspondence, and although he wrote well, it was with extreme difficulty and slowness, and innumerable corrections even in such details as grammar and spelling. A large proportion of his letters were political and diplomatic, rather than military in the strictest sense. A boy who was not only a ready and powerful writer, but who possessed in addition the instinct of a statesman and the spirit of a soldier, was an inestimable discovery. From the first he acted as secretary, sharing the duties of the post with one who became at once his devoted friend, 'the old secretary,' General Harrison. The affection of this colleague invented the nickname which has stuck—'the little lion.'[1]

From the first, also, he was employed to write important documents, and sent upon errands that required character and discretion. It is beyond question that the messages to Congress, and the correspondence with British generals, which impressed Europe with the dignity and power of the American leader, were mainly the work of Hamilton's mind. The official correspondence of Washington during this period had a wide audience and a great celebrity, and while we must acknowledge the credit due to his secretary in the vigour, the logical arrangement, the lucidity and the stateliness of these documents, we are no less bound to beware of the absurd explanation which has depicted the commander-in-chief as a kind of puppet. It is a favourite device of a certain class of commentators upon great men to attribute their excellences always to some one else, and Hamilton has not altogether escaped this indiscreet tribute, either during his life or subsequently. But certainly he never sought it,

[1] *Life*, p. 64.

nor gave the least colour to the legend. Washington was not the readiest of writers, but he held his opinions in a vice; and we may safely assume that if his vivacious secretary had happened upon any occasion to set forth his own views and not those of his chief, the despatch containing them would have been rewritten before it was signed. It is not unfair, however, nor is it any derogation from the splendid character of the commander-in-chief, to say that Hamilton began by writing to his instructions, and ended by divining, interpreting and anticipating his thoughts.[1] In counsel no less than in action, the greatest of Washington's qualities was his instinct for the true relation of things. Reasoning and argument were only a degree less irksome to him than composition and penmanship. It has been said of him by one who had acted as his secretary, that when some important document had to be acknowledged, he left his bewildered amanuensis to find not only the words, but even the answer itself. But to live on close terms with Washington was to be dominated by his opinions to such an extent that it would have been difficult to run counter to them.

Of one of Hamilton's services we have very ample records. At the end of October, after the news had come of Burgoyne's surrender, he was despatched to General Gates for reinforcements. He was in his twenty-first year, and had been acting as military secretary for a period of only eight months. Gates was a vain, envious and foolish creature, but he was also a victorious general. He had reaped where others had sown, and was enjoying an immense fame and popularity in consequence. His success at Saratoga was contrasted by shallow and impatient people with the defeat at Brandywine and the fall of Philadelphia. There was a strong Gates party, composed of his own henchmen and the ill-wishers of the

[1] Pickering to Coleman, *History*, ii., preface, p. vii.

commander-in-chief. Gates, in the first flush of conquest, had even permitted himself certain deliberate slights and discourtesies. Altogether it was a difficult embassy for a boy to accomplish with credit, and it may be taken as proof of the confidence which Washington reposed in Hamilton that he went armed with a letter, to use if there were need of it, clothing him with absolute power and leaving everything to his discretion.

Gates, as might have been expected, demurred to parting with two out of his three brigades, and pretended danger from Sir Henry Clinton in New York as his justification. He would give one of the three, which Hamilton, mindful of the diplomacies, was about to accept with a wry face, when he discovered that it was less than half the strength of either of the others, and liable to still further diminution at an early date through the expiry of the term of enlistment. Thereupon Hamilton had no option but to act upon his powers. His letter to Gates is a masterpiece of courtesy in the imperative mood. The victorious general, surprised in sharp practice, gave up more than he need otherwise have done, and added a second brigade.

With General Putnam, whom he met by the way, Hamilton dealt more cavalierly. Putnam was a better man than Gates, braver and more honest, but he had what in Scotland is called 'a bee in his bonnet.' With him high matters were a complete confusion, and the little things usually took precedence of the big. Like many brave veterans who are dimly conscious of their own lack of perspicacity, he was of a most touchy disposition. Orders given without any authority by a very youthful staff officer, commanding him forthwith to detach troops to the south when he had been planning a baresark descent upon Clinton in New York, were a great deal more than he could stand with equanimity.

Hamilton returned a few days later, after his encounter
with General Gates, to find that his august commands to General Putnam had not been carried into execution. His indignation was only equalled by his determination to be obeyed. He was shivering with fever, but such was the force of his youthful spirit that from his sick-bed orders went forth to Putnam's puzzled subordinates to march south immediately, and neither the unwillingness of one, nor the ingenious pretext of another that his men were undergoing 'an operation for the itch,' was able to stand against such persuasions.

In the following year we find for the first time murmurs against the undue influence exercised by Hamilton upon the mind of Washington. The charge was maintained till the end of his days, and in later years became one of the chief cries of the Democratic party. The power which Hamilton exercised over the minds of his fellows and over events is undeniable; but throughout his life he was ever suspected of an even greater personal influence than he possessed. The superior brilliance of his personality distorted the true proportions of every word and action. If something noteworthy was done, men were certain that he had pulled the strings; if something remarkable was said, that he had prompted. All admiration and odium were concentrated upon him, and it was conceived to be impossible for any colleague to retain his independence of will or judgment in such dangerous company.

Hamilton's correspondence during the period of the war is full of interest, and bears evidence to a clear and soldierly view of the situation. But what has been preserved is only a fragment, and where we should most desire his commentary there is usually a gap. In the early months of the year he was engaged at Valley Forge with a com-

mittee of Congress, drafting and redrafting their reports
upon the organisation and subsistence of the army.　He
kept up a regular but unofficial correspondence in his
own name, but on his general's behalf, with the friendly
party in Congress.　At the battle of Monmouth he
appeared once more as a soldier, protesting energetically
against the tactics of Lee and rallying the retreating
regiments.　Afterwards he was sent to interview Admiral
d'Estaing.

In the following winter ('79), while the army lay watching
the British, a plan for kidnapping Sir Henry Clinton was
hatched by some audacious spirits.　"The British general
' was then occupying a house near the Battery, in New York,
' situate a few yards from the Hudson river.　Intelligence,
' through spies, had been obtained of the approaches to his
' bedchamber.　Light whale-boats, with muffled oars, were
' to be placed under the command of Colonel Humphreys,
' of Connecticut; and the party, in full preparation, were
' waiting anxiously the approach of night for the execution
' of their purpose. . . . Colonel Hamilton, in the interval,
' became informed of the intended enterprise.　He observed
' to General Washington 'that there could be little doubt
' of its success; but, sir,' said he, 'have you examined the
' consequences of it ? '　The general inquired, ' In what
' respect ? '　' Why,' replied Hamilton, 'it has occurred to
' me that we shall rather lose than gain by removing Sir
' Henry Clinton from the command of the British army,
' because we perfectly understand *his* character; and, by
' taking him off, we only make way for some other, perhaps
' an abler officer, whose character and disposition we have
' to learn.'　The general acknowledged the force of the
' objection, and abandoned the project."[1] . . . There is
an almost preternatural sagacity in such reasoning.　The

[1] *Life*, pp. 218, 219.

scene appeals to the imagination so strongly that we
pray it may indeed have happened:—the solemn general,
with the weight of American freedom on his broad
shoulders, standing six feet two in his shoes and frown-
ing over his big, thick nose which turned to so bright a
scarlet in cold weather that intelligent strangers visiting
in the camp suspected the sobriety of his habits; the
little secretary, stretching to his full height of some five
feet six, delicate and dark-eyed, propounding with an
awful and relentless gravity the logical defects of this
exuberant plan—it is a situation filled with the spirit
of eternal humour. For beyond doubt either of the two
men would have given his ears to go, had his duty allowed
it, in the light whale-boat with muffled oars to steal Sir
Henry Clinton from his bed-chamber in that dark night
of February.

In December 1780 Hamilton was married to Miss Betsy
Schuyler, a girl of great charm and a quick and humorous
intelligence. Her father was that General Schuyler who
had held the important command of the northern army
until a few weeks before Saratoga, when Gates, by intrigues
with Congress, contrived to supplant him and to reap the
credit of his patient strategy. Despite his ill-treatment
Schuyler continued to serve against Burgoyne as a volunteer until the British surrender, when he showed the most
considerate hospitality to his defeated enemies. He was
a man of a noble and magnanimous nature, greatly trusted
by Washington, and possessing much political influence,
especially in his native state of New York, by reason of his
character, his old family traditions of public spirit, and his
wide possessions. To what extent this alliance added to
Hamilton's resources is uncertain, for he was of a fierce
independence with respect to money matters; but the
marriage, which had the hearty approval of his wife's

family, assured his position as an American citizen. It was, in other respects also, a fortunate and happy union to the end. For in spite of certain scandals that were brought to light in later days through the industry of political malice, the confidence and affection existing between the two was never shaken. The private shortcomings of Hamilton cannot be denied. He has himself admitted them gravely and with dignity, making neither reservation nor excuse; but as regards his loyalty there has never at any time existed even the shadow of a doubt.

The circumstances of Hamilton's resignation of his staff appointment have been made the subject of much fine writing. It is clear that even so early as the spring of 1780 he had grown somewhat impatient of his office, and had sought without success an independent command in the south, at a time when the fortunes of the colonists were by no means brilliant, and there had been much hard fighting and many serious defeats. It must be remembered that he valued himself more highly as a soldier than in any other capacity. He believed, whether rightly or wrongly can never be decided, that war was his true profession, and that if the chance were given he could prove himself to be a great commander. His post on the staff was a strict and literal secretaryship, more civil indeed than military. It was indeed ' the grovelling condition of a clerk,' which his youthful genius had contemned with such vivacity. The very excellence of his work made promotion nearly impossible; for Washington could find many capable men to lead columns, but what other to write letters to Congress?

The cause of the severance was simple enough, but, as the incident was dramatic, it has resulted that Hamilton has sometimes been accused of ingratitude to his benefactor. This rupture, or quarrel, assuredly did not produce the effect that such occurrences beget in the relations of common men; for within a week or two of the event we find Washington inviting his ex-secretary to be present at a private conference with Rochambeau, and signing himself 'yours sincerely and affectionately.'[1] Indeed, there is not the slightest evidence of any slackening in their mutual confidence either then or afterwards. The truth of the matter appears to lie in this—that a great man will not continue contentedly to be secretary to any one, not even to another great man many years his senior, at a time full of arduous enterprises and stirring events. It is a trying relationship, and must soon become intolerable to a vigorous and independent mind. Hamilton longed for a command in the field, and the work which in despondent moments he may have regarded as that of a conduit pipe became more and more distasteful to him. In the end he seized at an opportunity that let him escape into freedom.

The evidence against him is his own letter. He had the defects of his qualities. Not to write upon any subject which interested him was an impossibility; and he had the further Johnsonian failing that he made his minnows speak like whales. There is often a touch of the 'my-ambition-is-prevalent' in his early letters, and when he wrote to his admiring father-in-law, General Schuyler, to explain why he had ceased to be a member of General Washington's 'family,' his statement is more than usually pompous. The commander-in-chief had met him on the stairs and desired his immediate attendance. The Marquis de Lafayette had button-holed him as he was hastening to obey. Washington had exploded, as the best man will, at having been kept waiting; imagined it was ten minutes

[1] *Life*, p. 373.

when in fact it was but two.   The little secretary was
icily respectful under the tempest, but adamantine that
the incident must end his service.   As to the alleged
delay—'I am not conscious of it, sir; but since you
have thought it, we part.'[1]   Nor would any condescension
move him one hairsbreadth.   The good Washington went
further than any but a great man would have gone to
soothe the ruffled feelings; but it was unavailing, not
because feathers were ruffled, but because the bird longed
for freedom.   Doubtless each in his heart understood the
other, and in spite of some display of temper loved him
only the more.

Hamilton resigned his position on the staff in February
1781, and obtained command of a light corps late in the following summer.   In October, when Cornwallis was surrounded
at Yorktown, he found the chance that he had longed for.   It
was indeed too late in the day to dream of becoming a great
general; but the opportunity of proving himself a daring and
capable officer was still open, and Hamilton seized it, or it
might almost be said, snatched it out of the hands of
another who had been appointed over his head.   His assault
upon the first redoubt at Yorktown did not determine the
issue of the war; did not even determine the surrender of
Cornwallis.   It was only one of those brilliant and particular
actions of which military history has thousands on its
record, and will continue, we may safely believe, to inscribe
thousands more so long as there are wars in the world and
brave men.   But although from the general view of the
campaign it may almost be ignored, it was an effective deed,
and showed the highest qualities of swiftness, judgment,
leadership and courage.   It was valuable to Hamilton himself because it confirmed his confidence, and to his descendants as one of those personal heirlooms that will never be

[1] *Works*, ix. pp. 232-37.

forgotten even in a greater fame. The praise of Washington
was never lightly earned. "Few cases," he wrote of the
taking of the first redoubt, "have exhibited greater proofs
' of intrepidity, coolness and firmness than were shown on
' this occasion." [1]

[1] *Life*, p. 383.

BOOK II

THE UNION OF THE STATES

A.D. 1780–1788.   Æt. 23-31

F

*The greatness of an estate in bulk and territory doth fall under measure; and the greatness of finances and revenue doth fall under computation. The population may appear by musters; and the number and greatness of cities and towns by cards and maps. But yet there is not anything amongst civil affairs more subject to error, than the right valuation and true judgment concerning the power and forces of an estate. The Kingdom of Heaven is compared, not to any kernel or nut, but to a grain of mustard seed; which is one of the least grains, but hath in it a property and spirit hastily to get up and spread. So there are states great in territory, and yet not apt to enlarge or command; and some that have but a small dimension of stem, and yet apt to be the foundations of great monarchies.—*BACON.

BOOK II

THE UNION OF THE STATES

CHAPTER I

Political Writings during the War

THE second period of Hamilton's career began in the sixth year of the war. As military secretary he had seen his commander-in-chief hampered and distressed, the army starved and disheartened. He discovered the cause in the impotence, faction and financial discredit of a Congress which affected to represent thirteen jealous and discordant states temporarily and imperfectly united by a common danger. Being what he was, a confidential staff-officer, he viewed the matter in the first instance from that standpoint. He was impressed by the bad effects of misgovernment upon military affairs. He realised that the federal assembly lacked the power, the intelligence and the will to support its generals with vigour and consistency. He was confronted with that order of difficulties which arises when a debating-club is dressed up in the lion's skin of authority; when a deliberative assembly, upon a dubious warrant, endeavours to perform the high executive functions of government. The routine of his office brought him into daily touch with a bustling and eloquent sham. A military secretary, whose concern is with an army and its supplies, may be forgiven for unfavourable opinions of a government that can neither recruit nor provide. To discharge its proper share of the burdens of such

a time it needed to be of good credit, and to this end it
was essential that it should be honest, resourceful and
businesslike. In Hamilton's opinion it was lacking in all
these qualities.

In the autumn following the battle of Monmouth (1778)
he found time to undertake the flagellation of a certain
legislator of Maryland, who had made a corner in flour.
This gentleman was a member not merely of Congress, but
of the very committee charged with provisioning the army
and the French fleet. By Hamilton's account he would
appear to have been a worthy pioneer of the most
modern commercial developments. He played with his
committee, postponing its decision, while his emissaries
bought up all the available flour. Prices were thereupon
doubled, and the speculation wore a smiling face, when by
some means his sins were discovered. Over the signature
Publius,[1] which a few years later was to become immortal
in a nobler controversy, Hamilton is forcible enough, but
not in his happiest vein. The correspondence is a pompous
exercise in the manner of *Junius*, interesting less for its
intrinsic merits than for the simple fact which it records.
Little, indeed, is left of the offender and his corner in
flour; but we feel that such sentences as "notwithstanding
' our youth as a nation we begin to emulate the most veteran
' and accomplished states in the art of corruption,"[2] are a
trifle too grandiose for the occasion that called them forth.

Early in 1780 Robert Morris undertook the desperate
finances of the Federal Government. He was a rich man
and an able administrator, but he had to make bricks without straw. The great plan and the astute, particular resource were equally within the field of his practical energy.
He ruined his own fortune for the state, and a grateful
country allowed him in later years to gain experience in a

---

[1] *Works*, i. p. 199.   [2] *Ibid.* i. p. 202.

debtor's prison.   Money was harder to raise at this time
than ever before.   Supplies were more deficient, and the
army was mutinous.   Hamilton, who held Morris in great
and deserved respect, took the opportunity of his appointment to present him with an anonymous memorandum on
the financial situation.

It is amazing to find a soldier of three-and-twenty, with
his hands full of a laborious official correspondence, with no
experience of business beyond what he had gained as a boy
in a merchant's office, plunging into a detailed and forcible
argument for the establishment of a national bank.[1]   "The
present plan," he announces with modesty, "is the product
' of some reading on the subjects of commerce and finance,
' and of occasional reflections on our particular situation;
' but a want of leisure has prevented its being examined in
' so many lights and digested so materially as its importance
' requires."[2]   There is indeed proof of considerable reading
in this lengthy analysis, though how he can have found the
time for it remains a mystery.   But there is also something
a great deal more valuable.   It is an argument from experience.   It was but a small section of human affairs that
formed the basis of his theories—Cruger's ledgers and
the starvation of the federal army—but he viewed these
scraps of reality in a light of such intense understanding
that they were sufficient for the purpose in hand.   There is
eloquence in the letter, for it is a quality always present in
his writings, even upon the driest themes, but the fabric is
substantial and practical.   The bank is realised down to its
quills and ink-pots as vividly as in its grandest international
operations.   Mr. Law, he argues, was right in his main
idea.[3]   For Law had grasped the necessity of interesting the
moneyed classes to co-operate with Government, and his
policy was a failure only because Law was himself dishonest.

[1] *Works*, iii. p. 319.   [2] *Ibid.* iii. p. 341.   [3] *Ibid.* iii. p. 332.

In the following year Hamilton returned to his argument in a second letter to Morris,[1] this time under his own name. A national bank still appeared to him to be the only way out of the difficulty which had arisen owing to the lack of funds. He accordingly provided an elaborate plan, with articles of constitution. Britain, he argued, had failed to subdue the states by force of arms; she was within an ace of winning by their financial exhaustion. He urged the advantages of a national debt, a blessing if not excessive, and 'a powerful cement of our union.' The idea of an alliance with the moneyed classes, of taking hostages from them, was enforced once more. It remained to the end a fundamental article of his financial creed. Later on, in his own famous administration, he was able to realise it.

Morris in answer was polite and appreciative. He informed his correspondent that a bank was about to be started, following the lines of Hamilton's project, but upon a more modest scale. That a soldier should have sought to intervene in these weary matters with so much zest and vehemence may well have excited wonder in the mind of the statesman. The modern reader marvels to find a military secretary discoursing in his leisure moments on national resources and foreign loans, on imposts and taxes and the balance of trade, propounding a plan for a national bank, elaborating it with an exuberant energy, a comprehensiveness of vision, a directness and ease and force of expression which disclosed the blessed quality of youth in every line and turn. There are occasions in Hamilton's career when we are puzzled whether to laugh or to cry out with admiration at the boyish confidence undaunted by the grimmest difficulties. There is a heroic quality even in his longest letters on taxation. Their passionate sincerity, their joyful audacity, bridge the gulf of years and create an

[1] *Works*, iii. p. 342.

intimacy such as we have felt with our heroes of romance— with Quentin Durward and with d'Artagnan; a confusion of wonder with personal affection. For a true understanding of Hamilton's part in American history it is necessary to realise that he was loved by his contemporaries in this spirit.

A more famous letter was written between the dates of the two that have been mentioned. In August 1780 there was a general despondency, not wholly financial. French aid had arrived at Newport, but the second fleet which was looked to for complete supremacy lay in Brest Harbour blocked by the tyrant of the seas. Americans, with an easy lethargy, affected nevertheless to believe that Britain was finally exhausted. A few days later Gates was routed by Cornwallis at Camden.

'The fundamental defect,' wrote Hamilton to Duane, 'is a want of power in Congress.'[1] Three causes contributed to this misfortune: in the people a jealous excess of the spirit of liberty; in Congress a diffidence of their own authority and a want of sufficient means at their disposal. The clear duty of Congress was to usurp powers in order to preserve the Republic; but its courage stopped short of this solution. The confederation, as it stood, was fit neither for war nor peace.

Men, mindful of the pretensions of a British Parliament, were jealous of sovereignty; but the real danger of the states lay in too little sovereignty and not in too much. The defects of the situation were plain to any one who was not blinded by phrases or misled by distrust.

As funds were the basis of all civil authority, the central government must have the power to tax, which under the existing arrangement was denied to it.

A deliberative body was unfit to rule, for a powerful

[1] *Works*, i. p. 213.

executive must be few and not numerous; active, not merely loquacious.   Congress, from a kind of vanity, was averse from delegation to individuals.   The small powers it possessed were whittled down to an absurdity by delegation to boards; and boards, as John Stuart Mill pointed out in later days, are screens.

The fluctuating constitution of the army, the imperfection and inequality of its supplies, were consequences to be expected from such conditions.   " It is now a mob, rather ' than an army ; without clothing, without pay, without ' provision, without morals, without discipline.   We begin ' to hate the country for its neglect of us.   The country ' begin to hate us for our oppressions of them.   Congress ' have long been jealous of us.   We have now lost all con-' fidence in them, and give the worst construction to all ' they do.   Held together by the slenderest ties, we are ' ripening for a dissolution." [1]

The remedies were hard to achieve, though easy to name. Congress must have greater powers, either by taking its courage in both hands and seizing them upon the plea of necessity, or by a convention of the states empowered to conclude a real confederation.   Personal responsibility was an essential, and the only safety was to be found in the appointment of great officers of state, ministers for foreign affairs, for war, marine, finance, and trade.   Recruits must be enlisted for the period of the war, or at the least for three years.   Congress itself must have the duty of supply, and the means for exercising it.   Officers who sacrificed their prospects for patriotism deserved consideration.   The least they had a right to was half-pay for life.   But the question of funds lay at the bottom of everything. A foreign loan, a federal revenue, a tax in kind, and a national bank were Hamilton's prescriptions; and, as he added shrewdly,

[1] *Works*, i. p. 221.

they need not want for the first of these, since they could
coerce France with a threat of peace.

This letter to Duane is an important landmark. It shows
that even at this early date Hamilton had fully and firmly
grasped the essentials of the situation. In his cogent and
unambiguous fashion he led his various arguments up to
the final conclusion that the supreme need of the moment
was the need of a nation. The artificial nature of the states,
with their unreasonable sentiments, eternal jealousies and
disastrous pretensions to separate sovereignty, was no doubt
easier to understand and harder to excuse when viewed by
one who was an American only by adoption, and had become
a citizen of one of these rival communities almost by an
accident. His foreign birth was therefore an advantage,
since it enabled him to consider the problems and forces of
the time in a spirit of detachment, without the heat of
local prejudice and in their true proportions.

Hamilton, it will be remembered, resigned his appointment
as military secretary in February 1781, and it was not until
August that he obtained a command and marched south
against Cornwallis in Yorktown. During these seven months
of leisure he had time to meditate more deeply upon the
political situation. The fruits were *The Continentalist*,[1] a
series of six papers, of which four were written during this
interval, and the remaining two in the spring and summer
of the following year. It is an odd but magnificent way
of spending a short leave, after five years of uninterrupted
labour and hardship. For the great Washington was an
exacting taskmaster, and his campaigns were not conducted
with much regard for a generous diet, warm feet, or soft
lying.

In these letters, which contain the kernel of Hamilton's
theory of statesmanship, he goes further back into causes

[1] *Works*, i. p. 243.

in search of a cure for the national disorders. There is no contradiction of his former ideas, but only a greater completeness.

At the beginning of the war there was a lack of men experienced in government. The majority of this class adhered to the other side, and the influence of the small number who were available 'was too commonly borne down by the prevailing torrent of ignorance and prejudice.' 'An extreme jealousy of power is the attendant on all popular revolutions.' It was not marvellous, therefore, that both the people and the states were jealous of the authority of Congress; or that Congress, being subject to the epidemic timidity, was jealous of the army. With courageous iteration Hamilton returned to his old argument. The capital defect was a want of power in Congress. Unsupported by the confidence of its constituents, it had none to bestow upon its servants. There was a want of agreement as to the proper remedies; but every man admitted that the confederation was unequal either to a 'vigorous prosecution of the war, or to the preservation of the union in peace.' The great danger of a popular government is ever its jealousy of power. "In a government framed for durable liberty, not 'less regard must be paid to giving the magistrate a proper 'degree of authority to make and execute the laws with 'rigour, than to guard against encroachments upon the 'rights of the community; as too much power leads to 'despotism, too little leads to anarchy, and both eventually 'to the ruin of the people." [1]

In the case of a single state the commonest danger is that the sovereign, whether a monarch or a republican council, will make himself too powerful for his subjects; but in federal governments which have to deal with the affairs of a group of states the peril is of an opposite character.

[1] *Works*, i. p. 246.

A.D. 1781
Ær. 24

In such a case it usually happens that the members are an overmatch for the common head, and that the central power is lacking in authority sufficient to secure the obedience of the several parts of the confederacy. States subscribing to a league or union may have, or seem to have, at certain times an advantage in things contrary to the good of the whole, or a disadvantage in things conducive to the common weal. And under this aspect states are like private men who, when they have the power of disregarding the laws of their country, frequently find a sufficient reason for doing so in their own interest. But the danger that, upon a cool estimate, the members may discover a real or imaginary gain in disobedience to the titular sovereign, is not the end of the evil. Prejudice, vanity and passion have also to be taken into account. The ambitions of persons holding office in the several states foster ideas hostile to the confederacy, in order to preserve their own consequence; while the people tend also in the same direction, being more devoted in their attachment and obedience to their own particular government, which acts upon them directly, than towards the central power which can only touch them indirectly, and possesses no officers clothed in a calm assurance to enforce its laws.

When the war came to an end all danger from foreign aggression would temporarily disappear. Relieved from this menace, centrifugal tendencies would then run riot. Societies whose true aim and only security against attack lay in a close political union "must either be firmly united under ' one government, or there will infallibly exist emulations and ' quarrels; this is in human nature."[1] Even when Hamilton wrote, in the midst of war and of danger too serious for trifling, some of the states had evaded or refused compliance with the demands of Congress on points of the greatest

[1] *Works*, i. p. 254.

moment.   Peace would bring the danger of disunion much more near.

After the final defeat of British policy it ought to be the aim of American statesmanship to prevent and frustrate for all time European interference with the development of the states, and even with the destinies of the whole Northern Continent. It was only to be expected that the great powers would endeavour to obtain a foothold, and might therefore upon occasions have an interest in fostering internal contentions, jealousies and schisms; in instigating competitions with regard to boundaries, rivalry in commerce and disputes wheresoever a plausible pretext could be discovered.   Groups and minor confederacies would then begin to combine, and Europe would be allowed to come into American affairs as an ally of one or other of them.   From such an opportunity it was of vital importance that she should be rigorously excluded.   To a man viewing the thirteen states in a broad vision, as one nation, such a conclusion was too obvious for any argument.   To a man regarding the matter from the meaner standpoint of the interest of an individual state, the conclusion was no less clear if he would but project his mind a few years into the future.

"Our whole system," he continues, "is in disorder; our 'currency depreciated, till in many places it will hardly 'obtain a circulation at all; public credit at its lowest ebb; 'our army deficient in numbers, and unprovided with every-'thing."[1]   And while government was thus unable to pay, clothe, or feed the troops, things were happening in the Southern States which should have caused Americans to blush.   Cornwallis had won victory after victory, and was making steady progress, in spite of the fact that the whole British forces in the states were little more than fourteen thousand men.   And yet the population of those states was

[1] *Works*, i. p. 255.

greater than at the beginning of the war—more than two
millions and a quarter of white citizens. The quantity of
specie had also increased. The country abounded in the
necessaries of life and in warlike materials. There was no
lack even of foreign commodities, and commerce in spite of
everything was growing. A powerful ally co-operated by
sea and land, and paid the whole cost of supporting her
five thousand troops on American soil.

In these circumstances but one of two things could afford
an explanation of the disastrous situation—a general disaffection on the part of the people, or mismanagement on
the part of their rulers. The former alternative could not
be entertained, for the reason that it was contrary to notorious facts. The prime necessity therefore was to strike at
the root of the whole evil by a reform of government and
by augmenting the powers of the confederation.

The great defect of the constitution under another aspect,
was that it had no property; no revenue, nor the means
of obtaining it. Funds are the foundation of everything. 'Power without revenue, in political society, is a
name.'

At this point the series of letters was interrupted by
Washington's sudden campaign in the south against Cornwallis. After the fall of Yorktown in the autumn, Hamilton
retired into civil life, and in the following April and July
the argument was concluded in a different strain. From the
necessities of government he passed to the possibilities of
development; from a criticism of the theory to a discussion
of the practice of government.

"The vesting Congress with the power of regulating trade
' ought to have been a principal object of the confederation
' for a variety of reasons. It is as necessary for the purposes
' of commerce as of revenue. There are some who maintain
' that trade will regulate itself, and is not to be benefited by

94 ALEXANDER HAMILTON

A.D. 1782
Æt. 25

'the encouragement or restraints of government. Such 'persons will imagine that there is no need of a common 'directing power. This is one of those wild, speculative 'paradoxes which have grown into credit among us, contrary 'to the uniform practice and sense of the most enlightened 'nations."[1] There are laws which a government must observe in regulating commerce. Individuals may have objects in trade which it is the duty of a government to defeat. There may be prospects of national wealth which, since the capital of private persons is limited, only government help can inaugurate. The state will aim at a balance of the whole, favouring neither the cultivators of the land, nor the merchants, nor the manufacturers, nor the artisans and labourers. Under this aspect an excessive tariff would be as unstatesmanlike as no tariff at all. That trade can be trusted to regulate itself to the greatest advantage of the community is the prime paradox. All experience is against it, and proves that the influence of government is salutary if only government be wise and honest. The government of Elizabeth fostered the trade of England. Colbert laid the foundations of prosperous trade in France. In the opinion of some, who grant these premises, the separate states and not the federal power were the proper regulators of commerce; "but as they are parts of a whole, with a common interest in 'trade, as in other things, there ought to be a common direc-'tion in that as in all other matters."[2] With regard to any plan devised by human ingenuity, it will always be possible to argue that it is for the advantage of one unit, or of one state, rather than of another; but "unless we can overcome 'this narrow disposition and learn to estimate measures by 'their general tendencies, we shall never be a great or a 'happy people, if we remain a people at all."[3]

But supposing that the central power is prevented from

[1] *Works*, i. p. 267. [2] *Ibid.* i. p. 271. [3] *Ibid.* i. p. 277.

undertaking, or should be unwilling to undertake, the control of trade, what will happen? There will be a lack of revenue. There will be a risk of independence. The union will become precarious. The want of a wholesome concert and provident superintendence to advance the general prosperity will lead to a depression of the landed interest and of labour for the immediate advantage of the trading classes. Finally, the trading interest itself will fall a victim to bad policy. It is of the essence of statesmanship that burthens should be distributed and benefits shared. No class should be oppressed, for the interests of all are interwoven. "Oppress trade, lands sink in value; 'make it flourish, their value rises. Encumber husbandry, 'trade declines; encourage agriculture, commerce revives." [1]

"There is something," he concludes, "noble and magnificent 'in the perspective of a great Federal Republic, closely linked 'in the pursuit of a common interest, tranquil and prosperous 'at home, respectable abroad; but there is something pro- 'portionably diminutive and contemptible in the prospect 'of a number of petty states, with the appearance cnly of 'union, jarring, jealous, and perverse, without any determined 'direction, fluctuating and unhappy at home, weak and in- 'significant by their dissensions in the eyes of other nations. '. . . Happy America if those to whom thou hast intrusted 'the guardianship of thy infancy know how to provide 'for thy future repose, but miserable and undone if their 'negligence or ignorance permits the spirit of discord to 'erect her banner on the ruins of thy tranquillity." [2]

[1] *Works*, i. p. 231.   [2] *Ibid.* i. pp. 286. 287

CHAPTER II

Congress and the Conduct of the War

A.D.
1776–1783
Æt. 19-26 THE legend which was born out of the soaring fancy of the early chroniclers covers a much wider field than the mere origins of the rebellion. The influence of the epic can be traced no less plainly in the popular beliefs regarding the course of the war, than in the current estimates of the virtues of individuals and of the value of institutions. The image of the American Revolution which fills the mind of the average Englishman is smooth, definite and highly coloured, but it is a poor likeness of the event. In this picture the thirteen colonies are presented as one people, firmly bound together from the beginning by a confidence in one another, and a common sentiment of freedom far stronger than the forms and articles of any constitution. 'The League of Friendship,' as it was named by hopeful enthusiasts, is conceived to have had no parallel save in the Golden Age. The prevailing pattern of man during this virtuous epoch is imagined to have been George Washington. Congress, no less than the army, was cast in that heroic mould. The nation itself rises before a picturesque imagination like some vast audience in the Albert Hall, tier upon tier, a multitude of individuals, but a single type. Everywhere there appears the same austere patriotism and awful gravity, the same fortitude and the same simplicity. If any man were bold enough to suggest that comparison is possible between the British Parliament and the American Congress of that time, or that among the members of these two august assemblies there was anything approaching an equality of virtue, wisdom, or courage, popular opinion, nourished upon the

myth, would put aside the paradox without a smile, as a jest bordering too closely on profanity.

The Englishman, who never shows to best advantage in the apologetic mood, has accepted everything which the American epic required for its completeness. He has bowed in humility before the frequent scorn of its moral judgments, has received without demur its shallow and eloquent generalisations, and, clothed in a white sheet, has joined, with a taper in his hand, in the discovery of scapegoats and the making of heroes. It is no part of our purpose to enter upon a defence of British policy; but if we are to entertain a true regard for the fame of Washington and Hamilton, the difficulties against which they had to contend must be firmly grasped. If these be covered over industriously with rose-leaves, we may arrive at a very flattering estimate of the virtues of the American colonists; but in that case we shall be forced to undervalue the greatness of these two leaders, who both during and after the war had, according to the common history of mankind, their hardest difficulties to overcome from within and not from without.

Instead of this picture of a perfect patriotism, it is wiser to accept the plain facts. The American Revolution, after the war began, owed but little to Congress, much certainly to the patriotic spirit of the people, but most of all to a few great men. The countrymen of Washington, engaged in a prolonged and painful struggle, where fortune varied and hearts grew sick with deferred hope, showed the same high qualities and the same ignoble faults that might have been looked for in men of that race.

Throughout the whole period of the war, and for more than seven years afterwards (dating from the surrender at Yorktown), the states were not a nation, but merely a loose and jealous confederacy. It is indeed matter for amazement, not that the war should have run such a long and painful course, but that under such conditions it was ever conducted to a successful conclusion. We must admire the binding force of the desire for independence by which the ill-founded structure was kept together, and marvel at the ineptitude of British diplomacy that could drive no wedges of disunion into a fabric riddled with such dangerous gaps.

Until the outbreak of war none of the thirteen colonies had been, or had even claimed to be, a sovereign state. Sovereignty, for what it was worth, resided in King George, who exercised it upon the advice of his cabinet and through the agency of the different governors. Each state was independent of its neighbours. None was in a position of superiority to another. There was no machinery of law or custom for joint action through any central power. Franklin, indeed, had dreamed of federation in years gone by. The representative Congress which assembled to concert measures with regard to the prosecution of the war with France had arrived at a plan of union largely under his influence. The royal governors were favourable to the proposal; but it was rejected without hesitation by the home Government, which feared to call into existence so powerful a subject, and by the colonial legislatures, whose jealousy of one another seemed to be ineradicable.[1]

With the assumption of independence sovereignty therefore went a-begging. No federal power existed, only a Congress of the States, assembled in a great emergency to take counsel together and to speak, if possible, with one voice. In political virtue, courage and sagacity, this first Congress was a body of a remarkable distinction; but it was not a government, and it lacked both the authority and any precedent for creating one. The prevalent opinion was that sovereignty, having departed

[1] *History*, iii. p. 245

out of King George the Third and the British Parliament,
had entered into the individual legislatures of the thirteen
states.   A minority, it is true, held that by some mystical
process sovereignty had passed into the hands of Congress;
but all serious attempts on the part of that assembly to
exercise sovereign powers over the various states incurred
at once the odium of the selfsame tyranny against which
the revolution was directed.   Massachusetts, Pennsylvania
and the rest, were determined that they would no longer be
subjects.   Their aim in taking up arms was independence,
and they were no more willing to part with this precious
possession to their own Congress than to King George.
At a later date, when it was proposed to create a revenue
for support of the army out of a duty upon imports, a patriotic
opposition demanded a plain answer to the question as to
how this measure differed in principle from the Stamp Act
which had set two continents by the ears.

In spite, however, of this extreme jealousy, the severe
pressure of circumstances brought it about that from the
beginning many of the customary duties and functions of
a sovereign were performed by Congress.   There being, in
fact, no alternative, it took upon itself to create an army, to
build a fleet, to issue paper money, to raise loans, make
alliances and assert the independence of the United States.
But as Congress acted always upon sufferance, it lacked the
confidence which is given by real authority, and as a natural
result its procedure was feeble, irresolute and ineffectual.
Shortly after the famous declaration of July 1776, ' articles
of confederation and perpetual union' were submitted for
consideration, but until March 1781 they remained without
ratification.   The delay was a matter of but little moment,
seeing that this stately and sonorous document merely
defined in more precise terms the impotence of government.

Put in the shortest form, the evil lay in the want of power. 'Influence,' in the words of Washington, 'is not government.' Congress had no subjects. It was merely the council of an alliance. It could requisition supplies, and money and men; but if a state chose to fill its ears with wax and pay no heed, the central authority was without any remedy but patience. Over the individual citizens of the states it had no jurisdiction whatsoever. With the various legislatures its relations were those of a diplomatist. When it sought to create an army it needed to ask leave, and to accomplish its end was forced to submit to terms not only ignominious but contrary to reason. When a state saw fit to furnish a regiment, it claimed and exercised the right to appoint its officers. Military organisation under such conditions was clearly impossible. Efficiency would have been beyond hope had the commander-in-chief lacked the courage and personal force necessary for exceeding his functions.

Congress issued paper money, and its value sank after a few months to two cents in the dollar. It made alliances which could and would have been disowned by any state had it discerned a private advantage in the disavowal. When Congress finally came to make peace, the terms which it had agreed to were ignored and repudiated. In the harlequinade of human affairs no pantaloon ever exercised less discipline and authority.

The consequences of this want of power were certain. Men of capacity who desired to serve their country sought other opportunities, in the state legislatures, in diplomacy, or in the army. The ranks of Congress were recruited by mediocrities, most of them loquacious and many of them corrupt. It had the mysterious confidence of Chinese mandarins in the efficacy of ordinances and proclamations. It ordered victories and decreed an army of eighty thousand men; but, notwithstanding, Washington had to make shift with ten thousand that he and not Congress had the labour and credit of collecting. It meddled with appointments and promotions, and to every foreign " adventurer that came, ' without even the shadow of credentials, gave the rank of ' field officers." [1] It fumed over the question of supplies, leaving the army to perish of cold and hunger while it debated interminably and bungled its diplomacy with the states who were the real paymasters. Occasionally it had ideas. Officers, Samuel Adams argued, ought to be elected annually, so as to preserve the commonwealth from military despotism [2]—a view of the matter which, had it prevailed, might have ended the war at a much earlier date. His kinsman, John Adams, Chairman of the Board of War, discoursed on strategy and promulgated maxims. ' My toast is a short and violent war '; for he was utterly ' sick of Fabian systems.' George the Third, if he had happened to hear of these sayings, must have wished well to the Adams family. These rhetorical activities were their own reward. They found no shoes, blankets or victuals for the men who camped at Valley Forge and huddled round the fires at night, afraid to sleep lest they should never wake. Maddened by the ingratitude and ingenious persecution of congressmen, Arnold became a traitor ; [3] and Greene, who had a nature beyond treachery, was driven to resignation [4] by their consequential malice. In this buzz and hubbub of inferior minds Washington alone was able to endure, wearing down their folly and conceit by his resolute gravity.

This Congress, to which the great and constant general was obliged to defer and appeal, was clothed with a mock dignity and that fickle and uncertain power which rests entirely upon moral influence. It was meddlesome and

[1] Hamilton to Duer, *History*, i. p. 431.   [2] Cf. also *History*, i. p. 420.
[3] *History*, ii. pp. 50-52.   [4] *Ibid.* ii. pp. 39-42.

inefficient; was much addicted to fault-finding, to the giving of foolish advice, and to intrigue against its own officers. It stinted supplies and delayed action. While it endeavoured with certain ill results to assert its own vain and foolish authority in the conduct of military affairs, it showed a corresponding backwardness and timidity in grappling with the national credit and curbing the recalcitrancy of the states. Enjoying the exercise of its minor functions with a peculiar zest, it shrank from placing them in jeopardy by any bold attempt to develop its implied powers on the plea of a national emergency. To consolidate its position and assume or usurp the high executive rights of government was an ambition wholly beyond its mean horizon; but in the torment and obstruction of its servants it was an adept, jealous of its privileges and observant of the letter of its commission.

It is interesting, no doubt, to speculate upon the events which might have happened had the British Cabinet acted with more vigour, or had Washington been governed by less fortitude; but it is, perhaps, still more interesting to consider what might have happened had Hamilton been a member of Congress instead of a soldier. When we consider his daring and masterful spirit, and remember how at a later date, with less assistance from the pressure of events, and in the teeth of interests which in the meanwhile had become more widely vested, of prejudices which had hardened into hatred, of traditions of independence which had grown from saplings into timber, he still succeeded in prevailing upon his fellow-countrymen to accept a real union, it is hard to believe that in the case we have imagined the signature of peace would have found the whole work of federation still waiting to be done. It appears more likely that he would have taken the metal at a red heat in 1777, than that he would have waited for eleven years longer until

it had grown cool. That his attempt would have succeeded
is not beyond possibility, and had it succeeded it is conceivable that the constitution so created would have been a
more powerful charter and more in accordance with his own
political convictions than that which was subsequently
approved at Philadelphia.

The famous Conway Cabal (1777-1778) aimed at getting
rid of Washington and replacing him by Gates 'the hero of
Saratoga,' afterwards the hero of Camden, on which occasion he fled a hundred and eighty miles without looking
back.[1] Because all Americans at the present time entertain an affectionate reverence for the memory of their first
great leader, we are apt to assume that there must have
been an even livelier passion of loyalty in the breasts of
their ancestors who were his contemporaries. The reality
was somewhat different. It is well to remember that for a
time the opinion of a majority of Congress was in favour of
driving Washington to resignation.

In November 1777 that body was in the pride of its youth.
If it was powerless to supply Washington with reinforcements, it was equal to the task of complaint against his
failures and condemnation of his 'Fabian tactics'; if it
showed no alacrity in checking frauds in the commissariat,
it could still point a moral and deduce conclusions from the
victory of Saratoga and the defeats of Brandywine and
Germantown. It was inclined to a simple-minded worship of
success, without analysis or consideration of circumstances.

In the early spring thieves fell out, and the Conway
Cabal came to an inglorious end. It had reckoned
hopefully upon Washington's resignation, and had the
commander-in-chief been merely the good man and high-
spirited gentleman he was, and not something still greater
over and above, the plan would have had the best chances

[1] Hamilton to Duane, *History*, ii. p. 124.

of success. But, fortunately for his country, he looked upon his own position in a spirit of extraordinary detachment. He regarded domestic intrigue, discontent and calumny as natural incidents in the war; as things to be reckoned with, like floods, frosts and snowfalls, impersonally and without malice. As he had never sought power and honour, but merely accepted them when duty left no escape, he had no motive for resignation; for his duty was unchanged either by ingratitude or abuse. Under this attack his strength was weighted with another burden in that winter of suffering in the hills at Valley Forge, but he would have thought himself no less disgraced in laying down his commission before the clamours of Congress than in laying down his arms to a summons from Sir William Howe.

To have a clear understanding, not merely of the campaigns of Washington, but of what followed after, when peace was signed, it is necessary that the character of the government, the nature and extent of its authority, should be firmly grasped. The war languished and dragged wearily along from the want of power in Congress and from the lack of virtue in congressmen. In reality the second was merely a consequence of the first; for a position of prominence and publicity without powers commensurate to the office has no attractions for effective citizens who take statecraft seriously and are content to endure speech only as a means to action. But to the consequential classes, prominence, publicity and speech have ever appeared ends admirable in themselves. Such men are easily content with those shreds of power which consist in the giving of advice, in the finding of fault, and in setting their servants by the ears. We must therefore admire the constancy of the patriotic minority who held to Congress through good and evil report, bearing with the din of clap-trap for the chance of being able now and again to serve their country by the defeat of an intrigue or the destruction of a folly. Men like Robert Morris have a right to share in the fame of Washington. In a sense they have a double title to the gratitude of their countrymen, seeing that they not only withstood the mischief but endured the debate.

Putting aside all consideration of persons, putting aside also such aspects of the conduct of government as the ingenious bad faith which marked its action after the Saratoga capitulation, looking at the matter in the driest light, there can be no shadow of a doubt that the feeble constitution of Congress, with its attendant evils in the character of its members, was the cause of the long continuance of the war. Had Washington been supported with men and supplies, it is neither incredible nor even unlikely that the messengers bringing news of the surrender of Burgoyne, in October 1777, might have met halfway upon their journey riders from the south with word of the surrender of Howe at Philadelphia. The number of Washington's troops was at no time in proportion to the manhood of the country, nor were his supplies of food, clothing and pay ever commensurate with its wealth. Neither in men nor money was there a true measure taken of the spirit of its citizens. These difficulties dogged Washington to the end. In every year after 1775 there was a possibility of ending the war by a crowning victory had he commanded an army worthy in numbers and equipment of the resources of the United States.

It has been calculated by a thoughtful American historian,[1] that in the war between North and South, ninety years later, the federal troops towards the end of the struggle were in the proportion of one in every five of the men capable of bearing arms; more than a million

[1] *The Critical Period of American History*, by John Fiske, pp. 101-3.

soldiers were in the field for the defence of the union. In the War of Independence the numbers never reached so high a ratio even if the militia, who appeared and disappeared very much at their own pleasure, is included in the sum. Accordingly it has been maintained by certain writers, that in the war against Britain there was a weaker spirit of patriotism than in the War of Secession. In both cases there was a man of immense character acting disinterestedly to attain success. Lincoln and Washington may be held to cancel one another in the equation. The real difference is that in the one case there was government, and in the other there was not.

For if Congress could not bring into the field in such a cause men who were willing to serve, and if it could not provide for its soldiers, whom the country was well able to support, it was clearly an institution too contemptible to be described as a government. Allowing to natural conditions and the inertness of Britain their full force, the success of the colonists in the fight for independence was due to no political institutions, but only to the binding force of a common aim and the unmatched qualities of one great man. At the end of the war government was still to seek. The binding force of a common aim was then for the time being relaxed, for it had split into a thousand centrifugal forces of local jealousy and minor interests. But at least the one great man remained as before, and by good fortune another great man emerged in the nick of time to his assistance.

Neither Washington nor Hamilton was under any illusion with regard to the immediate consequences of peace. They foresaw dangers ahead of them more grave in character than those which had already been surmounted. They knew that the future of their country hung upon a firm union, and that a firm union was impossible without a strong

government. The existing government was a make-believe. A.D. 1776–1783 Æt. 19-26
It had been maintained in an appearance of authority only
by the determination of the people, and by an excessive consideration, a conscious and patriotic hypocrisy, on the part
of their leaders. It had no inward strength, but like a
sinking patient depended upon stimulants and doses for the
preservation of its feeble vitality.

As Hamilton had foretold, the ending of the war let loose
at once all the forces of disunion. Men ringing their joy-bells
as King George's fleet of transports shook out their white
sails in New York harbour forgot that independence, being
won, had still to be secured; or, if they did not actually forget,
indulged themselves in an easy confidence, longing for a brief
respite from all high endeavour. To Hamilton such indifference seemed as dangerous as the lethargy of the traveller
who sinks exhausted in a snowdrift. He believed that all
effective co-operation had ceased when Washington disbanded his army in the autumn of 1783; that the union
was then dissolved as a reality, and preserved in Congress
only as a tradition. The states were thirteen independent
sovereigns, whose jealousies left open the doors of the house
to foreign intrigue. Unless the people could be brought
to realise the gravity of their predicament, the natural
consequence of the War of Independence would be another
civil war.

During the spring of the year 1783 much correspondence
had passed between Hamilton and the commander-in-chief
upon this matter. Their minds were clear both as to the
malady and the means to a cure. "Unless Congress have
'powers competent to all general purposes," Washington
wrote, "the distresses we have encountered, the expense we
'have incurred, and the blood we have spilt, will avail us
'nothing."[1] "It now only remains," Hamilton replied, "to

[1] Sparks's *Washington*, viii. p. 391.

A.D. 1783
Æt. 26 for his own glory.   Such alliances are rare, but out of their conjunction great events are apt to be begotten.

Hamilton was justified in all his predictions.   The centrifugal forces, escaping from their cave, made such a tempest of disorder as may well have taken even the prophet himself by surprise.   Washington, in his wise optimism, held unmoved to the belief that 'everything would come right at last,' and compared the riot and extravagance of the states after the peace to that of 'a young heir come a little prematurely to a large inheritance,'[1] who by and by, under the pressure of circumstances, will return to his natural good sense, and successfully rebuild his dilapidated fortune.   As things went from bad to worse he grew graver, but never despondent. What perhaps weighed upon him most heavily was not so much any doubt of the result, as the peril of his most cherished desire.   He wished to live the rest of his days as a country gentleman, mending and enjoying his estate.   He loved his wide plantations, green forests and majestic river. The struggle with Nature for an antagonist delighted his great heart by its arduous intensity, its compatibility with silence, its freedom from the restlessness of camps and cities and the affairs of men.   But gradually it became clear that no union could ever be attained without him; and when it was at length attained, that no man but he could properly start it on its course; and afterwards, that no man but he could continue it with safety.   So in the end there remained barely three years for a reward to one who cared less than most men for the prizes of ambition, and loved to watch the seasons in his country home more than to lead victorious armies or to be a ruler over a great nation.

[1] Sparks's *Washington*, ix. p. 11.

CHAPTER III

Centrifugal Force and its Consequences

THE first trouble was the army, as has already been stated A.D.
1782–1783
Æt. 25-26 in a previous chapter.[1] Unpaid and unpensioned, it spoke openly of rebellion. Washington was urged to make himself king, not only by men who had claims and grievances, but by others who, while they loved order, considered this remedy to be the only means of obtaining an honest acknowledgment and liquidation of the various liabilities which had been contracted during the war.[2]

Soldiers in peace-time are at a disadvantage. They are rarely masters of effective speech. Their words lack the cunning of restraint. Their sincerity and their consciousness of injustice render them impatient of parties. Occasionally they are useful to the politician, but he discards the alliance immediately it becomes a question of recompense. Moreover, their misfortunes tend to bring them upon the rates. Their grievance being that the country has dealt with them ungenerously, the taxpayers of whom the country is composed are placed in what they would themselves describe as 'a delicate position'—the delicacy consisting in the fact that they cannot indulge their emotions without putting their hands deeper into their pockets. Consequently, in a democracy, though the wrongs of an army frequently call forth much sentiment, they rarely obtain substantial redress.[3] A pension-list for political purposes is the utmost that a reasonable mind will entertain.

Congressmen were very slow to respond. They continued

---

[1] Book I. Chap. vi. pp. 65-67.   [2] Fiske's *Critical Period*, pp. 106-8.
[3] Cf. action of Massachusetts, *History*, ii. pp. 494-5.

to draw their own salaries with a most punctual fidelity; but the claims of the army were a controversial matter which they professed to have scruples against settling offhand. It would be easier, they alleged with some truth, and more dignified, to discuss the question at leisure when the army was disbanded.[1] When mutinous murmurs reached their ears they looked askance at Washington, and made speeches upon the text, 'No Cromwells.' In plain words, they had no power, and what was even more, they had no goodwill. The debating caste was jealous of the warrior caste; feared it, and affected, not altogether insincerely, to regard the calling of arms with a kind of moral reprobation. Soldiers were under certain conditions a painful necessity, but, like a panther used for hunting, should be clapped in chains as speedily as possible after the quarry had been killed. Hamilton, writing to Washington from Philadelphia in the spring of 1783, describes the attitude of his fellow-congressmen without flattery : " But ' while I urge the army to moderation, I advise your ' Excellency to take the direction of their discontents, and ' endeavour to confine them within the bounds of duty. I ' cannot, as an honest man, conceal from you that I am ' afraid their distrusts have too much foundation. Repub-' lican jealousy has in it a principle of hostility to an army, ' whatever be their merits, whatever be their claims to ' the gratitude of the community. It acknowledges their ' services with unwillingness, and rewards them with reluct-' ance. I see this temper, though smothered with great care, ' involuntarily breaking out upon too many occasions. I often ' feel a mortification, which it would be impolitic to express, ' that sets my passions at variance with my reason. Too ' many, I perceive, if they could do it with safety or colour. ' would be glad to elude the just pretensions of the army."[2]

---

[1] *History*, ii. p. 496.   [2] *Works*, ix. p. 330.

The dangers of a military rebellion were avoided in the manner which has been already described. For success the movement needed a Cromwell; and there was only one Cromwell possible, who not only declined to serve, but by adroit and courageous management defeated the hopes of the revolutionary party. Hot as was Washington's indignation, much as he loved the army, his patriotism was too wide and well balanced to let loose the havoc of civil war, even though short of this remedy there was no hope of an adequate provision. It was said with truth that the defeated Government of King George dealt with the exiled and fugitive loyalists with a far greater liberality than the United States bestowed upon their victorious but impoverished army.

After the taking of Yorktown, Hamilton returned to Albany, and remained the guest of his father-in-law until the spring. General Schuyler offered pecuniary assistance, and there was some talk of a public appointment, but both were refused. Hamilton's determination was fixed to go to the bar. He resigned his commission in the army on the ground that he had obtained his command in the autumn only with great difficulty and after repeated applications. He was unwilling, now that the issue admitted of no uncertainty, to 'obtrude' his claims upon the commander-in-chief. At the same time he gave up his rights in the matters of half-pay and compensation. In the May following (1782) he accepted for the period of a few months the office of receiver of the continental taxes for New York state, but resigned it in winter, when he was chosen to be a member of Congress.

In 1782, after a few months of study, Hamilton was admitted to the bar. The age of twenty-five, which was his age at that date, is to-day the usual time of life for young men to enter upon this arduous profession. There is an odd contrast, however, between the typical student of

H

Lincoln's Inn or the Temple, and this strange, smiling, boyish figure, with the fine lace ruffles, who had already played the part and borne the responsibilities of a man in the affairs of a great war, who had dealt with statesmen in high matters of politics, and conducted with tact and firmness the diplomacy between the commanders of America and France.

When we read of his sudden success as an advocate, we are inclined to look for the reason in the smallness of the arena and the dearth of great practitioners. To a certain extent both explanations are correct. The population of New York state in 1782 numbered only about a hundred and seventy thousand persons, New York city some thirty thousand. The former leaders of the bar, for the most part loyalists or Tories, had been swept entirely out of the field.

But granting that the arena was small, it was not so with the issues which the conclusion of peace had brought up for consideration. Few courts of justice have ever been called upon to settle principles of higher moment to the state. Hamilton followed the Ciceronian tradition, mixing and interweaving law with politics. Through his advocacy in private causes he sought to affect, and to a large degree succeeded in affecting, public opinion outside the court-house.

The treaty of peace with Britain, like other documents of the kind, contained provisions of give and take. After signature by the commissioners in Paris, it was ratified with due consideration by the Continental Congress. The advantages which it secured were not merely of a sentimental nature, but material. It was justly regarded by enlightened citizens of the States as a triumph of diplomacy. The credit of Britain in the bargain was more of the heart than of the head. She was willing to concede substantial and important benefits in order to secure the lives and property of those colonists who had clung to the old tradition and had sustained her arms. Looking at the matter in a cool light, she blundered into sacrifices that were altogether needless even with this aim in view. Her discredit was a lack of knowledge, of foresight and of interest. The game was played, and she had lost. North America, in the eyes of her statesmen, was a strip of eastern seaboard; the great lakes were but dimly understood; the continent beyond the Mississippi was ignored. She gave much more than she needed to have given, both in east and west, to attain her honourable end; and what was more immediately distressing, she received little or no value in return for her liberal concessions.

"The *uti possidetis*, each party to hold what it possesses," Hamilton writes in the first letter from *Phocion*, "is the ' point from which nations set out in framing a treaty of ' peace. If one side gives up a part of its acquisitions, the ' other side renders an equivalent in some other way. What ' is the equivalent given to Great Britain for all the important ' concessions she has made? She has surrendered the capital ' of this state (New York) and its large dependencies. She ' is to surrender our immensely valuable posts on the ' frontier, and to yield to us a vast tract of western territory, ' with one-half of the lakes, by which we shall command ' almost the whole fur trade. She renounces to us her claim ' to the navigation of the Mississippi, and admits us to share ' in the fisheries even on better terms than we formerly ' enjoyed it. As she was in possession, by right of war, of ' all these objects, whatever may have been our original ' pretensions to them, they are, by the laws of nations, to ' be considered as so much given up on her part. And what ' do we give in return ? We stipulate—that there shall be ' no future injury to her adherents among us. How insigni- ' ficant the equivalent in comparison with the acquisition !

' A man of sense would be ashamed to compare them; a ' man of honesty, not intoxicated with passion, would blush ' to lisp a question of the obligation to observe the stipulation ' on our part." [1]

In return for these advantages Congress had most solemnly undertaken three things, and the people, wearied by the sufferings of an eight years' war, would have gladly purchased the blessings of peace at a much higher price. The first of these conditions was that no obstacle or impediment should be put in the way of the recovery of debts due to British subjects from the citizens of the Republic; the second, that in the future no fresh prosecutions or confiscations should be directed against loyalists; the third, that Congress should sincerely recommend to the legislatures of the various states a repeal of the existing acts of confiscation which affected the property of these unfortunate persons. On the last no stress need be laid. Franklin was candid as to the difficulties, and in all likelihood it was little more than a pious hope. But the first and the second were unambiguous, and by every man, honest or dishonest, were understood in the same sense when peace was joyfully accepted.

The forms of political knavery are beyond enumeration, but they fall into classes with certain conspicuous features, according to the development of the community. There is the knavery of the pure savage, which differs from that of the feudal baron; and there are knaveries peculiar to a bureaucracy, to a despot, and to a people without previous experience in international relations. The knavery of the American states was of the last-named order. They took the benefits of peace which the efforts of Congress had secured to them; they accepted the advantages of the treaty which their representatives had signed; they watched

[1] *Works*, iv. p. 239.

and waited until the troops of King George were embarked
in transports for England, and then proceeded to deny, in a variety of tones, all power in the central government to bind them in the matter of the *quid pro quo*. It was not a great thing which Congress had undertaken to do, or one which could be of any material advantage to their late enemy. All their promise amounted to was that they would abstain from the degradation of a petty and personal revenge, and this promise they proceeded to break in every particular.

As Hamilton wisely and nobly urged, the breach was not only a despicable perfidy but an impolitic act, since loyalists might become good citizens, and the states needed nothing more urgently than population. But no sooner was danger at a distance, embarked on transports, than the states assumed an attitude of defiance.   New York in particular proceeded to persecute the Tories by novel expedients and with redoubled energy.   The thirteen legislatures vied with one another in the ingenuity of measures for defeating recovery of debts due to British creditors.   They derided the recommendation to repeal oppressive acts and to restore confiscated property, and proceeded without regard either for honour or consequences to pass new acts of wider oppression and to order confiscations on a grander scale. It was the same spirit which had violated the terms of the Saratoga capitulation: the same which in later days preached the gospel of repudiation with its hand upon its heart.

The United States at this date were not independent of European assistance, but on the contrary stood urgently in need of it.   They required capital and credit, and, beyond everything, treaties of commerce; but until 1789, when the constitution was in being, they called their wants to deaf ears. European bankers and ministers of state, mindful of these events, evaded—sometimes with less of courtesy and circumlocution than was agreeable—all proposals for co-operation.

en their politest messages were unflattering. They com-
plained of the duality of a government that was one and
indivisible when it desired to purchase a favour or an
accommodation, but turned into thirteen recusants when
it became a question of paying the reckoning. They
declined to be captivated or tempted by the illusion of a
Congress that dissolved and faded under the pressure
of an obligation into a welter of truculent and con-
ceited legislatures, who pleaded their municipal statutes
against the law of nations, and denied the right of the
central power to do more than secure prepayment from
simpletons.

Against this flagrant and ruinous chicanery the nobler
spirits of the Revolution revolted, protested and fought,
but for a considerable period of years in vain. They had
no regard for popularity, and incurred much hatred.
Among its opponents Hamilton was foremost in writings
and action. Clinton, Governor of New York, became at
this time his enemy, and remained so to the end. Among
people who had no word upon their lips so frequently as
freedom, Clinton acted the part of a predatory despot by
playing ingeniously upon the greed and passions of his
constituents. It is impossible to withhold a certain degree
of admiration for this narrow, irascible, obstinate, masterful
precursor of Tammany, who maintained his domination
against a coalition of all the virtues and all the talents over
a prolonged term. In shrewdness, and not from cynicism,
he called his policy Democracy. Phrases never clouded his
illiterate and direct intelligence; but he was far from despis-
ing their utility in dealing with the electorate. Having given
his policy a name, not with the object of describing it, but
merely to please the public taste, he fixed it like a ring in a
bull's nose, and led the passive creature whithersoever it
pleased him.

Clinton loved his governorship with a passion that was A.D. 1783
entirely royal, and he hated Congress because it possessed Æт. 26
a semblance of superior power. When it was possible to
do so he thwarted that august impotency and treated it to
humiliation and contempt. He hated and feared the idea
of union, and fought against it tooth and nail; for union,
beyond any doubt, meant the curtailment of his power and
importance. He hated the loyalists and Tories because they
had once been his enemies. It is probable that after a
fashion he loved his own state of New York, was jealous of
her glory, desired to see her independent, rich and powerful,
as sometimes a man has a pride in his wife though he
ill-uses her.

Such a character holding the governorship of the chief
commercial state of the Union was the natural leader of the
revolt against treaty obligations, and in his action it is
likely that his hatred of Congress was at least an equal
motive with his hatred of loyalists. His first move was a
comprehensive measure for disfranchising every one who
had stayed of his own free will in places occupied by
British troops or under their nominal control; but the proposal was too crude a usurpation for the stomachs of his
more timid supporters. Then he attempted to impose an
oath as a condition of enfranchisement—an oath not of
loyalty in the present and for the future, which would have
been legitimate, but of immaculate patriotism in the past.[1]
He promoted an edict of perpetual exile against all Tories
who had left the state. He carried an act enabling citizens
whose property had been occupied or entered upon by others
under British authority, during the military occupation,
to bring suits for damages against such persons as tres-
passers. This measure struck at the roots of the settlement,
and such was the intention of the Clintonian party. It

[1] *History*, iii. p. 29.

also opened the doors to every kind of extortion working through prejudice against justice.

Hamilton contended boldly that the act was illegal, being contrary to the treaty of peace which Congress was within its legitimate powers in concluding. Clinton, with much adroitness, arranged for a test case in which a poor widow sought damages from a wealthy merchant.[1] Popular sympathy was on the side of Clinton's law, and the circumstances of this particular cause lent themselves to a sentimental treatment. The state courts were swayed by both considerations, and would gladly have found a way to enforce the Trespass Act and right the widow. But Hamilton left them no way. He fought the case upon the great principles of national obligation which lay at the root of the matter, and wrung a verdict for his client from the reluctant judges.

By this victory he smashed the Trespass Act; but the whole policy of repudiation was abhorrent to him, and he attacked it at large in the first of his letters from *Phocion*. One Ledyard, over the signature of Mentor, attempted a reply which drew from Hamilton a second letter upon the same theme. These two pamphlets are among the noblest and most persuasive of his writings. In personal invective he was not a great master. He lacked the delicacy of wit and melody of phrase which alone can render anger and contempt agreeable to a passionless and disinterested posterity; but when he writes, as in these, with deep sincerity, with candour and good temper, he is disarming and resistless. His simple object was to persuade all honest men that for them the Clintonian policy of oppression was impossible; and honest men, reading the pamphlets, put aside their prejudices and became slowly convinced. We find some measure of his success in the rage of

[1] *History*, iii. pp. 11-22.

the governor's faction. Never, even later when he spoke
disrespectfully of the French Revolution, was he hated with
so great a frenzy. A club frequented by Ledyard decided
to challenge Hamilton, each member in turn, until some
one at length should have the good fortune to put an end
to him. But Ledyard, who had, at least, the virtue of being
able to take blows in return for those he gave, entering
the club and hearing of this strange proposal, broke out
in loud indignation: "This, gentlemen, can never be!
'What? You write what you please, and because you
'cannot refute what he writes in reply you form a com-
'bination to take his life."[1] And so, reluctantly, the scheme
was abandoned by its devoted authors.

It was Hamilton's most fatal weakness as a politician, and
one of his chief virtues as a statesman, that he was indifferent
to popularity. The same passion for order and justice, which
had driven him as a boy to defend his enemies against the violence of an excited mob, armed him now against the threats
and abuse of Clinton's henchmen. He called himself a Whig,
following the practice of the revolutionary leaders, and his
definition of the name might almost have converted Lord
Thurlow himself. "The spirit of Whiggism is generous,
'humane, beneficent, and just. These men (the Clintonians)
'inculcate revenge, cruelty, persecution and perfidy. The
'spirit of Whiggism cherishes legal liberty, holds the rights
'of every individual sacred, condemns or punishes no man
'without regular trial and conviction of some crime declared
'by antecedent laws; reprobates equally the punishment of
'the citizen by arbitrary acts of legislation, as by the lawless
'combinations of unauthorised individuals, while those men
'are advocates for expelling a large number of their fellow-
'citizens unheard, untried; or, if they cannot effect this, are
'for disfranchising them, in the face of the constitution,

[1] *History*, iii. p. 45.

' without the judgment of their peers and contrary to the ' law of the land." [1]

Hamilton's career and merits as a lawyer have been discussed at length by men who were themselves great jurists. In the present essay, which is concerned with his political services, any elaborate survey would be out of place. His practice grew rapidly. Abilities that could win a verdict against the oppressed widow and the popular governor could not be safely overlooked by litigants, no matter what political views they might entertain. He was no mere advocate to dazzle twelve plain men in a box. With courts he was more successful than with juries; and the higher the court, the greater was his influence upon it.

We are apt, having rarely witnessed the phenomenon, to ignore the chief advantage of his circumstances. In the vigour of his youth and at the very summit of hope, he brought to the study of the divine precepts of law a character already trained and tested by the realities of life, formed by success, experienced in the facts and disorders with which law has to deal. Before he began the study of the remedies, he had a wide knowledge of the conditions of human society. Although still a boy in years and spirits, the memory of playing fields and debating clubs was faint and far off; for he had already contended and measured himself against characters who have left their mark on history.

It is characteristic of his quality that during the year in which he studied for the bar he wrote a text-book on law for the use of students. With a succeeding generation of students Hamilton's text-book remained in use,[2] not from any sentimental reason, for the party which he had led was extinguished and his own fame lay under a cloud of unpopularity, but solely on its merits.

[1] *Works*, iv. p. 231.   [2] *History*, ii. p. 282.

He practised at the bar for seven years before Washington summoned him to his cabinet, and for ten after he had resigned his office — altogether barely seventeen years. During the whole of this period he was occupied as much with public affairs as with his profession. Yet from what remains to us in the meagre reports, and in his own notes, abstracts and memoranda, from the testimony of his contemporaries and the criticism of men who followed after, there exists no doubt that he must be numbered among the great lawyers, one of the smallest societies of mortal excellence. With him, as with them (for it is the badge of their company), law was not so much a slow and arduous acquisition as a sudden discovery; not so much a painful effort of learning as the intuition of an eternal harmony: a reality, quick and human, buxom and jolly, and not a formula pinched and embalmed, stiff, banded and dusty like a royal mummy of Egypt. Reversing the rule of all academies, and following the invariable practice of greatness, he learned from the top downwards, not from the base upwards; and if he escaped drudgery, which we are too often inclined to place upon a separate pedestal and worship for its own sake, it was not at the sacrifice of thoroughness; for principles were a part of his being, and he found his details as he needed them, like a man seeking needles with a lodestone.

CHAPTER IV

Disorder and Anarchy

THE violations of the terms of peace which took place in New York were conspicuous, not so much by reason of their exceptional flagrancy, as from the commercial importance of that state, from the large number of Tories included in its population, and from the notable part taken by Hamilton in opposing a policy which in his eyes was one not merely of breach of faith, but of disintegration.

Up till this time the great difficulty had been to arrive at anything approaching unanimity among the states; but there was at once a perfect unanimity in refusing to repeal the acts of confiscation. There was also a practical unanimity in engaging in fresh persecutions of the loyalists, not merely by the enactment of oppressive civil laws, but even by denying them the protection afforded by a just enforcement of the criminal laws. In many districts these unfortunate persons were robbed, tortured, and even put to death with impunity, and over a hundred thousand were driven into exile in Canada, Florida and the Bahamas. Finally, there was unanimity among all the most important states in taking measures to defeat the recovery of private debts in cases where the creditors were Englishmen.[1] It was the same in Massachusetts and in South Carolina, in Pennsylvania, Maryland and Virginia, as well as in New York.

The recovery of private debts was indeed one of the stipulations of the treaty of peace, but in dealing with any nation which had evolved a public opinion capable of sustaining the most rudimentary code of personal honour it would have been superfluous, a thing which would have gone without saying. It is remarkable, however, that in this period of pristine virtue public opinion was at once so childish and so rotten, that we are at a loss whether to marvel most at its recklessness of credit or at its unvarnished dishonesty. Public opinion was entirely favourable to the idea of private theft, and the interest of rogues was considered with a tender compassion by the grave and respectable citizens who composed the legislatures of the various

[1] Fiske's *Critical Period of American History*, pp. 129-130.

states.   Measures were passed amid popular rejoicing to
obstruct the recovery of debts due to British merchants, and
to enable the fortunate Americans to revel unmolested in
the pleasant flavour of stolen fruit.

Such lack of morals in the people being added to the
lack of power in Congress, it is not wonderful that the
federal government gradually faded into a dim shadow.
Even the instinct of self-importance was insufficient to
keep it alive.   Having become wholly a farce, it sank
into indifference.   The legislatures of the thirteen states
treated it with frank contumely; acted in open defiance
of its authority; ignored its counsels; refused its requests,
and went their various ways in contempt.   Delaware
and Georgia, with stern economy, considered it to be a
waste of the public money to furnish delegates   During
the six years preceding 1789 the average attendance was
about twenty-five, out of a total of ninety-one.   Frequently
the meetings were adjourned, which harmed no man, for
want of a quorum.   "Our prospects," wrote Hamilton to Jay,
"are not flattering.   Every day proves the inefficiency of
' the present confederation; yet the common danger being
' removed, we are receding instead of advancing in a dis-
' position to amend its defects.   The road to popularity in
' each state is to inspire jealousies of the power of Congress,
' though nothing can be more apparent than that they have
' no power; and that for the want of it the resources of the
' country during the war could not be drawn out, and we at
' this moment experience all the mischiefs of a bankrupt and
' ruined credit.   It is to be hoped that when prejudice and
' folly have run themselves out of breath, we may return to
' reason and correct our errors." [1]

Hamilton took his seat in Congress during November
1782, and remained for eight months a member of that body.

[1] *Works*, ix. pp. 381, 382.

majority of modern writers, while the House of Commons, which refused to entertain his proposals, has been unsparingly condemned as narrow-minded, short-sighted and churlish.

In so far as its action was due to temper, the result was doubtless lamentable, since it has tended to obscure the cool motives of policy which were the real mainspring. It is not clear, however, that temper had much to do with the matter. Historians have perhaps tended to assume too readily that a nation which had been worsted in a long, costly, and somewhat ignominious war, would be in a mood highly unfavourable for considering measures which, while they might conceivably have conferred substantial benefits upon themselves, would have had the undoubted effect of conferring benefits, relatively much greater, upon their late antagonists. To a generation which has grown accustomed to regard all state regulation of international commerce as nothing better than a way of cutting off one's nose to spite one's face, it has seemed natural to conclude that the decision of the British legislature must have been dictated by no more respectable motive than ill-feeling. But this assumption rests more upon its inherent probability, according to modern ideas, than upon any contemporary evidence of repute.

Pitt's view, certainly the view of the later writers who have praised his foresight and breadth of mind, was not only that the purposed arrangement would have been commercially beneficial to Britain by enriching an eager and important customer, but further, that it would have excited a strong sentiment of gratitude in the citizens of the new Republic, and would have swiftly consigned to oblivion all the bitter memories of the war.[1] It has been assumed as an axiom that this admirable result must have

[1] *History*, iii. p. 57.

ensued; but at the best it was no more than a vague possibility, and upon the whole it seems more likely that nothing of the kind would ever have occurred.

For, in point of fact, it was in the states and not in England that revenge was elevated into a national object. The wholesale repudiation of the terms of peace would never have found its necessary support in public opinion had it rested merely upon the interest of private debtors. To pretend that the policy of Clinton was the result of the British regulations concerning trade and shipping is only possible to a profligate imagination, or to a memory unretentive of dates. The nature of these regulations was unknown, their effect had not begun to make itself felt, when the carnival began like some process of spontaneous combustion. Nor even had those things been known and felt would they have afforded a plausible pretext. For there was nothing invidious in the action of Britain. The policy she chose to pursue was entirely in accordance with the practice of all nations at that epoch. Commercial warfare was their normal condition. France, the ally of the states, was no less stiff in her enactments, and the hostility of Britain excited louder complaints only because Britain was of incomparably greater importance to the prosperity of the states than any of her rivals.

Had Pitt's measure been passed it would have meant a complete reversal of a policy which had been pursued with success since the days of Elizabeth. The refusal of Parliament to approve of so great a revolution implied no particular animosity to America, but merely an aversion from the sudden jettison of an approved tradition. It is credible, and even likely, that a system of unconditional free trade might have resulted in the enrichment of many British manufacturers and merchants, and in an increase of the volume of trade between the two countries: but it

I

would have been none the less a startling violation of a principle which had obtained for many generations. This principle laid it down firmly that the proper object of national policy was to bind together the mother country and her colonies in an empire which should be as nearly as possible self-sufficing and independent of the rest of the world. According to this view, it was a mistake to cherish our rivals, and strengthen their sinews, even for the sake of a pecuniary advantage to ourselves.

In this case, moreover, there were particular reasons which weighed with the majority both in the Cabinet and in Parliament against any relaxation of the traditional policy of Britain. Then, as now, this country was the chief maritime power, and then, as now, she was determined at all costs to maintain her supremacy. The conditions of this supremacy were sailors and ships, and for these she looked to the prosperity of her mercantile marine and of her building-yards. Gratuitously to invite America to take a share in the carrying-trade seemed little short of madness. The right policy was to exclude her from it to the utmost extent that was possible, seeing that of all others she was the rival who had the greatest natural advantages to support her competition. Materials were so plentiful and ready to hand that in those days ships could be built in New England for less than two-thirds of the price that was required in Europe.[1] The development of American resources and an encouragement of her shipping must, therefore, have meant within a few years the closing of British yards. These considerations lent an overwhelming force to the opposition directed against the free trade proposals, and it may even be that on second thoughts Pitt himself was converted by their logic. Certainly he never again submitted his Utopian scheme. British trade to and

[1] Fiske's *Critical Period of American History*, p. 137.

from British colonies was accordingly confined as rigidly as before to British bottoms.

The result entailed much hardship and widespread ruin in the states. In the old colonial days, American shipping had depended almost entirely upon the trade with Britain and her West Indian possessions. Under the new settlement, however, the latter were immediately closed to her vessels. The distress thus caused was genuine; but the complaints which it called forth were to a large extent unreasonable; for in fact the states, having voluntarily broken away from the Empire, could hardly claim with any justice to pursue the same profitable intercourse which would have remained open to them had they chosen to remain within it.

British policy, however, did not stop short at this point, but sought a further advantage which the unfortunate predicament of the states enabled it to seize without much difficulty. A bold attempt was made to confine all trade between Britain and America to our own shipping, and so long as dissension continued among the thirteen states the attempt succeeded, since no measures of reprisal, no unanimous and general counter-strokes, were possible. Duties upon imports coming from England, and dues upon English ships, could only become an effective weapon if they were universally levied at all the ports along the coast, and this was out of the question until the Union was something more than a mere name. Congress, urged to it by the chief commercial states, asked for powers, but asked always in vain. Each state was jealous of its neighbours. The southern states, who depended upon the export of their raw material, were distrustful of the northern states who owned the ships, and not without reason suspected a design to exclude the English carrying-trade from American harbours only in order that Yankees and New Yorkers might be enriched by exacting more burdensome freights for delivering the produce of the plantations to European consumers.[1]

Things accordingly became even worse than during the war. The carrying-trade then existed, though its risks were high; but now it was wholly extinguished by the competition of their former enemy in American ports. Shipbuilding, though no nation had more natural advantages of materials and situation, was likewise extinguished; for, with the loss of the carrying-trade, there was no market at home, and abroad the hostile duties made sales impossible. The free access to the fisheries which had been secured under the treaty was in practice but a small boon, since the profitable foreign market in the British West Indian possessions was closed to the sale of the salted produce.[2] And in spite of all the grievance and ill-feeling, a large demand arose for British goods. For these specie had to be paid down on the nail in all cases where wares or materials were not taken in exchange, since no British merchant would now give one pennyworth of credit, out of respect to the measures of the various states for the obstruction of the payment of British debts. Even when payment was taken in kind the rate of the exchange was ruinous to the American producer, for many of his commodities fell under the ban of the British tariff, and had to be reckoned, not at their market value, but at their market value less the amount of the import duties they would have to bear when landed in London or Bristol. It has been computed that in 1784 £1,700,000 of our manufactures were imported, and but £700,000 of native produce taken in exchange.[3] The balance was paid in hard cash. Specie flowed out of the country, so that, in addition to the ruin of the merchants, shipowners, shipbuilders and fishermen, there was added a

[1] *History*, iii. p. 110.   [2] *Ibid.* iii. p 108.
[3] *Cambridge Modern History*, vii. p. 312.

currency question that ultimately led to civil war upon a considerable scale.

Financial trouble had dogged the steps of Congress throughout the war. As the struggle dragged on, this problem increased in difficulty; but so long as hostilities continued, the difficulty was by some means overcome. It had been to the interest of France and Holland, and of the other enemies of Britain, to keep the war alive. They could not afford to let it perish of exhaustion. And a further reason was found in the argument that when the severe drain of war expenditure had ceased, prompt payments of interest and a speedy return of the principal would certainly be made. Creditors had therefore been sanguine and indulgent. But in fact all their calculations were upset, for with the declaration of peace precisely the reverse of all their forecasts came to pass.

The chief stimulus to contributions from the various states was gone, for the common danger no longer existed. Far from being in a position to deal handsomely with its creditors, Congress could barely support the small charges of the nominal government. The interest on foreign loans was still unpaid, and repayment of the capital became a remote and visionary possibility. European financiers were disinclined, therefore, to throw good money after bad. Not only were American applications refused; they were derided. In the end even the resourcefulness of Robert Morris could do nothing. He had in all likelihood achieved more than any other man could have hoped to achieve.[1] His disinterestedness no less than his competency was singular in that company, for, like Washington, he contributed his private fortune to the common stock. But the limit of his powers had been reached, and, hopeless of any speedy change in the constitution, he felt the position to be impossible. The

---

[1] Hamilton to Washington, *History*, ii. p. 503.

true remedy was discussed by Congress with ungrudging prolixity, but never seriously attempted, and with a fine sense of irony it appointed a committee to succeed to his functions when he tendered his resignation.

Commercial treaties were no easier to obtain than loans, so that this means of reviving and fostering commerce was also closed. No country would conclude a bargain with Congress, for the reason that the thirteen states could be relied upon to repudiate all parts of the arrangement which conferred an advantage upon the other contracting party.[1] Even the little commerce overseas which was retained lacked all security, and was endangered by the want of power to protect it. American ships were seized, and American citizens sold in slavery by Barbary pirates, while their countrymen at home were engaged in arguing the question of State Rights, and laying traps for the confusion of the central government. American diplomacy and American subjects were open to insults and injuries from the meanest antagonists. The voice of the Union had no authority among nations, any more than its bonds had credit or its promises were believed. It was indeed a somewhat humiliating pass to have come to, within a few years after having overcome the richest, proudest and most powerful people in Europe.

Power, prosperity and consideration, which all men affected to desire, were only to be had on terms which the states could not bring themselves to pay. The dignified entreaties of Washington, the unanswerable reasoning of Hamilton, failed to move their light minds. The number of the plagues was still incomplete. The citizens hardened their hearts; preferring, like Pharaoh, to endure the murrain, the locusts, and the darkness, rather than abandon their mean jealousies, their rivalries at once sordid and malicious;

[1] *History*, iii. pp. 87, 90, 91.

rather than part with, or delegate, a single shred of local sovereignty to clothe the shivering and naked form of the federal government. Finally in their madness they fell one upon another; each at the beginning looking merely for advantage to itself in injury to its neighbours, but as time went on seeking injury to its neighbours even as an end desirable in itself.

The thirteen states proceeded to indulge themselves in the costly luxury of an internecine tariff war. The states with seaports preyed upon their land-locked brethren, and provoked a boycott in return. Pennsylvania attacked Delaware. Connecticut was oppressed by Rhode Island and New York. New Jersey, lying between New York on the one hand, and Pennsylvania on the other, was compared to 'a cask tapped at both ends'; North Carolina, between South Carolina and Virginia, to 'a patient bleeding at both stumps.' It was a dangerous game, ruinous in itself, and, behind the custom-house officers, men were beginning to furbish up the locks of their muskets.

Wherever there is a boundary there are apt to be disputes, and the political conditions being what they were, it was not likely that this copious source of ill-feeling would run dry. The barbarities of the Pennsylvanians under Patterson, in the valley of Wyoming, outdid even the legends of British atrocities, and left a rankling memory in Connecticut. At one time war between Vermont, New Hampshire, and New York seemed all but inevitable.

Then there came the greatest of all the plagues in the not unusual disguise of a panacea. The general commercial ruin and financial collapse had all but extinguished credit. The drain of specie had all but extinguished the currency. Credit without currency might in theory work great marvels; but the lack of both is necessarily fatal. Barter became a common expedient. Tobacco, whisky, and salt pork served in different states as the clumsy medium of exchange. Every industry groaned under the calamity. But help was at hand. Towards 1786 the genius of democracy discovered a remedy. The sound political instinct of the people, which it was the fashion of the Clintonian school to uphold as equally fitted for a general judgment after the event, and for the nicest problems of expert knowledge, rose to the occasion and demanded paper money. Printing-presses in Georgia and the Carolinas, in Pennsylvania, New York and Rhode Island, obediently creaked out affluence in response to the resolutions of their various legislatures. All the states, save only Connecticut and Delaware, were more or less disturbed by the agitation which passed like a sudden wave over the whole Union.[1]

In the matter of knots the prudent statesman will discriminate. All are not of the Gordian character, and, as a rule, it is safer to unravel than to shear them through. The panacea met with a fate unworthy of the high hopes of its inventors. The paper currency showed an immediate tendency to drop to two cents, or thereabouts, in the dollar. Mutton chops could sometimes be obtained for four dollars apiece, and a good, wearable hat for forty; but more usually a prudent shopkeeper preferred to lose his customer than handle such precarious stuff.

Clearly something was wrong, and the people taking thought discovered that it was the shopkeepers who needed coercion. Laws accordingly were passed with this object, and when they were defied, the matter came before the courts. The judges, sitting amid the noisy demonstration of popular anger, decided nevertheless that the laws were invalid, and absolved the defendants.[2] Up to this point

[1] Fiske's *Critical Period of American History*, pp. 168-186.
[2] *Ibid.* p. 176.

there had been, if not unanimity, at any rate a huge
majority supporting the panacea; but now there was a
division.   One party grumbled, but owned itself defeated;
the other, with a stern logic, discovered that to complete the
system the judges must be done away with or intimidated.
In Rhode Island they were accordingly dismissed, and elsewhere there was dangerous rioting.   In Massachusetts
there was civil war.   Battles had been fought at Spring-
field and at Petersham, and upwards of eight thousand men
were bearing arms, before Shays's rebellion was finally reduced.
Congress rising to the emergency called out for troops; but,
by a stratagem more prudent possibly than dignified, pretended that they were for use against the Indian tribes.[1]

Paper money was the worst of all the plagues; and yet
the people still hardened their hearts. 'The League of
Friendship,' as it was affectionately named, had reached a
sad dissolution.   A union resting upon sentiment, a government depending upon the goodwill of its members, are only
the make-believes of amiable enthusiasts or the cheats and
counterfeits of quacks and sophists.   The only security for
union must be found in the strength of the central government, and such strength can only be given by the forms and
machinery of a constitution.   In America during these years
men thought otherwise, and the words of Washington and
Hamilton therefore fell unheeded.   It was believed that a
federal power could be preserved by occasional outbursts of
high emotion.   It was forgotten that a government depending upon emotion for its authority is more likely in the end
to be destroyed by that incalculable force than to be saved
by it.

[1] *History*, iii. p. 178.

CHAPTER V

The Power of a Vision

A.D.
1785–1786
Æt. 28-29

In the early spring of 1785 a modest but memorable meeting took place at Washington's country seat of Mount Vernon, between representatives from the states of Maryland and Virginia. The occasion was a conference in regard to waterways between the eastern settlements and the western unpeopled land lying in the valley of the Ohio and to the north-west. The greater portion of these vast territories had been ceded to the Federal Government by the various states who claimed them under their charters, or by virtue of a nominal occupation. To the south North Carolina stretched out in a wide strip to the banks of the Mississippi. Her western population being something more than nominal, had refused to be included in the cession, and after an unsuccessful effort to form themselves into a separate state under the name of Frankland,[1] had been compelled to return to their old allegiance.

The development of the western country was one of the great dreams of Washington's life. He foresaw the importance of these possessions at a time when few men were willing to give them much thought. They were the fruits of the great policy of the elder Pitt, in which, as a youthful soldier, Washington had borne a distinguished part. What the Treaty of Paris in 1763 had secured to Britain, another Treaty of Paris in 1783 had divided between Britain and the victorious colonists. This rich inheritance it was his fixed determination to weld into the confederacy. By speech and correspondence he had pressed the matter upon his fellow-citizens even before peace had actually been signed;

[1] *History*, iii. p. 121.

and throughout the whole of the turbulent period which A.D. 1785-1786 Æt. 28-29 ensued he continued to urge the need for development, and for the firm attachment of this estate to the rest of the Union.   When these means proved inadequate, being a practical man, he founded a joint-stock company to open up communications.

Even the peculiar advantages of this territory appeared to Washington to contain some not inconsiderable dangers. The splendid waterways of the Mississippi and its tributary streams were not an unmixed advantage, seeing that the mouth and the lower reaches were in the hands of Spain, who also extended a shadowy claim to the whole western bank and to the unknown region beyond.   The easiest course for the new settlers was to drift their produce down the broad current to New Orleans, and the dread of Washington was lest this tendency might induce 'a habit of trade' with a foreign power; an intimacy and a mutual interest which in the end might lead to a detachment from the Union. Consequently, at a time when the chief matter of political anxiety with regard to the western lands was the menace by Spain against the free navigation of the Mississippi, he was more concerned to develop the natural trade routes from east to west by clearing the waterways of the James, the Potomac, and the Ohio, and by the construction of a system of supplementary canals.

It was for the adjustment of certain differences, and to procure the co-operation of the two states, whose sympathies had already been enlisted in this enterprise, that the meeting took place at Mount Vernon in March 1785.   As the delegates had come together in a businesslike and peaceful spirit, other matters of mutual interest were brought tactfully under discussion—the advantages of a uniform currency and system of duties; the need for a general cohesion and mutual support among the confederated states.   Under the spell of

A.D. 1786
Æt. 29 a great character prejudice was for the moment forgotten, and invitations were issued to Pennsylvania and Delaware to join in the discussion. But good feeling expanded even further—once started on the course of reason it was easy to urge it forward—and it was ultimately decided to propose to all the thirteen states that in the autumn of the following year (1786) they should meet at Annapolis to discuss the whole commercial situation.

Before this date arrived the paper panacea had been pricked, and Shays's rebellion was in full blast. In addition, the disputes with Spain about the free navigation of the Mississippi had come to a head. Threats of the confiscation of American ships presuming to enter the lower waters had been followed up by action. The southern states were in a flame of indignation. Their northern neighbours were apathetic. The problems of the Mississippi did not touch their interests at any vital point. On the contrary, they desired nothing so much as a good understanding with Spain, for they had hopes that in this quarter their courtship might not be despised, and that a commercial treaty might at last be signed. All this pother about free navigation for the sake of a few backwoodsmen seemed to them to indicate a lack of the sense of proportion. Jay at the Foreign Office took this view of the matter, and, as a compromise, advised Congress to consent to close the river to free navigation for a period of twenty-five years.[1] The southern states were in no mood for such concessions, and threatened that if Jay's proposal were accepted they would secede and return to the British allegiance. The New England states, with an equal vivacity, threatened secession unless the recommendation were confirmed. The crisis was averted only by an indefinite postponement; New Jersey, Pennsylvania and Rhode Island siding with the South.

[1] *History*, iii. pp. 101, 104-5.

A.D. 1786
Æt. 29

The convention of Annapolis, though it met in stirring times, was but a thin congregation. Only five of the states appointed commissioners who attended; four appointed commissioners who did not attend, and the remaining four did not appoint commissioners at all. The last class included Maryland, which had joined in issuing the invitation; but what was more than all the rest, New York was represented by Hamilton, and Hamilton ruled the convention.

It is something of a shock to the finer feelings that this assemblage, the beginning of the movement which culminated in the constitution, should have been convoked for the consideration of purely material things; for the discussion of inland navigation, of customs duties and the currency. The folly of distracted effort was gradually making itself apparent. The advantages of combination were beginning to be dimly surmised. The farce of fiscal independence was played out. Even the stiff-necked citizens of New York had come to entertain doubts whether their private interests as a trading state would not be better served in the long run by the pursuit of the prosperity of the whole, than by a narrow policy of individual gain at the moment. It is notable that the immediate cause of the constitutional compact is to be sought, not in the higher spheres of political necessity, but in the practical needs of business men. Trade necessities, and these alone, were the occasion of their meeting and the purpose of their deliberations. By these 'sordid bonds' a loose confederation was in due time to be lashed together into such a union as the world had never seen.

In the short session at Annapolis it became evident to the delegates, under the searching analysis of Hamilton, that the only remedy for the evils affecting trade must be looked for in broad constitutional changes which their limited commissions gave them no authority to discuss.

Under the influence of his vigorous spirit the convention had a remarkable result; for out of its unanimous conclusion that it could do nothing great things came to pass.

Hamilton drafted an address which, after much modification, was adopted. It was his policy and habit to overshoot the mark; to compel the weaker brethren to consider plans that were too heroic for their natural timidity, confident that the diminished fabric would still be of an ampler proportion than if it had arisen from mean foundations. This document set out precisely the object of the convention— "To take into consideration the trade and commerce of the ' United States; to consider how far a uniform system in ' their commercial intercourse and regulations might be ' necessary to their common interest and permanent har- ' mony; and to report to the several states such an Act ' relative to this great object as, when unanimously ratified ' by them, would enable the United States in Congress ' assembled effectually to provide for the same." [1] New Jersey, he pointed out, had given a more liberal commission to her delegates, empowering them to discuss not only these, but ' *other* important matters.' A complete agreement among the thirteen states, which was the chief object of the meeting, was precluded by the mean attendance. "Your ' commissioners," therefore, "did not conceive it advis- ' able to proceed to the business of their mission"; but they place upon the record "their earnest and unanimous ' wish that speedy measures may be taken to effect a ' general meeting of the states in a future convention for the ' same, and such other purposes as the situation of public ' affairs may be found to require." [2] They submit "that ' the idea of extending the powers of their deputies to other ' subjects than those of commerce . . . was an improvement ' on the original plan, and will deserve to be incorporated

---

[1] *Works*, i. pp. 335-6.   [2] *Ibid.* i. p. 337.

'into that of a future convention.   They are the more
' naturally led to this conclusion as, in the course of their
' reflections on the subject, they have been induced to think
' that the power of regulating trade is of such comprehensive
' extent, and will enter so far into the general system of the
' Federal Government, that to give it efficacy, and to obviate
' questions and doubts concerning its precise nature and
' limits, may require a correspondent adjustment of other
' parts of the federal system." [1]   The address concluded by
recommending that " the states by which they have been
' respectively delegated would concur themselves, and use
' their endeavours to procure the concurrence of the other
' states in the appointment of commissioners to meet at
' Philadelphia on the second Monday in May next, to take
' into consideration the situation of the United States, to
' devise such further provisions as shall appear to them
' necessary to render the constitution of the Federal Govern-
' ment *adequate to the exigencies of the Union.*" [2]

Congress was fatuously indignant at such a usurpation; [3]
indulged in hair-splitting arguments upon legal rights and
the lack of authority in any body save themselves to
summon a representative council.   But things had come
into too bad a pass for the groans of Congress to produce
much impression upon the minds of men.   Amidst riots,
rebellions and threats of secession, on the very brink
of a war with Spain, people were in no mood to pay much
heed to the loquacity of angry impotence.   Congress,
deprived of all hope of a sufficient revenue by the contumacious wrangling of New Jersey and New York, [4] had
merely a Hobson's choice—they might consent to the convention or they might forbid it, but whatsoever course they
adopted the convention would nevertheless take place.

[1] *Works*, i. p. 337.   [2] *Ibid.* i. p. 339.
[3] *History*, iii. p. 236.   [4] *Ibid.* pp. 175-8.

A.D. 1786 Considerations of dignity seemed to point on the whole to
Æt. 29 acquiescence; but while the matter was still under debate
Virginia chose General Washington as one of her delegates
to the proposed meeting at Philadelphia. The tide was
running in over the flats of the firth, and a Congress with
any care for its popularity, had to gallop before it *ventre à
terre*.

The convention of Annapolis was the turning-point. The
reaction which had ensued when the war was ended, and
independence for the time being assured, had spent its main
effort.

The removal of a common danger had let loose at once, as
Hamilton had prophesied, all the forces of disintegration.
States had clamoured about their particular sovereignties.
Individuals, in a needless panic lest union should mean
some abatement in the pre-eminence of mediocrity, flung
all their influence into the centrifugal movement. Mean
spirits, hating the heroic and incredulous of magnanimity,
stirred up suspicion against those for whose services
gratitude was the only recompense possible or welcome.
Washington aimed at the title of king; Hamilton at the
reversion of the monarchy. No figment was too gross
for belief.

Providence, which is on the side of the big battalions,
appears to be also on the side of the great idea. Visions
that were at once noble in their proportions and consistent
within themselves have played a notable part in the history
of mankind; but there is this difficulty, arising out of the
conditions of the particular time, that a vision is wholly
without force to move a generation which is unprepared to
apprehend its meaning. The virtue of the seer who produces
a practical effect upon the fortunes of any nation is not that
he sees some image of surpassing splendour which no one
else has seen, but rather that he sees clearly something

which a large number of his fellow-men have already seen
dimly. His merit is that he removes a few of the wrappings
which conceal the pattern of life, and discloses a design
which though half suspected had lain till that time hidden.
The result is a vivid presentment, some startling re-arrange-
ment of familiar things, which contains the promise of relief
from an intolerable suffering, or adds a sudden value to life
by giving a nobler purpose to human endeavour. Michael
Angelo has said that he already saw in the unhewn block a
statue which to duller eyes remained invisible until his
chisel had removed the flakes of marble which concealed it.
The fabric of a vision which worketh great marvels is the
experience 'common men. Nothing is novel or surprising
in the material but only in the plan. When once an idea
of this order has taken possession of the spirit of a nation, it
will not be overcome by criticism. The forensic method,
argument and rhetoric undirected by a master thought, can
never hope to hold it back. For an idea can only be fought
by an idea. It is not sufficient that it should be crushed by
disproof; it must be expelled by some more powerful vision
which usurps its place.

The inherent truth or falseness of such a vision does not
seem to afford any measure of the effect it may produce
upon human institutions. What is shown in an alluring
picture may be incapable of achievement. Facts may be
distorted in the crystal until they become mere phantoms.
The motive and the goal of a great convulsion may be
nothing better than mirage. Two things only appear to be
essential to its potency—some exceptional gift of presentment in the seer, and an eager predisposition on the part of
men. The same strange expectancy, which greets the Mahdi
or Messiah, met Rousseau more than halfway, overwhelming
him in gratitude. His gospel immediately entered into a
place in men's hearts that was empty. He saw beautiful

K

things; he saw them clearly and believed them to be true: and although to a large extent his vision was pure fantasy, its triumph was almost as swift and facile as his dream. There are some rare occasions scattered about in history where, as if by a common impulse, humanity has paused at its work, and, leaning upon its spade, has looked round bewildered by a sudden hopefulness; aware dimly that something fortunate has happened, that a new man has appeared in the world, and that he is a friend.

Of all men who have sought to benefit their fellows by a change in the old order, Hamilton and Rousseau are probably the most opposite in character and aims. Hamilton was a man in a world of men, and the affairs of the world he lived in were to him an open book. The counters of his fancy were not shadows, but real people, real motives, and real things. His labour in accomplishment was severe, and, by comparison, slow; for a vision that is free and careless has an advantage over one that is burdened and hampered by the whole fabric of society. Rousseau, lying under a tree beside the road to Vincennes on a hot summer's afternoon, 'in an unspeakable agitation,' and Hamilton, meditating from day to day, as he struggled cheerfully and laboriously with the correspondence of General Washington, had little in common except the divine gift of revelation. Each beheld an immeasurable and splendid prospect, and what he saw he believed with an intensity and an unwavering faith that no logic could shake. To each his vision seemed to be the firmest truth that life contained. Neither the knowledge of new facts nor the experience of changing conditions ever raised a doubt or provoked a conflict in their minds, but like well-disciplined reserves swung swiftly into line, as if such reinforcement in the general movement had been from the first foreseen and preordained.

CHAPTER VI

The Convention of Philadelphia

THE Convention of Philadelphia was summoned for the 14th
of May 1787. In spite of the distracted condition of public
affairs, the arrival of the delegates was marked by no in-
decent haste. It was not until the 25th that a quorum of
seven states was assembled. All were ultimately represented, with the exception of Rhode Island, which held
aloof in ridiculous isolation. Of sixty-five delegates who
were appointed, ten never attended. The final draft of the
constitution was signed on the 17th of September by only
thirty-nine delegates, and out of the total number only
forty-two were then in attendance.

The sessions were held in private, and General Washington presided. No reports were issued of the debates, which,
from the notes and correspondence of Madison, Yates and
others who were present, appear to have been conducted
with great vivacity, and to have been influenced, not merely
by strong convictions, but by violent prejudice. Nevertheless, by virtue of the secrecy of the proceedings, speeches
were addressed mainly to the point, and but little to the
gallery. It is impossible to overestimate the advantages
of privacy in such an undertaking. When at last the
constitution emerged it was a complete thing; to be
judged by the nation, for whose salvation it was intended
to provide, as an organism, and not as a series of independent propositions.

The use and the misuse of popular judgment have been
subjects of much dispute among wise men from the beginnings of society. Popular judgment is a sound but
rough instinct, impatient of diplomacy, unfit for adjust-

A.D. 1787
Æt. 30

ment, and incapable of compromise. These are the functions of individual men, meeting inside closed doors, and if their work is to be of the best, it must be left undistracted by a running commentary of criticism and applause, by incitements to combat and appeals for consideration. The elimination of the partisan is of the highest importance, for the need in such a case is of negotiators, and champions of all varieties are a curse. The wider the audience, the harder for good feeling to be maintained and for good sense to conquer. Even in those days of slower publicity, the Convention of Philadelphia would hardly have succeeded in accomplishing its work had it been beaten upon day after day by a well-informed public opinion and a patriotic press.

The first labour of the Convention was to settle the foundation upon which the Union should be built up. Was it to be, as in the past, a confederation or league of states, or was it to be a fusion of men into a nation?

Its second labour was to draft a constitution that should rightly give effect to the principle which had been agreed upon.

In both stages the part played by Hamilton was powerful rather than conspicuous. 'He had not great tact,' it has been said of him, 'but he set his foot contemptuously to work the treadles of slower minds.'[1] The criticism is not entirely just, for contemptuous calculation is a quality that belongs to calmer natures. Moreover, in great matters he had something which is closely akin to tact; a knowledge of the dangers arising from his own eager and impetuous temper; a power of self-restraint where the argument was more safely left to a more conciliatory spokesman. His intervention, when he deemed the occasion favourable, was on the heroic scale; but even in the earlier debates he was an infrequent speaker, not only as compared with

[1] Schouler, *History of the United States under the Constitution*, i. p. 25.

Madison and Randolph, but also with others of the second
rank.

The importance of Hamilton's influence upon events at
this period is missed if we attempt to measure it either by
his speeches upon great occasions or by his writings.   His
pamphlets had borne fruit, his orations resounded in the
ears of men; but his most effective weapon was the private
conference.   The Convention did not meet until near midsummer, but early in the spring the federal Congress came
together in New York, and many of its members were
already nominated delegates to the assembly that was to
consider the constitution at Philadelphia.   Hamilton spared
no pains to prepare the ground.   He was not one of those
statesmen who make their rare, stately appearances in a
dramatic arrangement of lights and slow music.   His greatness was as confident and humane as that of Rabelais himself.
It did not fear the familiar encounter, or the good-natured
match of wits across the bare mahogany.   He loved society,
and rejoiced to meet his enemy in any gate.   His house was
open to all men without distinction of politics.   His hospitality was splendid in its simplicity and kindliness.   Men were
put off their guard by his wit and gaiety.   They were dis-
armed by his enthusiasm.   His eloquence took them prisoners.
The power of his intellect was hardly suspected under the
ambush of his extraordinary charm.   It is even claimed for
him that Madison [1] was his convert; and judging that
eminent man by his past record and his subsequent career,
it is difficult to account for the steadfast course of his
endeavours during the Convention upon any other hypothesis than that some more powerful nature had for the
time being cast a generous spell over his timid and grudging
disposition.

When the basis was at length a settled matter, Hamilton

[1] *History*, iii. pp. 239, 303, 323.

ceased from all public speaking, and even upon two occasions returned to New York to attend to professional
matters.[1] It has been alleged by his enemies that he was
mortified by the rejection of his own plan, and by his
apologists that, as his vote was nullified by the opposition
of his two colleagues from New York, his close attendance
would have been to no purpose. The real reason was that
by this time the power of his ideas was secure enough in
the minds of his party for it to be left without his presence
to work out the details of the constitution.

Four days after a quorum of states had assembled, the
Virginia Plan was introduced by Randolph. Its main principle implied a revolution. Government, to be effective,
must act directly on its subjects as individual men. To this
end it must be fully clothed in powers, not merely by
the unambiguous phrases of a constitution, but also by
the opinion of a united people. It was not sufficient
that its authority should be defined beyond a doubt; but
further, that the men who obeyed its laws and supplied its
revenues should feel their submission was rendered, not to
some remote tyranny or committee of oppressive rivals, but
to a government that was indeed their own. The essential
condition of popular affection and awe could be secured by
one means alone. The loyal support which had hitherto
been lacking would only be possible if the government
rested upon election by the people, and if, between the value
attaching to the votes of all citizens throughout the Union,
there was a rough equality. Election by the separate states
must cease; for clearly there could be no approach to equality
if a community of 70,000 free inhabitants had the same
power in the Union as one containing 700,000. Population,
therefore, whether tempered or not by the contribution of
revenue, was the basis of the Virginia proposals.

[1] *History*, iii. pp. 317, 322, 329.

The machinery of the constitution was to consist of an A.D. 1787
upper and a lower house, elected by the people. The executive Æᴛ. 30
government was placed in the hands of a single man, to be
chosen by this legislature. This governor or president was
to hold office for a short term, was to be removable only by
impeachment and conviction, and was not to be re-eligible.
The judges of the supreme court were likewise to be chosen
by the legislature, which had powers to create such inferior
federal courts as might be required.

The ideal of the *Virginia Plan* and of the national party
was a union of the people and not a league of states. The
ideal of the opposite party was precisely the reverse. They
cared nothing for the equality of the citizens, everything for
the equality of the states. On June 15, after prolonged
debate on Randolph's resolutions, the *New Jersey Plan* was
submitted to the Convention by Patterson. His proposals
were put forward avowedly for the protection of the smaller
states against their more powerful neighbours. His chief
concern was the pride and dignity of thirteen separate
nations, which required that no distinctions should be created
between the power and status of the contracting parties.
The logic of this policy was anti-democratic, since the unit
which it considered was not a man; nor even a particular
race or breed of men; but a mere boundary, always artificial,
and in many cases an accident. The Convention as a whole
was certainly conspicuous by its lack of any enthusiasm for
democracy; but the delegates who supported the doctrine of
State Rights carried distrust of the people to an extreme
which is remarkable not only in the light of modern developments, but of what happened only a few years later.
The Democratic party was then compounded by the genius
of Jefferson out of a sheer contradiction; for the ideas most
diametrically opposed in principle were those of State
Rights and the Rights of Man.

The New Jersey proposals were respectful to Congress. They aimed at strengthening in some particulars, but in principle maintaining, the existing arrangements. Their object was a binding alliance between sovereign states. They were utterly opposed to the idea of a nation. They contemplated a single house of delegates, voting by states. The executive was to consist of a council chosen by this legislature, but removable by the hostile vote of a majority of the state governments. The supreme court was to be appointed in a similar manner; but there was no power to constitute any inferior tribunals.

A plan like this could never be accepted, for it provided no cure for the evils that had brought the Convention together. Its fatal defect was the same lack of power which had made the original Congress impotent during the war and contemptible after peace had been declared. For it was impossible to preserve the sovereignties of the various states without denying to Congress any direct power upon individual men. If the central government was restricted to an indirect authority which could only operate through the state legislatures, it could only coerce at second-hand. In any case of recalcitrancy the procedure would be cumbrous and unworkable. The federal council would find itself obliged in such a case to direct the local government to compel the individual; and if the local government, for any reason, or upon any pretext, should refuse, the remedy would be the coercion of a state, which is not a constabulary business, but civil war.

On the other hand, it was urged with great eloquence that a reformed Congress, acting through articles of confederation, now most solemnly confirmed, revised, corrected and enlarged, would have upon its side a very powerful sentiment, and would exercise a prodigious influence. But Washington, who in his quiet mind always saw the big objects

clearly, had already settled that argument for ever. '*Influ-* A.D. 1787
ence is not government.' Sentiment is no adequate bond   Æt. 30
for a nation.

On the 18th of June, three days after the introduction of
the New Jersey plan, Hamilton submitted his own proposals
to the Convention. This famous statement occupied five
hours in delivery, and by all accounts was an achievement
far overtopping all other speeches made at the Convention in
force of reasoning, in courage and in eloquence. Unfortunately we have to estimate its quality at second-hand, for no
adequate report remains to us. His own notes are methodical,
but a mere skeleton or list of points to guide the speaker in
the order of discussion.[1] The argument is nowhere opened
out, and of the style and force which counted for so much
in the effect upon those who listened, no trace remains
under his own hand. The reports or notes that were taken
by Madison[2] and Yates[3] are not only condensed but imperfect. They do not cover more than a small portion of the
ground. The longer of them would occupy barely a column
and a half of the *Times*, while a verbatim report of the
speech itself would probably have filled about twenty
columns. Hamilton was an ample speaker; certainly not
verbose, but exhaustive of the facts and copious in illustration. His style does not lend itself easily to abridgment.

"He was obliged to declare himself unfriendly to both
'plans. He was particularly opposed to that from New
'Jersey, being fully convinced that no amendment of the
'confederation leaving the states in possession of their
'sovereignty could possibly answer the purpose."[4] People
had questioned the powers of the Convention to propose
anything beyond a mere amendment of the existing system;
but "we owed it to our country to do, in this emergency,

---

[1] *Works*, i. pp. 370-378.   [2] *Ibid*. pp. 381-393.   [3] *Ibid*. pp. 393-403.
[4] Madison's Report, *Works*, i. p. 381.

'whatever we should deem essential to its happiness. The 'states send us here to provide for the exigencies of the 'union. To rely on and propose any plan not adequate to 'these exigencies, merely because it was not clearly within 'our powers, would be to sacrifice the means to the 'end."[1] Having swept aside this plea of obstruction, he proceeded to examine and condemn the existing situation in terms and upon principles with which we are already familiar after a study of his previous writings. The *esprit de corps* of the various states had proved hostile to any superior government, and this principle was ineradicable, seeing that it was founded on human nature. The love of power in mediocrities, the ambitions of demagogues, and the local attachment of the people to their particular legislatures, set up a plain and obvious opposition which nothing could remove save a power in the central government to operate directly upon its subjects. If the weapons of coercion of the people were left in the hands of the states by their titular master, mastery would pass with the weapons, though the title might remain as an empty form. For coercion of a sovereign state was impossible by a mere abstraction calling itself the central government. The practical means were wholly wanting—armies and supplies. And even if these could be brought into existence, the remedy "amounts to war between the parties. Foreign 'powers will not be idle spectators. They will interpose; 'the confusion will increase, and a dissolution of the union 'will ensue."[2] A powerful influence, also, not necessarily amounting to actual corruption, was on the side of the states against the central power—the gift of places, the dispensation of honours and emoluments. These forces made a continuance of the existing system an impossibility, and the *New Jersey Plan*, which aimed at conserving and

[1] Madison's Report, *Works*, i. p. 382.   [2] *Ibid.* i. p. 384.

perpetuating the present institutions, should therefore be utterly discarded.

The complete extinction of the states would have simplified the problem and would have been productive of a great economy; but such a measure, however desirable in itself, was out of the question. Hamilton did not propose a revolution on so grand a scale, realising that the sentiments of the people made it altogether impracticable. Subordinate authorities and jurisdictions would still be necessary under the strongest government, and the state legislatures might well be used for this purpose.

He despaired "that a republican government could be ' established over so great an extent. . . . In my private ' opinion, I have no scruple in declaring, supported as I am ' by so many of the wise and good, that the British Govern-' ment is the best in the world; and that I doubt much ' whether anything short of it will do in America."[1] He quoted the opinion of Necker that "it is the only Govern-' ment in the world which unites public strength with ' individual security."

To Hamilton the term 'republic' stood for something different from the meaning attaching to the word to-day. His pattern of a republic was an assemblage in the market-place—the direct and turbulent practice of Athens and Rome. In 1787 it was this idea which arose most readily to the minds of men. The credit of republican institutions in the modern sense had yet to be established; and it is necessary to bear in mind that even at the present day the respectability of this form of government rests mainly, if not entirely, upon the success and stability of the American constitution. When Hamilton announced his distrust of a republic and his preference for a limited monarchy, he was using language as it was understood by his audience. He

[1] Madison's Report, *Works*, i. pp. 388, 389.

could not foresee the history of the next hundred years; but had he foreseen it he would have claimed with perfect justice that the success of the United States was based upon that monarchical element which he had spent such great efforts in establishing. Throughout the whole discussion the terms are used by both sides with a certain degree of ambiguity —sometimes as epithets of abuse, at others as quiet words of science. Hamilton himself speaks of a monarchy upon occasions as if it were synonymous with a despotism, a republic as an equivalent for a democracy of the market-place; while upon others the adjective monarchical is an epithet of praise, implying merely a salutary strength in the executive, and the word republic is innocently employed as the title of the proposed union.

It is also worthy of attention that his idea of the British constitution which was held up for admiration is oddly unlike the system under which we find ourselves at the beginning of the twentieth century. It was not even a correct picture of the facts as they stood in 1787. What he had in his mind was the British constitution as George the Third had tried hard to make it.[1] The king's policy working to increase the strength of the executive power had, as a minor accident of his policy, provoked the War of Independence. With the disastrous result of that struggle his attempt had failed. To a large extent his failure was due, as Hamilton saw, to a lack of central authority and to the obstacles that were created by an opposition not yet reduced to its proper functions in the state—an opposition whose sympathy and encouragement from the beginning to the end of the war had strengthened the hands of the rebellious colonists against the British king. His Majesty's opposition had been of great service to the rebellious colonists, but the danger of adopting such an institution was sufficiently obvious. The

[1] Sir Henry Maine, *Popular Government*, pp. 212-13.

aim of the American statesman was to create a system which A.D. 1787
should be free from the defects which George the Third Æt. 30
had laboured vainly to remove.   It is necessary to understand, not merely that Hamilton and many of the wisest
men engaged in the Convention of Philadelphia, including
the great Washington himself, held these views with a deep
sincerity, but, further, that their object was attacked by the
bulk of the opposite party not because of its conflict with
the principles of a democracy, but because of its antagonism
to the theory of State Rights.

Hamilton's ideal was, in fact, an elective monarchy, and
his guiding political principle a balance of authority. "Give
' all power to the many, and they will oppress the few.   Give
' all power to the few, and they will oppress the many.   Both,
' therefore, ought to have the power, that each may defend
' itself against the other.   To the want of this check we owe
' our paper-money, instalment laws, etc.   To the proper ad-
' justment of it the British owe the excellence of their con-
' stitution.   Their House of Lords is a most noble institution.
' Having nothing to hope for by a change, and a sufficient
' interest, by means of their property, in being faithful to the
' national interest, they form a permanent barrier against
' every pernicious innovation, whether attempted on the part
' of the Crown or of the Commons.   No temporary senate will
' have firmness enough to answer that purpose. . . . As to
' the executive, it seemed that no good one could be estab-
' lished on republican principles.   Was not this giving up the
' merits of the question, for can there be a good government
' without a good executive?"[1]

"Having made these observations, I will read to the com-
' mittee a sketch of a plan which I should prefer to either of
' those under consideration.   I am aware that it goes beyond
' the ideas of most members.   But will such a plan be

[1] Madison's Report, *Works*, i. pp. 389, 390.

' adopted out of doors? In return I would ask, will the
' people adopt the other plan? At present they will adopt
' neither.   But I see the union dissolving, or already dis-
' solved.   I see evils operating in the states which must soon
' cure the people of their fondness for democracies. I see
' that a great progress has been already made, and is still
' going on, in the public mind. I think, therefore, that the
' people will in time be unshackled from their prejudices;
' and whenever that happens, they will themselves not be
' satisfied at stopping where the plan of Mr. Randolph would
' place them, but be ready to go as far at least as he pro-
' poses. I do not mean to offer the paper I have sketched
' as a proposition to the committee. It is meant only to
' give a more correct view of my ideas, and to suggest the
' amendments which I would propose to the plan of Mr.
' Randolph, in the proper steps of its future discussion." [1]

Hamilton's plan may be summarised in a few words. The
legislature was to consist of two chambers—an Assembly
elected by the people for three years, and a Senate elected
by electors chosen for that purpose by the people. The
Senate was to hold office for life or good behaviour. The
supreme executive power was to be placed in the hands of a
Governor, elected in the same manner and upon the same
terms as the Senate, who should have the right to negative
all laws passed by the legislature, and who should hold the
office of commander-in-chief of all the forces of the Republic. With the advice and approbation of the Senate he
should be empowered to make treaties and to appoint all
the officers of the state, and the appointment of the cabinet
was to be in his hands without control. The Senate should
have the sole power of declaring war. The judges of the
supreme court were likewise to hold their offices for life or
good behaviour, and power was to be given to the legislature

---

[1] Madison's Report, *Works*, i. pp. 392, 393.

to create inferior federal courts in every state. The governor, the senators and all officers of the Republic were to be
liable to impeachment before the supreme court.   Laws
passed by the state legislatures, contrary to the constitution or laws of the United States, were to be void, and for
greater security the governors of each state, who were to
be appointed by the central government, should have a
negative upon all local legislation. No state was to maintain any warlike force on land or sea.

It is abundantly clear from Hamilton's own words that
he entertained no hope of carrying his plan; but equally it
is beyond a doubt that he sincerely held it to be better than
either of the others. To the New Jersey principles he was
utterly opposed. He accepted the main proposition of the
Virginia scheme, but desired to extend it further in the
direction of strength and permanency. His own proposals
were brought forward in no unfriendly spirit, but as a
reinforcement to the movement led by Madison and Randolph, with whom he was on terms of confidence and
alliance. His deliberate purpose, as at Annapolis, was to
overshoot the mark; to set up an ideal which should to
some extent compel the minds of men, even in their rejection of it; to terrify the champions of a loose confederation
with the formidable aspect of an alternative which was
vastly more disconcerting. At a somewhat later date he
drafted a complete constitution upon the basis of his own
proposals, and handed it to Madison for his guidance in the
subsequent discussion.[1]   It is worth while to compare it

[1] *Works*, i. pp. 347-369. The point whether Hamilton read his final
scheme to the Convention, or read only a skeleton of it, is not without
doubt. Madison's report of the proceedings is the main authority. He outlived all the members of the Convention, and when he published his report,
was beyond contradiction. J. C. Hamilton accuses him of suppressing
certain things, and garbling others, in order to justify the outrageous
attacks made by himself and his friends upon Hamilton during the first
administration, when their main charge was his alleged disloyalty to the

A.D. 1787
Æt. 30

with the actual constitution of the United States, for there are few more conspicuous examples in history of the maxim that when people are struggling towards a decision the man who will take the pains to think out and elaborate his own plan in a clear consistency is apt to reap a reward entirely beyond his hopes, in the domination of his drilled ideas over the undisciplined aspirations of his enemies.

The struggle was long and bitter between the *Virginia* and the *New Jersey Plans.* At times it seemed beyond possibility to avoid a deadlock which would have broken up the Convention. In the end there was a compromise. The legislature was to consist of two chambers, of which the Assembly was to be chosen by the people upon a basis of population, the Senate by the states upon the principle of equality among themselves. In the former, therefore, the *national* principle was to prevail, and in the latter the *federal.* The voting in both branches of the legislature was to be by the representatives and senators in their individual capacities, and not according to the method of the old Congress. The effect of the compromise was to concede certain powers to the central government; not, as Hamilton would have wished, to give all powers, except such as were expressly reserved to the state legislatures. Disappointed in this, his whole influence was exerted to make the intention of union clear, while keeping the conferred authority vague, indefinite, untrammelled and unlimited. He foresaw that administration could afterwards proceed to discover powers that were implied, though not precisely designated. Although the frontal attack had failed, there was still a way round.

Republic. The matter is not of great importance except to persons who are interested in the psychology of Madison, for no one believes those charges to-day, and it is hard to imagine that any one but the blindest partisans believed them at the time. Young Hamilton also maintains that Madison had no right to take notes at all, far less to publish them, as such actions were contrary to the spirit and the letter of the arrangement for complete secrecy. Cf. *History*, iii. pp. 284-6, 301-2, 338.

It was alleged against Hamilton at the time, and afterwards during his administration of the Treasury, incessantly
and with excessive bitterness, that he desired to establish
royalty, and that at heart he was an aristocrat.   There is
no colour for the first charge, and there is no doubt of the
second.   Hamilton made no secret of his belief in the
advantages of an aristocratic power in the commonwealth,
or of his reasons for that belief.   Apart altogether from the
need of stability and of deliberate judgment, he was deeply
conscious of the importance of honour in the history of
nations; and he was wise enough to grasp the truth that the
honour of nations ought to be of a composite character,
deriving its virtue out of the separate and peculiar virtues
of every order.   The people at large are ever eager to act upon
a sudden emotion of justice, resentment, or pity; ready to
accept the plausible coherence of an *ex parte* statement.
They are impatient of evidence, and wholly averse from the
consideration of what may be urged upon the other side.
The merchant classes, basing themselves upon contract, and
conscientiously examining into the extent and nature of
their rights under a bond, judging everything by that
supreme test, assert confidently that there is no place for
sentiment in business, and are full of a fine contempt for
mere tradition.   The lawyers bring everything to trial by
arguments and precedents, interpreting the bond, advocating
or questioning it with one eye on the immediate issue, the
other upon some general principle of society.   The people
see national justice as good fellowship.   The merchants see it
as common-sense.   The lawyers see it as law.   There is something beyond all this; not hostile to it, but different.   It
has received a variety of names, but none of them entirely
suitable.   The honour of a gentleman is perhaps nearest the
mark; the honour of a man whose position is secure, whose
authority is acknowledged, who is neither concerned nor

L

interested in any struggle for pre-eminence. His own personal dignity is the spring of his judgments, which are instinctive rather than reasoned. His opinions, like those of the people, are grounded on the feelings, but they are deeper and more constant. They may be contrasted with the sudden violence of popular sentiment as the current which flows underneath the waves. In addition, there is a touch of something conventional and fantastic. The parchment of the bond is less honoured than the spirit of it; and while he is jealous, almost unreasonably and to extremes, of certain punctilios, there is often present to his mind a generous sympathy towards the motives of his opponent, and a lofty consideration for his feelings. As an element in a republic the honour of a gentleman is of at least as much importance as the precedents of the lawyer, the honesty of the merchant, or the enthusiasm of the people. But while in a swelling and triumphant democracy the three last named are always certain of a great influence, it is not the same with the first, which requires the support of some strong convention if it is to render effective service to the state.

Hamilton was deeply concerned to make this element a force under the new constitution. His idea of a senate which, like the judges, should hold office for life or good conduct, was founded in this sentiment. Though not hereditary, and although resting upon popular choice, it was to be frankly, and in the best sense, aristocratic. The class from which he desired to exact political service was not likely, in his opinion, to be willing every few years to submit themselves to the calumny and fluster of contested elections; to canvass for votes and to court popularity. It is possible that his race and temperament had much to do with his view of this matter, but it is probable that his main reason lay in his experience gained in the conduct of the

war, and in the founding of the constitution. We are conscious of a strong current working throughout the war and
in the early years of the Republic always on the side of
constancy and strong government—of the sustained and
instinctive effort of a class, capable of cohesion and inured
to responsibility. Behind Franklin, Madison, Jay, Jefferson,
Gouverneur Morris, Randolph, Wilson and the other notable
spokesmen and writers, was a powerful order that cared
little for notoriety, but without whose silent and devoted
leadership the dominion of King George the Third might
never have been overthrown nor the Union of the States
achieved. From this aristocracy of squires and planters
Washington himself was sprung; and though circumstances forced him to the utterance of words, he was a
true type both in his natural silence and in his calm
efficiency.

Hamilton failed. The Constitution of Philadelphia has
proved itself to be of immense strength, but the principle
of aristocracy has no part or credit in it. In the light of
history we are forced to admit that Hamilton's lamentations
appear exaggerated; that his prophecies of disaster have not
come true; that the swing of democracy has so far been
able to keep the balance of the state unaided. But admitting so much, and even granting to American public
virtue most of the excellence which its patriotic pane-
gyrists have so lavishly claimed for it, it is still permissible
to speculate whether it might not have stood even higher
than it does in the opinion of the world had it possessed,
in addition to its other components, that element which
Hamilton struggled so hard and vainly to include.

His eagerness to secure an element of aristocracy in the
constitution of the United States was due much less to a
love of aristocrats, or to any tenderness for their privileges,
than to a conviction that it would prove a good bargain for

the nation. His aim was economic. Popular government
may secure at a cheap price the services of a large number
of men in easy circumstances, of superior education, and
with family traditions of loyal service to the state. If it is
not willing to pay the price, it must rub along as best it may
with the professional politician. The new Republic chose
the latter alternative, while Britain, by a most fortunate
obstinacy, adhered to the former.

It is easy to deride the House of Lords, the vanity of
titles and the custom of primogeniture. The philosopher,
regarding only the value of a man across a dinner-table or
in popular debate, easily justifies his derision. But there
is a practical as well as an academic side to the matter,
leading us to inquire further, if Britain has not gained much
by her illogical disregard of the principles of natural selection, and if the Republic has not lost much by a too
reverent observance of the Rights of Man ?

As a matter of logic the democratic argument is conclusive; as a matter of history it is nonsense. The principle
of aristocracy in a popular government is a very practical
device for making use of the upper classes. We use ours
while the Americans waste theirs. Titles and primogeniture
may be absurd, but the fact remains that the wealthier
classes in Britain recognise a public duty attaching to their
position, while in the United States they do not. The
tradition of the great English families, and of those whose
ambition it is to become great, is service of the state in
peace and war. The tradition of the great families in the
Republic is as yet, in the nature of things, less defined; but,
so far as it may be judged by a foreigner, it seems for the
most part unconcerned with the duties of government, and
is tending more and more towards the acquisition of commercial influence upon a scale such as the world has never
before seen. The public spirit of its wealthy citizens is

measured by huge donatives rather than by loyal service. A.D. 1787
They appear to entertain a cockney confidence that every ÆT. 30
obligation can be discharged by the signing of a cheque.
The conspicuous virtue in the one case is honour; in the
other, enterprise and industry; but if in a purely practical
spirit we endeavour to compute the advantage to the state,
everything is on the side of Britain, from the government
of a parish to the councils of the nation.

CHAPTER VII

The Federalist

THE constitution had been framed at Philadelphia with A.D.
an admirable patience; but there still remained the labour 1787–1788
of persuading the nation to accept it. The draft in due   ÆT. 30-31
course was reported to Congress, and by Congress the
decision was referred to separate conventions in the thirteen
states. As soon as nine had ratified the constitution, it
was to be at once adopted by those states themselves and
put in force. The delegates dispersed from Philadelphia in
September 1787, and the ninth state confirmed the Union in
June 1788. Between these two events lay a period which is
remarkable, not merely for the success of its achievement,
but also for the fact that it threw up as a by-product one of
the great books of the world.

The labouring constancy of Washington and Hamilton,
aided in their work by the plagues arising from misrule,
had ended the first period of the struggle for union at the
Convention of Annapolis. They had then succeeded in
awakening a powerful section of the people to the need
for a national policy. They had inspired a hesitating
world with confidence in its own instincts; had guided

events and managed interests till the meaning of each event and the security of every interest were made to point in one direction, and to produce and sustain the idea of an inexorable destiny barring every road save that alone which led to the desired goal.

The work of the second period was done when the draft of the constitution was signed by the delegates at Philadelphia. Their business had been to construct a system strong enough to fulfil the needs of the present, wide enough to admit those of the future.

The third period was occupied in convincing the people of the various states that the reality which had been attained in the heat of debate and by the practice of concession, corresponded with their various and conflicting ideals; that a document in matter-of-fact phrases, definite, precise, cold and formal was indeed a true translation into a practical shape of the vague but fervent spirit of their hearts. They had to be persuaded on the morning after marriage, that Leah was a bride no less desirable than Rachel. It was during this period, and while the state conventions were being held for the purpose of ratifying the constitution, that the *Federalist* [1] was written.

It has been said, and probably with truth, that in every state there was, at the beginning of the agitation, a majority against the new constitution. To the friends of union its weakness was a disappointment. To the defenders of State Rights its usurpations appeared an outrage. But the alter-

---

[1] The word itself is a concession. Up till the compromise between the Virginia and the New Jersey plans the opposition was between the *Nationalists* (the party of Hamilton and Madison) and the *Federalists* (the party of State Rights). Satisfied with material victory, the former took the name of their opponents, but before twelve months had passed they became nearly as odious under the new title as they had been under the old one. The upholders of State Rights thereupon took the names at first of *Republicans*, afterwards of *Democrats*. It is under the latter title that they are referred to throughout this essay.

native was nothing less than anarchy and dissolution, and against so menacing a combination there was everywhere an even larger preponderance, if the real issue could but be clearly stated. The object of the opposition was to confuse the actual choice. Its leaders were active and unscrupulous, strong in a ready-made party organisation of state legislatures. The work remaining to be done was therefore harder than any that had yet been accomplished.

"Among the most formidable of the obstacles which the ' new constitution will have to encounter," Hamilton wrote in the first number of the *Federalist*, "may readily be dis ' tinguished the obvious interest of a certain class of men ' in every state, to resist all changes which may hazard a ' diminution of the power, emolument, and consequence of ' the offices they hold under the state establishments; and ' the perverted ambition of another class of men, who will ' either hope to aggrandise themselves by the confusions of ' their country, or will flatter themselves with fairer prospects ' of elevation from the sub-division of the empire into several ' partial confederacies, than from its union under one govern ' ment." To convert these two classes was impossible ; but 'the honest errors of minds, led astray by preconceived ' jealousies and fears,'[1] Hamilton considered it to be within the limits of human endeavours to remove. The attempt was made in the *Federalist*, one of the most remarkable of political documents.

The idea of the work was Hamilton's. Something more, indeed, than merely the idea—the spirit of the whole enterprise was his. It was his energy that carried the thing through, as it was his wisdom that had planned it; and without detracting from the deserved renown of his two contributors, the lion's share of the credit must rest with the creator. Out of eighty-five short essays, which appeared

[1] *Works*, xi. p. 4.

at intervals of a few days during the autumn and winter of 1787-1788, more than fifty were written by Hamilton himself.[1] Of the rest, the greater number were by Madison; a few by Jay. The crowning merit of these papers, which were produced under great pressure — often while the printer's boy was waiting in the office[2]—is that they succeeded in accomplishing what they set out to accomplish. They were the greatest force that worked on men's minds to make them consent to the adoption of the constitution.

It is difficult to bear in mind, as we read the vigorous pages of the *Federalist*, distinguished by their hopefulness no less than by their conviction, that Hamilton was by no means satisfied with the constitution. But his mind was of a practical cast. His military experiences had intensified his natural horror of schism and lukewarm co-operation; and in big things, at all events, magnanimity was a stronger force than any personal consideration. From the moment when he attached his signature to the Philadelphia draft he became its champion. He accepted it as a whole and without reserves. If in precise terms it did not achieve all he had hoped, he saw, nevertheless, that it contained huge possibilities. Courage and patience might still contrive to supply many of the omissions. As it realised many of his dearest aims, he received it in a spirit of wide compromise and wise opportunism, thrusting his preferences upon one side, and looking only to the gravest fact—that the chance of union was never likely to recur save as the outcome of a bloody war.

The most striking difference between Hamilton and the constitution-makers of France a few years later is the absence of all illusions regarding the magic of a mere document. A constitution was to him but a skeleton; and had it been put

---

[1] *History*, iii. p. 371, says sixty-five.
[2] *Ibid.* p. 370.

together by the wisest men, in the coolest hour, there would still have been no virtue in it until it was inspired with life. Its strength lay not in the written words, but in the tradition that was still to seek. The first administration would have greater powers in moulding the destinies of the nation than the whole Convention of Philadelphia voting unanimously. For the title-deeds of all political authority are elastic. Courage will stretch them, and the process will appear inevitable; but with a timid possessor they will shrink into a feeble formula. In the one case the intention will ever override the words; in the other even the words themselves, like teeth in old gums, will be useless for the lack of their natural support.

The *Federalist* is pure advocacy, but it is the greatest and rarest advocacy, for it appears to the reader to be a reasoned judgment. Confident in their cause, the authors never shrink from a fair statement of opposite opinions; so that, to the modern, its wisdom and justice are apt to obscure the amazing skill of the counsel who conducted the case.

Hamilton had two aims—the adoption of the constitution, and its security. He sought to establish the first by an exhaustive explanation of the practical conveniences and advantages of the Philadelphia plan, by a full exposition of its merits, and by showing in contrast the existing paralysis, unsettlement and danger. But for the security of the new institutions it was necessary to prove also that they were founded upon broad and eternal principles, harmonious with the ideals of his countrymen.

A self-respecting nation, as it stands at the cross-roads, will deliberate, demanding to be satisfied under both heads; requiring to be shown clearly that its convenience will be well and promptly served; asking, further, for full assurance that the remedy for present ills is not contrary to nature, or likely to induce at a future time some morbid disaster. It occasionally happens that a political party is able to snatch a hurried decision on the first ground alone, on some temporary personal advantage, truly or falsely alleged; but a verdict given in this fashion lacks stability. Having no foundation in the real nature of things, it is easily shaken. No sanctity adheres to it. When men, despite the promises made to them, experience disappointment, they will pull it down without reverence, for it draws no aid from a noble tradition.

A democracy at its best is not content with a proof of self-interest, even though it extends to its grandchildren. Mere practical considerations may be clearly shown to possess a certain permanency, but are not, by that reason alone, enough to make a strong tradition upon which men will act as it were by instinct, to which they will defer as to the precepts of a revealed religion. Public opinion is at once a man of affairs, dry, grudging, sceptical of all sciences save arithmetic, and an idealist who will reject the most fortunate balance of material profit, if the attainment of it is in conflict with the national honour. There is a need for some spiritual element; for some ideal, informing policy. The politician, ignoring these things, involves us in endless debate; but the statesman, fully aware, is unsatisfied with a favourable vote which, given inconsiderately, does not set the seal upon the upholding principle. It was not enough for Hamilton that the constitution should be accepted, unless men firmly believed it with their minds and cherished it in their hearts.

The United States have been fortunate in the possession of a great and constant tradition, compounded of an intense belief in their institutions, in their destiny and in themselves. It has carried them safely through much rough weather, and it is not idle curiosity that puts the question how, being so young a nation, they came to gain it? The

Pangloss opinion does not hesitate: that as their institutions were good, their destiny favourable, and they themselves were born valiant and virtuous, it was impossible that belief could be withheld, the conditions being so obvious. But the inquiry is still unanswered, for their institutions are not conspicuously better than those of other nations that have come and gone, except precisely in this, that they are more steadfastly believed in. Their destiny likewise could have worked no wonders until men had faith in it, which in 1787 was far from being the case. Few men even surmised it, and still fewer then held to it firmly—not even Madison, anxious and defensive, but only Washington, Hamilton and Franklin, who found no great number of visionaries to understand their meaning.

Without this tradition the emigrants who flocked into the states during the nineteenth century, overwhelming and outnumbering the descendants of the old colonists who fought against George the Third, would never have been compacted into a great people. In these exiles and outcasts there resided no superior virtue, but rather the reverse. It was not merely the pure spirit of adventure, but suffering, weakness, despair, discontent, turbulence and crime that swept them together out of the dusty corners of Europe, and shook them out, Celts and Saxons and Latins and Slavs, in the seaports of the states. It is impossible to conceive of any immigration more lacking in unity and cohesion, or containing elements more dangerous to human society. Had the same men landed instead in the disunited states of the southern or central continent, they would have swollen the forces of disorder. But if they came on shore at Boston, Philadelphia, or New York, they were met at once by a tradition so universally held and so despotic that disagreement and resistance appeared equally absurd.

This tradition has the defects of its qualities: extrava-

A.D.
1787–1788
Æt. 30-31

gances, excesses, and upon occasions a preposterous assurance which strangers may fairly deride. But men of our nation can laugh with good humour because, being governed by a like tradition of their own which leads them at times into similar absurdities, they can also admire without envy. Questioned as to the origin of our faith, we find it hard, when taken unawares, to make any suitable reply. We know vaguely that we have scrambled to it somehow; slowly, over a long period, through a series of events which, viewed carelessly, look almost like accidents. We are inclined to believe that its foundations must have been deliberately laid by a few great men working in reasonably good material. We have a backward vision of Alfreds and Henrys and Edwards, far off, 'like misty warders dimly seen.' But in our sober moments we do not claim that the tradition which governs us so despotically can be fully explained and accounted for by our splendid opportunities, by our noble laws, or even by the virtue of the mass of our citizens. These things are rather the results of the tradition than the causes which have produced it. In periods of extreme complacency we have perhaps inclined to overlook the most remarkable excellence of the British race, which is its fertility in leaders; and leadership is the true cause of the tradition no less in the history of a nation than in the annals of a regiment.

Under this aspect America is an admirable example and a useful reminder. The great interest which attaches to her experiment is that during the whole of its development it has been under a close and rigid observation; for the time is short, and records have been kept. If we choose to look we can see the founders of the tradition at work like bees in a glass hive, careful, industrious and ungrudging. From Washington to Lincoln there is no obscurity anywhere. And great as was the practical achievement of the *Federalist* in procuring the adoption of the Union, its glory is even greater in having established it among those firm things which a nation with loving reverence has determined to place beyond all question.

For the rest of the world who are not the subjects of the Union the *Federalist* has the value of a great book, and this not merely for the style in which it is written, or even for the wisdom it contains. Style is a wonderful pickle that is able to preserve mediocrity of thought under favourable conditions for many centuries. Ingenious and consistent thought will frequently preserve itself even in the teeth of obviously uncomplying facts. The greatness of the *Federalist*, though it is lacking neither in style nor consistency of thought, is something different, something altogether unique. Men speak of it in the same breath with *L'Esprit des Lois* and *Il Principe*; and it has at least this in common with those works, that it deals with the problems of government, not merely on the surface with a tidy ingenuity, but fundamentally. Like them, it has had an immense influence both upon thinkers and upon men of action. But the contrasts are also valuable. Montesquieu was a curious analyst, a man of wit and eloquence; but he was almost at the opposite pole from the visionaries. He expounds a situation, explains it, comments upon it, and sums it up with the charming attribute of French writers, that his conclusions seem inevitable even on the occasions when we know his premises to be inaccurate. But he is always outside the actual controversy; keenly interested, but entirely detached; calm and impartial in his demeanour, even if in his heart he cherished certain preferences. He is considering other people's affairs all the while; never concerned in vindicating anything for which he is personally responsible. The conspicuous quality is his fertility in suggestion; the book is oftener on the knee than in the hand, and the reader far away on the wings of his own thought.

Machiavelli, on the other hand, is always the man of action—the would-be man of action—or at least the counsellor of men of action. In a sense he is an idealist, and would have built up a state; but he lacks the true spirit of the revolutionary, for he never contemplates, nor ever appears to desire, any change in the rules of the game. He is of opinion that he could play it better and more intelligently than his contemporaries; and it is not derogating from his genius to say of him that he writes somewhat in the manner of Cavendish on Whist. Assuming the conditions which exist—the nature of man and of things—to be unchangeable, he proceeds in a calm, unmoral way, like a lecturer on frogs, to show how a valiant and sagacious ruler can best turn events to his own advantage and the security of his dynasty. If we can conceive of Montesquieu and Machiavelli set upon the same problem, the construction of an ideal state, the former would have sought for the wisest balance, the latter for the strongest prince.

The morals which Montesquieu draws out of his analysis, the maxims which Machiavelli prepares from his experience, are entirely different from the method of the *Federalist*, which advocated a plan; explained and justified it; prevailed upon a nation of practical men to make a trial of it. This plan has now been at work for upwards of a hundred years, and its strength appears to-day to be greater than it was at the beginning. A book which has helped to produce a phenomenon of this order would possess an interest for mankind, even if it were not, as the *Federalist* is, a classic at once in style and thought.

The science of political philosophy in recent times has drawn in its horns, setting an example of modesty which its economic sister shows some disposition to imitate. Its

pretensions are to-day less confident than in the England
of the seventeenth century, or the France of the eighteenth.
Since Edmund Burke it has wisely chosen to waive its
early ambition of absolute power, accepting a position of
influential dignity rather than of executive authority. In
its present mood it is ready to agree with the Law of
England that a superior virtue resides in judgments delivered upon particular issues, and that *obiter dicta*, however
entertaining, are not sound rules to go by. The author
writing on themes of government, as it were at large, without direct responsibility for the result, and chiefly for the
edification of the intelligent classes and the general improvement of the world, can still enjoy an ample reward
for his fancy and his industry. But the statesman whose
effort is to explain, to justify and to recommend a particular
policy, is on a different plane. If his plan in the end
succeeds and becomes notable, the words in which he urged
its adoption command a deeper attention. He challenges a
verdict not merely upon his principles, but in their result;
so that if his work has stood, the statement of his belief on
which it was based has a superior authority with succeeding
generations.

The opponents of Union had no artillery of sufficient
weight to reply to the *Federalist* and to withstand its
tremendous attack. They trusted vainly to the machine;
relying upon intrigue in the state legislatures, upon light
calumny and incredible misstatement. Confronted with a
real issue which for the moment has touched men's hearts,
even the strong management of a modern party has found
itself discomfited. An organisation is an excellent thing in
itself, but at such times it cannot fight ideas with bogeys.
People refused to believe that Washington wished to be
a king. They refused to believe that a state would deprive

its subjects of freedom and install a tyranny were it to part
with a portion of its sovereignty to the central government.
They were told, in the hallowed phrases which have done
duty since the days of Cleon the demagogue, that the
Convention of Philadelphia aimed at making the poor poorer,
and the rich richer; at the domination of the few and the
slavery of the many;[1] but men remained unconvinced even
by this familiar eloquence.   It was urged upon the maritime
states that to part with a shred of their fiscal independence
was to make over a portion of their natural wealth for the
benefit of their neighbours;[2] but even their faith in this
plausible appeal began to crumble before a wider vision and
a nobler aim.   Finally they were assured that the plan
was fantastic and unworkable; that it was but the wild
experiment of 'visionary young men.'   Every pamphlet and
every platform of the opposition echoed with this tremendous charge, and young men who see visions may, if we
consider the result, take comfort throughout the ages.

On the 17th of June 1788 the Convention of New York
state met at Poughkeepsie to consider the draft constitution.   This event stands in somewhat the same relation to
Hamilton's political career as the taking of the first redoubt
at Yorktown to his military service.   It was a brilliant
episode, a gallant action upon which popular imagination
has fastened, attracted by the spectacle of enemies meeting
one another in the gate.   'Two-thirds of the Convention,'
Hamilton wrote, 'and four-sevenths of the people are against
us.'[3]   Governor Clinton was his opponent, not himself an
orator, but a character of impressive size.   Even in private
conferences he was hardly articulate, but he knew clearly
the direction in which he had reasons for not travelling.

---

[1] *History*, iii. p. 449, also pp. 452-4.
[2] *Cf.* Clinton's policy in New York, *History*, iii. p. 174.
[3] *Works*, ix. pp. 432-3.

He controlled a majority of forty-six against a minority of nineteen.[1] But there comes a time in most struggles that are prolonged when it is not enough to direct the battle, when the leader who is willing to risk a personal encounter prevails over his opponent who seeks to control the movement from a windmill. Clinton was strong, narrow, unscrupulous and very stubborn, but he had in him nothing of the stuff of a paladin. His military career had been inglorious, and in debate he pushed others forward to do the fighting, lashing them into combat with a surly condemnation.

Since our narrative of the events at Poughkeepsie is mainly drawn from the notes and journals of the opponents of union, we may believe that the accounts of Hamilton's prowess are not exaggerated. He fought every point, and was at first beaten upon every point. His eloquence could make no impression upon the mechanical majority. He drew tears from his audience, both sides alike; spoke for hours at a time, and all men hung upon his words. But still, at the vote, forty-six hands went up against nineteen. The system on which the discussion was conducted is very puzzling. The constitution was rejected by a clear majority, and next day Hamilton returned undaunted to advocate it once more. Again it was rejected, and again he refused to accept the decision as final, arguing for delay, hoping that the news of ratification by other states would gradually wear down the obduracy of his opponents.

A friend finding him one day alone, " took the liberty to ' say to him, that they would inquire of me in New York ' what was the prospect in relation to the adoption of the ' Constitution; and asked him what I should say to them. ' His manner immediately changed, and he answered : ' God ' only knows. Several votes have been taken, by which it

---

[1] *History*, iii. p. 483.

' appears that there are two to one against us.' Supposing
' he had concluded his answer, I was about to retire, when he
' added, in a most emphatic manner: ' *Tell them that the*
' *Convention shall never rise until the Constitution is*
' *adopted.*'" [1]   Minorities are to be measured by spirit as
well as numbers, and the buoyancy of the nineteen who
followed Hamilton was disconcerting.

Suddenly there came a collapse.   Melancthon Smith, the
able leader in debate of the Clintonian party, announced
his willingness to ratify 'upon conditions.' Hamilton refused
to entertain the idea of a compromise, and wisely took the
admission as a signal for a more vehement assault.   The objections that were made to a complete acceptance " vanished
' before him.   He remained an hour and twenty minutes on
' the floor.   After which Mr. Smith, with great candour, got
' up; and after some explanations, confessed that Mr.
' Hamilton by his reasoning had removed the objections he
' had made." [2]

In spite of this defection, Clinton refused to budge, and
for a time it appeared as if his silent legion would stand by
him in sufficient numbers to ensure his victory.   But day
by day the news of ratification by other states came to
strengthen the weaker party.   All eyes were turned upon
Virginia, where the influence of Washington was pitted
against the open opposition of Monroe and the puzzling
advice of Jefferson, who wrote from Paris that he was in
favour both of acceptance and rejection.   But when at
last, over the dusty summer roads, Hamilton's triumphant
gallopers brought word of the adherence of the great
southern state, the battle was decided against the strong.
On the 25th July the minority of twenty-seven was changed
into a majority of three.

While we may accept without hesitation Hamilton's

---

[1] *History*, iii. pp. 522-23.   [2] *Ibid.* iii. p. 524.

estimate that four-sevenths of the population of New York state were opposed to the Union, we must also believe the contemporary accounts, which assure us that on his return to the city it seemed as if a unanimous people had come out to celebrate his victory.   It was not only the Convention of Poughkeepsie which had been conquered by his masterful and persuasive influence.   The minds also of the men who welcomed him with hymns and banners [1] had been subdued and fascinated by the dramatic spectacle of a ' visionary young man ' struggling against the discipline of overwhelming odds, day after day for six weary weeks, and in the end overcoming all opposition, by the prowess of a great character strung to its highest pitch by the inspiration of a great idea.

[1] *History*, iii. p. 528.

BOOK III

THE FEDERALISTS

A.D. 1789–1791

The feudal system may have worn out, but its main principle, that the tenure of property should be the fulfilment of duty, is the essence of good government. The divine right of kings may have been a plea for feeble tyrants, but the divine right of government is the keystone of human progress, and without it governments sink into police, and a nation is degraded into a mob.—DISRAELI.

BOOK III

THE FEDERALISTS

CHAPTER I

President Washington

CONGRESS met at New York in April 1789. Upon a canvass of the returns from the electoral colleges, it was found that General Washington had been chosen President by a unanimous vote.

"As he approached the Hall of Congress, he was seen to
' retain the firm, elastic step of a yet vigorous soldier's frame.
' His thin hair of hazel brown, covered with powder, was
' clubbed behind, in the fashion of the day. His dress was of
' black velvet. On his side hung a dress sword, and around
' his neck a ribbon to which was attached, concealed, a minia-
' ture of his wife, worn, it is stated, from his nuptials until his
' death. 'Time,' wrote Fisher Ames, 'had made havoc upon
' his face. He addressed the two Houses in the Senate
' Chamber; it was a very touching scene, and quite of the
' solemn kind. His aspect grave, almost to sadness; his
' modesty, actually shaking; his voice deep, a little tremulous,
' and so low as to call for close attention—added to the series
' of objects presented to the mind, and overwhelming it, pro-
' duced emotions of the most affecting kind upon the members.
' I sat entranced.'"[1]

[1] Fisher Ames, 3rd May 1789, *History*, iv. p. 8.

The first President had the gift of seeing into the heart of a situation better than most men, and he therefore doubtless understood that his unanimous election was not the beginning of the Millennium. He had a just pride in his fame in the world, an honourable concern for the good opinion of his fellow-countrymen, and it needed no prophetic instinct to perceive that in this new adventure both were to be placed in jeopardy. Even in his own trade of soldier it was hardly possible that he could have added to his laurels by fresh enterprises, and in the unknown trade of politician it was not unlikely he might suffer total eclipse. Nor could he hope in this hazardous undertaking to retain the all but universal affection which had rewarded his conduct of the war. Popular government in its working was predestined to result in a cleavage, and he who had been the leader of the whole people would find himself before long only the leader of a party. Beyond these considerations was a fervent desire for rest after an arduous life. 'The business of America's happiness,' in Hamilton's phrase, 'was yet to be done.'[1] It was a true statement of the case, and to the younger man, whose aim was not peace but achievement, the prospect appeared radiant and delectable. With Washington, however, it was entirely different. No action of his life shows a finer patriotism than his acceptance of office; for he foresaw both the danger and the labour, and judged notwithstanding that duty left him no escape.

The constitution which had been framed at Philadelphia, and afterwards accepted by the people, was as yet a lifeless thing. At the most it was only a licence to begin governing, granted to a few energetic characters who had faith in their own capacity to make the experiment succeed. Nothing appeared more likely than that this licence would be promptly withdrawn if the early years were marked with

[1] *History*, iv. p. 2.

failure, or even if delay occurred in achieving some conspicuous success. The life of the Union being bound up in
the strength of its government, the first thing to be done was
to establish that strength upon sure foundations by the bold
use of the powers which had been bestowed. In the weak
hands of men afraid to act upon their warrant, afraid to
construe it widely and even to exceed its strict and literal
intention, the constitution compacted with so much care
and accepted with so much misgiving must infallibly have
gone to pieces. In twelve months the states, which were as
yet united only upon paper, would have split again into
disunion. There was no magic in the charter itself that
could have drawn order out of the existing chaos. The
document signed at Philadelphia was little more than an
opinion and a hope. It was by the vigour and courage
of Washington's administration, and by the interpretation
placed upon the constitution by his boldest minister, that
the United States ultimately became a nation.

The enemies of Union both within and without were
hopeful that a weak government would undo the work of
the Convention. France, who conceived her interest to lie
in a distracted league, was unfriendly to the idea of an
American nation, and incredulous of the accomplishment of
such a miracle.[1] The 'French' party in the states bestirred
themselves in bringing forward the name of Benjamin
Franklin, whose advanced age alone was a sufficient obstacle
to his efficiency. The minority, who had vainly opposed the
act of union, were equally averse from the appointment of
a strong president, and endeavoured in a timid and subterranean fashion to promote this impossible candidature.
The adherents of Gates, whose personality appears at all
times to have exercised a fatal fascination upon impotent
intriguers, were favourable to any nomination which would

---

[1] Instructions to De Moustier, *History*, iii. p. 559.

have excluded Washington from power. But in fact the only question worth an answer was whether Washington himself would consent to serve. In this case the issue was a foregone conclusion. The real obstacle was neither France nor Gates, but Washington's own reluctance, his 'great and sole desire to live and die in peace and retirement on my own farm.'[1] In the letters which passed between Washington and Hamilton during the summer and autumn of the previous year[2] there is proof of the genuine aversion of the former from the cares of office, and of the determination of the latter that he must be compelled to make a sacrifice of his inclination.

It is clear that Hamilton grasped the importance of immediate effort. The enemies of the constitution, though temporarily discouraged, were numerous and powerful. They would gladly have obstructed the creation of any government, but as that had not been possible, they were prepared, as soon as occasion offered, to pervert its intention. Hamilton thoroughly understood the value attaching to the early acts of an administration charged with the perilous inauguration of a brand-new system. While he was well aware of the fatal consequences of any serious mistake, he was also aware that any delay on the part of the executive in exerting its authority would be construed as hesitation, and would restore the strength and spirit of the opposition. He sought, therefore, to impose his own policy at once, and to entrench it in such a fortress of precedents that only a revolution would be able to dislodge it. While men of slower natures were looking about them stunned by defeat, or bewildered by success, unsettled and disorganised—like an establishment of servants brought up to town and deposited in a new and unfamiliar mansion —he alone, and at once, grasped the opportunity afforded

---

[1] *History*, iii. p. 553.   [2] 1788. *History*, iii. pp. 550-58.

by these circumstances to a self-possessed and energetic character with a clear knowledge of his own mind. While public affairs were in this plastic condition, purposes could be achieved with but little difficulty that at a later date would have required stupendous efforts for their accomplishment. At such a time things might also be done which could never be undone.

National unity was in a sense already attained; the principle had been accepted in the most solemn fashion; but the constitution, where it was vague, imperfect, or inadequate, had still to be defined, developed and extended. The financial position was rotten. It was of paramount importance to place it at once on a sound and honest basis. The natural resources of the empire were enormous, but they needed the care of a strong and watchful sovereign to bring them into early prosperity. A continent upon the eastern side of the Atlantic, distracted by jealous rivalries, invited the American people to flattering but deadly alliances, in which Hamilton dreaded to see the new Republic entangled either by reckless sentiment or by a spirit of inveterate revenge.

With these objects he set himself at once to extend the power and prestige of the federal government, and to curb and diminish the importance of the states; to provide for or discharge all debts according to the strict letter of the bond; to pursue the deliberate advantage of his own country among nations, equally unmoved by affection for France and by hatred of England, and equally indifferent to the enthusiasm of most men, and to the indignation of a few, as the Revolution in Paris pursued its startling career. And in all circumstances, at every turn of events and clash of interests, he kept before his eyes the subordination of classes, industries, and states, to the national purpose and the advantage of the commonwealth.

The complete sovereignty of the central government over all citizens and states of the Union had been the chief subject of controversy from the beginning. This principle, not altogether unintentionally, had been to some extent put out of sight during the discussions at Philadelphia. It was not fully admitted even by the clauses of the constitution. Still less had it been accepted by the people with all its unforeseen consequences when they ratified the action of the majority of their delegates. It was the chief object of Hamilton's policy to establish this principle so firmly that it could not be overthrown or even questioned. The chief object of his opponents was precisely the reverse. They aimed at limiting the central sovereignty, while he sought to extend it. Where the terms of the compact admitted of a doubt, they endeavoured to construe them in a sense favourable to the state legislatures, unfavourable to the federal government. Both parties admitted the need for a balance of power as a check upon rash administration, but while Hamilton was determined to produce this balance out of the forces which existed within a single nation, the opposite party held no less fervently by the old idea that the end in view could only be successfully accomplished by the competing interests of many nations within a league.

This difference in political faith was fundamental. Long after Washington and Hamilton had passed away, cheerful, well-meaning men and despondent, wise men endeavoured vainly to adjust by compromise what could only be settled by victory. Any solution of the antagonism between the Federalist ideal and the pretensions of the State Rights party was wholly beyond the reach of concession or accommodation. For the policies were in direct opposition, like two men whose sole but essential quarrel is simply for the upper hand. Bland mediation, soothing make-believe, patched-up temporary arrangements, were hopeless negotiators, for there was in such a case no choice of alternatives. In the end one man must prevail, the other must submit.

It is conceivable that had the times been more propitious, had Hamilton been as admirable a party leader as he was a statesman, had he lived, or had the Federalist party at the beginning of the nineteenth century discovered some other chief capable of sustaining their spirit and guiding their counsels, the difference might have been settled by a political victory. But each year of delay added to the danger by complicating the issue with fresh interests. The growth of population, the development of territory, the increase of wealth, added strength and confidence to the opposing parties, so that by the time Lincoln came to undertake the government of the country[1] there remained only one possible solution—the stricken field. 'In campaign, battle, hospital, and prison,' it has been computed that a million of human lives were sacrificed,[2] in order 'that this nation, under God, shall have a new birth of freedom.'[3] Certainly it was not a cheap victory. The thing which commands our admiration is that three-quarters of a century later a man should have arisen, the equal of Washington in character, of Hamilton in perspicacity, who had the courage to maintain the Union even at this staggering price.

A great nation does not for any mean or trivial difference split into two camps of eager volunteers and engage in civil war until one of the sections yields through mere exhaustion. Long before four campaigns had ended, the virus of personal hatred would have spent itself, the pretensions of a mere phrase would have been detected. The War of Secession would never have been fought by men,

---

[1] March 1861.   [2] *Cambridge Modern History*, vii. p. 453.
[3] Lincoln's Address at Gettysburg.

bewitched by rival logicians in dispute regarding the abstract propositions of constitutional law. The spirit which combated against union in the Philadelphia Convention, in the early Congresses and in the cabinets of Washington, was the same spirit, and engaged in the same struggle, in the cabinet of Buchanan and on the field of Gettysburg, seventy years later. It is a spirit that compels respect from its most determined opponents—a spirit of an impracticable ideal, but still an ideal. But between the fanatics for State Rights whom we condemn, and the upholders of the dignity and utility of local authorities whom we have been taught to admire, there is in fact only a difference of degree. A commonwealth in which this spirit had ceased to exist might be safely marked as a dying race; but in the view of the statesman it can never be allowed the upper hand. Like the steam in a boiler, it serves its purpose by its efforts to escape from imprisonment and control; but if these efforts are successful, there is an end of the utility.

The struggle between Federalism and State Rights soon made a wide cleavage in the first cabinet. Washington's own convictions and sympathies were on the Federal side; but he considered that his supreme duty as a Federalist, no less than as a patriot, was to compel the new constitution to prove itself capable of being worked. The country had to be governed, a political system had to be inaugurated at all costs. With this end in view he set to work reluctantly and wearily, composing differences and enduring obloquy, with the same calm judgment and undramatic courage that had directed his conduct of the war. The weight of this immense and unfamiliar character was not to be resisted. While Hamilton laboured at the foundations, Washington helped him to keep the enemy at bay, and approved the work, step by step, as it was accomplished.

It may well be doubted whether without this fortunate
co-operation the constitution would ever have existed except
as a historical document.

CHAPTER II

The Threefold Policy

THE governing principle of Hamilton's policy, of Washington
who supported Hamilton, and of the whole Federalist party
who followed him, was to establish a supreme sovereignty.
The first step towards the accomplishment of this object
was dull but arduous. Out of nothing the whole machinery
of government had to be called suddenly into existence.
Controversy was silenced for the moment by an overwhelming necessity. At this stage the difficulties were
mainly those inherent in the nature of the task, and were
not to any important extent the result of the spirit of
faction. But so soon as the machinery was contrived,
departments organised and provision made for the pressing
needs of the Union, the governing principle became visible,
and according to the dispositions of men it appeared admirable in the eyes of some and hateful in the eyes of
others.

Hamilton sought his prime object by a threefold means.
The idea of his financial policy was the welding of the
Union, of his commercial policy the development of the
estate, of his foreign policy to confirm independence. Each
of these undertakings was planned upon the heroic scale in
accordance with the nature of its author; but all were
subordinate to his main end, and never, even in the dust
and heat of political controversy, were they permitted to
escape from their true proportions.

The period during which Hamilton's ideas have directed the course of American history has not yet ended, and is not likely to end in our day; but the time during which his personal influence controlled the policy of government is reckoned only at twelve years, while his official career lasted for but little more than five.[1] The administration of Washington began in April 1789 and ended in March 1797. Upon his retirement from political life, John Adams, also a member of the Federalist party, was chosen to succeed him. Adams was no friend to Hamilton, but his cabinet did not allow him to break the spell during the term of his administration.

In March 1801 Thomas Jefferson, the founder and leader of the Democratic party, having defeated the Federalists, became President of the United States. For four-and-twenty years from that date the highest office in the Union was occupied in turn by three men[2] who not only held the whole trend of Hamilton's policy in abhorrence, but were among the bitterest of his personal enemies. The Federalist party, seriously crippled even before the death of its leader,[3] gradually crumbled into discredit when deprived of his support. In these circumstances it was only natural that the ideals of Hamilton earned but a scanty respect. Much was said about the need for undoing his work, and something was attempted towards that end; but, fortunately in one respect, his fame was so completely obscured for the time being by the superior radiance of his successors that it was judged unnecessary to signalise the triumph of the Democrats and the ruin of the Federalists by the inconvenient process of destroying institutions which were already perceived to be indispensable to the prosperous management of affairs.

[1] Federalist Administrations (Washington and Adams), April 1789–March 1801 ; Hamilton Secretary of the Treasury, September 1789–January 1795.
[2] Jefferson, Madison and Monroe.   [3] Hamilton's death, 11th July 1804.

The ultimate object of the threefold policy was to establish a set of principles, by weaving them into the fabric of the national tradition, before the opponents of strong government should have the opportunity of office. Hamilton sought to accomplish his ends by a series of legislative measures and by a course of steadfast conduct on the part of the executive. If these measures and this course of conduct were to fulfil his ultimate object, it was necessary, in his opinion, that each separate act should succeed in a conspicuous manner in achieving its own particular and immediate object. Good results must be shown forthwith. The great mass of the citizens must be affected by a sudden and fortunate contrast, with a sense of a great benefit due unmistakably to the federal arrangement. And yet it was equally necessary that the policy should be wise and well grounded. For although a rapid improvement was for every reason desirable, it was above everything desirable that the measures of the first administration should possess the quality of permanence. It was essential that their purpose should not be impaired at a later date by the need for frequent alterations and adjustments which in careless or hostile hands might have endangered the existence of the essential principles. If Hamilton's threefold policy succeeded in detail, the result, in his opinion, would be to produce throughout the country a feeling of gratitude and even of reverence, not to himself personally or to his party, but towards those new institutions which were standing upon their trial. In addition to this general aim, there was also a particular intention in many of his acts, notably in those which dealt with the funding of the debts and other problems of finance, to enlist powerful interests and classes upon the side of the federal government by assuming obligations and responsibilities towards them which had previously been distributed among the separate states.

N

A.D. 1789
Æt. 32 It may also be said of Hamilton's policy, viewing it from a different standpoint, that its object was the same as that of the war itself. The struggle with Britain had been for the sake of independence, and for that alone. After immense sacrifices the states had succeeded in getting rid of every vestige of direct external control. Hamilton's aim was to secure the measure of independence which had been thus attained, and to extend the work a stage further by getting rid of all influence from without, not only direct but indirect, not only political in the strict sense, but general.

The aim of his financial measures (in which he succeeded) was to make the nation independent of external creditors, of European usurers, bankers and governments who had supplied the funds necessary for carrying on the war either at onerous rates, or, as in the case of France, in order to gain an influence which would enable them to promote their own political ends.

The aim of his foreign policy was independence of European intrigue, and the exclusion of its diplomacy, not merely from all direct appeals to the individual states, but from a position in which it could exercise pressure upon the federal power. And in his practical and foreseeing mind he clearly understood from the beginning that if the Old World was to be kept from interference in the affairs of the New, it could only be by a stiff and unyielding refusal upon the part of the Union to be drawn upon any pretext into the quarrels of the European continent. In this aim also he succeeded; for if he did not actually secure the formula which is now known as the Monroe Doctrine in the definite phrases of a state document, he none the less by irrevocable acts laid the foundations and raised high the edifice of that foreign policy which his country has pursued from that day to this.

Independence was likewise the aim of his commercial

policy, which was framed with the deliberate intention of creating a self-sufficing nation. American industry was to be made as free from the hazards of European markets as American politics from the influence of European governments. His method was to arrive at a balance between the production of food and raw materials on the one hand, and manufactures, shipping and other forms of commerce upon the other. It was possible, in his opinion, with the prudent assistance of legislation, to come speedily to a point at which all the necessities of life and instruments of labour, and even the greater part of the luxuries that were in common demand, should be supplied from the fields and farms, the mines, mills and workshops of the new republic. A nation which was content to drift along the path of least resistance must suffer the inconveniences and dangers of a lop-sided development. A nation in which the manufacturing or the agricultural interest was in an overwhelming predominance would never be proof against foreign hostility or catastrophe, as a nation might hope to be which maintained the principle of a strong internal market for commodities of every kind.

Hamilton's desire to establish his commercial policy did not succeed. It is true that he has set forth his ideas in one of the most memorable reports ever made to Congress. It is true also that his proposals were welcomed by the great majority of his own party as well as by many of his opponents. But although in certain isolated cases he was able to introduce his system of national development, it was so little advanced when his power ended that the proportions of the fabric did not affect the imaginations of men so as to impel them, willing or unwilling, to complete the work. Unlike his foreign and financial policies, his commercial policy did not crystallise into a tradition or an institution. The foundations were not even laid, but only staked out;

and although the elevation and the working plans existed ready to the hand of the builder, they were laid aside and soon forgotten. All that can be claimed is that the idea was perfect in his own mind. But only after many years had elapsed did it begin to assert an authority among men who, under the pressure of circumstances and not by means of their own clear foresight, had begun to travel slowly in the same direction.

The fate of Hamilton's threefold policy after his death is worth noting at this stage. That part of it which dealt with finance was accomplished during the term of his office. Although his opponents had blustered heroically about their intentions, it was never undone, because it was too strong to be pulled down by peaceful means. The principles of his foreign policy were fully accepted in practice before the retirement of Washington. Their sound patriotism was too obvious to be disregarded by his successors, who, when their passions were cooled and the malice of rivalry had died away, completed the structure and confirmed the tradition. But of his commercial policy the plan only was bequeathed to future generations. His policy, therefore, succeeded in accomplishing the greater number of the particular objects it set out to accomplish. In no instance was it defeated. It was only delayed. Even when some counter idea for the moment overcame it, the victory was never followed up by effective occupation. It is true that his commercial policy did not prevail, but the doctrine of Free Trade did not usurp the vacant place. Free Trade was never even set up with success as an alternative to his commercial policy. The obstacle was merely a kind of lethargy which descended upon men in what has been termed 'the era of good feeling,' an indisposition to decide upon any new and definite policy. The spirit of the times was an easy contentment with existing institutions, even though these were obviously incom-

plete Men preferred to live in an unfinished palace, despite
the dangers and inconveniences attaching to their lazy
occupation, rather than to engage in any strenuous efforts
to complete the structure.

When we come to consider further what was to Hamilton
the main and ultimate object of his threefold policy—the
firm establishment of a supreme and sovereign government
—we find that here also he has been successful—successful
even beyond his own hopes, but still not wholly successful.
The Union still exists. The forces of disintegration have
been kept at bay. This result, however, has not been
attained by the peaceful means which Hamilton had planned,
but only as the outcome of civil war waged upon a tremendous scale. In placing these limits upon the renown of his
achievements, we must in fairness take into account the
prodigious nature of his ambition. We are bound to
remember also this fact, that if the Union, for which he
sacrificed his own life, was not preserved without the further
sacrifice of a million lives, it was, beyond any doubt, from
the love of the institutions he had raised, and by the
force of the tradition made by his great spirit, that men
were found willing to pour out their blood like water to
secure all that he had won for them, and nearly all that he
had dreamed of winning.

When we consider the course of events during the first
quarter of the nineteenth century, it is impossible not to be
struck by the prevalence of lethargy in the counsels of
Hamilton's successors, and even in the people themselves.
There is a tendency among the statesmen who followed him
to leave his work for the greater part where he had left it;
if complete, complete; if half-done, half-done; if only
planned but not begun, to lay the plan aside. Hamilton
was as great a builder as he was an architect, as necessary
in the one capacity as in the other; and for more than half a

A.D. 1789 century after his death no man was found equal to the task
Æt. 32 of finishing the work. When a further advance was required by circumstances, his successors, like the architects
and builders of an inferior age, were apt to carry out the
original intention in a feeble, grotesque, or disproportioned
style. In the case of the commercial policy this tendency
is everywhere conspicuous. The plan lay ready to hand,
but when Hamilton's successors came to put it in execution
they showed at first a futile hesitation, and in the end a
riotous extravagance, owing to their inability to see the
problem as a whole. The fine symmetry and the noble
purpose which existed in the mind of Hamilton were
entirely missed. Under the shelter of his name, what he
dreaded most has come to pass, and the advantage of
interests and of classes has been preferred to the wellbeing
of the nation. His system of foreign policy had less to
fear from mutilation, for it was not only planned, but for the
most part already built. Yet even here it is impossible not
to detect the absence of the master's hand. Although his
ends have been achieved, his wise maxims have been ignored
even upon grave occasions. "There appears to me too much
'tartness in various parts of the reply," Hamilton wrote at
the crisis of the negotiations with Britain. "Energy without
'asperity seems best to comport with the dignity of national
'language. The force ought to be more in the idea than in
'the expression or manner."[1] And again, 'real firmness
is good for anything; strut is good for nothing.' The
note of his system was a quiet adherence to essential things
and a contemptuous aversion from exasperating methods.
His preference was for the aristocratic spirit and ritual. A
courteous and dignified demeanour was to his thinking a
better weapon than the self-conscious, highflown aggressive-
ness which delighted the hearts of the Democrats. The

[1] *History*, vi. p. 5.

Monroe Doctrine and the modern tariff policy of the United A.D 1789
States are both in a certain sense direct inheritances from Æt. 32
Hamilton. But, viewed under another aspect, both contain
an element of caricature, not only in their style, but even
in their methods and ultimate aims. We miss the grand
manner which despised provocation. A certain bustling
assurance, with all its loud talk of business principles,
does not reach the high level of his energy, while it
misses many things which were firmly held in his luminous
and well-proportioned view.

CHAPTER III

Hamilton's Difficulties

AN attempt has been made to explain the Federalist
principle and to draw a rough outline of the policy by
which Hamilton purposed to establish it as a precedent for
future governments and as a part of the national tradition.
Even this inadequate account will have been enough to
indicate the splendour and audacity of his enterprise; but
for a true understanding of his character it is necessary that
we should bear in mind the difficulties which surrounded
him on every side.

The first of these is the shortness of the period in which
the work was done. Five years and a few months was the
brief term of Hamilton's official career. Within seven
years after his retirement from Washington's government
his enemies came into power.

Nor was shortness of time the greatest of Hamilton's
difficulties. We must realise also that, except for the few
months between his appointment as Secretary of the
Treasury in September 1789 and the meeting of the second

session of Congress early in the following January, there was hardly a day during the whole of his administration when he was not challenged and obstructed at every turn by a powerful opposition.

While it is true that throughout the remaining term of the first Congress[1] parties were not yet organised upon a strict system, and that the cleavage was uncertain and not wholly partisan ; yet this fact had its disadvantages as well as its benefits, for the members, lacking discipline, were often and easily persuaded to sacrifice a principle to a passing sentiment. Accordingly, although upon the whole the Federalists who followed Hamilton were in a considerable majority, it happened on more than one occasion that Hamilton's measures were defeated, and it was the exception when any important Act was carried without some mischievous alteration or illogical curtailment.

In the second Congress[2] the opposition was organised, fanatical and unscrupulous. Not only Hamilton's policy, but his personal integrity, was constantly and bitterly assailed, and although these attacks were on every occasion rolled back with disaster upon their instigators, the pertinacity of these enemies was untiring. Apart from the distraction and annoyance, the mere time occupied in the defeat of the eager malice of the Democrats was a serious impediment to his labours.

In the third Congress[3] there was, if possible, a still more savage and relentless temper. The difficulties of administration were enhanced by the fact that the Federalists now no longer held a majority in the House of Representatives,

---

[1] The *first* session of the first Congress lasted from the beginning of April to the end of September 1789 ; the *second* session from January to August 1790 ; the *third* session from December 1790 to March 1791.

[2] October 1791 to March 1793.

[3] December 1793 to March 1795.

but were outvoted on every party division by the Democrats. Moreover, during this period Hamilton was occupied
for several months with the suppression of the Whisky
Rebellion,[1] which had been excited by the blundering intrigues of the opposition. A military expedition, headed by
Washington, was required to restore order, and although
Hamilton accompanied the Federal forces without a military
command, the direction was mainly in his hands.

The rapidity with which parties came into existence is
hardly a matter for surprise. The ordinary man is apt to
cry out lustily whenever he is hurt or inconvenienced, and,
unless he be perpetually reminded that his complaints are
unreasonable, there is always a danger that he will settle
down into a regular opposition.

The process of union or confederation must always be to
some extent a painful business. As in the case of badly
set limbs, bones have to be broken by the surgeon and
reset before the patient can regain his proper shape and
the full use of his members. It was not only bad citizens
and dishonest rascals, not only men who sought a profit in
disunion or in the repudiation of debts, who composed the
Democratic party. There were also included in it all those
who still clung, many of them unconsciously, to the doctrine
of State Rights, and dreaded as if by instinct the rule of a
central government which in their panic they identified with
tyranny. And to these were added, in a remarkable alliance,
the adherents of the new-fangled and fashionable doctrines
of the Rights of Man.

Gradually but swiftly, therefore, a party, compounded of
malcontents of every variety and enthusiasts belonging to at
least two incompatible faiths, grew up and consolidated in
antagonism to the policy of the administration. To say that
this party was hostile to the Union would be too sweeping

[1] 1794.

a charge; but it is none the less true that it was hostile to the conditions upon which the very existence of the Union depended, and in time it became even more hostile to the personal forces that were engaged in maintaining the Union. In many minds the necessity for strong government was only admitted at particular moments under the lash of adversity. People who had called out for a true sovereign during the crisis of the war became careless as soon as peace was declared, and many likewise who had been clamorous for Union in the intolerable disorders of 1787 grew lukewarm in the comparative tranquillity of 1790. The constant tendency among this class of citizens was to be content with an instalment of comfort. They grudged paying the full price which would have ensured them a permanent possession of the whole benefit.

Parliamentary opposition was neither the last nor the worst of Hamilton's difficulties. Before many months had passed the cabinet was divided no less sharply than Congress, till in the end the majority of its decisions were arrived at by the casting vote of the President. In such circumstances a perfect loyalty among its members would have been a difficult achievement had they been men of the nicest honour. But even an outward show of cooperation proved to be quite unattainable. Confidence was entirely destroyed. The opposition out of doors was directed, encouraged and comforted from within. The measures of government were damned in advance by a zealous Democratic press well supplied with information by its supporters in the Cabinet.

It must be admitted, after the event, that Washington's original conception of cabinet government was founded on a capital error, and even that his management of his administration was marred by very grave mistakes. There

is little cause for wonder and none for reproach in such a
verdict; for though Washington was by nature a statesman
as well as a soldier, neither by nature nor by training was
he a politician. His instinct did not foresee the pitfalls that
were hidden in parliamentary institutions of an entirely
novel and unprecedented type.

His idea of a strong cabinet was a representative cabinet.
Not only was it his desire that it should be representative
of geographical divisions, of north and south, of Virginia,
New England, and New York,—in itself both a sound and
a politic aim,—but he wished also to make it representative
of the various currents of political thought, and this was
necessarily disastrous. It may be urged that at the time
when he chose the members of his cabinet there was no
sharp division of opinion; that to all appearance differences
had been successfully ended by the compromise of Philadelphia; that the whole country was in an optimistic mood,
and proceeded upon the assumption that every good man
had rallied once and for all to the support of a government
charged with the task of establishing the Union. It is
difficult to withstand an enthusiasm of this character, but
in Washington, who had a wide knowledge of mankind in
general and of his own countrymen in particular, we must
suspect a certain measure of incredulity. For he had seen
the two opposing principles at work from Lexington to the
Convention of Philadelphia, and was well aware of their
force and essential hostility.

The confidence of any people in its government is grounded
in the opinion that the government knows its own mind. A
cabinet which is representative of conflicting ideas can only
hope to tide over some sudden crisis. Its existence supposes
a common enemy. When the crisis is past it can only
maintain itself by the most rigorous inaction. For withstanding some temporary danger it may have considerable

virtues, but for carrying through a policy it is a miserable instrument.

The result of this attempt to reconcile irreconcilable ideals was a bitter disagreement which ended in an open and public scandal. Had the opposing forces been equal, the functions of government must have been suspended by hopeless paralysis. Only the overwhelming character of Hamilton rescued the administration from disastrous failure. Washington, whose influence in a united cabinet would have been a tower of strength, was put out of action at the height of the battle. His convictions were on the side of the Federalists, but his sense of duty forced him to play the arbiter. At moments when a bold pronouncement was the thing most needful, he was engaged in a conscientious examination of arguments. In political matters his mind worked slowly. Having provided himself with a ministry of conflicting principles, he felt bound to consider their conflicting advice. By his delay in coming to a decision he frequently lost the advantage of prompt action, and raised suspicions that there was room for doubt upon the merits of the case.

But, further, he was guilty of a tactical error in retaining colleagues with whom he was in utter disagreement, whose characters he had come to distrust. He seems to have cherished the illusion that by adopting this course he would disarm their hostility, and would pin them down to an approval of his measures. The result was altogether disappointing. The reluctance of Jefferson, the Secretary of State, and of Randolph, the Attorney-General, was published upon the housetops. The scrupulous deliberation of Washington bound them to nothing, but merely tolerated the presence of informers in his own camp.

The well-meaning plan of a representative cabinet was therefore in the working of it a complete failure. The broad

basis proved to be a mere will-o'-the-wisp. The great matter
was that the federal idea should get clear away, and to this
end the necessity was a cabinet of perfect sympathy, even
though it was chosen upon a narrower principle of selection.
The mistake of Washington lay in imagining that the
strength of a government was determined by the number
of its friends at the beginning. Disillusionment came too
late, when he found the opposition to his administration
was led by his own ministers.

In addition to these difficulties arising out of the gigantic
nature of the task, the shortness of the time, the growth of
parties, the hostility of Congress, and the dissensions in the
cabinet, Hamilton was further impeded by the rules adopted
by the two Houses for the transaction of their business. If
ever it may be said with safety of any man that, given the
opportunity, he would have been a great parliamentarian, it
may confidently be said of him. He had the true genius
for debate in addition to his other and nobler qualities. His
management of the Convention of New York[1] is in itself a
sufficient proof of his capacities in this direction. A man
who could carry his party to victory against a majority of
two-thirds of the convention and four-sevenths of the people
would hardly have failed in persuading the triumphant
Federalists in the first and second Congresses to pass in
their integrity the measures necessary for the conservation
of the republic. When, therefore, it was determined by the
legislative bodies that not only were ministers to be excluded from debate, but even their reports and recommendations were to be made in writing, it was as if on the eve of
battle a general were to be forbidden to make use of his
artillery. Under this regulation the business of a minister
was merely to prepare his measures for the consideration of
Congress. The defence and explanation of the policy was

[1] At Poughkeepsie, 1788, *ante* pp. 176-179.

taken altogether out of the hands of its author and left to friends who, however devoted and intelligent, could hardly be expected to understand its bearings in all their width and depth. Objections that should have been dealt with at the moment were left to wander at large. Opponents who should have been smitten hip and thigh upon their first hostile movement were often allowed to hold the field for want of a proper challenger. Principles were obscured by irrelevant issues, and by sudden appeals to sentiment or the authority of phrases. But the chief evil was the exclusion of that personal force which transcends all argument and tactics, which causes its will to prevail in popular assemblies not so much by an appeal to the emotions or even to the reason of men, as by the direct impact of character, asserting its mastery like the lion-tamer by some inexplicable quality inherent in the eyes, the voice and the demeanour.

CHAPTER IV

Secretary of the Treasury

THE bill to establish the Treasury department passed into law on the 2nd of September 1789, and Hamilton was appointed to the Secretaryship on the 11th of the same month. In view of the condition of the public finances, it was the hardest post under government. Having regard to the disposition of mankind when called upon to pay taxes, it was the most perilous. And under every aspect it was the most important. Friends endeavoured in vain to dissuade him from accepting a position which, while it involved the sacrifice of a lucrative practice for a stipend inadequate to cover the expenses of his household, might also destroy a career of brilliant promise by engaging him in an undertaking foredoomed, in their judgment, to failure.

The story goes that Washington consulted Robert Morris,
the late Superintendent of Finance, upon the dismal prospects of his department. 'What are we to do with this heavy
debt ?' 'There is but one man in the United States who
can tell you,' Morris replied; 'that is Alexander Hamilton.
I am glad you have given me this opportunity to declare to
you the extent of the obligations I am under to him.' [1]

Hamilton was appointed Secretary of the Treasury at the
age of thirty-two, and found himself a great minister of
state, with a salary of £700 a year. He gave up his profession before he had been able to effect any substantial
savings, in order to undertake the office of Chancellor of
the Exchequer to an embarrassed and almost bankrupt
nation, impoverished by a long and costly war. There was
neither treasury nor treasure, revenue nor staff of experts,
system of accounts nor practice of audit—only a crowd of
solicitous and noisy creditors, and a government without the
means of paying even the modest expenses that had to be
incurred from day to day. The currency was in disorder.
Commercial credit, the fundamental condition of progress
and prosperity, had ceased to exist. The minds of all men
were filled with uncertainty, and the life of every industry
was threatened by the national insolvency.

One great advantage Hamilton certainly possessed, for
there was nothing to undo, no creaking system and stiff
traditions to be destroyed; but against this may be set the
disconcerting fact that he was without even the skeleton of
a service or the remnant of an organisation. Not only had
he to devise a method, create a machinery, find and train
his servants; but he was peremptorily required to furnish an
immediate revenue, and, while providing it under so great
pressure, to think out and establish a permanent financial
policy with which these hasty expedients should not be at

[1] *History*, iv. p. 30.

discord. Beyond all this he was determined so, to fashion the measures of his department that they should contribute, directly as well as indirectly, to the strength of the constitution which was on its trial. He found himself, therefore, confronted with a labour of drudgery and detail. At the same time he was clearly aware that in his hands lay the power of affecting the destiny of his country far beyond the scope of his particular department. The distracted Congress turned to him as a saviour, and within ten days after his appointment demanded a report on ways and means.[1]

The confidence with which all men regarded him in these days of confusion is a strange phenomenon. Hamilton enjoyed even at this date a great financial reputation; but when we come to investigate the basis on which it rested, and the means by which it was acquired, it is impossible to suppress a smile. His sole practical training for administering the finances of the republic had been those few years spent in a storekeeper's office in a West Indian sugar island, between the ages of eleven and fifteen. He was favourably known to many as a charming and handsome young soldier, who had written General Washington's despatches in a most admirable style; who had very gallantly taken a redoubt at the crisis of the war; who had been called to the bar, and had at once sprung into a great practice; who, ever since he was a college student, had written political pamphlets, memoranda and letters; who had had a large share in framing the constitution, and an even larger share in procuring its adoption by his countrymen. But these characteristics, qualities and accomplishments, however admirable in themselves, hardly seemed to warrant the confidence with which men saw him undertake the hardest office in the first administration.

But beyond this what was there to show? Only, so far

---

[1] *History*, iv. pp. 32, 45.

as can be gleaned from history, the fact that while he was Washington's secretary, harassed by the want of supplies and the ill conduct of affairs, he had written and talked about finance and figures, revenue and credit, with an ease and decision that made people gape with astonishment. He had no credentials save his conversation and his letters. He was wholly without training, and had never borne an ounce of financial responsibility in the whole course of his public career.

Of all political reputations the reputation for financial ability is the easiest to acquire and to lose. A man of any notoriety can almost have it for the asking. If he has but a small eminence from which to show himself to his fellow-countrymen, and a persuasive tongue, or even a sufficiently solemn aspect of silent wisdom, he need not fear that his fitness will be too severely scanned at the beginning. It is almost enough to have been a banker in order to be believed a financier. To have become suddenly wealthy by speculation, by manufactures, or by keeping shops, places his intellectual fitness beyond question, and people then only demand to be satisfied of his integrity. For the world hates boredom, and to be forced to do arithmetic is for nine-tenths of humanity the gloomiest and the most irritating of all forms of boredom. And the world also hates, except in rare moments of spiritual exaltation, to look its indebtedness in the face, fair and square. The suspicion of insolvency lurking in the heap of bills intensifies its natural disgust with the subject. If a persuasive man suddenly appears, talking fluently of sinking-funds and conversions, saying, " Gentlemen, leave it all to ' me. I see my way. I promise you everything will ' come right," or if a silent person, who is known for his private success, be pushed forward by his admiring friends, the world is usually willing, especially when times are bad, to let the dismal burden be strapped upon his shoulders.

But if confidence be easy to win in this department of human affairs, it is even easier to lose. Bankruptcy has a penetrating quality which disconcerts the efforts of the bravest charlatan who seeks to banish it with incantations. Two months before Hamilton entered Washington's cabinet the Bastille had fallen, and the ancient monarchy of France was rocking upon its foundations. For that great disturbance of society it may be fairly claimed that persuasive financiers had as large a share of the credit as incompetent monarchs or extortionate nobles or any other class of mankind.

In what precisely the quality of state financier consists it is difficult to say. Only one thing is certain about him, that he must be persuasive in an altogether remarkable degree. This is not to lay down the rule that he must be smiling and bland and full of amiable prognostications of fair weather; but he must be able to inspire confidence, not only in the tax-payers whose affairs are in his charge, but also in the moneyed classes with whom the duties of his office place him in relations. To speak in terms of his department, his credit is of even more importance than his cash. Under a certain aspect it almost seems as if, given persuasiveness, a scrupulous adherence to copy-book precepts will do the rest. A moderately clear head, infinite pains and a stiff back will carry him a long way. In a nation already enjoying prosperity these qualifications have often proved quite adequate to the purpose; but in other and more difficult circumstances we are conscious of something beyond, which, as it is too volatile for definition, we allude to vaguely as genius. Two or three men whose names are recorded in history have possessed it, and Hamilton is one of these.

The results in such cases are the only proof; but when, impelled by curiosity, we attempt discovery of the methods by

which this peculiar success has been achieved, they continue
to elude us. In Hamilton's fluent reports everything appears
so simple, so obvious, so entirely in accordance with common-
sense; everything is so orderly and neat and inevitable, so
exactly what we should ourselves have recommended unhesitatingly in similar circumstances, that the intelligent
reader, almost from a kind of modesty, and being accustomed
to associate genius with a mist or an obscurity, becomes
sceptical of its existence where nothing of the magician
is allowed to appear. The cloak, and the hat, and the
wand, and the air of mystery are all absent, and there is
nothing at all remarkable except a certain lucidity.

Hamilton set himself to work, and the principles of
finance, like the principles of law, immediately surrendered
to him. His instinct grasped the few essentials of his task
firmly and clearly. When these were once established,
industry and firmness did the rest. Swiftly and unhesitatingly he proceeded to grapple with the multitude of important details, inevitable trifles, and pure irrelevancies; not
in a spirit of sightless drudgery, but like some traveller on
a frosty autumn morning who sees before him on the sunlit
plain the spires and steeples that are his goal, and steps out,
brisk and cheery, in the full swing of his stride, whistling
and singing on his way.

With insight, and with what in a sanguine financier is
even rarer and more wonderful—with sufficient foresight,
yet not too much—he devised his method and constructed
his machine. He collected his staff as best he could,
and imbued them with his own orderly and indefatigable
spirit; arranged a system of audit, checks, records and
divisions, good enough for his immediate purpose, and, as
the event has proved, good enough for the United States
until the present day.

Regarded merely as an official Hamilton is a great man,

for he constructed his department upon principles that have never needed to be altered because they have never hampered the national development. Nothing of this work has ever been undone by succeeding generations of public servants, but has merely expanded and unfolded under the pressure of circumstances. When we consider the rapidity with which the United States have grown in population, wealth and intricacy since 1790, far exceeding the progress of any people recorded in history, and even far beyond the hopes that Hamilton himself entertained, we are amazed at the qualities of practical wisdom that enabled him to create the Treasury. For his contrivance was like no human-made garment that is soon worn threadbare and outgrown, but rather like the bark of a tree, that from the very nature of its being is never inadequate, since it is a part of the living organism which it covers.

Our admiration increases when we remember that he was not left in peace like a mathematician in his study to construct a system, and to emerge by and by at his leisure and apply it deliberately to the phenomena of life. He was rather in the position of a camp cook who, under a sniping fire, is required to build his oven and to supply baked bread. Congress was impatient for advice upon a multitude of questions and for practical suggestions in a great variety of perplexities. And not only the urgency of Congress, but the pressure of hard facts rendered delay impossible.

At the time Hamilton accepted office the cabinet was still incomplete. Knox, the Minister for War, and Randolph, the Attorney-General, were both subordinate figures. The most important office in the first administration, after the Presidency and the Secretaryship of the Treasury, was the Secretaryship of State.[1] The most important character

---

[1] *i.e.* for *Foreign Affairs*. It is not intended to suggest that constitutionally the Secretaryship of the Treasury is the superior office, but only that in the peculiar circumstances of the time it was the more important.

in the first administration, after Washington and Hamilton,
was Thomas Jefferson, author of the *Declaration of In-*
dependence, a prominent legislator of Virginia and Minister
of the United States at the court of France, who accepted
the post of Secretary of State shortly before Christmas 1789.
The nomination of Jefferson, who was widely respected, had
been pressed by Madison and welcomed by Washington.
The new minister was, however, unable to enter upon the
duties of his office until the following March, when, upon
his arrival at the seat of government in New York, he
found Congress plunged in an eager discussion of Hamilton's comprehensive plans for dealing with the public
credit.

It was said of Hamilton by his enemies at a later time,
that he took an unconstitutional and arrogant view of his
own position, and that he regarded himself not merely as the
head of a department responsible solely to the President,
but as something in the nature of a prime minister responsible on the one hand to the President, as to a monarch,
and on the other hand to Congress. Although this statement is an ill-natured exaggeration, it is none the less true,
not only that he threw the net of his department as widely
as possible over the waters, but that his activity extended
and his influence predominated far outside the limits of
his own office. Every important proposal brought forward
by his colleagues was minuted and reviewed by Hamilton,
and it may be added that a large number, if not the
majority, of these proposals were offered at his instiga-
tion, and were drawn upon lines which he had already
sketched out. From the beginning to the end of his official
career the cabinet was literally overwhelmed by his wide
interest and untiring industry; and although in a short
time his insistence provoked a violent resentment in certain
quarters, in the main issues his policy prevailed, and the

government submitted to the force of his will, whether the various ministers liked it or not.

The power of getting work done was one of his most remarkable qualities, and excites our astonishment alto-gether apart from his force of character. The diversity of his occupations during the first ten months of office, between the date of his appointment and the end of the next session in Congress, is little short of appalling. He organised the Treasury Department and the revenue system. He sifted and analysed the various debts, reported on the public credit, and recommended a policy with regard to it. He provided supplementary reports at every stage of the Fund-ing and the Appropriation Bills; further reports on the much-needed amendment of the Revenue Act, and on the voluminous and intricate claims of individuals against the Treasury. He issued circulars to the collectors of customs, and framed an Act to provide more effectually for the duties on imports and tonnage. These were matters which came naturally within the scope of his department, and we marvel only at the amount of the work accomplished. When we remember, however, that no permanent service of experi-enced officers stood at his elbow to provide him with the necessary assistance, we marvel even more.

But this activity was not the sum of his labours. During the same space of time he made a digest of the navigation laws; reported on the depreciation of the currency, on the purchase of West Point for military purposes, and on the Post Office department, with regard to which he drafted a bill. He drafted bills as to official foreign intercourse, remission of fines and forfeitures, and for the establishment of lighthouses. He also made a summary of the acts for registering and clearing vessels, and drew up a plan for the sale of public lands. Nor must it be thought that the first ten months was a period of exceptional industry. He continued the same course until he resigned his office, and during the later years, when foreign affairs and domestic disorders became the chief cares of government, when the attacks of his opponents were levelled, not only against his measures, but against his personal honour, the burden of work was far heavier than in this earlier period of comparative calm.

CHAPTER V

The Public Credit

WHEN Congress met at the beginning of the new year,[1] it was obvious that the chief subject of its deliberations must be the disordered finances of the Republic. During the war with Britain both the Federal Congress and the governments of the various states had contracted a variety of onerous debts for the advantage of the common cause. The total sum that had been borrowed in this way amounted to some sixteen millions sterling. When it is a case of raising the wind at a time of national difficulty, it is beyond reason to look for a clear and uniform system. Financiers, both state and federal, had to get money how and when they could, and the result was a bewildering confusion of accounts, creditors, securities, rates of interest and principles of repayment. In many cases payment of interest was heavily in arrear, while any repayment of the capital was almost too remote a contingency for contemplation. 'We are in a wilderness,' wrote Madison sadly, 'without a single footstep to guide us';[2] and Ames puts the same thought in more grandiloquent language: 'We perceive a great, unavoidable confusion ' throughout the whole scene, presenting a deep, dark and ' dreary chaos, impossible to be reduced to order without

[1] 7th January 1790.   [2] History, iv. p. 47.

' the mind of the *architect* is clear and capacious, and his ' power commensurate with the occasion." [1]

Fortunately, ' the mind of the architect' was well suited to the needs of the problem. Fortunately, also, there was a promptitude in his action which, in the particular situation of affairs, was invaluable. On the day after Congress assembled Hamilton announced that he was ready to submit a full report on the public credit, and desired to be instructed whether he should discharge this duty by speech or in writing. According to some commentators Congress feared lest they might come too much under the spell of his eloquence, and it was for this reason that they signified their wish to consider a written statement of the national finances. The report was immediately placed upon the table, and the House of Representatives proceeded to consider its contents a week after they had met.[2]

The principle of Hamilton's first series of financial measures was a copy-book heading; the most universal, indeed, of all that family of aphorisms—*Honesty is the best Policy*. He held that nations should pay their debts punctiliously, both as a matter of honour, and because it was wise.

The federal debt was due partly to foreign, partly to domestic creditors; and there were besides the various debts due by the several states. Hamilton's simple and comprehensive plan was that the central government should recognise all these liabilities at their face value, should undertake full responsibility towards the various creditors, and should see to the discharge of all arrears of interest in accordance with the bonds. With these objects he proposed to consolidate the whole in a National Debt, with a proper provision for redemption by means of a sinking-fund. As the new constitution now gave a much greater security to

[1] *History*, iv. p. 47.   [2] 14th January 1790.

the lenders for the principal as well as for the punctual payment of interest, he considered himself entitled to propose, as an equivalent for the assumption of these responsibilities by the federal government, a reduction of the varying and exceedingly onerous terms of the original bargains to a uniform and more moderate rate.

About Hamilton's proposals for dealing with the foreign debt there was little disagreement;[1] but a fierce contest arose with regard to the domestic debt, and one still more fierce on his scheme for the assumption of the state debts by the central government.

In the case of the federal domestic debt it was contended with some truth that there had been speculation. Many of the original holders had parted with their securities much below the face value under the pressure of necessity or through hopelessness of redemption. The deserving patriots who had lent money, or parted with money's worth in goods or services on behalf of the national cause, would not receive the chief benefit under the proposed arrangement. A tribe of gamblers, usurers and speculators who had bought up the paper at a huge discount would derive an unholy profit. The evil was grossly exaggerated. Hamilton maintained firmly that whether honest men or rascals held the bill, a promise to pay remained a promise to pay. A self-respecting nation, like a self-respecting merchant, must honour its signature and meet its engagements as to interest and principal alike. With this solid argument he answered every opponent—the loose-tongued, loud-voiced demagogue who loved repudiation for its own charms; and the fantastic sentimentalist who believed, in all sincerity no doubt, that hardship might be set right by injustice.

It was Hamilton's fate to encounter the doctrine of repudiation at many points in his public career, and when-

[1] *History*, iv. p. 50.

ever he met with it he gave no quarter. It was abhorrent to him as a gentleman. As a statesman he judged rightly that if successful it would prove ruinous to his country by the destruction of credit, and by corrupting the character of its citizens. This doctrine of repudiation has had a singular vitality in American politics, and has appeared on a variety of occasions in suitable disguises. Sometimes, as in the present instance, it was a moralist, eloquent upon the unworthiness of the creditor; at others it was a strategist arguing in favour of dishonesty as a form of warfare,[1] threatening nations who had incurred the displeasure of the United States with the cancellation of all public bonds and private debts due to their subjects.

Madison, Hamilton's old colleague of the *Federalist*, came forward with an amiable and well-meaning plan for a division between the original and the present holders of domestic federal debt.[2] By this means he pretended that the sufferings of the army might be equitably recognised. He argued warmly that soldiers who had disposed of their warrants for arrears of pay at large discounts were justly entitled to receive a further benefit when at last a stable government was in a position to redeem the pledges of its predecessor. This view of the matter was pressed upon Washington not only by Madison, but by the Secretary of State.[3] Fortunately the plausible but unsound plea ended in failure. The 'poor soldier' argument, like the 'poor widow' argument, was destroyed by Hamilton's vigorous common-sense. The case was well put by one of his supporters: 'The original holder has no claim upon the justice of the government. His claim is on its humanity.'[4]

But unfortunately 'humanity' implied further taxation, and this attempt upon the part of Madison to shift the

[1] e.g. *History*, v. pp. 523-24.
[3] *History*, iv. pp. 129-30.
[2] *History*, iv. p. 76.
[4] Lawrence, *History*, iv. p. 79.

burden of recompensing the army from the shoulders of A.D. 1790
Æt. 33 the citizens to the shoulders of the creditors of the Union was only repudiation in a more ingenious form. The niggardly individual, anxious merely to withhold as much as possible from the tax-gatherer, does not easily find a plea that lends itself to noble-mouthed rhetoric. A society for the avoidance of personal obligations would not be felt to rest upon a strong moral basis; but if it can be pretended that not a private but a patriotic motive is involved, a better stand may be made. According to the practice of demagogy, the doctrine of repudiation was in this way raised to a higher moral plane. In the twilight of words and phrases the seductive idea, like a lady of doubtful virtue and waning beauty, was arranged in a charitable and becoming shadow, and honesty was insulted by her lovers.

Madison has been bitterly assailed, and not without excuse, by the admirers of Hamilton. Much has been made of apparent contradictions in his course of conduct, and of changes in his attitude, towards men and ideas. His steadfast advocacy of the Union at the Convention of Philadelphia has been contrasted with his refusal during the first period of federal government to support the measures by which alone the Union could be turned into a reality. And from this it has been argued that a sour jealousy, and not any earnest conviction, directed his actions during Washington's administration. But viewing the contest from a remoter standpoint, these contradictions and changes become of less importance. The accusation of a flagrant and interested inconsistency fails to convince the modern reader of its justice.

Madison was an upright, unimpassioned man, but he was an idealist only under compulsion. Diffidence was his most remarkable characteristic. The impression he makes upon the mind is of something unusually formal and precise. It

A.D. 1790
Æt. 33
appears altogether incredible that he was upon any occasion untidy in his dress; that he ever mislaid a penknife or a memorandum; that he ever shook with laughter or shouted with joy. He is the type of the elderly young man who has pleasure only in sedate company. His intellect was powerful but full of cobwebs. We contrast it with the intellect of Hamilton, which excites a certain measure of distrust because of its preternatural and appalling perspicacity. Men of slow wits have admired Madison for his defects, have judged him wise because he shared their own infirmities, and prudent because he ran away from the consequences of his opinions. He loved discussion, though he was averse from wrangling. In spite of his temperament he never shrank, as Jefferson always did, from meeting his enemy in the gate. He was no less conspicuous for his personal courage than for his timidity as a statesman. " I ' think him a little too much of a book politician, and too ' timid in his politics," wrote Fisher Ames. ". . . He seems ' evidently to want manly firmness and energy of character."[1] The reproach, upon analysis, seems to resolve itself into this —that he was wanting not so much in the courage of his ideas, as in ideas. It was an epoch of construction, and he was deficient both in boldness and in imagination. As a critic he never lacked confidence, but criticism was not the supreme need of the moment.

Madison was also peculiarly subject to personal influence. It has been considered amazing that, having supported a national policy at Philadelphia, he should have run counter to it almost from the beginning of the federal government. But it is really more amazing that he took the line he did during the convention. For his course before that event was entirely consistent with his subsequent action. It almost

[1] Fisher Ames, *History*, iv. p. 75.

seems as if at Philadelphia he was under some kind of A.D. 1790
enchantment, and advocated a policy which was discordant Æt. 33
to some extent with the natural mood of his mind.   It is no
surprise, therefore, that he fell speedily under the influence
of Jefferson, whose procedure was far more sympathetic to
his disposition. We have a feeling that even at Philadelphia
Hamilton frightened him.   Hamilton's methods were too
swift, his manner too peremptory; his very confidence was
provocative of doubt and hesitation.   Madison was by nature
suspicious of the constructive statesman, and inclined to the
belief that inaction was usually wisdom and action folly.
Consequently he was attracted by the Jeffersonian policy of
drifting into danger, preferring it to strenuous efforts, even
though these had for their object to escape from the fatal
current.

It may be true, but if true it is unimportant, that he was
jealous of Hamilton; for he was in essentials too honest
a man to be guided by such considerations.   If his temperament had been sympathetic to the policy of Hamilton, we
may believe he would have supported that policy even
though he had hated its projector.   Even after reading the
seven volumes of Hamilton the younger we decline to be
convinced that Madison was anything but a good man.   He
was a good man in the most intolerable sense. His excessive
virtue deprived him of charity.   He appropriated all virtue
to himself and his followers.   His sincerity upon this point
would be detestable if it were not so ludicrous.   He believed
fanatically that his opponents were utterly corrupt.   He
made and permitted to be made, under the shelter of his
name, the grossest charges against their personal honour,
charges which his common-sense must have told him clearly
were nothing better than rubbish had he not been wholly
possessed by this illusion as to his sole property in virtue.

From the date of his opposition to Hamilton's proposals

for dealing with the debt his course of action towards his former friend is wanting not merely in generosity but in candour.   At every point his constitutional antipathy to constructive statesmanship appears; but there is also a more bitter and personal accent of hostility which can be traced to the resentment of one who, having been temporarily led out of his natural course by the influence of a superior character, has returned to his ancient habits and looks back upon his aberration with horror.   His manner towards Hamilton from this time forward is always grudging.   His favourite weapon is that of the common politician—the suggestion of motives so mean that they are wholly incredible.   The triviality of his attacks is painful.   The disinterested reader turns the pages quickly, anxious not to dwell too long upon the humiliation of a worthy gentleman, whose friends, had they been true ones, would often have drowned his eloquence in a discreet tumult or would have led him away to recover his sense and his dignity.

In the end Hamilton carried his point as to the federal debts, and vindicated the sanctity of contract all along the line. He routed with equal success the people who wished to escape taxes, though they had profited by the loans, and those others who professed themselves willing to pay, provided that a portion of the funds were taken away from the legal holders and given in charity. The federal debts, both foreign and domestic, were in the end recognised and consolidated, and provision made for full payment of all the arrears of interest.

The assumption of the state debts was a harder matter. States which had incurred small debts, or none, upon account of the war, were persuaded without much difficulty to regard it as monstrously unfair that the large debts of their neighbours should be saddled upon the Union. The mere difference in the amounts stank of injustice to the simpler class of citizens, while for the more refined there A.D. 1790 was the argument that the heavily indebted states must Æт. 33 have been negligently administered. Opponents of the government policy clamoured for a hostile and searching scrutiny of reasons, expenditure and accounts.

By such means it was made to appear that a certain corporate dignity was outraged by Hamilton's high-handed procedure. Finally Congress,[1] by a majority of two, refused Hamilton's proposal to take over the war debts which the states individually had incurred for the common good.

Hamilton determined to have this decision reversed, and he accomplished his end in a characteristic fashion by giving a civility in exchange for a loaf of bread. It so happened that the states of little debts, and therefore disposed against assumption, were for the most part southern states, while those of big debts were mainly northern. Each of these parties desired, for sentimental reasons, that the capital of the Federal Republic should be fixed within its own boundaries. Hamilton spoke with Jefferson, who was of the southern party, and Jefferson gave a dinner-party. Being, according to his own account, but a child in such matters, he remained silent, and allowed his guests to talk. As the result a compact was arrived at whereby the majority adverse to assumption of the state debts was converted into a minority,[2] and the south in return was allowed to possess the honour of the capital city of the Union.[3]

In his treatment of the debt Hamilton was not concerned merely with the honour of his country, nor did he regard the matter only with the merchant's eye to the advantages of good credit in case of further troubles. His measures were something more than financial. They had a deliberate political intention. The constitution, as has been stated

[1] 12th April 1790.   [2] July 1790.   [3] Ford's *Jefferson*, i. pp. 161-62.

already, did not entirely satisfy him.   He felt that the plain meaning of its terms did not convey sufficient power to the administration, nor secure beyond question solidarity in the Union.   His efforts accordingly were directed towards supplementing its deficiencies.

The political object of his financial policy was to bind the moneyed classes firmly to the central government ; to induce them to look to that quarter for the security of their capital and the punctuality of their dividends; to fix their interests in it rather than in the state governments.   The interests of this powerful class being thus made dependent upon the existence of the Union, it was natural to suppose that they would cherish it and contribute to its strength, as the family of a man whose wealth is in annuities zealously and tenderly endeavours to prolong his days in peace.   It was a legitimate aim, but it could hardly hope to escape opposition when once its purpose was fully detected.

Hamilton claimed for his measures that they would ' cement more closely the union of the states' and ' establish public order on the basis of an upright and liberal policy.' [1] He was fully aware that, if successful, they would strengthen the central government in comparison with the state governments—to a large extent, indeed to the detriment of the latter—by assuming a great portion of their respon- sibilities, and by identifying and allying the safety and self- interest of the creditors with the power and permanency of the federal authority.   It was a deliberate aim, and it succeeded.   The champions of State Rights who had opposed the constitution naturally strove against these extensions of its hated principles with the energy of despair. This zealous panic swept many of the timid and hesitating off their feet, Madison among the number.   It gathered up also in its course all the disappointed, all the feeble, critical

[1] *Works*, ii. p. 232.

the hard facts of the year seventeen hundred and ninety-one
when it was written. It is restrained and reasonable, persuasive and disarming. Its eagerness and hope stamp it as
having had an immediate object and not a remote one. A
man does not write like this to give advice to posterity, but
only to wring the necessary consent from to-day. Haste is
visible in every page, but nowhere impatience. The document has the appearance of a letter that has been written
at unnecessary length, because the occasion was pressing
and the writer lacked the leisure to prune it to a more
sententious form. It recalls the correspondence of Bismarck
with its rough, careless logic and vigorous redundancy. It
is wanting in compactness but never for a moment in
lucidity. He repeats the same argument in slightly different
forms, but there is never the slightest doubt either as to
what he wishes to do or as to why he wishes to do it. As a
state document it stands in the first rank, not only by virtue
of its quality of thought, but by reason of its ultimate
authority. The report on Manufactures is filled with the
personal charm of the author and with the hopefulness and
sincerity of youth, but at the same time it is as clear and
shrewd as the letters of a banker to his agent or a merchant's
valuation of his stock. It is a strange but distinguished
figure among state documents in all their great variety;
but perhaps still stranger and more distinguished when it is
remembered that the theme on which it is written has been
named ' the dismal science.'

Adam Smith's *Wealth of Nations* had appeared in 1776—
the first year of the American Revolution. Hamilton had
studied the book with care, and had written a commentary
upon it, which unfortunately has been lost.[1] The contact of

[1] Mr. Sumner doubts this, but his argument does not seem conclusive
against J. C. Hamilton's statements, *History*, ii. p. 514, on the authority of
P. S. Duponceau (1783). The commentary was written while Hamilton was
still a member of Congress (Sumner's *Hamilton*, p. 108).

two brains so fresh and original, and so free from cant, was too valuable to have gone into the dust-heap. Adam Smith, the absent-minded student and philosopher, educated at a Scots university, matured by seven years' study at Oxford, had been appointed in due time to lecture upon Logic and Moral Philosophy to the undergraduates of Glasgow. Friendly, interested and clear-eyed, he mixed in the society of the merchants and manufacturers of that thriving city, drank their claret and joined in their discussions; and while he continued to lecture on logic and ethics, on rhetoric and the *belles lettres,* in accordance with the terms of his foundation, his mind began to revolve the problems of the wealth of nations as a subordinate part of "an immense design of ' showing the origin and development of cultivation and ' law; or, as we may perhaps put it, not inappropriately, of ' saying how, from being a savage, man rose to be a Scots- ' man."[1] Whatever may have been the case with the rest of his speculations, those affecting commerce were founded upon the study of the facts at first hand.

Adam Smith published a book on the *Moral Sentiments,* and on the strength of the reputation it produced, was appointed bear-leader of the young Duke of Buccleuch, whom it was decided to send upon the grand tour. In this capacity he travelled for three years in Europe, spending most of his time in France, and studying the conditions of humanity everywhere with an eager eye. When he returned, he lived for ten years quietly with his mother in the village of Kirkcaldy in the ancient kingdom of Fife, meditating upon the plan of his life's work without excessive impatience. When sixty-three years of age he published the *Wealth of Nations,* the first instalment of this great plan and also the last; for the fame of it procured him the appointment of Commissioner of Customs, and during the

[1] Bagehot, *Biographical Studies,* p. 255.

remaining fourteen years of his life he lived very comfortably in Edinburgh society, performing a task for which he was entirely unfitted.

Adam Smith cannot have been conscious of the immense influence his famous work would afterwards exercise upon the fortunes of his country. He was an elderly philosopher contemplating the conditions of an old world, that had not yet begun to renew its youth, in a spirit of gentle curiosity. Hamilton was a young statesman considering the future of a great continent which he had the ambition to mould, not only by the force of his thoughts, but by the vigour of his acts. In Adam Smith he found a lucid analysis of causes he had been revolving, a discussion of systems he had been constructing in his own mind with a determination to bring them into operation as soon as opportunity should make it possible. In their conclusions there was doubtless some disagreement, but they were at one at least in their method; in their preference for observation of the facts at first hand over all the other and easier ways of arriving at conclusions in political science.

Hamilton's report urges the importance of the immediate establishment of manufactures upon two fundamental reasons — military security and national development. "Not only the wealth but the independence and security ' of a country appear to be materially connected with the ' prosperity of manufactures. Every nation, with a view to ' those great objects, ought to endeavour to possess within ' itself all the essentials of national supply. These comprise ' the means of subsistence, habitation, clothing, and defence.

' The possession of these is necessary to the perfection of ' the body politic; to the safety as well as to the welfare of ' the society. The want of either is the want of an important ' organ of political life and motion; and in the various crises ' which await a state it must severely feel the effects of

' any such deficiency.   The extreme embarrassments of the
' United States during the late war, from an incapacity of
' supplying themselves, are still matter of keen recollection;
' a future war might be expected again to exemplify the
' mischiefs and dangers of a situation to which that incapacity
' is still, in too great a degree, applicable, unless changed by
' timely and vigorous exertion.   To effect this change, as
' fast as shall be prudent, merits all the attention and all the
' zeal of our public councils : it is the next great work to be
' accomplished." [1]

But national development requires, no less than military
security, manufacturers and traders in addition to farmers
and planters.   It is a question of good husbandry.   The
human and material resources of the imperial estate must
both engage the attention of government.   If military security
calls for a self-contained and self-sufficing confederation,
commercial security and national wellbeing demand a development which shall be symmetrical and not lopsided,
a society of varied enterprise and multitudinous employments.   A nation of specialists, whether farmers or bankers,
manufacturers or traders, lacks the essential condition of
permanency, for its various parts do not afford an adequate
support one to another.   Its wealth depends upon its intercourse with foreign nations.   If circumstances should arise
when this intercourse is violently interrupted, if its supplies
are cut off, or its surplus goods refused, it will experience
a shock, ruinous to a greater or less extent.   The wars,
disasters and policies of strangers are a constant menace
to its prosperity.   It is at the mercy, not only of the malice
of its rivals, but of the misfortunes of its friends.

But there is an argument beyond mere commercial safety.
The development of a nation will be much more rapid if it
encourages a town population to support its country people;

[1] *Works*, iv. pp. 135, 136.

artisans to consume the produce of the fields, farmers to employ the output of the mills. The establishment of work-shops will therefore prove a benefit to the United States by ' creating in some instances a new, and securing, in all, a more certain and steady demand for the produce of the soil.'[1]

Moreover, in a fully developed community the natural genius, aptitude and inclination of every man desiring to earn his living will readily find work suitable to his character. It clearly makes for the wealth of any country if it can 'furnish greater scope for the diversity of talents and dis-positions which discriminate men from each other.'[2] In such a state also employment will be found for classes of the community not hitherto engaged in business : for the wives and daughters of husbandmen who would otherwise be idle, or insufficiently or less remuneratively employed.

The immigration of good citizens will be stimulated. Manu-facturers and workmen of the Old World, impatient of its 'burthens and restraints,' attracted by their "greater personal ' independence and consequence under the operation of a ' more equal government," tempted also by the boon of "a ' perfect equality of religious privileges . . . more precious ' than mere religious toleration," will flock into such a state if only they can be inspired with the hope of being able to pursue their own trades and industries there 'with an assurance of encouragement and employment.'[3] But these men, the best and the most intelligent of the middle and working classes of Europe, will not transplant themselves without excessive provocation, if by emigrating they have no alternative to engaging in agriculture, an avocation to which they have served no training, and the pursuit of which would entail the sacrifice of all their technical skill and inherited experience.

[1] *Works*, iv. p. 87.　　[2] *Ibid.*　　[3] *Ibid.* p. 92.

To this composite and self-contained state will also accrue the advantages of a scientific division of labour, whereby the national prosperity is increased through men becoming experts in particular departments. And as the minds and characters of the people are like a natural field of various soils that may be cultivated, well or ill, suitably or unsuitably, just as much as swamps of rice, or acres of corn, or plantations of tobacco, the state which develops at the same time in a multitude of directions will reap a benefit in a political as well as in a commercial sense—both directly in its wealth and indirectly in the character of its citizens. Its varied opportunities will "cherish and stimulate the ' activity of the human mind by multiplying the objects ' of enterprise."[1] The imaginations of the restless and ambitious spirits will be touched with a magic wand. " Every new scene which is opened to the busy nature of ' man to rouse and excite itself, is the addition of a new ' energy to the general stock of effort. The spirit of enter- ' prise, useful and prolific as it is, must necessarily be ' contracted or expanded, in proportion to the simplicity or ' variety of the occupations and productions which are to be ' found in a society. It must be less in a nation of mere ' cultivators than in a nation of cultivators and merchants; ' less in a nation of cultivators and merchants than in a ' nation of cultivators, artificers, and merchants."[2]

With the utmost care and tenderness, avoiding the contentious phrase and all words of provocation, Hamilton examines in turn a variety of arguments and opinions that had been urged and held at different times against the establishment of manufactures in general, and in the peculiar circumstances of the states. The old doctrine of Quesnay and the *Économistes*, that agriculture is more profitable than the labour of the mill and workshop, because in the fields

[1] *Works*, iv. p. 94.   [2] *Ibid.* iv. pp. 94, 95.

man works with Nature as a partner, but in the other case man works alone, is examined at a length and with such respect as somewhat amazes us at the present time. Hamilton meets the contention that labour would be diverted from the land, and that the narrow capital of the new empire would be insufficient for engaging in a competition with Europe, and other arguments of the same character with a respectful eagerness and a good nature that are full of persuasiveness.

Having established the necessity of manufactures on the grounds of military security and national development, having proved the advantages, direct and indirect, to wealth and character, to stability and progress, of a composite and well-balanced industrial society, he comes to the practical consideration—how is such a condition of things to be created?

It had never been allowed to exist in the colonies, but it showed hardly greater signs of life in the free republic. It might never exist. It certainly would not come to pass speedily if left to the action of individuals. To consummate the federalist policy a rapid prosperity was of the highest importance, and this would only be attained under the care and direction of government. It was the function of the state, according to Hamilton's argument, to provide inducements that would make men engage readily in manufacture; to sustain the young industries against the ruthless and deliberate assaults of more powerful communities; to meet the commercial regulations of foreigners with a vigorous and consistent policy of national defence.

He viewed his country ever as a whole. States and divisions meant nothing to him. Local sentiment affected him with so little sympathy that he failed, except on one occasion,[1] even to use it as a weapon. In his imagination there was a

---

[1] *Ante,* p. 223.

great continent united by a miraculous good fortune into one state, of unknown extent, of undefined limits, unexplored and uninhabited save for a fringe along the Atlantic seaboard, but surmised to be habitable and fertile throughout the length and breadth of its territories. The rapid development of this great inheritance meant much more to Hamilton's mind than the mere addition of so many families and so much wealth to the national stock. It meant the obliteration of state rivalry and the sweeping out, as by a flood, of the litter and decay of ancient jealousies. Its ultimate intention, like all the rest of his policy, was union. His vision was of one great nation, capable of producing within its own wide borders everything that its citizens would require for life, for comfort, and even for luxury. Independent of its neighbours, it might hope to escape from embroilment in their quarrels; dependent on the co-operation of its members, it would be secured in the possession of internal peace. But a lopsided expansion, an absorption of nine-tenths of the inhabitants in pastoral and agricultural pursuits, was in his opinion neither a swift nor a sure means to this end. Such a development was more likely to occur, was in a sense easier and more natural than the other; but as a gardener will take pains to secure an even and symmetrical growth in his plantation, by pruning, by the removal of obstacles at the roots, by the admission of light, by the destruction of oppressive neighbours, by defence against the winds and storms; so, he argued, should the state regard it as one of its most important duties to promote a healthy industrial society of varied employments which gave mutual support.

The reply of the economist that all this would come to pass in good time if it were really desirable, failed to satisfy him. There is no such great hurry, argued his opponents. The intelligent self-interest of the individual will produce manufactures in their proper season. His opponents spun amiable theories on the nature of the economic man—and hazarded sanguine prophecies of his glorious destiny, if left to his own devices, without help or hindrance from government.

Hamilton believed in the possibility of a commercial policy. The doctrine of *laisser faire* did not appeal to him any more than it would have appealed to a tobacco-planter in reference to the cultivation of his estate. The effort, it is true, can only come from the individual, as the sap can only come from the soil; but the direction of effort, if it is not to run to waste, must come from elsewhere. There are things desirable in commerce too big, and by their nature impossible, for private citizens to achieve even in combination. In the frankest terms he disputed the pessimist creed of leaving things alone and letting men blindly wander round in hopeless circles of wasted effort. He contended that a commercial policy in a positive and not in a negative sense was necessary in the circumstances of the case.

Hamilton had definitely committed himself to this solution of the problem when he founded the National Bank with the avowed object of creating commercial credit. It would be incorrect to say that the report on Manufactures carries this policy one step further; for in reality it travels to the very end of the journey. It contains both the science and the art of modern commercial development. The policy that has slowly and awkwardly struggled into existence during the last quarter of the nineteenth century, which is pursued every year with greater confidence and perspicacity by all the great industrial nations, with the exception of the United Kingdoms, is Hamilton's policy. He thought it out for himself, keenly contemplating the commercial facts of New York and the New World, by much the same method as Adam Smith, the basis of whose speculations was the trade

of Glasgow and the Old World. The reality and force of
the writings of both men are derived from their intimate
thoroughness. The foundations of their practical experience
were narrow, but they were firm. Their theories grew out
of the facts themselves and not out of the theories of other
men.

The state, in Hamilton's view of the matter, may create
the industrial conditions it desires, precisely as a landowner
goes about his forestry. The effort truly comes from the
nature of man in the one case and of trees in the other; but
if, possessing a waste of good land, you would provide a high
arching forest of oak for your great-grandson to cut, where
now there is but a thin straggle of stunted trees, you will not
leave the achievement of your design to random gales sowing
acorns fortuitously from the sparse, indigenous trees; but you
will trench and drain, and plant, and provide artful shelter,
and clear the choking undergrowth. You will not create
the great woods, it is true, for that is the work of nature's
unintelligent force; but your direction is none the less a
condition of its creation, without which it might never have
been, or at the best would have taken as many centuries for
its growth as under your plan it will require decades. Un-
combined human effort is nearly as blind and unintelligent
a force as the nature of trees; and the functions of the state
and of statesmen were in Hamilton's opinion the same as
those of the squire and his foresters.

Having established his principles, that it is the interest of
the state to possess the most varied industrial society, and
also its duty to attempt the creation of such conditions, he
plunged into a detailed discussion of the ways and means to
this end in which it is unnecessary to follow him. Duties
and bounties and premiums have their various uses for
different objects. Landways and waterways are to be
improved and extended at the charge of government.

A.D. 1791
ÆT. 34

Inspectors of produce are to be appointed to guard 'the good name' by seeing that quality is maintained. Inventions are to be carefully secured to the inventors. A board with ample funds at its disposal is to devote itself to the encouragement of arts, agriculture, manufactures and commerce.

Hamilton was out of sympathy with the orthodox French economists of the eighteenth century. He found but little virtue in their uncreative logic. He disbelieved in the Economic Man—a being without bowels, with an interior like a clock, accurately ticking the progress of the human race under the impulse of the magic spring of enlightened self-interest, and never needing to be either wound or regulated. The besetting vice of the economists was their preference for argument over observation. They based their reasoning upon axioms when they should have gone to the facts. They conceived that they could treat the wealth of nations by a series of propositions like those of Euclid. At each stage they became more and more the victims of words that did not correspond with realities, of syllogisms that under analysis were little more than mere arrangements of phrases. To a large extent their ideas were completely dead things, like the conclusions, paradoxes and truisms of the ingenious schoolmen of the middle ages; as painfully industrious, as technically exquisite, as those samplers which were sewed by our great-grandmothers, and of nearly as much use and benefit to the world.

Hamilton, on the other hand, saw the facts themselves in a magic crystal. His clear view held the closer objects in an easy and true proportion; but also, in the full meaning of the splendid common phrase, it went 'far and wide.' It was a vision of bold extent and distant range. He beheld a unity, where all objects fell into place as in a picture. What his mind grasped and concerned itself with was not the advantage of a single trade or group of trades, of a single state or group of states, but the advantage of the whole inheritance. His idea of good statesmanship was good stewardship; an active direction and continuous effort towards an unmistakable goal. It was not enough, in his opinion, to remove obstructions. You do not necessarily render a river navigable for all time merely by tearing out the snags and other foreign impediments that lie there blocking the water-way. For there are sandbanks to be dug away, channels to be dredged, banks to be protected with piles, buttresses and groins. There are precautions against flood and drought. There are shiftings of the course, natural but unforeseen; conditions that change on a sudden, and a constant wear and tear. To give the greatest freedom to the force of the river may have the undesired effect of creating, as the final result, a wide impracticable shallow through which no barge of commerce can ever hope to penetrate.

CHAPTER VII

Stewardship of the Estate

THE wisest commercial policy that ever came out of the human brain could never hope, it was contended by Hamilton's opponents, for a richer fruitfulness in its effect than to benefit certain classes at the expense of the community, certain trades to the detriment of commercial society, certain towns, districts, states, or groups of states against the best interests of the nation. This proposition being laid down with greater or less plausibility by many speakers and writers as one of the laws of nature, unalterable by any contrivance of man, their argument proceeded in perfect order to the inference that Hamilton's real but unavowed intention must therefore be the advantage of private individuals and particular sections.

Hamilton met his opponents upon both grounds. With much detail he proceeded to show how a commercial policy was capable in intelligent hands of benefiting the nation as a whole. As for the personal accusation, his career from first to last had been such as to render it incredible to any sane man, but more especially to his present critics, who, in former contests, had incessantly taunted him with his indifference to local privileges. Much more vehemently than his opponents, Hamilton held that the duty of the state in every circumstance was to look beyond the interest of the individual and the section to the general advantage. For the state to benefit one of these units, be it merely a man or half the empire, is an evil if that benefit is the sole intended result of its action; but, on the other hand, the state should never shrink from conferring such an advantage upon particular trades or classes, if it clearly foresees that this course will ultimately conduce to the swifter development, the greater prosperity and the firmer security of the nation.

An advantage given to one man does not necessarily mean, when it is fairly examined, a corresponding burden imposed upon another. You cannot argue safely from physics to politics. But even if such were the case, the burden of this year may nevertheless become a benefit in that which follows. The burden of one generation may build up a fine estate for its successor. What a man to-day is compelled to forgo may be recovered by his children and grandchildren with heavy accumulations at compound interest.

There was, Hamilton maintained, a habit of exaggeration in the argument of his opponents that the immediate increase of price which his proposals might entail would prove oppressive to the consumer. There was a tendency also to ignore the advantage which all alike would derive when the general object of his policy was attained. The doctrine that in helping one person you are necessarily injuring another has in it a pinch of truth, but a pinch only. It is subject to many qualifications. It is alleviated from the beginning by countervailing benefits. But supposing that it were true in that wide and absolute sense which is claimed for it by its professors, what is the alternative? If the state is to fulfil the purpose for which it was called into being, it must act; and by its every action it must cause more or less of injury to some of its citizens, more or less of benefit to others. A complete paralysis is the only alternative. It is not only in matters affecting trade that this argument holds good, but in every department of government, and perhaps more in that of public defence than in any other. The question that awaits an answer upon the introduction of any measure is always the same: Will the proposed reform promote the health and vigour of the nation?

The action of the state ought therefore to be guided calmly to one end—the advantage of the whole in the present and in the future. All men are agreed that appeals from any class for favour should be coldly regarded. What has not been so generally perceived, is that the complementary duty is of equal force; that prayers for government to stand still, to hold its hand, and to abstain from interference with existing conditions, lest a benefit should thereby accrue to some interest or industry, must be ruled by the same tests and as resolutely set aside upon the same grounds.

But if division of labour among men is the cause of a rapider increase of wealth than under conditions where each has to perform for himself a hundred tasks for which he has no inclination and but small capacity, surely, urged the opposition, the same argument applies to nations ? Let each people therefore attend to those labours in which they are most proficient, in which nature and their own inclinations will render the most admirable assistance. Hamilton conceded the justice of this argument, but upon one condition —'if the system of perfect liberty to industry and commerce were the prevailing system of nations.'

"In such a state of things each country would have the 'full benefit of its peculiar advantages to compensate for its 'deficiencies and disadvantages ... a free exchange mutually 'beneficial, of the commodities which each was able to supply, 'on the best terms, might be carried on between them, 'supporting, in full vigour, the industry of each. ... And 'though the circumstances which have been mentioned, and 'others which will be unfolded hereafter, render it probable 'that nations, merely agricultural, would not enjoy the same 'degree of opulence, in proportion to their numbers, as those 'which united manufactures with agriculture, yet the pro- 'gressive improvement of the lands of the former might, in 'the end, atone for an inferior degree of opulence in the 'meantime; and in a case in which opposite considerations 'are pretty equally balanced, the option ought, perhaps, 'always to be in favour of leaving industry to its own 'direction.

'But the system which has been mentioned is far from char- 'acterising the general policy of nations. The prevalent one 'has been regulated by an opposite spirit. The consequence 'of it is, that the United States are, to a certain extent, in 'the situation of a country precluded from foreign commerce. 'They can, indeed, without difficulty, obtain from abroad 'the manufactured supplies of which they are in want; 'but they experience numerous and very injurious impedi- 'ments to the emission and vent of their own commodities.

'Nor is this the case in reference to a single foreign nation
'only. The regulations of several countries, with which
'we have the most extensive intercourse, throw serious
'obstructions in the way of the principal staples of the
'United States.

'In such a position of things, the United States cannot
'exchange with Europe on equal terms; and the want of
'reciprocity would render them the victim of a system
'which should induce them to confine their views to agri-
'culture, and refrain from manufactures. A constant and
'increasing necessity, on their part, for the commodities of
'Europe, and only a partial and occasional demand for
'their own, in return, could not but expose them to a
'state of impoverishment, compared with the opulence to
'which their political and natural advantages authorise
'them to aspire.

'Remarks of this kind are not made in the spirit of com-
'plaint. It is for the nations whose regulations are alluded
'to, to judge for themselves, whether, by aiming at too much,
'they do not lose more than they gain. It is for the United
'States to consider by what means they can render them-
'selves least dependent on the combinations, right or wrong,
'of foreign policy. . . . If Europe will not take from us the
'products of our soil, upon terms consistent with our interest,
'the natural remedy is to contract, as fast as possible, our
'wants of her." [1]

One may be permitted to doubt whether Hamilton would
have made even this concession had he been confronted with
a situation of perfect liberty in commerce between the nations.
For it conflicts, to some extent, with his master principle of
a varied society and multitudinous employments as the condition of healthy and rapid development. Even had every

---

[1] *Works*, iv. pp. 100-102. See also draft of Smith's speech (January 1794)
by Hamilton, *Works*, iv. pp. 205-24.

gateway been open throughout the world, it is probable
that on this ground he would still have judged it wise, in
the special circumstances of the United States, with their
vast natural wealth, their undeveloped resources and uninhabited fertile tracts, to pursue a strictly national rather
than a cosmopolitan policy in matters of commerce. But
this condition of perfect freedom did not exist, was not
likely to exist, and has in fact never existed. On the
contrary, the strictly national policy has imposed itself
gradually, piecemeal, but in the end completely, upon all
the nations of the world save only upon Britain. Opinion
has often halted. Motives have rarely been without confusion. The waves have slipped back upon the sand; but
the tide has ever continued to advance. The concession of
the principle, guarded by an impossible 'if,' was wise argument; for granting the foundations of his opponents'
contention, accepting their theory under ideal conditions, he
was able with still greater force to establish the validity of
his own counsel.

Another argument with which modern ears are not
unfamiliar, is " the proposition that industry, if left to itself,
' will naturally find its way to the most useful and profitable
' employment.   Whence it is inferred that manufactures,
' without the aid of government, will grow up as soon and as
' fast as the natural state of things and the interest of the
' community may require.

' Against the solidity of this hypothesis, in the full latitude
' of the terms, very cogent reasons may be offered. These
' have relation to the strong influence of habit and the spirit
' of imitation; the fear of want of success in untried enter-
' prises; the intrinsic difficulties incident to first essays
' towards a competition with those who have previously
' attained to perfection in the business to be attempted; the
' bounties, premiums, and other artificial encouragements with

'which foreign nations second the exertions of their own
'citizens, in the branches in which they are to be rivalled.

'Experience teaches, that men are often so much governed
'by what they are accustomed to see and practise, that the
'simplest and most obvious improvements, in the most
'ordinary occupations, are adopted with hesitation, reluctance,
'and by slow gradations. The spontaneous transition to new
'pursuits, in a community long habituated to different ones,
'may be expected to be attended with proportionably greater
'difficulty. When former occupations ceased to yield a profit
'adequate to the subsistence of their followers, or when there
'was an absolute deficiency of employment in them, owing to
'the superabundance of hands, changes would ensue; but
'these changes would be likely to be more tardy than might
'consist with the interest either of individuals or of the
'society. In many cases they would not happen, while a bare
'support could be insured by an adherence to ancient courses,
'though a resort to a more profitable employment might be
'practicable. To produce the desirable changes as early as
'may be expedient may therefore require the incitement and
'patronage of government."[1]

An endeavour has been made to describe the main purpose
of Hamilton's report, but the effort is quite inadequate to
the occasion. In a condensed form his eager advocacy is
stripped of all its charm and much of its persuasiveness.
The leading quality—its practical intensity—is dimmed by
the omission of a multitude of instances drawn from the predicament of commerce at the time when he wrote. It would
be altogether impossible to follow his methodical analysis and
defeat of minor objections; his examination in detail of the
industries which, in his opinion, it was possible advantageously
and at once to establish in the United States; his review

[1] *Works*, iv. p. 104.

and consideration of the various means and resources of which government might make use for planting and foster- ing manufactures; his enumeration and criticism of taxes conducive and inimical to commercial prosperity—for to attempt such an undertaking would result in reprinting at length the whole of this voluminous document.

In none of his measures does Hamilton show more remarkably the great force of his instinct for reality, his piercing insight into the true conditions of things, his grasp upon the facts of the case. Like Adam Smith, he will look at matters with his own eyes in the first instance; and having made his survey, then and only then, he goes for counsel and a second opinion to the works of others who have considered the same problems in a similar spirit.

For the skilful craftsman, quick of eye and ready with his hands, tired out and hungry after his day's work, it is an irksome effort to study out of books the science of his avocation. He is aware, or at any rate he is frequently reminded, that by so doing he would sharpen his intelli- gence, improve his output, and derive much collateral profit. But under the influences of fatigue and repletion he is disinclined. Sleep steals upon his eyelids. In point of fact he is lazy, but he justifies himself by affecting to view all book-learning with contempt. For the man who works not with his muscles but with his mind, be he statesman or philosopher, laziness sits in the other scale. Books and words and syllogisms are as easy to him as the brace-and-bit and the plane to a carpenter. He is under an everlasting temptation to substitute the lazy methods of logic for the hard and uncongenial processes of observation. In his library he is happy; but you derange his whole life, and render him miserable, if you condemn him to a week's work in a merchant's office.

In economic science mere syllogisms have never been

enough. Political insight requires some more substantial food than the insight of other men. The philosopher is required to sacrifice his leisure, to observe the facts of the world he lives in as well as to reason about them, if the results of his labour are to serve the nation and to endure. Hamilton accepted this necessity like a cheerful, winter-morning bather, plunging daily into the actual confusion of things. His opponents drew the bedclothes up to their noses, turned lazily upon the other side, and dreamed dreams of an Arcadia while a very different world was astir.

BOOK IV

THE DEMOCRATS

A.D. 1791-1794

'BY-ENDS.—*Why they, after their headstrong manner, conclude that it is their duty to rush on their journey all weathers; and I am waiting for wind and tide. They are for hazarding all for God at a clap; and I am for taking all advantages to secure my life and estate. They are for holding their notions, though all other men be against them; but I am for religion in what, and so far as, the times and my safety will bear it. They are for Religion when in rags and contempt; but I am for him when he walks in his silver slippers in the sunshine, and with applause.*'—THE PILGRIM'S PROGRESS.

BOOK IV

THE DEMOCRATS

CHAPTER I

Thomas Jefferson

THOMAS JEFFERSON is one of the most remarkable figures in history. Of Welsh descent, he was born in Virginia in the year 1743. At his father's death he inherited a small estate, and to this he added by shrewd purchases, so that at the date of his marriage, in his thirtieth year, he was the owner of some five thousand acres and fifty slaves. He was bred to the law, and enjoyed a lucrative chamber practice which was the chief source of his income; but at the same time he cultivated his own land, and, like Washington, had more happiness in this pursuit than in any other. In Virginian society he was not eminent either by reason of his birth or wealth. He was merely a substantial country gentleman. His circumstances were easy from the begin‐ ning; and shortly after his marriage the death of his father-in-law was the means of adding largely to his resources. Hardship, therefore, of the pecuniary sort, had no share in his education. Until near the end of his days he was undisturbed by anxieties arising from any lack of funds.

Jefferson was a patriotic citizen who served his country

with ungrudging labour for close on half a century. He was a member of the House of Burgesses in his own state, and of the Continental Congress both before the war began and after its conclusion. For two troubled years[1] he was the Governor of Virginia; for five[2] he was minister at the Court of France; for four[3] he was Secretary of State in Washington's cabinet. He was Vice-President of the United States from 1797 until his election to the Presidency in 1801, and only retired from official life at the end of his second term in 1809. He died in his eighty-fourth year By a dramatic coincidence his death occurred upon the fiftieth anniversary[4] of the famous *Declaration of Independence*, of which he was the author.

He is described by his biographer[5] as 'thin and raw-boned,' with 'red hair, and freckled face and pointed features.' His height was well over six feet. He was large in frame and loose-limbed. We are told that he was studiously unkempt, and even slovenly in his dress and person; 'made up' elaborately, as his enemies suggest, for the part of a sterling democrat. His uncouth disorder upon high occasions, his disregard of the ordinary conventions and ceremonies of state, slippers down at the heel, corduroy breeches very much the worse for wear, neck-cloth awry and not overclean, do not impress the modern reader as they appear to have impressed the admiring citizens of his own day. We are not struck by the sincerity of a great nature contemptuous of trifles, but rather by the ingenuity of a great actor who had carefully weighed the value of the meanest accessories.

The portraits of Jefferson are of a considerable variety, and difficult to reconcile one with another. There is dignity in all of them, and kindliness in most. But there is also an expression of anxious vigilance. The face suggests

[1] 1779-80.   [2] 1784-89.   [3] 1790-93.
[4] 4th July 1826.   [5] Tucker

a sensitive and shrinking nature which, by the sport of circumstances, or by a perverse ambition, has been led to play the wholly unintended part of a man of action. Jefferson was a bold horseman, but in every other sphere where courage and swift decision are usually looked for, he was dilatory, timorous and unready. He was an affectionate friend, adored by his familiars, and brilliant under the glow of their sympathy. But as an enemy he was less admirable: untiring, but unchivalrous; never fighting in the open where he could avoid it, and never taking blows without a whine. He hated to hear any man applauded who was not under his immediate patronage; and, what is perhaps his strangest quality, seeing that he was a scholar and had much experience of the world, he detested whole classes of his fellow-creatures for no better reason than because they were invested by tradition with some kind of respect.

When Jefferson first came into prominence certain ideas were in the air, and these ideas were believed by their lovers to be capable of forming the solid foundations of states. By their enemies, on the other hand, they were denounced as pernicious nonsense, impossible to be translated into political action save at the cost of anarchy and disorder. The poetry, religion and philosophy of the revolutionary epoch had a great vogue for nearly three generations, and when Jefferson, as a member of Congress, drafted his famous *Declaration of Independence*, they had been in men's minds for a quarter of a century. The dominant note at this time was the love of mankind, no less intense because of its vagueness, and a bitter indignation against officers and institutions that were deemed to be the cause of human suffering.

When Jefferson for a second time appeared in distinguished pre-eminence as Secretary of State these ideas were in their second period, of which the note was a blind and

bloodthirsty rage that had its origin in failure. Despite
the prophets the millennium had not yet arrived. The
contrivances of despots, the zeal of their minions, the
cowardice of doubters, were assumed to be the causes of
the delay. Ultimate defeat was held to be impossible, for
the stubbornness of the facts themselves had not then
begun to be suspected.

To this age of impatience there succeeded an age of comparative peace. The violence of emotion had produced
a natural exhaustion. A dim perception of the things that
must be rendered unto Cæsar had somewhat abated the
confidence of poets and the dogmatism of philanthropists.
The manners and hearts of men became the objective of
such revolutionaries as still maintained their faith. The
institutions of the state would be moulded in the end
through the awakened conscience of mankind, when the
spots of the leopard were changed and the Ethiopian had
become white.

Roughly the revolutionary epoch lasted for three-quarters
of a century.[1] Its first period was one of brotherhood, the
second of rage, the third of a mild and patient aspiration.
Jefferson was prominent in each of these phases. His
sympathy never wavered, his hope never failed. In his
own country certainly, and in other countries possibly, the
majority of good men was with him from the beginning to
the end of his career—the majority of the idealists, the
unselfish, the thoughtful, the articulate and the unwise.
They were not practical men, but they were sincere, and
Jefferson was their champion and exponent. Fidelity to
ideas rather than success in action was their concern. They
judged their leader more by the eloquent orthodoxy of his
messages and manifestoes than by any test of efficiency in
office.

[1] 1750 to 1825.

This is the first, and the greatest, and the most worthy of the causes that made Jefferson a famous character. He was a kind of Don Quixote; with this difference, that half the world shared his illusions.

A further cause was the political exhaustion that followed upon strenuous effort. Jefferson came as chief magistrate to a people longing for peace after war, rest after revolution.[1] Independence was secured, union accomplished, a constitution created and set in movement. The natural temper of men in such conditions is towards the enjoyment of what has been won by so great sacrifices. They desired to go about their business, to cultivate material prosperity, to have leisure and to breathe freely.

This condition in the United States coincided with the third phase of the revolutionary spirit throughout the Western world. Public opinion, while deprecating violent action, conversion by fire and sword, and all attempts upon the grand scale to translate its aspirations into statutes, was grateful to one who kept its faith alight by *obiter dicta*, and persuaded mankind by his glowing deliverances that the triumph of these principles, though postponed, was inevitable. Martyrdom during the first quarter of the nineteenth century was not prized among friends nor inflicted upon enemies. The period was one of easy faith. Men searched for welcome signs of conformity in their neighbours rather than for spots of heresy. The little outward forms of democracy in which Jefferson took an uncouth delight were in fact better tribute-money than a stern and rigid adherence to the formulas of equality and fraternity. The literal observance of the Rights of Man had, to tell the truth, become inconvenient and embarrassing. The virtuous citizen, while cherishing the ultimate hope, abstained from the pedantic practice of perfect brotherhood.

[1] 1801.

Finally, there is the sound practical reason for Jefferson's pre-eminence that, very fortunately for his reputation, he had fallen upon an age of dwarfs, which had succeeded to an age of giants. After the defeat of Adams, the deaths of Washington and Hamilton, the ostracism of Burr, there were no possible rivals. We look in vain for any sign of lusty nature among his conspicuous lieutenants and successors. Madison and Monroe belong to a different breed of men. Jefferson was the last of the giants; and consequently, while he continued in life, he was secure of his reputation, through the absence of all competition. A kind of sanctity encircled his head. He was the grand keeper of the Touch-stone of Democracy. Men voyaged from long distances, and put him to exorbitant expenses in grateful entertainment of them, merely to look upon his features and boast of it to their grandchildren; and in the end he died, as he had lived, in the odour of phrases.

It is better to concede all Jefferson's faults, and having done so to make a single bold claim that few will be found to dispute, though to some it will appear as an explanation of his success rather than as a proof of his virtue. There was a quality in him which Hamilton and other great statesmen of the constructive school have usually lacked. It is the old battle of the moralists against the evangelists, of salvation by works or by grace. Jefferson believed in humanity without any reservations, and the causes of his great influence must therefore be sought for in his faith and not in his acts. Hamilton disbelieved in humanity, unless it had the support of strong laws and the leadership of great men. To the people, craving for an affectionate confidence, these limitations implied distrust. The world which needed his works and profited by them forgot him for the time in favour of a rival who was not merely barren of achievements, but who also lacked the gaiety, courageous bearing and charm of manner which are in the usual way strong aids to popularity.

Hamilton was a master; but Jefferson men felt to be a friend. He lived in their hearts. It was useless to point to the ledger account of benefits conferred. The mass of citizens was not ungrateful to Hamilton, nor wilfully disrespectful to his memory; but towards Jefferson there was a homage of a wholly different order. His love for them was sincere, his faith in them was constant. Freedom and fraternity were ever on his lips, so that not only his followers in the North, but possibly even he himself, came to forget that he was a Virginian slave-owner to the last.

That the manner of his climbing into power, and his way of dealing with his enemies, do not conform with his own ideals of virtue, cannot fairly be brought as evidence that he was insincere. In the case of every public character wide allowance must be made for divergence between his public professions and his private practice. He has a right to plead an imperfect world for much apparent inconsistency. And for Jefferson it is necessary to make a further excuse. In his own timid disposition he had more to fight against than most men. It led him constantly into situations from which he chose to escape by some mean device, or on some disingenuous plea, or even by plain untruth. But if it be some excuse for him as a man that he was found continually acting under the influence of his fears, it is also his severest condemnation as a servant of the state.

According to one of his bitterest critics, "Jefferson was ' a practical theorist. His theory was the general credulity ' of mankind. Upon this credulity his life was the success- ' ful practice." [1] This judgment is true up to a certain point, but misses, as prejudice usually does, the real interest of his character. It is true that he practised successfully

[1] J. C. Hamilton, *History*, iv. p. 463.

R

upon the credulity of mankind, but his art was to a large extent unconscious. For no man was ever yet born so clever that he could live upon popularity merely by his wits. To succeed at the game it is necessary that he should be himself a dupe. The appeals of Jefferson were in many cases so absurd that they could never have earned even a temporary assent, had he not himself believed in them with the utmost sincerity. For all his shrewdness, his character was one of an extraordinary simplicity. The things in which he believed are possibly astounding, but the fact of his belief in them is beyond all question.

In observation no statesman has excelled, and very few in the whole history of the world have equalled, Jefferson. The whole of the uppermost, emotional nature of individual men was an open book to him. Their vanities, their enthusiasms, their ambitions, needed little study and no reasoning. He felt them by a kind of sympathy. His instinct within these limits was unerring. The profounder depths he did not understand. He saw only what was reflected in the mirrors of his own feelings. The sterner qualities of mankind were hidden from him. Steadfastness under discouragement and amidst the doubt of friends, renunciation that was silent and undramatic, volcanic passions and cold equity he could not see, for his own nature held no glass to reflect them. He did not fully understand Hamilton. He was baffled by his frankness and miscalculated, convinced it must be a cloak to conceal some interested motive. He never understood Washington beyond the fringe of his character. He was incapable by his nature of understanding the personal dignity of a Scots shepherd, or of a Jew pedlar, or the unbreakable loyalty of a blackguard. But he looked into most men, if he did not look entirely through them. He was as superior to Walpole, who traded mainly upon their meanness, as he was inferior

to Chatham, who knew how to use their virtues. In prac-
tising upon the emotions no man was ever more adroit and
at the same time less self-conscious, and no man ever reaped
a greater profit on his genius.

Jefferson's greatest skill was in dealing with men as individuals; but he was also a capable analyst of mankind
in the mass. To his credit it must be set down that
he made no attempt at bribery. He did not offer doles
and never hinted at spoliation. There was no grossness in
his method. The harmonics that he fiddled were entirely
upon the strings of sentimentality. He had a *flair* for
what was or might be made popular. He understood and
interpreted what was felt at the moment, and he had the
gift to foresee what would be felt at the next moment. It
was less art with him than a kind of instinct, which is
shared by the theatrical manager and all great showmen.
He knew what the public wanted, and he knew also what
it was easy and possible to educate it to want; and what it
wanted or might want he was always ready to provide.

The charge against him in this respect is not dishonesty,
for if any of his beliefs were sincere his belief in the *Vox
populi, vox Dei* theory is entitled to respect. If the popular
voice was truth, the part of a wise and virtuous statesman
must be to listen and obey, to anticipate and prepare. It
may appear to us amazing that any man should have held
such views; but granting that he did, it is impossible to
impeach him upon the accusation that he pandered to popularity. The real difficulty is at a later stage. The popular
voice uttered such discordant judgments that obedience to
them all would have seemed to most men to force the
abandonment of the divine mansion of reason. But in
Jefferson's case there was apparently no struggle. He ex-
ploited an emotion until it showed signs of flagging, and
then passed on to another which he had helped to kindle.

Disaster was forgotten not only by himself, but by his constituents, in the hope and excitement of a new venture. So quick was he to seize and interpret the mood of the moment, that a grateful people easily overlooked the fact of his having championed with equal fervour some prior emotion of which they had come to repent.

But just as Jefferson failed to penetrate the profound and noble qualities in his personal friends and enemies, so he missed the essential things in national affairs. The desires, indignations and enthusiasms of the majority of citizens in any country at a given moment are not necessarily synonymous with the material or spiritual needs of the people. In the former he was a sharer, and as he lived in a period of peace and not of stress (when unreality must have found him out), he had an immense reward for his sympathy. But looking beyond this sympathy what is there to show? What institutions owe their origin to his efforts? What problems did he solve? The record of his actual achievements is almost negligible. The opportunities which he missed entirely dwarf his meagre accomplishment.

The irony of events forced or permitted Jefferson to assume the rôle of a leader of men. Whatever the virtue of his qualities, it was not an executive virtue. Yet he put himself to slavery for many long years, endured endless mortifications, and, according to the computation of one of his editors, wrote upwards of forty-five thousand letters, most of them long ones, to achieve a triumph which, viewed as statesmanship, was nearly, or wholly, barren. Reading his correspondence, we doubt whether he even enjoyed the pleasures of the pursuit, for he was not a combative man or a sportsman. It seems rather that he was haunted by a sense of duty impelling him to snatch power out of the hands of certain dangerous characters who had proved their iniquity by deriding a set of phrases which were more to him than all religion. His success was conspicuous but tragic. In the end he ousted his enemies and cast down the revilers; but his phrases played him false. No power could translate them into policy or law, because they did not correspond with any translatable human facts. For the greater part they were only words, and for the rest they were the fancies of a poet.

Although Jefferson outlived Hamilton by more than twenty years he was his senior by fourteen, and this fact accounts for much of the bitterness which marked their relations. When Jefferson arrived at New York in March 1790 to take up his duties of Secretary of State, Hamilton had been already at work for six months. His fame was in the mouths of all men. He was the hero of the particular crisis. Jefferson was not used to subsist upon the crumbs of applause. That he genuinely hated Hamilton's political ideals there can be no question; nor that he hated his methods and his pre-eminence even more than his ideals. Hamilton's swift, practical way of setting to work and accomplishing his ends without allowing his opponents the luxury of phrasemaking and prolonged debate was wormwood to him. The temperaments of the two men were as far asunder as the poles; not different in the sense that they were complementary, which might, under favourable circumstances, have made them fast friends, but in that they were intensely antipathetic in every particular, from the philosophy of life to the cut and fashion of their clothes. And beyond all this there was the same personal rivalry which disturbed the peace of the archangels. Jefferson, the writer of the *Declaration of Independence*, which it had been the custom to consider the noblest and most famous document in the whole history of the world; Jefferson, the minister at the court of the most Christian king, the friend of philosophers, the philosopher of fine ladies, the counsellor of the most eminent statesmen of Europe—for such a man in the prime of his life to be dragged at the chariot wheels of an energetic young upstart was altogether intolerable, and Jefferson must have been something more than human had he accepted the position with magnanimity.

It has been suggested that Hamilton regarded himself in the light of a prime minister. It is certain that he insisted upon making his policy operate in every department of the state. His clearness of thought, swiftness of decision, cogency in argument, whether spoken or written, gave him an enormous advantage, both with the cabinet and Congress. His faculty for getting his own way was little short of miraculous. Washington was his staunch supporter. General Knox, the Minister for War, always followed his lead. Even Randolph, the Attorney-General, with the bravest intentions, was constantly detached from his allegiance to Jefferson by the magnetism of his rival.[1]

If it were possible to consider Thomas Jefferson and Alexander Hamilton quietly, as types of human temperament and modes of thought, stripped of all personal rivalry, the whole pageantry of the times swept aside, and all the husk of fashion, prejudice and affectation torn from each character, there would still remain a violent and eternal opposition. The small accidents of their official relations merely provided a dramatic setting to an enmity which was as fundamental as that of fire and water.

The ideal of Hamilton was the hive, the ideal of Jefferson was the bee. To the former the state was everything; to the latter, the divine nature of man. To Jefferson an individual was much more important than a state, a state much more important than the Union. In proportion as human life took on a corporate character and strength,

---

[1] Jefferson to Madison, *History*, v. p. 344.

he became less interested in its fortunes and more apt to regard it with jealousy and suspicion. In his honest and sincere belief, a man as an amiable, prosperous individual, not the state as an aggregate of self-sacrificing men, was the true goal of politics.

Never in the history of the world has there been a full realisation of Hamilton's dream. The nearest approach to it is the popular conception of the Empire of Japan—a mass of intelligent humanity, reckless of their lives, yet filled with the joy of life, eager for distinction, hungry for success, alert, practical and merry; but at the same time subordinate, humbly and piously subordinate, to a pure abstraction. With a people inspired to so high a pitch, the triumph and security of the race would dominate every individual aim, interest and affection. The maxim of such a polity is combination; but the inevitable corollary is caste.

If, as Hamilton's enemies contended, his passion for order and strong government would certainly, in the event of its full success, have bound the United States of America into a conservative Venetian republic within the space of a few generations, Jefferson's counter policy, with the same fortune, would assuredly have plunged them into anarchy and bloodshed within a decade. The passion of Jefferson was individual freedom. Often it amounted to a formula— sometimes to a quite extravagant formula; but there was a reality underlying it. He had a genuine belief in the goodness of humanity viewed as individuals. He hated the idea of the hive. He could never understand the fascination of its abstract glory, or realise that it possessed any practical utility. Sacrifices to such an end were not even a puzzle to him, but merely a foolish paradox. His nature was impervious to any national anthem. What was important to him, and holy, was the free growth of men, restricted no more than was absolutely necessary by laws or conventions.

He desired to see them grow up in their natural shapes, and believed that these shapes would be more 'natural' on a bleak, wind-swept moorland, or in a crowded forest, than in any cared-for park or sheltered garden. He was an enthusiast, who hoped for good with so fervent and extreme a faith, that he openly avowed a preference for government by newspapers and disparaged the virtues of a settled constitution. It is hardly exaggeration to say that he would have rejoiced to see the state a dismasted hulk, so confident was he that by the action of beneficent and eternal currents, she would drift for ever upon a smiling sea, within bow-shot of the delectable islands, without the aid of sails or rudder. Hamilton lacked the same enthusiasm, was entirely wanting in such confidence. His passion was good seamanship, trim tackle and a hearty crew. To drift was for him ever the greatest of all evils; and the advocate of such policy was in his opinion a madman, an incompetent, or a coward.

Under the British system of government Hamilton must necessarily have been a head and shoulders above all other statesmen of his time and country. Jefferson, on the other hand, would not have taken any rank whatever among statesmen, but would have arrived at eminence in some different sphere. Our parliamentary plan has many faults, but certain compensations. It hinders the work of a minister and wastes his time, but at least it enables him to defend his own measures. And there is this safety in it, that our party leaders must always be men of courage. Sometimes in our haste we may permit ourselves to speak disparagingly of debate, and if the result of debate were merely the prevalence of eloquence over silence, of good arguments over bad ones, it might justly be contemned as a means of selecting men to govern the country. But debate is something a great deal more respectable. The glory of the British parliament is that men subdue it by their characters to a far greater extent than by their arguments. It is required of a leader that he must be prepared at any moment to stand up to his enemies, to give blows and to take them. This test can never be escaped. Occasional brilliant appearances will never put any man in power, or keep him in power if he has happened to arrive there by some accident. Private influence or intrigue, literary gifts of the highest order, are all in vain. The system is sound, although of necessity it excludes many aspirants of shining talents. The rule is absolute that, before a man may be permitted to govern the nation, he must have proved himself capable of prevailing over his rivals in single combat and face to face.

Jefferson did not shine in controversy. He hated it—it is not unjust to say that he feared it. His abstinence from debate has been explained by a huskiness of the voice, but in reality it was much more a matter of temperament. He avoided personal strife whenever it was possible to do so, and upon the whole his foresight to that end was amazingly successful. But when occasionally the unexpected happened and he found himself confronted with a determined adversary, he never hesitated to escape, nor gave much thought to the dignity of his demeanour.

Many instances are alleged against him,[1] and of these the most conspicuous is his failure as governor of Virginia during the war. It is not credible, as his enemies have insinuated, that Jefferson feared for his life, or would have hesitated in the extreme necessity to give it for his country. But in any crisis he was unprepared, and emergency always

[1] " He deserted from Congress instantly on hearing of the battle of Long Island. He abandoned the chief magistracy of Virginia while the enemy were in possession of that state, and when an impeachment was hanging over his head ; and he retired from the Department of State (January 1794) when everything indicated imminent peril to his country."—*History*, v. pp. 438-39 ; also v. pp. 339-55 ; iii. p. 65.

found him in a fluster. He was a quiet, studious, patriotic and unwarlike citizen, but as a governor, called upon suddenly to repel a bold invader supported by a mere handful of men, he was a lamentable failure. He could inspire no confidence in his legislators, because he was utterly unable to collect his own wits. He lacked the clear and practical sense of an objective, the swiftness of decision, the cheerful and cool resourcefulness that the occasion demanded. The policy of his life was to toss phrases into the ears of mankind, like honey-cakes to Cerberus. But it was impossible to deal with men who carried muskets by this easy prescription. Jefferson proved himself incompetent as governor of Virginia to repel the British troops under Arnold, and by reason of the same defects in his character he would have been no less incompetent to deal with the funding of the national debt, for creditors are an equally obdurate class of antagonists.

The contrast between Hamilton and Jefferson is forced upon us at every turn, in acts as well as in theories, in trifling fashions and in serious beliefs. Nowhere is it more remarkable than in the style of their writings. Jefferson is flowing, desultory and familiar. He has an entertaining spice of peevish humour and captious satire; an aptness in outflanking his opponent by some ingenious digression. Hamilton, on the other hand, is ever grave and eager; formal if not actually distant; terse, vigorous and direct in attack, preferring the frontal to all other methods. He never deals in trivial annoyance. If he wounds it is not because he desires to hurt, but because his intention is to destroy.

The contrast is as obvious in their opinions as in their style. Hamilton made his party round his convictions. The men who thought as he did, the men who were won over by his appeal, came to him and attached themselves.

Jefferson's opinions, on the other hand, cannot escape a suspicion of having in many cases been chosen deliberately in order to attract a party to follow him. There is no single instance where he stood out boldly against a popular cry. Hamilton, on the contrary, was more often found fighting against the sentiment of the moment than in agreement with it. He never hesitated to risk his favour with the people if his ideas of justice were opposed to their passions. He was always a leader. Jefferson at his best was never more than a patron, and usually he was only a purveyor. His unique faculty for self-persuasion alone saved him from actual dishonesty.

It has been the custom to excuse Jefferson, and even to praise him, on the grounds that his feelings were stronger than those of ordinary men. But the difference was really less in the strength of his feelings than in the weakness of his control. He had the shrewdness to make a merit of a vice, and he succeeded so well that he has not only been forgiven for his lack of self-command, but has built upon it the proof of his sincerity. Like many persons who profess the widest philanthropy and are beset by loose emotions, he was vindictive and at times ferocious. He exulted over the suffering and degradation of individuals and classes against whom he had merely a theoretic grudge. His apologies for all that was worst in the French Revolution are painful reading. We miss not only an intelligent estimate of these events, but any semblance of magnanimity. His most solemn judgments are tainted by a morbid spirit of literary revenge; they never arrive at that pitch of authority which overawes, and although he is often cruel, he is never stern.

To search for the explanation of a great renown, and to find so little that corresponds to our ideas of a hero, is disappointing. We are wearied by apologists who concede nothing to Jefferson's dispraise except his inconsistencies, and attribute even these to an excessive honesty; who keep harping upon his half-virtues, and would persuade us that after all tact is a kind of leadership, and perseverance a sort of courage; that eagerness for popularity is but a healthy love of approbation, and that untruthfulness which springs from timidity or the imagination is less heinous than if its origins were in some sinister ambition.   It is hard, listening to such instructors, not to go the whole way with the Federalists and to rate him as a mere mountebank whose title to fame consists not in the value of his work, but in the skill with which he imposed upon his own day and generation.   The ambition of a man like Hamilton is to get certain things which he believes in done, of a man like Jefferson to keep himself poised upon the top of a wave. In spite of his eloquent morality he held no opinion so firmly that he would risk his popularity to achieve it.   In spite of his belief that the greatest work of God is a man and not a polity, he hated minorities, and hated even more to be in a minority.   In spite of his admiration for rational as opposed to traditional government, he not only distrusted reason as many wise men have done—he detested it.   An argument drawn from experience was almost as offensive to him as a hard fact.   He was satisfied that he had penetrated to the heart of any matter when he had ranged it under one or other of his ready-made formulas.

It is easy to understand why Jefferson should have hated Hamilton.   Two so different dispositions were bound to disagree, and to disagree with bitterness.   What is difficult to understand, unless on the ground of a peculiar temperament, is the inveteracy of Jefferson's malice.   He outlived Hamilton for more than twenty years, and during the whole of that period his popularity had been prodigious and uninterrupted.   Towards the end of his life he became the object of a hero-worship almost religious in its character. Men came from all parts to gaze upon his countenance, and the name of Hamilton was for the time being forgotten.

In this serene and blissful atmosphere Jefferson set to work upon the revision of his correspondence and memoirs. It was with him no perfunctory task of notes and dockets, ordering of dates and filling in of initials; but a very serious and painstaking effort to leave the golden memory of the author without a single smut or stain. Passages were re-written. Incidents where some tarnish had fastened were industriously scrubbed. His share in ancient controversies was explained in a new light. His case was fortified by evidence that flowed easily from the cells of his resourceful memory. In the end it may be believed he was well satisfied with his work, and felt entirely confident that he had painted such a portrait of a virtuous citizen as the world must ever afterwards accept as the highest type.

The intended portrait of the virtuous citizen is a dull and lifeless presentment in thin and fading tints. On the canvas behind it, glowing through the transparency, is the true Jefferson in strong lines and gorgeous colours—Jefferson the skilful politician, the ingenious sophist, the intriguer against his enemies, the distorter of evidence and of facts; above all, perhaps, Jefferson the unforgiving. The *Anas* and the Autobiography give us a masterly, but too savage like-ness, and it is no wonder that his friends and admirers have never ceased to lament their publication. The Confessions of Rousseau are less convincing, because at times we cannot keep back the suspicion that a dramatic instinct of self-abasement has inspired his candour. The value of Jefferson is not his candour, for there is none, but his inadvertence, which is without a parallel. In his efforts to enhance his own glory he considered it essential to blacken the reputations of his enemies, and as a consequence he has given us a description of his own character to which his bitterest enemy would not wish to add a line.

CHAPTER II

The Origin and Growth of Parties

THE Democratic party which came into existence during the year 1791 (although it did not acknowledge its existence until considerably later) was lineally descended from the Conway Cabal.[1] It had its origin in the intrigues of which Horatio Gates was the hero, and "an intimate connection with ' the project of forcing General Washington from the com- ' mand of the army."[2] The conduct of the war required an efficient direction of the united energies of the states. "The ' friends of Washington were, therefore, the friends of ener- ' getic counsels. His opponents resorted to the usual instru- ' ment of disaffection, an appeal to jealousy of power."[3] In the period which preceded the convention of Philadelphia the dividing line was still the same. It was the same during the sessions of the convention; the same when a national government undertook to work out the salvation of the union.

"From the very birth of the colonies, jealousy of power ' had been the dominant thought of the American mind. . . . ' This feeling produced the Revolution. This feeling pro- ' longed its struggles. This feeling postponed the com- ' pletion of the Confederation. This feeling prevented its ' invigoration. This feeling produced the compromises of ' the Constitution. This feeling delayed and almost pre-

[1] *Ante*, p. 103.   [2] *History*, iv. p. 417.   [3] *Ibid*. iv. p. 418.

vented its establishment. The majority of the American
people were against it. Its founders were in a minority.
'Its supporters were a conservative party dealing with the
'masses. Of this party, while Washington was the head,
'avowing himself a Federalist, Hamilton was the exponent,
'both of its theory and of its practice."[1]

The division was between the upholders of State Rights
on the one hand, and the friends of a strong government on
the other. During the Conway Cabal, throughout the
'League of Friendship,' and in the Congress which met in
the autumn of 1791, the chief issues were ever the same.
The same fustian was talked about liberty. The same
catchwords were invoked 'to call fools into a circle'; and
to a large extent the same men were engaged in the contest,
and the same methods were set to work.

Jefferson accordingly found a State Rights party ready-
made when, outraged by the rivalry of Hamilton and offended
by the rejection of his own advice in the matter of the
National Bank, he determined to undertake the organisation
of an opposition to the government of which he was a
member. His genius in the manipulation of political forces
thereupon effected a strange alliance between the party of
State Rights and the party of the Rights of Man. He succeeded, by his consummate tact, in inducing those citizens
who hated and feared the tyranny of the Union to co-operate
with those others whose guiding principle was a hot affection
for the French Revolution. It was a work which earns the
praise of an incomparable dexterity, for at the beginning the
mistrusters of strong government were far further removed
than their opponents, the Federalists, from any admiration
for democracy;[2] while the Democrats would have found
little to object to in Washington's administration had it been
willing to support the arms of France and do homage to the

---

[1] *History*, iv. p. 463.   [2] *Ibid.* pp. 436-38 and 444.

principles of the Rights of Man. The cause of the cohesion of this oddly compacted party was to a large extent the endurance for twelve years of a government which both sections detested with an equal cordiality, though originally for widely different reasons. Before the end of this period the supporters of State Rights had for the most part become hearty Democrats, while the Democrats had succeeded in persuading themselves that a system of contumacious states would prove more favourable than a powerful Union to their ideals of liberty, equality and fraternity.

All the sections who composed the Democratic party had a common ground in their hatred of Monarchy. It mattered little that even upon this point their agreement was more a matter of a word than of things. It is true that monarchy to the lovers of democracy meant the personal rule of a king, and to the upholders of State Rights a strong rule of any kind, even one which rested on manhood suffrage. But as party leaders are well aware, an ambiguous word is often good enough for the purposes of an opposition. It is only when the 'outs' exchange places with the 'ins' that the double meaning is apt to become the cause of embarrassment. Every act done or supposed to have been inspired by Hamilton, was branded as a covert design to overturn the Republic and establish a Monarchy. The confusion of mind which associated the quality of strength in government with the idea of a despot was sedulously encouraged by the leaders of the opposite party. It is not credible that either Jefferson or Madison believed that Hamilton aimed at setting up a king, but for political purposes they fostered the suspicion in simpler minds,[1] till finally the charge of treason against the Republic became the burden of every Democratic speech and pamphlet. The objects of the invective were at first the Secretary of the Treasury and his corrupt adherents,

[1] *History*, iv. pp. 459-60.

but in the end the President himself was openly and fiercely A.D. 1791
attacked for his 'mimickry of kings.' ÆT. 34

In the same month which saw the end of the first Congress, Jefferson and Madison started upon a northern tour. They visited New York, and held interviews with Livingston, who had been disappointed of office, with Clinton, who detested the whole policy of union, and with Aaron Burr, whose predominant passion was intrigue, and whose constant experience was defeat. From New York the two emissaries passed on to Vermont and Connecticut. The object of their journey was to create an opposition to Hamilton's policy and the results became obvious as soon as the second Congress assembled in the autumn.

In June 1788, when ratification of the constitution was on hand, Madison had written to Hamilton a remarkable letter,[1] in which he warned him of the dangers to be apprehended by all true lovers of the Union as soon as the first administration should begin its labours. " Notwithstanding ' the fair professions made by some, I am so uncharitable as ' to suspect that the ill-will to the constitution will produce ' every peaceable effort to disgrace and destroy it. . . . My ' conjecture is, that exertions will be made to engage two- ' thirds of the legislature in the task of regularly *under-* '*mining* the government." This letter, which is signed 'yours affectionately,' is a startling forecast of the course which was to be pursued less than three years later by its author.

The anti-federal party soon rallied. Its defeat at Philadelphia had never become a rout. The spirit of State Rights was still a powerful force. To Jefferson, who had aided Hamilton, timidly and doubtfully, it is true, during the session of 1790, to carry his financial measures, it soon became apparent, not only that a rival had thereby been

---

[1] *History*, iii. p. 480.

strengthened, but that the policy of this rival was directed against a set of maxims which represented Jefferson's most cherished ideals. Jefferson was by nature all in favour of loose ties and a vague optimism. He despised institutions. Preferring as he did the guidance of newspapers to the rule of cabinets, he considered that mankind could only be governed fortunately by rhetorical appeals founded upon the Rights of Man. His natural dislike to precision in thought, definiteness in policy and force in execution, was excited by a competition and strengthened by an opportunity.

Jefferson was a man of singular astuteness, and it was not long before he realised that although for the moment power, and even an appearance of popularity, were on the side of his rival, there was a strong and very bitter party hostile to the Secretary of the Treasury on personal grounds and opposed with an equal detestation to the general trend of his policy. These persons felt that they had been outmanœuvred at the Convention of Philadelphia and overwhelmed in the popular agitation which followed it. They considered that their ruin was in process of being completed by the audacity and vigour of Washington's minister of finance. These malcontents were disorganised and leaderless. Madison, their most respectable figure, had contributed to the disaster by assisting Hamilton to mould the constitution and to write the *Federalist*. Although a statesman of undoubted ability, Madison lacked the qualities needed for inspiring confidence in common men, for party intrigue and for bold attack.

Jefferson therefore set himself actively to work in opposition to Hamilton. In spite of his want of personal courage, he was a dangerous antagonist. Conversations with 'old friends,' private letters well seasoned with political counsel, the mildest but the most indefatigable pulling of wires,

advice that was never too much forced or obtruded, gradually compacted a party in opposition to the government of
which he was himself a minister. Everything was so
gentle, it hardly earned the title of an impulse. He appeared
to act sadly, and from a sense of duty. Only a depraved
spirit could suspect him of ambition. His sole desire was
to do good stealthily. He wished for nothing so little as
the fame of a notorious attack; but merely induced the
younger generation to come forward and to speak their
minds, glad if the advice and encouragement of the 'wave-
worn mariner' could be of some small service to them.
Accessible and genial in a private circle, Jefferson acquired
an influence by the strangest method that has ever been
practised in public life. In the peculiar circumstances
which now began to develop, he was an unmatched party
leader. Timid, but untiring; ingenious, subterranean and
resourceful, he played his game, unaffected by the hatred,
suspicion and contempt of his immediate associates; and
in the end he won it by a strange mixture of virtues and
vices, of tenacity and cunning, by a wonderful knowledge
of the less admirable emotions of men, and by an unwavering confidence in their importance under any system of
popular government.

The Democratic party, which from the beginning of the
second Congress offered a vigorous opposition to all the
measures of the administration, was planned, concentrated,
organised, named and inspired by Thomas Jefferson, the
Secretary of State. It was an anomalous arrangement, but
for the attainment of its object, which was the destruction
of the government, it had very obvious advantages.

The reasons of Jefferson's bitter opposition' to Hamilton
were both public and personal, and there is no great difficulty
in understanding either. As a statesman Hamilton stood for
Federal Government against State Rights; for a strong execu-

tive against the Rights of Man; for the actual inequality against the philosophic equality of human creatures; for business against nonsense. The literary brain of Jefferson employed its leisure with the invention of names[1] to convey his iniquity. An intention to subvert republican institutions was constantly alleged. The idea of a king was suspended as a constant menace; but it was always difficult to give substance to the threatened dynasty. Hamilton's frankly expressed admiration for certain British institutions enabled Jefferson to foster the suspicion that he desired to bring about a union with that country, and to replace the necks of free Americans under an odious yoke.

Like many other great men, Hamilton had a polar quality which attracted love and hatred with a force that meaner natures are exempt from. His capacity for uniting his enemies was inferior only to his gift for inspiring devotion in his friends. He was great in the simple manner; not at all astute, but merely overwhelming and irresistible. He was one of the greatest strategists, but only, very rarely, even a respectable tactician. Every man, enemy or friend, saw how his course was laid. He never divided his enemies by conjuring up a timely mist upon the waters. He was combative; loved the giving of blows and cared little about receiving them. In the matter of smiting he had a heavy hand. On great occasions he was capable of a great restraint, but his natural character was eager and vehement, intolerant of fools and impatient of prudential management. His youth made it unforgivable that he should be so outspoken. Many envied his success; some certainly hated his ideals; and there were others, grave men, important among their neighbours, who had felt over their shoulders the lash of his contempt.

[1] 'Monocrats,' 'Anglomen,' etc. etc.

A few months later,[1] the results of Jefferson's northern tour and his collaboration with Madison became manifest. A journal was started to assail the government. Its editor was one Freneau, a gentleman of a light and caustic vein, with a turn for metrical satire. The Secretary of State appointed him to a subordinate post in his office. The pay was small; so small that the appointment has the appearance of a blunder. The patronage was of such a trifling sort, as far as money went, that the moral support assumed the chief part. Freneau's paper with great vivacity proceeded to assail all the acts of the administration except those which could be attributed to the impulse of his patron. Hamilton's financial policy was fiercely attacked. The charge of corruption figured constantly in the largest type; though the nature of the bribe, and the persons who had been bought, were involved in mystery. The briber alone stood out clearly for execration.

Under Jefferson's able inspiration Freneau played the game of indefinite slander with great vigour. From corruption he passed on to treason. Hamilton and the Federalists were scheming to subvert the Republic and impose a monarchy. The temper of the times was jealous, and the plain man accordingly did not always dismiss the charge as incredible; but hearing it often repeated came at last to think there must be something in it.

During Hamilton's remaining years of office his chief work in connection with the Treasury department was the defence and completion of his financial policy. But in addition he was forced to undertake a more irksome labour. His character was persistently assailed, at first upon the vague charge that, out of the public funds, he had corrupted others, and when that had failed, upon the cruder accusation that he had manipulated loans, and made away with

[1] October 31, 1791, *Works*, vii. p. 239.

millions for his private benefit. There was never even a *prima facie* case under either head. The accounts were so perspicuous, the records so complete, that no honest purpose, however blundering, was capable of misunderstanding their import. Jefferson and Madison, who instigated these attacks and drew a profit from them, can never have been unaware that they were false; but they argued wisely that for their immediate purpose truth or falsehood was not a matter of any great importance. What was of paramount importance was that Hamilton should be hindered in his work, and if possible should be driven out of public life.

Even had there been no dangers to the state arising out of the progress of the French Revolution, these departmental and personal concerns would have left Hamilton but little time for the prosecution of his commercial policy upon a grand scale. When the occasion presented itself, as in the case of the fisheries [1] and the system of import duties,[2] he did not hesitate to advance a few steps towards his end, but it was entirely out of the question to attempt the realisation of his dream of " erecting one great American system, superior ' to the control of transatlantic force or influence, and able to ' dictate the connection between the Old and the New World."[3] The report upon Manufactures, presented to the second Congress, within a few weeks after its assembly, was therefore left by him, reluctantly, without any serious effort to carry it into accomplishment.

Jefferson's attitude towards this commercial policy was hostile at every point. He hated it for two very good reasons : it was obnoxious upon different grounds both to the party of State Rights and to the enthusiasts for the Rights of Man. The former saw in it a new attempt to aggrandise the Federal power, the latter were up in arms

---

[1] *History*, iv. pp. 361-62.   [2] *Ibid.* pp. 392-95.
[3] *Ibid.* iv. p. 314.

because it offered an affront to the phrases of liberty. The A.D. 1791 first objection was grounded in the facts, the second was Æt. 34 based upon a purely verbal misconstruction; but for the purpose of an opposition the one was as good a weapon as the other.

Jefferson was a free-trader, as one would have expected him to be, but it is more than doubtful if he knew what the phrase meant. It was enough that a doctrine paid a kind of lip-service to the idea of freedom for him to subscribe to it without a second thought. For those who will not observe the conditions of their own time, the formula is ever the proper weapon. Jefferson was a reader of books, a weaver of fanciful philosophies, an accepter of general principles, a worshipper of words, a hater of the confusion of things. He loved everything that was 'free,' or that called itself 'free,' with the passionate unreasonableness of a collector of Stuart relics. His fundamental belief (if we may use these words to describe opinions which never at any point touched a firm bottom, but merely swam like a kind of 'sud' upon the stream of expediency) was a set of formulas which he had learned by rote during his official career in France. It was bad enough, according to the precepts of this philosophy, that free citizens should be required to pay taxes of any kind whatsoever. It was intolerable that imposts should be levied except to supply the barest necessities of the simplest form of government that would fit the needs of the time. He would have derided the idea that any country could be taxed into prosperity, or that under any circumstances a system of duties could become an aid to national development. A scheme which had for its object to place the industry and commerce of the states under the care of the federal government was either visionary and absurd, or else was the cloak to some ulterior end. Had it been possible to prove to him that such a scheme was in fact attainable and would produce great benefits to the community, his opposition would still have remained the same. It was more important, in his opinion, that private men should be left free to manage their own affairs, than that the affairs of men in the aggregate should be well managed.

The system of Jefferson prided itself upon a consistency that scorned compromise. All men were equal, and, with the exception of black men in certain favoured latitudes, they were born free. All countries were the same. If it were not for the injurious artifices of government, friendliness would be the rule among mankind. Truth was a flat and easy projection like Mercator's, not a rough crystal with a thousand planes. In the navigation of his fancies Jefferson allowed neither for wind nor current, neither for deviation of the compass nor for the tide that is in the affairs of men. He could not love a man who would dissect a beautiful theory; Hamilton, on the other hand, would not away with arguments unless they were based upon a knowledge of the conditions. To Jefferson, liberty, equality and fraternity were the pillars of the temple, and free trade seemed for the moment to be a necessary consequence of the plan. A few years later, it is true, fashions in thought and rhetoric underwent a change. The doctrine of free trade ceased to be an article of the Democratic faith. Its place was taken, under Jefferson and his successors, by a crude and spasmodic protection which was hardly less opposed to the national principle of Hamilton than to the original highflown professions of his rival. Those erratic efforts formed no part of a permanent and noble purpose, but were merely the hand-to-mouth expedients of compliant demagogues.

Jefferson's attitude towards the financial policy of Hamilton was at the beginning by no means unfavourable. It was only when he came to realise the strength and permanence of the feelings aroused against it that his opposition was

declared in unmistakable terms. Even as late as the spring
of 1791, after his quarrel with Hamilton over the National
Bank, we find clear expressions of approval, and a sound perception of the benefits which the country had derived from
the measures of the previous sessions.[1] It is necessary to
discriminate very carefully between the feelings which
Jefferson gave utterance to at the time when these measures
passed into law, and those other feelings which he was led
to entertain a short time afterwards, when the exigencies of
creating a political party became his chief concern. And it
is necessary also to discriminate between what Jefferson
really felt in 1790 and 1791, and what in later years he had
the audacity to maintain that he had felt during that period.
It is not too harsh a judgment to condemn the account contained in the *Anas* as unworthy of belief. The misrepresentation of the chief incidents of the time and of Hamilton's
measures, motives and methods is not less remarkable than
his undeserved depreciation of his own astuteness.

It is true, however, that Jefferson was entirely ignorant of
finance. He not only confessed the defect in his intelligence,
but made a merit of it. To understand finance was a thing
only possible for rogues. We are not unfamiliar with the argument at the present day. The rhetorical censor, baffled and
brought to book, invariably rushes to this classical asylum.
" You are too clever for me. You can prove anything. But
' all the same, the plain man knows very well that my
' charges are true, and that you are a knave." This method
argues a great reliance upon the opacity and indolence of
a democracy, but there is no gainsaying the fact that it
occasionally attains its purpose.

Jefferson alleges in his letters and *Anas*[2] that Hamilton's
measures were grounded in corruption and dishonesty; but
his own moral sense was never a very trustworthy guide,

[1] *History*, iv. pp. 486-87.   [2] Ford's *Jefferson*, i. p. 160.

and upon any question concerned with finance, his intelligence was as inadequate as his conscience. There was not merely a looseness in his judgment on this subject, but that real mental impediment which prevents most women and many men from being able to understand the simplest balance-sheet. When he disliked anything or anybody, he picked the handiest word from his vocabulary, and corruption was the most apposite term of abuse to employ in a case where money was in question. His own views upon national finance are of a charming crudity. In magniloquent and persuasive language he strove to persuade his followers to contest the whole matter of the debt, basing their arguments upon the proposition of Thomas Paine, 'that no generation has the right to bind posterity.' With an amusing precision he calculated a generation to exist for a period of nineteen years, and he earnestly recommended that any debt which had remained undischarged for such a time should be cancelled.[1] Posterity was to be allowed to enjoy private freedom and political safety; but the present age must either discharge the bill in full, or the bill itself must be wiped off the slate. He protested that although he aided Hamilton to carry 'assumption' in the manner that has been already explained,[2] he almost immediately came to regret it. He would persuade us that, at the time, he entertained no very decided convictions, and that his childlike simplicity was practised upon by his unscrupulous colleague. He explained in vivid but unconvincing detail the manner in which he was 'duped' by Hamilton.[3] Jefferson, indeed, is unique in his misfortunes, inasmuch as, at the time, he endured considerable unpopularity (to his mind ever the worst of all possible human calamities) through his supposed complicity in financial integrity,[4] and after his death discarded the reward of

[1] Ford's *Jefferson*, ix. p. 389.   [2] *Ante*, p. 223.
[3] Ford's *Jefferson*, i. pp. 161-62.   [4] *History*, iv. p. 449.

his martyrdom by allowing it to transpire that his sympathies
were wholly upon the side of repudiation. For posterity, looking back upon the deeds of its great-grandparents, is always a stern moralist, and in this matter of the debt unhesitatingly approves Hamilton's action and condemns the opposition he was forced to endure.

The first session of the second Congress did not meet under the most promising conditions. It is true that the country was enjoying a prosperity which had passed the dreams of the optimists. It is true also that, upon the whole, there was a disposition to support the Union, and to acknowledge the benefits which the administration of Washington had already conferred upon the nation. The composition of Congress reflected this general feeling, and the Federalists were in a considerable majority, though by no means firmly bound together upon party lines. But, on the other hand, there was an ominous lawlessness in Pennsylvania, where Gallatin had begun his evil work of agitation against the excise; while Virginia, the proudest of all the states, was deeply offended by the superior strength and dignity of the central government.

It was evident from the beginning that there was an organised party, far superior in discipline to the supporters of the government, determined to offer opposition to the Federalist principle at every point. The character and policy of the Secretary of the Treasury were the main objects of attack. He brought forward proposals to give effect to the decisions arrived at during the previous sessions; but no matter how obvious or how formal were his recommendations, they were made the occasions of factious opposition. Reason and consistency had no concern in the matter. It was sufficient that Hamilton was favourable to any measure for it to be obstructed by all the forms of Congress, and by all the invective of the opposition. Whether he proposed to

A.D. 1791
Æt. 34 increase the debt by a small sum in order to render the process of 'assumption' complete and equitable, or to decrease the debt by providing for its rapid discharge by means of a sinking fund, the settled hostility never varied. His proposals for the discharge of obligations due to foreign officers who had served during the War of Independence were assailed with objections as fierce and as captious as his proposals to provide a revenue adequate to the exigencies of the Union by means of an excise. An attempt was even made by Madison, in the full hope of success, to prevent the House from asking the Secretary of the Treasury to report upon Ways and Means. The insolence of the suggestion was deliberately designed to force Hamilton to resignation. Jefferson in private conferences endeavoured to detach a sufficient number of the Federalists, while Madison in Congress coloured the argument with a show of reason. The manœuvre was in the nature of a surprise, but in the end it was defeated by a small majority.[1]

From its inauguration in January the *National Gazette* pointed out the way and cheered on the antagonists of the administration. Jefferson, in addition to his quiet labours among the weaker Federalists in Congress,[2] turned his persuasiveness to the task of instilling a suspicion of Hamilton's integrity in the mind of the President.[3] The swashbucklers of the party were incited to make attacks in Congress, and Madison reinforced their ingenuous philippics with a more solemn malice and a more lingering innuendo. The charge of treason gradually gained strength. The charge of corruption passed into a new phase. At first it had been alleged upon the grounds that unworthy men who had bought up the obligations of the states and the confederation at a discount were, by Hamilton's system, to be paid off

[1] *History*, iv. p. 389. [2] *Ibid.* iv. pp. 388-90.
[3] *Ibid.* v. pp. 34-35 and 38-40.

at par. That was felt to be a straining of the meaning of words, and accordingly, as the charge was one too profitable to be withdrawn, Madison invented an accusation which he rightly considered would not be unworthy of the epithets his followers had employed. Clearly, though in an indirect form, he accused Hamilton of having bribed the members of Congress who were fundholders, and the moneyed classes generally, by creating an artificial price. Stock had been bought, it was alleged, on behalf of government for the purposes of the sinking fund at a price higher than the true market price.[1] It would be unfair to Madison's intelligence to suggest that he believed in the truth of his accusation, and equally unfair to his cool nature to put forward the excuse that he was carried away by a perfervid temperament. It is only fair to judge Madison to some extent from his own standpoint. There was no confusion in his thoughts, or heat in his action. He was merely an intolerably good man whose object it was to rid himself and his country of a bad man. He was willing to pay a price for this benefit which would have staggered meaner natures, and to his own conscience it is conceivable that he excused the means he employed on the grounds that the game of politics, like the game of war, leaves veracity out of its rules.

CHAPTER III

Charges of Corruption

THE Democratic party was planned and organised during the spring and summer of 1791, and its efficiency was well proved in the session which followed; but until after the scandals of August 1792 the opposition made no parade of their strength, acknowledged no leader either in Congress or

[1] *History*, iv. p. 528.

in the Cabinet, and would not even have admitted that they had any formal existence. Everything was wrapped up in secrecy, and it was intended that an excellent discipline should wear the appearance of a perfect spontaneity.

During the earlier part of the previous session [1] the loose ranks of the Federalists had been unprepared for any concerted attack. They had continued as before to indulge their private fancies, acting upon the assumption that in every division members would vote according to their sentiments and not by order. As a result, government measures had suffered defeat and alteration upon more than one occasion, and critical issues had often been determined by dangerously narrow majorities. Gradually it had become clear that some secret caucus was pursuing a consistent course with the firm intention of forcing Hamilton to resign. This attempt, having ended in failure, had been succeeded by a second attempt, the object of which was to tarnish his honour. The friends of the Secretary of the Treasury, stirred with indignation, had demanded a frank exposure of the hidden enemy; but in this they had been discouraged by their leader, who held that in the interests of the Union it was necessary for the moment, at all costs, to conceal the divided counsels of the Cabinet and the antagonism of the joint authors of the *Federalist*. Perhaps it would have been better had Hamilton continued of this mind for a twelvemonth longer; but patience under attack was not with him a natural quality, and the ingenious malice of his enemies was a remarkable thing even in the history of politics.[2]

Hamilton's view of the situation after the session had ended is set forth with his customary frankness in a private letter to Colonel Carrington.[3] He was then fully aware that

[1] 24th October 1791 to 8th May 1792.
[2] *e.g.* the St. Clair incident, *History*, iv. p. 416 and v. pp. 122-27.
[3] 26th May 1792, *Works*, ix. p. 513.

the obstruction of his measures and the attacks upon himself had not been mere casual explosions, but part of a pre-
concerted scheme. He had taken office against the advice
of his friends, confident that he would have the hearty
support of Madison, whom he knew, from Madison's own
assurances, to be in agreement with him upon all essential
points. Madison had been in favour of a funded debt, and
of the assumption of the state obligations. He had been
opposed on principle to discrimination and to repudiation in
that or in any other form. He had advised strongly that an
excise was a proper means of raising revenue. But from the
very beginning of the administration he seemed to have
gone back upon all his former opinions. Hamilton was surprised and chagrined, but nevertheless had received with
incredulity the tales of gossips who alleged a personal
animosity, and had refused to believe that so sincere a lover
of the Union could have been turned from his principles by a
crabbed jealousy. But after the work of last session it was
impossible to doubt any longer that Madison had exchanged
friendship for enmity, had thrown consistency overboard,
and had cast in his lot with the party which would have
gladly seen the *Federalist* burned by the common hangman.

It was clear also that Madison was co-operating day by
day with Jefferson. The similarity of the views put forward
by the Secretary of State at cabinet councils, with those put
forward simultaneously by the actual but unacknowledged
leader of the opposition in Congress, was too marked to be
the result of a mere accident. Jefferson's enmity was altogether unveiled. He held conversations with all and sundry
upon the iniquities of the Treasury policy. His particular
friends were the most active assailants of Hamilton's integrity
in public discussions and private talk. The virulence of
Freneau's paper was unceasing, and it was notorious that
Jefferson and Madison had been the promoters and were

still the patrons of this enterprise. In the whole of Madison's conduct there had been a more uniform and persevering opposition than Hamilton had been able to resolve into a sincere difference of opinion.[1] But even Madison's speeches in Congress afforded no adequate measure of his hostility. During the coarser and more violent attacks, as a rule, he had lain '*perdu*,' and had put up others endowed with a more reckless effrontery to do the dirtier portion of the work. On one occasion, however, he had departed from this prudent principle,[2] and had made a direct imputation of dishonesty against the Treasury.

Hamilton's letter goes on to enumerate his various disagreements with Jefferson and Madison since the inception of Washington's government. In all these disagreements the object of his adversaries had been to narrow the interpretation of the constitution and to abridge and curtail the federal power. In no case had they been able to achieve their ends, and Hamilton surmised that this constant current of success on the one side, and of defeat on the other, had made the opposition furious, and had produced a disposition to subvert their competitors, even at the expense of government.[3]

In conclusion, Hamilton pointed out the hollowness and insincerity of the clamours which had been raised against the tyranny of the central power. The real danger lay not in the possible suppression or extinction of the states, which were things beyond the wildest terrors, but in the preservation of the federal government which was engaged in a struggle for its very life. At every moment fresh attempts were being made with an untiring audacity to pare down the powers and whittle away the sovereignty of the Union. The constant attempts at encroachment on the part of the larger states were now becoming more and more difficult to with-

[1] *Works*, ix. p. 520.   [2] See *ante* p. 285.   [3] *Works*, ix. p. 530.

the mere fact of his survival compels a certain degree of
admiration.   Hamilton's popularity rose with the vehemence of the counterstroke. The Federalists were elated.
Washington, who vainly desired peace, was perturbed to the
point of remonstrating with both parties. The letters of
his two ministers in reply are worthy of consideration.
Hamilton is frank and fierce, but says he will endeavour
to comply—when he has finished with the business: like
some panting, victorious dog that is chidden by its master
for a street brawl. Jefferson answers at great length and
with a stammering affectation of serenity; as if he had
been in no wise ruffled,—a whine, a snarl and a great
flow of eloquence about his wrongs and his virtue.   It
has been doubted whether the controversy on Hamilton's
part was altogether dignified.   For the time it served its
purpose.   It was rough cudgel play; but it must be remembered that an outraged minister has no such safety-valve
in the United States as is provided by the British House of
Commons.   He is debarred from speechmaking, and has no
opportunity of defending himself in debate.   Under these
restrictions, to trounce a not too scrupulous adversary in
the newspapers is certainly excusable, and, according to
circumstances, it may even be good policy.

The history of the two sessions of Congress[1] which
followed upon these events is not a pleasing retrospect
either to the patriotic American or to the sanguine lover
of popular government. Hitherto the assault had been of
a somewhat general character. The demerits of Hamilton's
policy had been under review. Corruption had been freely
alleged, but the argument had depicted the Secretary of
the Treasury as the disdainful tempter, offering rosy-

---

[1] The second session of the second Congress (5th November 1792 to 3rd
March 1793), and the first session of the third Congress (2nd December 1793
to 9th June 1794).

cheeked apples to the lips of greedy followers. The new method was an accusation of personal dishonesty, veiled but unambiguous. A great concern was displayed for the fullest information with regard to the disbursements of the exchequer. A full explanation was required of this matter, a precise account of that one. The reports that were demanded covered the whole field of expenditure and finance since the Federal Government had come into existence. These demands were in themselves innuendos, and the multitude of the demands was designed to overpower the efforts of the responsible minister to reply to them, and to obfuscate the judgment of public opinion.

There is a dreary monotony in the records of Congress. Resolutions were moved and defeated. Reports were demanded and supplied. Committees inquired and reported. But the result was invariable. There was always an answer which left no possibility of doubt in the minds of those who were at the pains to consider it. Like a gambler who doubles his stake after each reverse of fortune, the opposition increased in violence as often as their charges were proved clearly to be calumny. Every fresh exposure made them more desperate. They never learned caution, and it must be admitted to their credit they never lost heart. Persistency in anything, even in calumny, has some hope of success if it is prepared, no matter how the luck runs, to double after every loss. The insensibility which refuses to be routed upon the proof of falsehood may commend itself in the long run merely as a good fighter; for a popular audience is apt upon occasions to be more interested in good fighting than in the pursuit of truth.

The hero of this period was Giles of Virginia, a preposterous, pugilistic character, to whom notoriety was much, and failure in calumny merely failure and not disgrace. Behind him we have a vision always of Madison with a

A.D.
1792–1793
Æt. 35-36

sponge, a basin and a towel. Madison does not cut a very dignified figure, but we excuse his solemn anxiety, for he had heavy wagers on the event. It was natural that he should nurse his 'fancy' with the most sedulous attention. He was not much of an ally, had little share in the glory of the encounter, but was reserved for the humiliation of defeat, in which the heroic Giles was unable fully to participate by reason of the grossness of his nature. Jefferson, in the meanwhile, hating controversy, shook his head; muttered suspicions to the President; averted his gaze from the eyes of men, and studied his square toes, while the mischief proceeded which he had so ingeniously set to work.

In spite of his violence, his reckless disregard of truth, his unconcern for the feelings of his enemies, Giles does not offend the moral sense to the same degree as his employers offend it. It is difficult to think of him without a smile, and the smile is not altogether unfriendly. He was a squat, untidy, blackavised little man, with a prodigious vitality, a quick eye and a shrewd instinct in a melée; a stout fellow with loud lungs. In a combat he was entirely without scruples, and, allowing for certain pasteboard conventions of rhetoric, equally devoid of highflown professions. Politics to him was a mere game, and the pleasure he derived from it was not the sordid results of success, but mainly the joyful exercise of his talents. He went into Congress as a man enters the ring, and finding himself there he hit out just as hard as he could. The more eyes he blacked, the more noses he caused to bleed, the more complacent he became. He did not rate himself highly, except upon his particular gift in the matter of the 'knock-out.' His attitude towards Jefferson and Madison was a mixture of good-humoured condescension and absurd respect—the attitude of the prize-fighter to the 'toffs' who have put their money on him. His attacks were in the brutal manner, his violence was outrageous, but he does not produce the impression of malice. He was vain, and Jefferson, for the time being, flattered his egotism. He was fluent, and Madison guided the torrent of his eloquence. Quick in mean manœuvres, shrewd in small issues, unscrupulous, reckless, persistent and 'game,' he combined the sharpness of the old-fashioned country attorney with the hardness of the old fashioned fox-hunting squire. No fence was too high, no hedge too thick, no joke too broad, no blow too heavy, no plea too desperate. He had none of the finer feelings, and, to do him justice, he believed that all mankind were made in his own image. He was a gamester in politics, but it is not to be denied that he was passionately attached to his own state of Virginia, and that he sincerely detested the constitution with the whole force of his nature.

During the session which began in the autumn of 1792 and ended in the spring of 1793, the energies of Giles were kept fully employed. Speaking generally, all measures which emanated from the Treasury, even the most formal and necessary provisions, were opposed and obstructed. Shortly after Congress assembled Hamilton introduced proposals of a far-reaching character for the reduction of the debt. Finding upon every side the evidences of a remarkable prosperity, he considered himself well justified in calling upon the country to bear a somewhat heavier taxation to diminish the national indebtedness. The credit of the United States with European bankers stood at a remarkable height. Loans had been issued at Amsterdam during the autumn which bore interest at the low rate of four per cent.[1] But in spite of these favourable conditions the Democrats, unwilling that Hamilton should have the renown of so conspicuous a reform, encountered his sugges-

[1] *History*, v. p. 109

tions with a determined opposition. The discussion, by one means or another, was put off from week to week, until the expiration of Congress put an end to the opportunity. It was an extraordinary spectacle. Hamilton, who had been reproached with the utmost bitterness for his supposed desire to perpetuate the debt, was now seen exerting all his influence to discharge it, and did not shrink from the odium of new taxes to attain his object. His opponents, on the other hand, who had clamoured so loudly against the debt, resisted every measure proposed to carry their own recommendations into effect, and offered no substitute that would have met the case.[1]

Immediately after Christmas, Giles and another were put up to ask for statements showing how the moneys derived from the various Dutch loans had been applied, for further statements covering the whole field of borrowing, and for returns of all the employees of the Treasury with their salaries and other particulars. Within ten days all this information was supplied.[2] Then the Senate became anxious for information about the National Bank, the appropriations of surplus revenue, and a variety of kindred matters. The following day its curiosity was fully satisfied.[3] Finally, in the fourth week of January, Giles opened his general assault. Taking for his text a purely technical point as to the authority under which certain foreign loans had been raised, he called for five reports to be made by the Treasury.[4] The speech of Giles admitted of no misunderstanding. 'Candour induced him' to make it quite clear that he accused the Secretary of the Treasury of malversation. He definitely alleged that the accounts submitted by Hamilton to Congress a few weeks earlier had been deliberately cooked, and that there was in fact an unaccounted for balance, amount-

[1] *History*, v. pp. 144-46.
[2] *Ibid.* v. pp. 174-77.
[3] *Ibid.* v. p. 177.
[4] *Ibid.* v. pp. 178-200.

ing to a million and a half of dollars. The Democratic press hastened to join in the chorus, teemed with articles upon corruption, and even pointed to the President as an accomplice in the frauds.

The campaign, it is needless to say, had been planned by Jefferson. He was anxious to bring pressure to bear upon Washington, and to break up the alliance which so far had defeated all his efforts. The resolutions which Giles moved were drafted by Madison in his own hand.[1] Hamilton, weary but imperturbable, issued his instructions, and the Federalists joined with the Democrats in voting for the fullest inquiry.

Hamilton's organisation and system served him well. The Treasury and its chief had to work for a month long after hours, but by the third week of February, Congress had before it a full statement of all receipts and disbursements since the beginning of the national government. The accounts were stated so clearly and simply that it was impossible to mistake their import. The answer to the opposition was cold, businesslike and complete. In so orderly a proceeding we do not look for genius, but only for lucidity. The lucidity of Hamilton was a thing to be dreaded. In his hands it became a weapon of destruction. His demeanour was quiet and formal as he proceeded to explain the system of his accounts and vindicate the integrity of his procedure; but indirectly, and apparently without resentment, certainly without temper, he explained the motives of the inquiry, and exposed the tactics of his enemies.

Hamilton as a controversialist had an altogether exceptional gift for the counterstroke. Regarded merely as a fighter on behalf of his own honour, he is far more admirable in defence than when he delivers the attack. Eighteen

---

[1] They still exist in the State Department, *History*, v. p. 18

months before, he had fallen upon Jefferson and driven him moaning, out of his entanglements; but that was a clumsy achievement by comparison.   In attack he had a tendency to get too much heated; to hit too hard and too promiscuously; to rely too much on his muscles, too little on his eyes; but in defence he is consummate. Quiet, and grave, and self-possessed, he yields nothing and overlooks nothing; but as the attack pauses and begins to reel, he steps forward in the same quiet, grave and self-possessed manner, without an appearance of haste, or enmity, or effort, and places his blows so gently that it is hard to believe he is putting forth his full strength.   Every touch is a shock, and the end of his enemies is ignominious disaster.

The rout was completed when the Democrats played into his hands by a false manœuvre. Anxious that Hamilton should not be formally acquitted, anxious also that if possible the charges should be kept hanging over his head while the elections for the new Congress were in progress, the indefatigable Giles was put up to move nine resolutions of censure which it was intended should be debated until the term of the second Congress had elapsed,[1] but not put to the vote. In this scheme he was defeated by the sudden outburst of feeling not only in the House itself, but out of doors. At the last moment the Democrats wished to withdraw the resolutions, but the triumphant Federalists refused to allow their opponents this means of retreat. The nine accusations were accordingly carried to the vote, and Madison and Giles kept one another company in a series of ignominious minorities, as a frail curate and a drunken roisterer might keep one another company in the stocks after a Saturday night's carouse.

The next session was a dreary echo of its predecessor. The only important change in the situation was that in the

[1] 4th March 1793.

lower House the Democrats, thanks to the French Revolution, held a clear majority. But as regarded the attacks upon Hamilton, the course of events was a dull repetition of the manœuvres of the year before.

Hamilton's short letter to the Speaker gave a formal challenge: "It is known that in the last session certain ' questions were raised respecting my conduct in office, ' which, though decided in a manner most satisfactory ' to me, were nevertheless, unavoidably, from the lateness ' of the period when they were set on foot, so accelerated ' in the issue, as to have given occasion to a suggestion ' that there was not time for a due examination: un- ' willing to leave the matter on such a footing, I have con- ' cluded to request the House of Representatives, as I now ' do, that a new inquiry may without delay be instituted ' in some mode, the most effectual for an accurate and ' thorough investigation; and I will add, that the more ' comprehensive it is, the more agreeable will it be to me.

'I cannot, however, but take the liberty of assuring the ' House that a like plan to that which was pursued in the ' last session will never answer the purpose of a full and ' complete inquiry, while it would lay on me a burthen, with ' which neither a proper discharge of the current duties of my ' office nor the present state of my health is compatible. The ' unfavourable effect upon the business of the department ' of the very considerable portion of my time which was engrossed by the inquiry of the last session has not yet ' entirely ceased." [1]

This letter was written upon the 16th of December, and the challenge was immediately taken up. Giles, loyal to his employers, and unaffected by the ruin of his previous efforts, made a gallant attempt to pursue the charges of corruption, founding his arguments upon the testimony of a clerk

[1] *Works*, iii. p. 179.

who had been dismissed from the Treasury. His success in this endeavour ended with the appointment of a select committee to inquire. Upon the 29th of the same month its report was issued. The conduct of the Secretary was justified at all points, and by a body in which his opponents held a majority against him, the charges were pronounced to be 'wholly illiberal and groundless.'[1]

Towards the end of February, Giles returned to the attack. A committee was appointed to inquire into the conduct of the Treasury. Although two-thirds of this committee were members of the opposition, and none of Hamilton's more capable supporters were chosen to serve upon it, but only new members filled with awe of their more famous colleagues, it is improbable that the sordid labour was undertaken with any great hope of success. After an exhaustive and hostile inquiry this packed tribunal was obliged, like all its predecessors, to report not only a complete exculpation of the minister, but praise for his loyal and upright service. Congress, therefore, had no alternative but to accept this verdict without a dissenting voice.[2] " It was a cruel thing ' in Congress," Colonel Heth wrote to Hamilton, "and ' somewhat unprecedented, I presume, to oblige your per-' secutors and prosecutors to sit as your judges; and what ' was still more ill-natured, to compel them to make a report ' by which they were obliged to convict you of purity of ' conduct, unshaken integrity, and a constant watchfulness ' over the public interest."[3]

But still the opposition to all Treasury measures upon whatsoever principle was unbroken. Everything was contested, and yet in this assembly where the Federalists were in a minority the essential things were in the end accomplished. "You are strange fellows," wrote a good-natured Democrat to one of his opponents; "formerly you did what

---

[1] *History*, v. p. 425.   [2] *Ibid.* vi. p. 33   [3] *Ibid.* vi. p. 34.

' you chose with a small majority; now we have a great ' majority and can do nothing. You have baffled every one ' of our plans."[1] It was not a matter of tactics. The opposition was forced to yield in the end always by the manifest good sense of the proposals of their great adversary.

When the same Congress met again in the autumn of 1794, Hamilton notified the Speaker of his intention to retire early in the new year, in order that any inquiries into his conduct which might be deemed necessary should be set on foot without delay. But by this time even Giles was surfeited with defeat, and Madison was too much relieved at the thought of Hamilton's withdrawal from office to engage in any new intrigues. Hamilton's plans for providing further support to the public credit were of course opposed, but the opposition was perfunctory. In the end his project for the redemption of the debt was carried, and on the 31st of January 1795 he retired from office. "In every ' relation which you have borne to me," Washington wrote upon this occasion, "I have found that my confidence in ' your talents, exertions and integrity has been *well placed.* ' I the more freely render this testimony of my approbation, ' because I speak from opportunities of information, which ' *cannot deceive me,* and which furnish satisfactory proof of ' your title to public regard."

The opposition to Hamilton during the period under review had been the extreme of political hatred. His measures were attacked in the first place, his character in the second. With the principle of the former no fault can be found except the fault of bad judgment; nor must the spirit in which it was pursued be judged too harshly. Patriotism has a vague boundary; and if the Democrats were frequently found far beyond the debatable land, they were not different in this particular from

[1] *History,* v. p. 588.

political parties all the world over. Misrepresentation of
the meaning and effect of measures, misrepresentation of
the motives which produced them, are conditions unfortunate enough, but inevitable, of all government by party. A
strong minister pursuing a clear policy must be prepared for
such assaults, and his admirers will do well to pass them by
without too much emphasis.

But the second method falls under a different category.
It is bad leadership that assails the private honour of an
opponent, as Jefferson did, relying upon the abstruse-
ness of accounts and the confusion of the subject, when
debated in heat before a popular audience, to make it
impossible for his opponent to get clear away. He says
in his memoirs that he believed Hamilton to be a man of
unblemished personal integrity,[1] and there is no reason to
doubt that in this case he was speaking the truth. Indeed,
to any one in close personal relations with the Secretary of
the Treasury, however hostile his disposition, this fact was too
obvious for argument. But none the less it was Jefferson who
launched the charges of corruption against his colleague, in
the same manner as he had attacked his measures—through
the mouths of his well-drilled partisans. When Hamilton
rolled up this furious assault with the same crushing
disaster to his opponents that he had dealt out to their
previous more legitimate efforts; when, to the amazement
even of his friends, he so disentangled both accounts and
charges that plain men not only escaped from the confusion, but perceived that it had been intended, and the end
to which it had been devised, the reaction for the time
being against the opposition and their leader was sharp
and scornful; and had it not been for other considerations,
which will be dealt with in the following chapters, it must
have been overwhelming. Hamilton's defence of his per-

[1] Ford's *Jefferson*, i. p. 166.

sonal honour, no less than his defence of his national policy, was complete. At no single point was he touched. The victory exacted enormous labours. It damaged his health and interfered seriously with his administrative work. But the result of the one is as satisfactory to those who hold his memory in respect as the result of the other was fortunate for his country. In an age when the charge of corruption was the commonest, and as a rule the most reliable weapon of attack against a minister, Hamilton resisted with success every effort to attach the shadow of a suspicion to the uprightness of his administration. But, unfortunately, the very commonness of the charge made men overlook the recklessness and the malice which alleged it without just cause. Hamilton, indeed, came out of the struggle unscathed, and for the moment a hero; but no infamy attached, as it would have done to-day, to his accusers. Jefferson and Madison did not, strange as it may appear, suffer in their reputations as honourable citizens. Giles continued unashamed to be a great figure in debate. Full justice was not done at the time, great injustice was done in the years which followed, and only in comparatively recent days have the actors in this drama come to be rated at their true values.

So in the earliest years the great constitutional doctrine that it is the duty of an opposition to oppose was fully grasped. These heroes of freedom were faithful to the logic of this principle, if faithless in later days to the logic of their own precepts. They had condemned the funding and assumption of the debts because they placed a burden on posterity, because the idea of a permanent federal debt was inseparable from corruption, and because they were charged with a rate of interest which it was possible to represent as intolerable. When Hamilton, finding the credit of the country good beyond his expectations, its

wealth rapidly expanding, and confidence secured both at
home and abroad, proposed to extend the operation of the
sinking fund, to borrow at a lower rate of interest, to increase taxation so as to pay off the heavy-interest, short-
loan stock and to redeem the whole debt at an earlier date,
the same opponents, with different cries, condemned the
proposal and secured its defeat.

Within a decade the opposition came into power, holding it for many years without a break. Jefferson, Madison
and Monroe, three of Hamilton's most relentless critics,
were presidents in succession, each for a double term of
office. But under their rule Hamilton's organisation of the
Treasury was preserved. His financial methods were maintained. His system of audit, which had been derided as the
intended accomplice of corruption, was accepted as a fit safeguard of the exchequer. His principles of national credit
and taxation were adopted and afterwards extended. Even
the bank charter after remarkable vicissitudes was renewed.
All the main pillars of his hated administration were kept
intact, partly because no one was found bold enough to
change them, but chiefly for the reason that there had never
existed, except among the ignorant, any belief that they were
fraught with danger.

CHAPTER IV

Foreign Dangers

IT appeared to Hamilton, taking stock of the situation in
the third year of his office,[1] that the unexpected was in
course of happening, and that the plan of his campaign must
be changed accordingly. To his credit stood the policy of
the Treasury, organised, in working order and successful far

---

[1] January 1792.

beyond even his own sanguine anticipations. Sound finance, the foundation of the independence of states, was now likely to maintain itself, and to strengthen its tradition year by year. The commercial policy was before the world for discussion; enthusiastically approved by some, vigorously denounced by others. To carry it, however, would have taken more time and effort than had been necessary in the case of its predecessor. All political conditions had hardened in the meanwhile, and any proposals which Hamilton might now have introduced were certain to be opposed by the whole weight of an organised party.

It is a fair question—Why did Hamilton leave the idea of his commercial policy as a kind of legacy? Why was the thing not accomplished during his administration? If he truly loved his idea, why was it set on one side to be tardily undertaken by a third generation? He was an indefatigable minister against whom no resistance could make head. Had he chosen to urge it, surely success must have ensued? But he did not choose to urge it, and from this some people have argued that he came to think better of his first opinions.

The true answer is somewhat different. The French Revolution upset many well-laid plans. The stately policies of the Old World were tripped up and stumbled; the eager projects of the New were arrested by it. All the nations, except the Chinese, held their breath and, like men in an earthquake, waited with their hands on the latches to make fast, to undo, or to escape.

Pitt dreamed a great dream as to how he might reap in peace what his father had sowed in war. The consolidation of an empire, the development of its resources, were the objects which attracted his ambition; but the realisation of this ideal required as its condition a Britain aloof and unconcerned in the affairs of its neighbours. Against

A.D. 1792
Æt. 35

kings and the old diplomacy, had these institutions continued to exist, he was fully secured. But the dynasties began to topple headlong, and the new systems which took their place disturbed all calculations. A great peace minister was therefore forced against his will to become a war minister. The defence of the empire, and not its development, was his unexpected task; and the boundaries which he had never wished to widen were set further and further over the face of the earth.

Hamilton no less than Pitt desired to give himself wholly to the task of husbanding the national estate and gathering in the harvests of prosperity. He aimed at being independent of his neighbours and at peace with them. It may be believed that he cursed the French Revolution as a fisherman curses a gale which suddenly opens upon him just as he has overtaken the shoal. The energies of both statesmen were diverted from a fruitful object to a barren defence, necessary, but in their eyes most lamentable. There is no difficulty in understanding the disappointment of such a transfer, though we recognise clearly a fertility in their efforts which the dust and heat obscured to some extent from the actors themselves. The tradition of Pitt is not sterile, and although Hamilton was forced to abandon his vision of industrial development, he has earned the credit of establishing the principles of foreign policy over a period which has not yet ended.

The quality of permanence is the most remarkable virtue in Hamilton's statesmanship. What he did at his leisure after much planning, as well as what he did hastily under great pressure, work which he imposed upon himself because he loved it, and irksome labours forced upon him by events, have the same character. They endure. Men, so far, have been unable to alter them. Enemies had but a short time to wait for the opportunity. They came eager and exultant, with axe and crowbar, furiously raging, but hardly a stone of the edifice was displaced.

In the making of the constitution, in the establishment of public credit, in laying down the plain rules of reason for the relations of the United States with the outside world— in each case we find the same quality of permanence. The cause is not difficult to trace. Hamilton knew what he wished to accomplish. He knew what forces could be employed for the purpose. He valued them accurately, and so disposed and arranged them, that out of its own vigour each gave to the others its due support. He built like a good bridge-maker, so that the stress confirmed and strengthened the fabric. This is only possible to a man who has the instinct of reality; who patiently considers things, not as he wishes them to be, but as they are; who works not with words, but with actual forces. A phrase-maker is often serviceable in a work of destruction. He is of considerable use when it is a question of clearing out slums and rookeries; but as a builder he is of little value, except occasionally to sing cheerfully while the other men are at work.

To the opposition the French Revolution came as a god-send. The ferment which this event excited in men's minds, the difficulties of government in steering through the typhoon, afforded an opportunity of putting a term to the triumphal progress of Hamilton's administration. At a time when all men are furiously taking sides upon the affairs of a stranger, rulers have commonly found it hard to keep a true course. While one set of partisans denounces their lukewarm apathy to noble sentiments, the other set contemptuously derides their timid respect for popular fanaticism. In such circumstances an astute opposition finds its most favourable opportunity, and the new Democratic party was accordingly highly favoured by events.

Everything turns, at this critical moment, upon the relations of the United States with Britain on the one hand, and with France on the other. From 1783 to 1793, from the Peace of Versailles to the declaration of war by France against Europe, the tendency of American policy had been a vivacious unfriendliness to Britain and a sedate attachment to France.

The legacy of the War of Independence was a strong resentment towards the mother country. The British view of the matter was that we had been beaten, but that the beating had not changed the face of affairs to any serious extent. Our position with regard to the great European powers was hardly affected by it. We had not put forth our full strength. A remote dependency had broken away, and there was an end of the matter. It was annoying that we should have lost our colonies, but a naval defeat in the narrow seas would have been a matter of incomparably greater importance. Americans, on the other hand, were exasperated because Britain would not treat its own calamity in a more serious spirit, and because King George's cabinet, until the Union, six years later, made difficulties about accepting the thirteen states as a real nation in spite of their famous victory. An aristocratic government, polite and correct, showed by numerous indications that it did not intend to deal with them as with an equal. To this grievance was added the injury inflicted by the commercial regulations of Britain during the period of disunion. Neither of these causes of anger was serious. A firm union was the obvious cure for both, and almost as soon as Washington's administration was formed the remedy began to work. The thing which really mattered was the non-fulfilment of the treaty of peace. Britain still held the frontier posts, alleging as her justification the breach of faith in regard to the payment of British debts, and the ill-treatment of the loyalists.

To France, on the other hand, there was an attachment, but until 1791 or even later, it was an attachment of a political rather than of a sentimental kind.   King Louis xvi. had been an ally in the past because an alliance had suited his own interests.   That fact was clearly understood by American statesmen, who considered that France was likely to continue her alliance in the future for the same reason.   But gratitude to France was never the attitude of the government of the states towards the government of Paris during this period. Gratitude was not due, seeing that the service rendered had not been in any sense disinterested.

Consequently, until the spring of 1792, when the Revolution was in full blast, such a sentiment would have been ridiculed had it ever been seriously urged.   Americans, while the idea of democracy was still in the background, viewed the assistance which had been given by Louis xvi. in its true light.   His government had no affection for the rebellious colonists, but merely desired to distress a dangerous rival. The conduct of France during the negotiations for peace had been viewed none too favourably by the new Republic, and, it must be added, the conduct of the new Republic had been viewed none too favourably by the ancient monarchy.

The ending of the war left no debt outstanding as between nations, except an account which was recorded in dollars, and this, thanks to Hamilton, was in process of being rapidly wiped out.   France had aided the American arms, and her ample reward had been the wounds thereby inflicted upon her European enemy.   The treaty of alliance was complete within itself.   Its terms constituted a fair bargain.   In case the American possessions of King Louis were attacked without provocation, the states were bound to come to his aid; and in case the United States were menaced in their freedom or possessions, France was to render a similar service.[1]

---

[1] *History,* ii. p. 417.

Therefore, though it is true that, during the ten years A.D. 1792
following the signature of peace, Americans regarded Ær. 35
Britain with dislike, it is altogether untrue that they
regarded France with any emotional fervour. Until the
French Revolution brought certain ideas into prominence,
'gratitude' to France never assumed importance as a
popular cry.

Beyond this there was a legal question. Louis was dead
and his system was ended. That in itself was enough to
have done away all obligations under his treaty with Congress. But to make the case clearer, his successors in the
government had passed the scythe over all his promises.
The Revolution had denounced and solemnly torn up all
the treaties made by the fallen monarchy.[1] Nothing stood.
A new reckoning was opened, and all the old accounts were
sponged off the slate. And it was only after these events
had occurred that the treaty between France and the United
States was invoked with frenzied zeal as a holy and binding
arrangement. It was then claimed by eloquent people on
both sides of the Atlantic that the American treaty had
been impliedly excepted from the massacre of the old
diplomacy; that it was a debt between nations and not
between rulers; that the conditions of a defensive war and
danger to the American possessions of France were to be
ignored upon a generous interpretation; and that, in plain
words, if France chose to go into war with any adversary or
upon any pretext, the United States were bound in honour
to follow her to the ends of the earth.

At the conclusion of the War of Independence, Hamilton,
as we have seen, pressed upon his countrymen, in season and
out of season, the sanctity of their treaty obligations. The
principle of loyal observance of engagements was a fundamental article of his creed. The obligations incurred

[1] *History*, v. p. 239.

'for ever' under the original treaty with France, when French aid was the only hope of final success in the struggle against Britain, were no less and no more sacred in his eyes than the obligations incurred towards Britain when the treaty of peace was signed; for valuable consideration had been given in both cases. He viewed the situation, however, without malice or excitement, and arrived early at the conclusion that circumstances, which were by no means unlikely to occur, might easily 'effect a revolution in the state of our foreign politics.'[1]

To France under the monarchy, her alliance with Spain was a far more precious asset than her alliance with the United States. If these alliances at any time should prove incompatible, the ministers of King Louis would never hesitate for a moment which to choose. The European situation must necessarily be regarded before the American. Nor was it unlikely that such a conflict would arise between the treaty obligations of France with Spain on the one hand, and with the Union on the other; for, of all nations, Spain was the most probable antagonist of the Union. The dangers caused by the troubles with Britain on the Canadian border were trivial as compared with the menace from the South. Spain held a strong position at the mouth of the Mississippi. She claimed the right to control the navigation of that river, and if her pretensions could have been enforced, the development of the states would have been throttled. She claimed, moreover, all the wide but undefined territories lying between the western bank of the Mississippi and the Pacific coast.

It was clear to Hamilton's mind that sooner or later this conflict of interests would have to be settled, and it seemed probable that the mode of settlement would be a war. In such case France would be compelled to choose which of

[1] *History*, iv. p. 194.

her allies she would retain, and it was unreasonable to
suppose that she would sacrifice the more valuable of the
two.   On the other hand, if war broke out, the aid of
Britain would be as serviceable against Spain as the aid
of France had in former times been serviceable against
Britain.   Nor was it likely, in the circumstances which
have been imagined, that it would be difficult to obtain the
co-operation of King George's government.

Hamilton was therefore anxious, while maintaining friendly
relations with France, to cultivate good, if not precisely
friendly, relations with Britain.   On commercial as well as
on political grounds he was eager to arrive at a good understanding, for he saw clearly the enormous benefit which
would accrue to the states by a treaty to facilitate trade.   The
first step towards this end was to get rid of the disputes,
charges and countercharges which had arisen out of the
treaty of peace.   It was of the first importance that the
atmosphere of hostility and distrust should be changed, so
that the negotiation might be undertaken in a frank and
reasonable spirit.   Hamilton had the lowest opinion of
provocative methods even in dealing with his enemies.
When it was a question of promoting neighbourly relations,
provocation seemed to him a form of insanity.   While he
would not have hesitated to adopt commercial regulations
that would have benefited his own country at the expense
of Britain, he was utterly opposed to the popular demand
for legislation which would have injured and irritated
Britain without bringing any advantage to the states.   To
Madison's proposals[1] for an invidious tariff which would
have injured both Britain and the States for the benefit of
France and Holland, he was even more strongly opposed, and
by his influence with the senate he succeeded in securing
their defeat.

[1] May 1789, *History*, iv. p. 7.

The sound sense of Hamilton's policy seems obvious enough to-day, but it is not difficult to enter into the feelings of those who held a different view. Their judgment was clouded by the memories of the war. To recompense the ally and to injure the enemy appeared in the temper of the times a very natural and proper course of action. Even Washington was at first inclined to look with favour upon Madison's proposals.

Union and the establishment of a federal government had changed the attitude of the British Cabinet towards the States. Britain was not slow in testifying a respect for the new order which it had denied to the old. This change of attitude was not more remarkable in the case of our own country than in the case of others; but as our enmity or friendship was, in commercial matters at all events, immeasurably more important, the contrast was more remarked. The success of Hamilton's financial policy in raising the credit of the nation produced as great and favourable an impression in London as in Amsterdam or Paris. In the autumn of 1791 Hammond was accredited as the first British minister to the United States. A few months later an American minister was sent to England.

In these events Hamilton saw a favourable opportunity for breaking down the ancient prejudices. But Jefferson, in whose department the matter lay, held opposite opinions. He had no wish for friendly relations with Britain, but, on the contrary, desired, as he states quite clearly, to keep 'alive an altercation' with that power.[1] In all likelihood he sincerely believed this to be the best means of inducing Britain to deliver up the frontier posts which she held as hostages for the fulfilment of the terms of peace; but if so, he misjudged the conditions. For Britain was incomparably less

[1] *History*, v. p. 8.

inconvenienced than the States by the non-settlement of the
differences. The matters of dispute were so remote that
they easily passed out of recollection. If London merchants
were aware in a dim fashion that the treaty of peace had not
been carried into effect, they were also sensible that, thanks
to the hitch, they enjoyed a very practical benefit in the
monopoly of the fur trade, which would cease so soon as the
frontier posts were given up. In the States, on the other
hand, the disadvantages of the situation were felt keenly, and
the whole problem, with its annoyances and humiliations,
was viewed at much closer range. The diplomatic position
of the Americans was a disadvantageous one, for the important reason that they were impatient while Britain was
indifferent. The right means of adjustment was to create
an atmosphere in which both parties could come together
good-temperedly to remove a serious danger.

Jefferson's diplomacy was bad because he misjudged the
immediate interests of the two countries. It was also bad
because he allowed his personal ties with a certain section of
Parisian society to colour his whole view of the situation.
In Hamilton's opinion, both Jefferson and Madison were
radically unsound and dangerous in regard to foreign politics.
"They have a womanish attachment to France, and a
' womanish resentment against Great Britain. They would
' draw us into the closest embrace of the former, and involve
' us in all the consequences of her politics; and they would
' risk the peace of the country in their endeavours to keep us
' at the greatest possible distance from the latter."[1] If these
gentlemen were left free to pursue their own course, 'there
would be, in less than six months, an open war between the
United States and Great Britain.'[2]

Throughout the spring and summer of 1792 we find
Hamilton constantly pleading for a candid, good-tempered,

[1] Hamilton to Carrington, 26th May 1792, *Works*, ix. p. 527.   [2] *Ibid.*

businesslike attitude.[1] He desired a commercial treaty with Britain which, in the circumstances, would have been more productive of benefits than commercial treaties with all the rest of the world. But Jefferson, and not he, was foreign minister. A confused thinker with a settled purpose is one of the most formidable opponents. Jefferson was constantly overruled by the cabinet, but unfortunately no power could take the 'atmosphere' out of his department. The temper of the discussion was in his hands so long as he was allowed to retain his office. It was comparatively easy to force an alteration of the purport of a despatch, but less easy to introduce a more cordial spirit when the medium of negotiation was his rasping phrases.

The progress of the French Revolution was a heavy handicap to Hamilton's efforts towards a good understanding with Britain. The popular sentiment had hitherto been dislike of Britain for her supposed hostility to the interests of the States. But now affection for France trumped up a plea of gratitude, and Britain, who was correctly surmised to be on the brink of war with her European neighbour, was hated with a much greater fervour for the sake of France than even from the memories of the War of Independence, or for her retention of the frontier posts.

To this gospel of unreality Washington, the fortunate inheritor of the temperament of an English squire, was as deaf as the uncharmed adder; but to Hamilton, cursed with the *perfervidum ingenium Scotorum*, the eloquent and invulnerable confusion was a maddening opponent. As the crisis developed he concentrated his efforts upon foreign affairs. Jefferson, in his ministerial capacity, became a reluctant conduit for the decisions of the cabinet. These decisions were in the main Hamilton's. Jefferson did what he could—grumbled, and delayed, and obstructed in council;

[1] E.g. *History*, v. pp. 1-20.

foamed over in indignant private correspondence, which was intended to have a wide publicity. But Hamilton's main ends were achieved, and his opponent was forced in the end, willy-nilly, to register his decrees.

The outburst of popular feeling in favour of France was the result of two sentiments, neither of which was well grounded in the facts. The American people were stirred with gratitude on account of an imaginary generosity and were flattered by an imaginary imitation. In the crisis of their own fortunes they had derived efficient help from Frenchmen and from French policy. Many persons held that the alliance had provided what was absolutely indispensable for the achievement of independence. And now, some ten years later, it appeared to the ordinary citizen that the glorious example of the American Rebellion was the type and model of the French Revolution. The spirit that animated the philosophers and the 'speculatists' was acknowledged, somewhat too readily, for the same goddess who had presided over the highly practical deliberations of Philadelphia.

The situation is crammed with paradox. The alliance with the rebellious subjects of King George the Third was the royal policy of King Louis the Sixteenth, whom the Revolution held a prisoner, covered with insults and was shortly to decapitate. The active sympathy and personal sacrifice in the cause of the States came from the aristocrats, from Lafayette and from others, some of whom the Revolution sent fleeing for their lives, while others less fortunate it put to death. What had benefited the colonists, if we may borrow the felicitous phrase which Jefferson subsequently adopted to describe the most unfortunate of monarchs, had been the cold-blooded calculation of 'a human tiger.' What had comforted their hearts had been the 'high-flown chivalry' of comrades in arms, to whom France now offered the generous choice of furtive exile, the dungeon, or the guillotine. The debt of American gratitude was due, if at all, to a king and his nobles, but by an effort of the popular imagination the bill was made payable to the assassins of the true creditors.

The resemblance of the National Assembly to the Convention of Philadelphia is visible only to the eye of faith, gazing over a thousand leagues of ocean. To the cool observer, untouched by cynicism or sentiment, the two assemblages stand out in the most remarkable contrast both in methods and results. In the one case there was a competition with a gallery for judges:—limelight, rhetoric, general ideas, Rights of Man, paper constitutions, quack prescriptions, applause, heat and chaos. In the other there were closed doors, practical speech, disagreement, compromise and a working plan. It needed a superlative degree of self-deception to perceive any imitation, conscious or unconscious, by which it was possible to be flattered.

Yet if it happens that men are in the mood to display gratitude, skilful politicians, interested in fanning their emotions, will never find any serious difficulty in making a respectable bonfire with worse materials than the superficialities of resemblance that lay to Jefferson's hand. His forces were strengthened by the fanaticism of the phrasemonger. Finance and commerce he did not understand; but in 'general principles' he was an expert. The popular enthusiasm was duly fed with literature and speeches. A new edition of Tom Paine was brought out as an antidote to John Adams, who had propounded the sturdy view that France for the moment was little better than a rubbish-heap. The government was blamed for its coldness. The growing distrust of the Federalist party towards France was ascribed to their vicious inclination towards royalty. The judicious neutrality of Washington was

explained by the malign, hypnotic influence of Hamilton. So
the tide rose, tubs were thumped, banquets held, toasts drunk,
the tricolour became fashionable, newspapers indulged in
dithyrambic prose and doggerel, and Jefferson all the time
sat writing his forty-five thousand letters and guiding the
storm.

CHAPTER V

The French Revolution and the Declaration of Neutrality

THE opinions of Hamilton and Jefferson with regard to the
French Revolution afford a remarkable contrast. No other
occasion shows a sharper difference between the insight of
the two men into the causes and consequences which are
the business of statesmen.

Than Jefferson, no man out of France ever gave himself
greater airs of knowledge. He was a sort of godfather to
the convulsion. His official career in Paris had lasted from
the middle of 1784 to the end of 1789. When he arrived,
the monarchy seemed firmly established. Before he left,
the Bastille had fallen. His opportunities for observation
were altogether exceptional, and yet there was hardly an
event in all the startling series which he foresaw, or for
which he was prepared.

He undertook a famous journey through the French
provinces, in the course of which, while pursuing the most
admirable methods, he arrived at no suspicion of the storm
that was brewing. His admirers have praised his practical
shrewdness, as described in his own narrative. He invaded
the privacy of the peasants, supped their coarse broth,
tasted their black bread, questioned them beside their
own hearths, turned over their bedding when they were
looking the other way, and by every means that occurred
to him investigated the conditions of their existence. But

although he practised the methods of common sense, he arrived at nothing worth finding out. He noted never a sign of approaching disaster; thought the peasants in certain parts were not so well off as in others; compared them favourably with their fellows in Italy; was of opinion that things would be very much better if their leases were longer; moralised at considerable length upon general topics, and ended his expedition over the crust of lava completely satisfied that no aristocrat would ever have seen into the heart of things as he had done. There can be nothing but praise for his methods. His freedom from disdain, from class prejudice, from pedantry, was admirable. His easy familiarity makes a pleasant picture; but there is the end of the matter. It is merely the idyl of a virtuous citizen holidaymaking. There was no discovery. And yet he started upon his tour in the month following the first Assembly of Notables, at which he had been present, and ended it only two years before the fall of the Bastille.

Jefferson was in Paris during July 1789; but in the events that were taking place around him, in the bloodshed, in 'the leading in triumph' of King Louis, he heard no tremendous mutterings. The situation was difficult, and in a sense dangerous, but to his hopeful mind it was not beyond solution by maxims. So far as his notes on France have a real human interest, it is purely as a record of the gossip of the court, the tattle of political intrigue, the entertaining superficialities. When he came to examine matters of a different order he was blind. The profounder movements were concealed from his gaze. He neither understood the nature of the passions that were wrenching at the masonry, nor the value of the blocks that were being angrily torn out. His philosophy entirely misconceived the fabric of society, and to the end he remained confident of a bloodless amelioration, not of social conditions, but of the forms of government.

Hamilton had a truer perception. In a letter to Lafayette in the same year, but before the news of July[1] had reached America, he writes:—" If your affairs still go well when this ' reaches you, you will ask why this foreboding of ill, when all ' the appearances have been so much in your favour. I will ' tell you. I dread disagreements among those who are now ' united (which will be likely to be improved by the adverse ' party) about the nature of your constitution; I dread the ' vehement character of your people, whom I fear you may ' find it more easy to bring on, than to keep within proper ' bounds after you have put them in motion; I dread the ' interested refractoriness of your nobles, who cannot be ' gratified, and who may be unwilling to submit to the ' necessary sacrifices. And I dread the reveries of your ' philosophic politicians, who appear in the moment to have ' great influence, and who, being mere speculatists, may aim ' at more refinement than suits either with human nature or ' the composition of your nation."[2]

This is no gibing of a partisan, but the high seriousness of a wellwisher. Lafayette and Hamilton had been loyal and affectionate comrades since they first served together on Washington's staff. The letter is not a state document, but the casual correspondence of friends: four or five pages of news hurriedly written on the morrow of his appointment as Secretary of the Treasury. Some years later Talleyrand used of Hamilton the remarkable phrase that he had 'divined Europe,' although he had never left the shores of America. The quality of his mind was to see the essentials of any situation in great simplicity. From poor and incomplete accounts his imagination was able to construct a picture of the event in its true proportions. His thoughts seemed to

---

[1] 1789—Fall of the Bastille.   [2] *Works*, ix. p. 460.

work without the support and encumbrance of other men's theories, directly upon the facts; very patiently, but also very swiftly.

Jefferson meanwhile, with all the advantages attaching to first-hand knowledge, saw in these 'speculatists' the hope not only of France but of the world. Flattered by their confidence, he participated with immense gusto in their councils and discussions. The company was indeed worthy and congenial, for no 'philosophic politician' in Paris could have excelled the American minister in the fashionable drawing-room entertainment of spinning the foundation stones of society out of the gossamer of intelligent conversation. He went daily to listen to the debates of the National Assembly, and was even asked to join the deliberations of the committee charged with drawing up another constitution. He patched up coalitions and adjusted differences between discordant 'speculatists.' He advised that a *séance royale* should be held, and the king come forward with a Charter of Rights in his hand; and so great were both his zeal and his knowledge, that he drew up an elaborate sketch of a charter suitable to the occasion. His motives were in every case beyond reproach. His discretion under circumstances that were doubly trying, in their own nature and in his, was admirable. He made many friends and no enemies. He returned to his own country with an enhanced, though somewhat vague, reputation; but living five years in France he had seen only the surface of events, while Hamilton, Washington, Adams, Jay, Gouverneur Morris, and other men living in America, no less well-wishers to France than himself, dependent upon belated despatches and tardy packets for their information, penetrated much deeper into the realities of the revolution that was proceeding, and entertained much graver fears of its results.

The feeling of Hamilton from the beginning was that the French had gone the wrong way to work; that people of the greatest influence were engaged in the hopeless endeavour to fit facts to their own principles, instead of looking for principles that would fit the facts. In the eloquence and impatience of these unpractical leaders he saw the gravest dangers lurking, and with each arrival of fresh intelligence his judgment found confirmation. There was no hostility to France, but, on the contrary, a very cordial wish for her prosperity. She had been a faithful and valued ally in time of war, and the alliance had continued after the restoration of peace. It was the interest, therefore, as well as the sentiment, of the United States and of Washington's government, that French disorders should be brought to a prosperous conclusion. Naturally, also, Americans were in sympathy with reforms that aimed at admitting the popular element into the constitution; but having themselves only recently arrived, after years of struggle and compromise, at what they hoped might prove to be a strong and enduring government, they were keenly alive to the dangers of haste and sceptical of the value of general principles.

When Jefferson landed in America in the winter of 1789 he found himself in an atmosphere of doubt and apprehension, very different from that irresponsible elation which he had left behind him at Paris. The lack of confidence in general principles, of belief in the virtues of enthusiasm, of admiration for popular debate and the eloquence of tribunes, filled him at first with amazement and shortly with disgust. Having taken no part in the great Federal struggle, he might well have been excused if he underrated the difficulties of setting up a strong government. But beyond this important fact it is necessary to bear in mind that his supreme object in the making of constitutions was not a government which should be strong, but a

x

people that should be free.   His ideal was an executive
nation, inspired by noble emotions.   The functions of the
ruler, or the first citizen, were merely to expound and
interpret from time to time in sonorous language the sentiments latent in every righteous breast.   The Revolution in
France had not then become a party question in the
United States, but with such a divergence of opinion upon
essentials political division was bound to be the result.

When a man returns from his travels he looks to have
his opinions on climate, scenery and manners treated with
respect.   He resents nothing with a deeper mortification
than that people who have never stirred from home should
assert contrary views based upon a knowledge at second-
hand.   The perspicacious, well-informed person of sedentary
habits is as much the natural enemy of the credulous and
inquisitive globe-trotter as a cat is the natural enemy of
a mouse.   No punishment is harder to bear with than
correction by fellow-creatures who have had opportunities
of knowledge inferior to your own.   Jefferson may therefore
be forgiven if he felt uncharitably towards the cold critics
who declined to share his enthusiasm.

He hoped, and not in vain, for a better disposition and a
more favourable judgment in the people at large.   From
the date of his return until the middle of 1792 (two and
a half years later) the popular tide of sympathy rose
rapidly, and for nearly two years more it stood at the turn.
In these matters his *flair* was usually to be trusted.   He
gauged the rhetorical possibilities of any cause with the
eye of a general selecting a position.

The great cleavage came during 1792, and parties were
then divided with that peculiar bitterness which frequently
attaches itself to causes which are remote and ill understood.
The fact which caused public opinion to precipitate was
the certainty that France was preparing for war.   Phrases,

maxims, and general principles were no longer the predominant partners; for having admitted violence to be a
member of the firm, they found themselves ousted from
all influence and direction. As was natural the party of
physical force was gradually gaining the upper hand, while
the more timid revolutionaries, who were willing to debate
interminably but shrank from action, were daily growing
in discredit. In comparison with paper constitutions and
edicts which nobody heeded, even riots and massacres
appeared to be preferable; for the temper of the times was
weary of speeches and cried loudly for simple solutions and
definite achievements.

The extreme party desired war because they had determined on a Republic; and as Lafayette also desired war, for
the reason that he aimed at a duly regulated monarchy, it
was to be predicted, in view of such an alliance, that war
was likely to ensue. Exiled princes were making trouble on
the Rhine, and upon this menace in April war was declared
against Austria. In August, France was invaded by the
Duke of Brunswick. Prussians and Austrians menaced
general principles and the millennium with advancing
cannons. Tyrants, screamed the party of Jefferson, were
about to throttle Freedom. But by the end of October
jubilant salvos announced that the sacred soil of France
was freed from the hirelings of despotism. To the panic
of the early autumn there succeeded an exaltation and
self-confidence that was worth many army corps. The arms
of France were offered magniloquently to the service of all
men who would spurn the base condition of slaves and rise
against their rulers. 'All governments are our enemies; all
peoples are our friends.' On the first day of February
1793 war was declared on Britain and Holland.

Upon these facts glowingly expanded, American opinion
was persuaded to rivet its attention. The coalition against

liberty was drawn and coloured according to the rhetorical
probabilities, so that a statement of the dull truth was
disbelieved. That the Emperor would have preferred most
things to war; that the King of Prussia saw nothing in it
but an uncomfortable disturbance; that Pitt detested the
idea with his whole heart; that the outbreak was the contrivance of Jacobins anxious for external enemies, in order
that they might add the count of treachery to the indictment
of their king, and of scatter-brained Lafayette, whose gift
it was to pursue his ends by means that secured their
defeat—these simple facts had no chance of persuading a
heated opinion that had already settled by geometrical
principles the nature of tyrants on the one hand, and of lovers
of liberty on the other.

In these circumstances the rumour of war not unnaturally
excited a thrill of sympathy. The declaration of a Republic,
the retreat of the allies, the victories of Dumouriez and
the conquest of Savoy, evoked a frantic outburst of applause.
Stripped of all mendacity, the situation was great enough to
have moved men's hearts to wonder and admiration; but
under the inspiration of Jefferson's luxurious fancy it became
something akin to a religious frenzy. When in February
(1793) Britain, the oppressor of American freedom, was forced
reluctantly into the confederacy of tyrants, indignation, unmingled with surprise, excited popular sensibility to the
highest pitch. Not only in the classes addicted to indulgence
in clamour and sensation, but among the general body of
citizens, a large majority were ready to take up arms upon
a sincere impulse of fraternity, though upon an erroneous
plea of alliance.

In Europe other incidents of this ominous autumn and
winter had arrested a gloomier attention. Even men who
were eager to excuse the excesses of the 10th of August,
and to applaud the declaration of the Republic, were struck

dumb by the September massacres and the execution of the
King. With a boundary no broader than the Rhine or the
Channel it is not easy to shut out the noise of murder, or to
listen patiently to the edifying discourses of theorists who
complacently account for it on general principles. For the
moment the roar of the Paris mob drowned the apologies,
explanations and bluster of 'the Society of the Friends of
the People,' the 'London Corresponding Society,' the 'Society
for Constitutional Information' and the 'Sons of Freedom.'
But in the states three thousand miles away Jefferson found
himself but little inconvenienced by the doings of Robespierre,
Danton and Marat. So much had been already discounted
of possible horror by the judicious language of Jefferson and
his immediate friends, that the public opinion of clubs and
newspapers was fully prepared, not merely to condone or
approve, but even to exult in the most violent forms of
purification by blood.[1]

In a small society it is impossible for a man of eminence
and many friends, a great talker, a prodigious letter-writer,
accessible at all times to his political supporters, patron of
the arts and letters and inspirer of journalists, to keep himself free from the condemnation of history on the plea that
no public speech or state document can be alleged against
him. If his indulgent opinion of homicides, his hopeful
rejoicings over the millennium did not actually claim fresh
glory from what was happening at Paris, at least they found
an easy explanation in the depravity of tyrants. You
cannot, if you are a man of Jefferson's eminence, be held

---

[1] *History*, v. p. 259. When it was reported (untruly as it turned out) that
the American ambassador (Gouverneur Morris) had been murdered at Paris,
the supposed murder was excused by the Democratic papers on the ground
that the sentiments of their minister were favourable to the fallen dynasty.
Astonishment was even expressed that he had been 'suffered to live so long,
under the protection of an American diploma, to triumph in unexampled
folly and impertinence.'

irresponsible for the results of your confidential communications, made to all men and sundry, merely by labelling them as 'private.' For he intended that they should produce a public effect. He was no incontinent babbler when he used the nomenclature of natural history to inform the popular mind, and described the classes of society that had incurred his reprobation as lions, and tigers, and kites, and mammoths, and hydras, and hyænas, and wolves. Jefferson understood his times, and the method which we should now consider to be somewhat banal, was an admirable success.

The preparation had been so complete that upon the occasion of the September massacres Jefferson was able to soar unflustered into one of his noblest flights of perverse unreality. " In the struggle which was necessary, many ' guilty persons fell without the forms of trial, and with ' them some innocent. These I deplore as much as any- ' body, and shall deplore some of them to the day of my ' death. But I deplore them as I should have done had ' they fallen in battle. *It was necessary to use the arm of* ' *the people,* a machine not quite so blind as balls and bombs, ' but blind to a certain degree. A few of their cordial ' friends met at their hands the fate of enemies. But time ' and truth will rescue and embalm their memories, while ' their posterity will be enjoying that very liberty for which ' they would never have hesitated to offer up their lives. ' The liberty of the whole earth was depending on the issue ' of the contest, and was ever such a prize won with so little ' innocent blood ? My own affections have been deeply ' wounded by some of the martyrs to this cause, but rather ' than it should have failed I would have seen half the ' earth desolated; were there but an Adam and an Eve left ' in every country, and left free, it would be better than ' as it now is. I have expressed to you my sentiments

'because they are really those of ninety-nine in a hundred
' of our citizens." [1]

Fourteen hundred persons—men, women and boys—were
murdered or executed in Paris between the 3rd and the 7th
of September 1793, among them, inadvertently, some malefactors who already inhabited the prisons when the packing
was begun. For the rest, they were selected with much care
by the most vigilant and discriminating of ruffians; herded
together thoughtfully and without haste (as was only seemly
when 'the liberty of the whole earth was depending on the
issue'). Only the manner of their death lacked the appearance of premeditation, and this was in accordance with the
plan. 'A few of their cordial friends met at their hands the
fate of enemies,' is Jefferson's complacent comment, with
finger-tips devoutly pressed to finger-tips, and eyes turned
heavenwards. But except the dozen or two poor devils of
malefactors, what 'cordial friends' had Robespierre among
the victims? It would be impious to attach such meaning
to the words of Jefferson, a man who was twice President
of the United States, and believed in the love of humanity;
but for any other meaning we search vainly in the vacuity
of his rhetoric.

King Louis, 'the friend of America,' had been for Jefferson
a subject of much praise during his ministry in France.
His dispositions were solidly good. He was capable of great
sacrifices. All he wanted was to be assured it would be for
the good of the nation. He was the honestest man in the
kingdom, and the most regular and economical; a true
friend to liberty.

On January the 21st the head of the honest and solidly
good man was taken off by the grateful nation whose wellbeing was his chief care. Jefferson retained his heroic
calm:—"We have just received here the news of the

[1] Ford's *Jefferson*, vi. pp. 153-54.

' decapitation of the King of France. Should the present
' foment in Europe not produce republics everywhere, it will
' at least soften the monarchical governments by rendering
' monarchs amenable to punishment like other criminals,
' and doing away with that rage of insolence and oppression,
' the inviolability of the king's person." What wonder that
Madison, under the influence of such noble precepts, should
become almost tepid in his enthusiasm ? ' If he were a
traitor he ought to be punished as well as another man.' [1]
What wonder that simpler people with no official reticence
should carry the principles of their excellent master to a
more fantastical conclusion ? We read of a dinner of the
Second Regiment of Philadelphia Militia, to which Governor
Mifflin and the French ambassador were invited, at which
" the head of a pig was severed from its body, and, being
' recognised as an emblem of the murdered King of France,
' was carried round to the guests. Each one placing the
' cap of liberty upon his head pronounced the word ' Tyrant!'
' and proceeded to mangle with his knife the head of the
' luckless creature doomed to be served for so unworthy a
' company." [2]

If it be the proof of a really great man that he can look
upon the consequences of his works approving and undismayed, Jefferson's reputation needs no other establishment.
For all this bloodthirsty inanity he had no reproaches, but
only for his own government that refused to be drawn into
the war. The excitement that was making was, in his judgment, the flood-tide to float him off an uncomfortable sandbank into power; but, in spite of all his letters and intimate
conversations, the ebb came and he was still fast aground.

The Cabinet disagreements, noted by Hamilton in his

[1] *History*, v. p. 222.
[2] Hazen, *American Opinion on the French Revolution*, p. 183.

letter to Carrington,[1] increased in bitterness during the autumn and winter of 1792. The news of victories gave strength to those partisans of France who sought to entangle their country in a war with Europe, more perhaps for the purposes of an opposition than even for the sake of the sentiment. In the peculiar situation of the United States, having regard to the youth and complexity of their institutions, an exemption from war was no less necessary for the development of their natural resources than for the security of their political system. Upon the preservation of peace, Hamilton believed with good reason that the success of the experiment in republican government would depend.[2]

Leaving out of account the fact that the French Revolution had deliberately cancelled all the international obligations of the monarchy, and admitting in its fullest latitude the argument that a nation has the right in its own discretion to change its form of government, Hamilton firmly denied the further right which was claimed " to involve other ' nations, with whom it may have had connections, absolutely ' and unconditionally, in the consequences of the changes ' which it may think proper to make."[3]

The plea that the friendship of France for the United States was of so exceptional a character that it ought to override the natural interpretation of the treaty, could not be supported for a moment. Judged by its actions the government of the Revolution was no less oppressive than the government of King Louis had been towards the commerce of their ally. Its restrictions, in disregard of frequent assurances of attachment, were firmly enforced. Advances towards a more liberal policy had even been met with insult and menace.[4] The government of King George, which it was the popular habit to execrate on all occasions, was a gentler task-

---

[1] May 1792, *Works*, ix. p. 528.   [2] *History*, v. p. 215.
[3] *History*, v. p. 238.   [4] *Ibid.* v. p. 215.

master and a more generous client. In Hamilton's opinion there was therefore nothing in the interests of the United States, or in the obligations of the treaty, or in the demeanour of France, which could justify engaging in a war for her support.

The news that war had been declared on Britain reached Philadelphia in the early days of April 1793. A month earlier the second Congress had come to an end, with the signal defeat of the first great campaign of Madison and Giles against the integrity of the Secretary of the Treasury. In the ordinary course of events the new Congress would not meet until the early winter, and therefore the sole responsibility of dealing with the emergency was fortunately placed upon the shoulders of the Cabinet.

In the war which France had undertaken in the previous autumn against Austria and Prussia there were no dangers for America. There had been a strong sympathy towards the revolutionary campaign, a great rejoicing in its success; but there the matter ended. The citizens of the United States had no desire to take up arms in the quarrel, and had they so desired it would have been a practical impossibility to gratify their impulse. But when war broke out between France and Britain, every day found more people in a belli-cose mood. Circumstances had unfortunately placed no barriers against the realisation of their object. War with Britain was only too possible, both by sea and land.

It was therefore necessary, if war was to be avoided, that the government should take up a strong and decided line. Four days after the news arrived, Hamilton wrote to Jay urging the need for a declaration of neutrality, and asking him to draft an instrument suited to the occasion. Wash-ington was in full agreement that it was the duty of the executive to impose a strict neutrality upon its subjects. The Cabinet met, and the matter was discussed. Jefferson, as may be supposed, was altogether hostile to any measures which might give offence to the susceptibilities of France. He argued strongly for his favourite policy of drift. He accused Hamilton of aiming at a defensive alliance with Britain. His organ, the *National Gazette*, started simultaneously a skilful campaign, the object of which was to identify Hamilton, and even Washington, with 'a British party.'[1] It exulted in the execution of Louis XVI., and pointed a moral for the benefit of all tyrants and imitators of royal ceremonies.

Washington was slow in certain matters. Finance was always a laborious effort to him; but upon this issue his vision was clear, his judgment swift. He had no doubts or scruples, but at the first glance knew his own mind through and through. The United States were on no account to be dragged into a war which did not touch their interests at a single point.

Hamilton, with his customary energy, made all the preparations and found most of the arguments. He drafted the questions for the consideration of the Cabinet which met on the 19th of April to consider the tremendous issue. Jefferson opposed neutrality on principle, and was defeated. He urged delay, and was again defeated. He then argued the matter on constitutional grounds. The President had no powers, without the consent of Congress, to take such a step as was contemplated. He favoured calling a special meeting of the two Houses to debate the matter. This advice, had it been accepted, must have meant war. For delay of any kind meant war, and further, the new Congress contained a majority of the Democratic party.

The Cabinet was firm. The Declaration of Neutrality was agreed to; only, as a concession to Jefferson's feelings,

[1] *History*, v. pp. 218-22.

the word 'neutrality' was left out.   The substance was
secured, but the offensive description was omitted.   On the
22nd of April it was promulgated.

It has been said that when Washington issued his Declaration of Neutrality he could not have been more violently
execrated by the Democratic party had he proclaimed a monarchy.   When we recall Washington's services in war and
peace, his clear and disinterested character, and then turn to
the political literature of the day, we are once more struck with
admiration for the rapidity with which the United States
had assimilated the fashions and procedure of government
by party.   Merciful opponents excused the President as
a man of weak intellect hypnotised by Hamilton, his evil
genius.   More vigorous and less refining orators brushed
aside such excuses, and advocated dealing with the iniquitous despot in the simple manner of Robespierre and
Marat.

It is unnecessary to dwell upon the extravagance of the
period, further than to mark it for a dangerous and considerable force.   It was as much an epidemic as the yellow
fever.

The sequence of events during this fateful year may be
briefly chronicled.   The Minister of France, Citizen Genêt,
arrived in Charlestown on the 8th of April, and proceeded
by leisurely steps to the seat of government at Philadelphia,
where he arrived in the middle of May.   Jefferson was
overflowing with kindness—a contrast to the calm correcti-
tude of his chief.   In the face of British protests against the
infringements of neutrality that were occurring every day,
it was necessary to communicate the firm intentions of the
Cabinet to Genêt, who was the prime instigator of these
events.   A week after his arrival he was at loggerheads
with the government to which he was accredited, and
Jefferson, who in private was everything that was agreeable

and indiscreet,[1] was compelled reluctantly, in official A.D. 1793
correspondence, to repel the outrageous pretensions of his ÆT. 36
friend. By the month of June Genêt began to talk of
'appealing to the people,' and Hamilton had published
the first numbers of his famous letters of *Pacificus*.

The sympathy of Jefferson was misleading. The popular
ferment which saluted the French minister on every hand
was even more misleading. The situation was dangerous,
and it was also intolerable. In all the great seaports were
seen tricoloured ensigns floating above the American standards. French ships of war were moored so as to command
the feeble batteries. The coasts were lined with privateers, and
cruisers roamed the high seas commissioned to capture every
neutral vessel. An internecine party, rallying against their
own government, tendered homage to a foreign minister.
The foreign minister was found rebuking Washington as a
violater of the laws, dictating to him his duty, and appearing
to divide with him the affections of the people. The Cabinet
was often in discord, while Britain, with every justification,
was threatening reprisals. Hamilton urged the necessity of
prompt and vigorous measures against the French minister,
and in the end his counsels prevailed.[2]

At the beginning of August, Hamilton's draft of the rules
of neutrality was agreed to by the President and the majority
of the Cabinet. It was determined to ask for Genêt's recall.
Hamilton was in favour of making public the correspondence
with this strange ambassador, confident that the announcement would appeal to the good sense and dignity of the
nation. Jefferson was opposed to this step, and again
advocated the calling together of Congress.

Jefferson, fearful of the consequences which seemed
imminent, spoke of resignation in the following month;
but Washington, indignant at the attacks of the Democratic

---

[1] *History*, v. p. 262. [2] *Ibid.* v. pp. 314-15.

party and their press, and determined to pin the Secretary of State to the policy of the government, refused to entertain his retirement before the end of the year. This attitude was natural; but it is difficult to see in what way it was of any benefit to the administration. The chief advantage in the arrangement has accrued to the reputation of Jefferson in modern times. His animosity against the Federalist policy of aloofness from European quarrels is now usually over-looked. What is remembered is that he was Secretary of State when, at the height of revolutionary enthusiasm, it was wisely decided, in the teeth of the popular frenzy, to pursue a course of neutrality. It is also remembered that he was the mouthpiece through which Genêt was censured and exposed. By reason of Washington's compulsion Jefferson has accordingly earned a great credit for sagacious statesman-ship of which he was not only entirely innocent, but the most determined and hysterical opponent.[1]

Throughout August Hamilton pursued his success. It was decided that British prizes wrongfully captured were to be restored and compensation given. Jefferson's doctrine that 'French ships of war and privateers with prizes may come and go freely, English may not,'[2] was emphatically repudiated. Hamilton drafted letters to Genêt of no amiable tenour, and to the United States ambassador in Paris, de-manding Genêt's recall. To these documents Jefferson was obliged meekly to append his signature. Finally, at the very end of the month Genêt's unwary insolence completed the victory. He launched a public attack upon Washington and his administration. The *National Gazette* clamoured indignant approbation of his action. But the country viewed the matter in another light. Suddenly, from all sides, there

---

[1] *History*, v. p. 337. Cf. also Reddaway's *Monroe Doctrine*, pp. 15-16.
[2] *History*, v. p. 232.

was a rally. A foreign agent had dared to insult the chief
officer of the Union.

By December, Genêt had sunk to the sad plight of a
blackmailer. He wrote angry letters threatening disclosures;
had instalments struck off, and demanded that they should be
officially circulated in Congress. Jefferson, on the eve of his
retirement, was anxious to escape the pain of sending the
necessary reply. But Washington was obdurate, summoned
a hasty Cabinet on a Sunday, and the last act of the
Secretary of State was a reluctant but emphatic denuncia-
tion of his former confederate.[1]

On the 31st of December Jefferson, with a sigh of relief,
relinquished his office. The *National Gazette* was dis-
continued, and the Democratic party arrived at the wise
decision that in the present state of popular feeling they
would no longer champion the cause of France against their
own government.

To support the policy of neutrality against the fanatics
Hamilton wrote the letters of *Pacificus* which, apart from
their special argument on the facts, will ever remain a classic
of wise, dignified, illusionless, unprovocative statesmanship.
Gradually, in the face of an indomitable resolution, the
violence died away. Once more Jefferson (now no longer in
office) saw the assault that he had planned and cheered on
thrown back with disaster. Common sense had prevailed.
The citizens of the United States had come to realise that the
policy of safety was a higher patriotism than the indulgence
of any sentiment. A consciousness that their antics had
been somewhat ludicrous, a suspicion that for two years
or more they had been the dupes of a parody of freedom, began to steal upon them; and with these the slow
conviction that a government they did not love had all
the time succeeded in keeping its head in spite of threats

---

[1] *History*, v. p. 436.

and unpopularity. They began to remember that after all they were for the most part Anglo-Saxons, and that for such a stock it was possibly unbecoming to caper round poles of liberty, to embrace in the streets, to guillotine emblematical pigs and to wear tricolour ribbons.

Citizen Genêt, the ambassador of the French Republic, came to America with the deliberate object of engaging the Union in a war against tyranny. The disposition of the shouting portion of the populace was altogether favourable to the purpose of his mission. Had the rule of the country which accredited him held good in that to which he carried his credentials, he might easily have fulfilled his hopes.

He was a gay and sanguine gentleman of pleasing address and a facile eloquence in several tongues. Handsome, debonair and audacious, with a fine ruddy complexion and busy and bustling manners, he advanced to the assault of the position unencumbered by the gyves of experience, or suspicion of any variety, racial or climatic, among citizens who gloried in their freedom. With a sublime air of condescending fraternity, as became one who had arrived by express from the fashionable Metropolis of Liberty, he wore his tricolour ribbon with a good-natured swagger, and played the lofty gentleman to open-mouthed rustics of virtue. He was not so much an ambassador to Washington's government as its patron; less of a diplomatist than the vice-gerent of the Rights of Man. His portmanteaux were stuffed with letters of marque. He had hardly stepped upon the quay before he began putting privateers in commission. The enlistment of American subjects was a regular item in his daily routine. For this well-born and accomplished youth, with a fresh experience of the instability of the most ancient and glorious of European Governments, the resistance of any human institution to his summons seemed a chimæra as ridiculous as the virtue of Clarissa to

Lovelace. With the government he was civil, of course,
and good-humoured, as a gallant in a Restoration drama
with the husband, or the father, of his mistress; kindly, but
contemptuous, letting it be understood that he considered
official dignity to be somewhat in the way.

He was in no hurry to present his credentials. To do
him full justice we must endeavour to put ourselves
into his point of view, and to realise that the power
to which he conceived himself to have been truly accredited
was the Sovereign People. The forms of diplomacy
lingered, but these were merely survivals, harmless if
every one understood their symbolism, but otherwise to be
torn down and destroyed like other pasteboard rubbish of
the feudal era. In his opinion, the proper business of an
ambassador was to be in close touch and direct communication with the Popular Master to whom, in any respectable
state, the executive, legislative and judicial powers stood
in the relation of humble servants. Nor when forms were
tedious and involved delay did he consider it necessary to
observe them pedantically. Where there was such absolute
good feeling, such a perfect understanding as was proved by
the enthusiastic uproar of his reception, to tie the hands of
all men and his own by the punctilious observance of ceremonies would have been to chill ungratefully the warmth of
his welcome.

And so without delay Genêt proceeded to his business,
taking the parade and shoutings as sufficient warrant
for his vigour. Privateers were desirable to prey upon
the commerce of Britain and her allies. He accordingly
chartered and fitted them out, providing them with stores
and munitions of war. Privateers needed officers and crews
to man them; so that logically he was compelled to give his
attention to enlistment and commissions. Prize courts in
safe and comfortable American harbours were conveniences

demanded by civilisation; so with French consuls for judges he established these tribunals. Everywhere as he went he spoke with enthusiasm of 'the alliance' between the two Republics as a thing already in existence; of mutual sacrifices, loans, and subsidies; of French help that had been given to colonists struggling for freedom; and of the obligation of a grateful return, seeing that the debtors were men of such well-known honour and probity.

Among his hearers, while the progress lasted, there was no one to say him nay; but on his journey northward he learned that Washington had issued his Declaration of Neutrality. Genêt read the terms of this document with incredulity and horror. Privateers, enlistment and prize courts were things that must altogether cease. British merchantmen must not be seized in American waters, and if so seized must be immediately released. Some mind, evidently not that of Jefferson or of the Sovereign People, was forcing this reluctant minister to utter very hard and definite forbiddings, which were an outrage not merely upon the decency of gratitude, but upon the very chastity of freedom.

To all lovers of fine comedy Genêt will ever be a hero, miscalculating so buoyantly, suspecting nothing, clothed always in a smiling dignity, till suddenly Jefferson, his confidential valet, and Jeffersonism, the credit-balance of his account, faded into thin air, and a grim Washington supported by a grave and polite Hamilton appeared in unlooked-for authority.[1] Altogether in the background stood his friend Jefferson, perturbed and deprecatory, with an anxious recollection of sundry letters and conversations 'as between friends' which it might be inconvenient to reconcile with his official duty, if an irate emissary, outraged in his office and feather-brained by nature, should

[1] *History*, v. pp. 335-37.

entertain no scruples with regard to publication. The
scruples of an angry Genêt were but pea-sticks against a hurricane.[1]

Facts following the written words began to take place. Force under severe provocation at last stretched out a paw, making it clear that the warning was to be supported by the aid of constables and prisons, or if the lamentable necessity should arise, even by gunpowder and cannon-balls. The private sympathy of Jefferson was consoling to Genêt as a man; but when it became apparent that the sentiment was merely 'as between friends,' and not politically efficacious in the smallest degree, it is hardly to be wondered at that contempt succeeded to amazement, and wrathful revelations to contempt.

Genêt may be forgiven for finding the situation somewhat puzzling. Looking around him he saw still the same fervour of popular demonstration; anger loudly expressed and almost equal to his own against the Declaration of Neutrality. Not only the people, but their leaders, Madison and Monroe, spoke of the act with horror,—'a most unfortunate evil'; injurious to 'the national honour by seeming to disregard the stipulated duties to France'; wounding 'the popular feelings by a seeming indifference to the cause of liberty'; violating 'the forms and the spirit of the constitution '; a ' millstone ' round the neck of Washington's reputation, and so forth and so forth.[2] Even the Secretary of State himself made no secret of his opinion that he viewed it with detestation, speaking of it openly as 'an English neutrality.'

Genêt grew daily more bewildered by his environment. He was in a strange land; not free, as he had supposed, but governed by a baleful paradox. The Will of the People was

[1] *History*, v. p. 374.
[2] Madison to Jefferson, 19th June 1793; *History*, v. p. 285.

not then really supreme. Ministers carried out measures which they privately denounced. What power sat over the heads of the citizens ? Why and by whom were they thus compelled and coerced ? The one clear thing in the situation was that the lesson of liberty had been learned only by halves. Tyranny held the reins in a misnamed Republic. In the New World things were even more topsy-turvy than in the Old, for here the theory of the Rights of Man walked hand in hand with the dark practices of despotism.

Only a touch seemed necessary, only a bold word, and the shackles of paradox would be struck for ever off the limbs of struggling Democracy. To him, Genêt, minister plenipotentiary of the French Republic, the glorious duty was clearly appointed by destiny. So, without undue hesitation, he struck manfully at the encumbering chains.

The result was not what he had foreseen, but as nearly as possible the reverse of it. He appealed directly to the Sovereign People, which might have been endured, but for the fact that the appeal was by its nature an attack upon the President of the United States, and this was unforgivable in any foreigner.[1] Thereupon paradox deepened to a tragedy. The Sovereign People was shocked beyond all words capable of expressing it; Jefferson and Madison and Monroe were seen publicly and privately wringing their hands and casting ashes on their heads.[2]

To Citizen Genêt, logically pursuing the path of General Principles, it appeared that he was in the land of the mad. His gallant effort had miscarried. Failure descended upon him and his mission. Letters of recall arrived in time to prevent further mischief. He passed rapidly out of sight in a haze of banquets and sympathy, blustering eloquently in a swiftly dying fall. Dreading what might befall him if he returned to France, he became an American citizen, and

[1] *History*, v. pp. 357-58, also p. 377.   [2] Jefferson to Madison, v. pp. 342-45.

married Governor Clinton's daughter. He had come near A.D. 1794
to provoking a revolution in the United States; but although Ær. 37
he found himself well placed for combustibles and had acted
with great spirit, he did not arrive at his object. He had
blundered into an error of tact for which his origin and
experience afford sufficient excuse; for how was a French-
man to understand a wilful race which rated its institutions,
even in their first youth, far beyond logic?

CHAPTER VI

The Treaty with Great Britain

THE danger of a war, undertaken out of sympathy with
France, may be said to have ended with the retirement of
Jefferson and the discredit of Genêt. But two dangers were
still to be dreaded. The one was internal disorder; the
other was a war with Britain, arising partly out of the
unsettled grievances and partly out of fresh provocations.
The year 1794 was therefore a period hardly less critical
than its predecessor.

Britain, engaged in a struggle for life or death, judged it
sound policy to take advantage to the uttermost of her
naval supremacy. It was her object to cut off all supplies
that came by sea to France, and to this end she adopted a
procedure with regard to neutral shipping that neutrals had
every right to resent as high-handed and oppressive. The
question has been argued as if it were one of morals, but
in reality it was purely a matter of military expediency.
Which was the greater evil from the standpoint of Britain:
to allow her enemy the advantage of sea-borne commodities,
or to provoke the United States to take up arms? The
principle of the calculation is easy to state, but the sum
itself was less easy to work out. The fact that Britain

modified her action from time to time, that orders were issued, amended, withdrawn, and renewed, seems to indicate that she was by no means certain as to the wisdom of her policy. There was a wavering note. Things hung in the balance. It is perhaps safe to assume that had her relations with America been frank and friendly, the regulations would never have been pressed to a point at which they could have caused serious offence. But the reverse was the case. While it was true that the attitude of Washington's government was correct, the feeling of the nation was notoriously hostile, and all the power of the executive had been unable to keep the people within bounds. In addition there were the outstanding disputes with regard to the non-fulfilment of the treaty of peace. While these were left unsettled it was beyond hope to get rid of mutual distrust.

Early in March, particulars of the latest orders to British men-of-war became known in Philadelphia. Their character was so oppressive that common men, and even the coolest members of the government, judged them to be altogether intolerable. The day following the receipt of this information, Hamilton put his views into writing and submitted them to Washington. He urged the importance of fortifying the chief harbours, raising troops, and placing certain special powers for the time being in the hands of the President.[1] When so sincere a friend of peace as Hamilton was found denouncing the grievance as 'atrocious,' it seemed much more likely than not that war would break out.

Still he did not abandon hope. He was as anxious as ever to pursue an honourable neutrality if it were practicable; but he judged it wise to prepare for war, with the double object of impressing Britain with the earnestness of American intentions, and of putting the country on a footing to prevent injury, and to strike an early, decisive blow

[1] *History*, v. pp. 507-8.

if it were assailed.[1] At the same time he advocated a frank A.D. 1794
discussion with the British government. The language and ÆT. 37
temper of the protest should be firm and determined, but
provocation should be studiously avoided. He was in favour
of a special mission to England to negotiate for the withdrawal of the oppressive regulations and the removal of the
old grievances of the loyalists and the frontier forts.

Washington approved this policy at every point, but the
Democrats, under the leadership of Madison, opposed it root
and branch. They lamented among themselves that their
enemy should have been beforehand with them in advocating resistance to Britain.[2] They defeated the Army
Bill. They accused Hamilton, possibly with a grain of
truth, 'of turning every contingency into a resource for
accumulating force in the government.'[3] In private they
admitted that war was probable,[4] but in Congress they
pretended that Britain could be brought to reason by commercial pressure.[5] While they were eager to engage in
provocations that must inevitably lead to war, they were
resolute that no preparation for the consequences of their
action should be undertaken. If a commercial campaign
proved insufficient, there still remained the weapon of
repudiation. The debts due to British citizens should be
sequestrated.[6] This plan was proposed upon various occasions and with difficulty defeated; but it had the chief
weight of the Democratic party behind it, and was warmly
supported by Monroe.[7]

Washington, determined to put an end to the danger if it
were at all possible, accepted Hamilton's proposal for a
mission to England. He wished Hamilton to undertake

[1] *History*, v. p. 516.
[2] Livingston to Monroe, *History*, v. p. 507.
[3] Madison to Jefferson, *Ibid.* p. 517.
[4] Madison to Jefferson, *Ibid.* p. 517.
[5] *History*, v. p. 516. [6] *Ibid.* v. p. 523. [7] *Ibid.* v. p. 570.

the duty—'an abler and an honester man they cannot find.'[1] The whole Federalist party would have accepted this nomination with enthusiasm; but the clamour that had been raised against Hamilton was too strong,[2] his unpopularity among his opponents was too great, for the appointment to be made. In the peculiar circumstances it would have been unwise to send to London the man who was constantly denounced as the leader of the British party. He himself refused on these grounds to entertain the idea, and a further reason for his refusal is found in his desire to be free to advise the Cabinet in the crowd of impending difficulties which he clearly foresaw.

In the end, upon Hamilton's advice, Jay was nominated by the President. By way of speeding him on his mission, the opposition brought forward motions in Congress for non-intercourse with Britain, and their supporters outside Congress burned him in effigy. But during April conciliatory despatches arrived from London, the Senate approved of the mission, and before the middle of April the minister sailed. Time at least was gained by this measure. The opposition was outmanœuvred. For the moment the British bogey dropped out of sight, and another set of troubles came into prominence.

For several years a dangerous agitation had been in progress against the excise. The centre of disturbance was Pennsylvania, and the leading mind, if not the leading character, was Gallatin, who in Jefferson's subsequent administration succeeded to the office of Secretary of the Treasury. The ostensible cause of rebellion was the duty on whisky. The real danger was a widespread terrorism and an armed defiance of the powers of the Union. The example of the French Revolution had strengthened the natural disposition

[1] Washington to Taylor, *History*, v. p. 535.
[2] *Ibid.* v. p. 533.

of a large body of the people to regard strong government as identical with tyranny. When laws were felt to be irksome by any considerable number of the citizens, it became excusable to render them null and void by non-compliance. Force might justifiably be encountered by force. The basis of any true republic being, according to the prevalent ideas, the voluntary obedience of the people, it was clear that the cardinal principle of Union was violated if taxes were imposed by Congress upon whisky. For to such an exaction Pennsylvania, and other districts also, were violently opposed. It seemed to infringe their private interests. Their consent was therefore involuntary, and it followed that they were entitled to withhold it if they desired so to do.

These doctrines had been disseminated far and wide by the industry of the secret democratic societies, whose connection with the official Democratic party was intimate if informal. In Congress the opposition had been overcome by an invulnerable alliance between Hamilton, the ablest mind, and Washington, the most revered character in the Union. There are reasons for the belief that in many quarters a physical resistance to the tyranny of the central government was regarded as the only means open for securing freedom. But it is clear that the chief sympathisers with these loose principles of anarchy did not regard the time as fully ripe. By temperament they were averse from reasoning out the consequences of their propaganda, and ever shrank from a definite course of action when it could be avoided. Their preference for a policy of drift was not confined to dealings with foreign nations, but was equally notable in domestic affairs.

In July lawlessness came to a head. Hamilton's opinion was in favour of mobilising an army of twelve thousand men by the 10th of September, and issuing a proclamation calling upon the rebels to disperse. The majority of the Cabinet concurred in this view. The only dissentient was Randolph, who had succeeded Jefferson as Secretary of State. His arguments are highly characteristic of the Democratic party to which he belonged. He doubted whether the rebellion was serious; doubted also the legality of the course proposed to be taken; doubted if the troops would serve; doubted if public opinion would support the measures of government. He was afraid that the insurgents might enter into an alliance with Britain, and concluded with the sagacious observation that the expedition would certainly cost a great deal of money.[1] Although Randolph had not then fallen into disgrace, his judgment was disregarded. It was afterwards alleged that he had been friendly to the rebellion, but judged it premature and feared it might miscarry from a lack of funds. A year later it transpired that at this very time he had made an extraordinary request to the French ambassador for money,[2] and Washington forthwith dismissed him from his office. Randolph published a vindication which earned the approval of Jefferson, joined the Democratic attacks on Washington's character which were then in progress, and likened his late chief to Tiberius and an assassin. Washington's opinion was less rhetorical but no less emphatic: 'A damneder scoundrel God Almighty never permitted to disgrace humanity.'[3]

In spite of Randolph's opposition, fifteen thousand troops were assembled on the appointed day. Washington was in chief command, and Hamilton, without any military rank, seemed nevertheless to direct the whole of the proceedings. It was he who had proposed the prompt and overwhelming display of military force. The policy was his, and so also were the matters which flowed from it—the Cabinet

---

[1] *History*, vi. pp. 70-71.   [2] *History*, vi. pp. 72-73, also p. 247.
[3] *History*, vi. p. 309.

A.D. 1794
Æt. 37

opinions, instructions to state governors, proclamations, reports and vindications necessary for the purpose of informing and guiding public opinion. The conduct of the war, if the short and bloodless campaign can be described by such a title, seems also to have been in his hands more than in those of any of the generals. When Washington, towards the end of October, returned to Philadelphia, Hamilton remained for several weeks longer guiding the movements of the expedition. The situation has its humorous side—Hamilton's appetite for work and responsibility is so prodigious that his comrades in the campaign, no less than his colleagues in the Cabinet, appear to have resigned themselves to his direction and to have left everything in his hands.

Most, if not all, of Randolph's prognostications proved untrue. The insurgents did not seek to enter into an alliance with Britain. Public opinion did not withhold its support. The troops did not refuse to serve, but, on the contrary, turned out with enthusiasm and in greater numbers than were required. The rebels faded away, overawed by an overwhelming display of power, and by the fourth week of October their unconditional submission was accepted. The wisdom of providing forces adequate to the worst contingencies was never more admirably exemplified. What might with more timid counsels or a more foolhardy confidence have proved to be a serious and bloody contest, rending the Union from one end to the other, was quietly extinguished and left no bitter memories behind it.

The campaign in suppression of this rebellion was bloodless. The opposition of men who had issued terrible manifestoes in praise of freedom and all its consequences, who had shown the boldest enterprise in the tarring and feathering of revenue officers, melted ignominiously before the progress of the army. The importance of the incident lies in two facts. Under one aspect it was the vindication, by a display of armed force, of sane government against the vague and disorderly clamour of the party which aimed at an alliance with the revolutionary government of France. Under the other it was the first stern proof that the central authority of the United States was able and willing, without the aid, or favour, or goodwill of any intermediary legislature, to put forth its strength and to exercise a direct and overwhelming coercion against its rebellious subjects. Under both aspects it was a salutary demonstration, and neither Washington nor Hamilton was blind to the double intention and effect.

Meanwhile there was good news from Jay. In November the government learned of the probable success of his mission. Hamilton's resignation took effect at the end of January 1795. Early in March the draft of the treaty reached Philadelphia. The Senate met in June to consider it, and after a fortnight's discussion accepted it conditionally. The terms having become public through the indiscretion or bad faith of a senator, the country was plunged immediately in an agitation which had not been exceeded in violence even by the outburst of sympathy with France. Jay was accused of having accepted bribes. Hamilton, when he addressed a meeting in New York, was stoned and hooted down. Washington was attacked for 'his mock pageantry of monarchy and apish mimickry of kings.'[1] He was taunted with being the tool of Hamilton, and was even accused of peculation.[2] An impeachment of the President was loudly demanded.[3]

The Democrats were bolder in Congress, upon platforms and in the press, than they had shown themselves in the field. From the date of the Whisky Rebellion to the end of his term of office Washington was the object of their constant attacks. His censure of the secret Democratic

[1] *History*, vi. pp. 282-83.   [2] *Ibid.* vi. p. 296.   [3] *Ibid.* vi. p. 283.

societies in his opening speech to Congress had the effect of extirpating these pests, but the official Democratic party fiercely resented his action and forced him to endure various petty discourtesies at the hands of the legislature. Gallatin, the ex-rebel, was now the most prominent figure of the opposition. He had succeeded Giles, who had become old-fashioned, as the chief fabricator of injurious innuendoes, and Madison, whose creaking constitutional prolixity had grown somewhat wearisome, as the intellectual leader of the party in debate. Under his inspiration the campaign of words, spoken and written, was conducted with a zeal and a measure of success which partly retrieved his timid and ignominious disaster in the rebellion. Nor must it be lost sight of that all the while Jefferson, from an unassailable obscurity, was still directing the movements of the party.

Washington issued his *Farewell Address* in September 1796, and John Adams succeeded him in the Presidency in the following March. The Democratic press excelled even its past records upon the occasion. "The man who is the 'source of the misfortunes of our country is this day reduced 'to a level with his fellow-citizens, and is no longer possessed 'of the power to multiply evils on the United States. If 'ever there was a period for rejoicing this is the moment." The name of Washington would no longer continue to give currency to political iniquity and to legalise corruption. In the retrospect of his eight years of administration it was considered marvellous that a single individual could have cankered the principles of republicanism in an enlightened people, and should have carried his designs against the public liberty, so far as to have put in jeopardy its very existence. The eloquent writer concludes that the day of Washington's retirement should be commemorated as a day of jubilee throughout the Union.[1]

[1] *The Aurora*, 4th March 1797, *History*, vi. p. 607.

A. D. 1797
Æт. 40 The new President sat in the Speaker's chair, and alone, in front of the judges, sat the late President. John Adams made his address, took the oath of office, and retired. During the short ceremony Washington remained standing and when it was over made a courteous bow to the vast throng of onlookers and returned to his home on foot. The assembly dispersed silently, many of them in tears, and followed him on his way. He smiled gently at this spontaneous exhibition of affection and turned to acknowledge it, but could find no words. "It is the general report," John Adams wrote, "that there was more weeping than ' there ever has been at the representation of a tragedy. ' But whether it was from grief or joy, whether from the ' loss of their beloved President, or from the accession of an ' unbeloved one, or from the novelty of the thing, or from ' the sublimity of it, arising from the multitude present, ' or whatever other cause, I know not. One thing I ' know. I am a being of too much sensibility to act any ' part well in such an exhibition. Perhaps there is little ' danger of my ever having such another scene to feel or ' behold."[1]

CHAPTER VII

The Foundations of Foreign Policy

BEFORE the end of Washington's administration the foundations of foreign policy were laid as firmly as the foundations of public credit, of order, and of the executive power. The Declaration of Neutrality and Jay's treaty with Great Britain were the two most noteworthy acts in the chain of bold conduct, whose tradition has maintained itself in subsequent times. The thing done, rightly claims the chief place, but the reasons for the doing of the thing are hardly less impor-

[1] *History*, vi. pp. 606-7.

tant. Hamilton's writings during this period are therefore deserving of close attention, both because of the effect they produced at the time and because they set out the broad principles upon which his policy was founded.

The letters of *Pacificus* were written during the summer and autumn of 1793, to stem the tide of feeling in favour of France; the letters of *Americanus* in February 1794, to stem the tide of feeling against Britain. In July 1795 he wrote the letters of *Horatius*, and began the series over the signature of *Camillus*, to justify the ratification of Jay's treaty by the Senate and the President. In September 1796 Washington issued his *Farewell Address*—one of the most famous documents in American history—and this also was from Hamilton's pen.

These Latin names are somewhat absurd to our way of thinking, but they were then the fashion. Every one knew that *Pacificus, Americanus, Horatius* and *Camillus* were Hamilton, just as every one knew that *Helvetius* was Madison. The writers made no secret of their identity even as they wrote; but clearly the practice must have conciliated some notion of propriety, for it was universally adopted except by Tom Paine.

It was impossible, in Hamilton's view, for a nation to act towards other nations as a man of warm feelings would act towards his neighbours. A nation cannot afford to indulge itself in hatred or affection, magnanimity or revenge. In deciding upon its course of action, sentiment is as irrelevant a consideration as malice, and wars of chivalry are as iniquitous as wars of religion. The statesman who bends to an emotional outburst of public opinion as richly deserves to be shot as a general who surrenders a city out of compassion for the inhabitants. The stern test of the righteousness of a war is the permanent security of the state. A government which goes knight-erranting out of sympathy for foreign nations is like a trustee who subscribes to charities out of the property he has undertaken to administer. A government, like a trustee, is responsible for the estate. Its business is sound investments, not the encouragement of deserving institutions or the succour of honest, poor men overwhelmed by adversity. Pity and prejudice are equally out of place when ministers, in whom king or people has placed the serious confidence of decision, come to determine the tremendous issues of alliances and wars.

Some philosophers, indeed, have discovered a distinction in the case of a Democracy. A nation which goes mad is surely free to do as it likes. But a nation, in Hamilton's judgment, is in the position of a tenant for life who must be restrained from spoiling the timber, pawning the heirlooms, and dilapidating the estate for his successors. In such issues there is room only for the charity of individuals who may deal as they please with their life interest, and be praised unreservedly for their sacrifice. They may give their own lives, and their own money if they choose, to the side which engages their approval, but out of the trust funds not a penny and not a grenadier. Lord Byron was all right; Exeter Hall, as a rule, is all wrong.

Aloofness from the struggles of other nations has been freely judged to be uncharitable and ungenerous; but what government that has fully realised its responsibilities will ever engage in crusades and adventures? It is reasonable to expect that ministers should have wiser and cooler heads than the electors, and the courage necessary to stand out against the tumults of popular indignation, that are often ready, upon a sudden impulse, to risk the safety of the state and even the freedom of future generations.

Nor does a man need to have lived for many years in a free country to realise that in such outbursts there is apt to be much hollowness and considerable error. What did the citizens of the United States actually know of the conditions of Frenchmen three thousand miles away? Tardy and irregular packets brought news with a fine gloss of rhetoric on the facts. Battles and revolutions made good reading and stirred the blood; but the causes were more lightly touched upon and less eagerly studied. Phrases and ideas were translated by glib pedants who had no suspicion of a difference between the Gallic and the Saxon scale, between the Liberté of Paris and the Freedom of New England.

When one nation is swept by a violent admiration or by a tempest of hatred for another, it is nearly certain that the situation has not been truly understood. Nations are not like the characters in a novel. They are rarely fit subjects for chivalry; still more rarely are they odious. Partisans—and more particularly remote partisans—are ever blinder and more furious than their principals. They are mesmerised by the dramatic and led to conceive of friends impossibly good, enemies impossibly bad, and both impossibly uniform throughout—nations of devils and nations of angels. No man ever sees his own countrymen under this homogeneous aspect; for there is always the candour of the Opposition and the obvious imperfections of his neighbours to correct and temper the illusion.

That Hamilton profoundly distrusted the French Revolution, and heaped scorn upon its pretensions with regard to liberty and the Rights of Man, gave point to his arguments, but did not in the least affect his main position. Had his sympathies been entirely in the other scale his principles of statesmanship would still have compelled him to advocate the same policy which he pursued.

In the struggle of France against the world, the sole concern of Washington's government was the true interest of the United States. Gratitude to Frenchmen was a worthy feeling for private men to entertain; but gratitude to France was a meaningless phrase. French aid had been politic, not sentimental. The object of their statesmen was neither love of American freedom nor hatred of British tyranny, but merely the warrantable desire to injure and embarrass a dangerous enemy by comfort extended to its subjects in rebellion. So long as the interests of France and the interests of the states lay along the same line, it was wise and patriotic to join forces; but at a later time, when the ways diverged and the benefits of such co-operation would have accrued only to one side, the risks and the dangers to the other, it would have been a breach of trust for government to yield to popular clamour and to enter into a new alliance out of consideration for the advantage which had been reaped from a similar engagement in former times.

The counter policy of Jefferson was in Hamilton's opinion a huge bubble blown up by windy rhetoric and a purely verbal enthusiasm. Gratitude was not due even to the King of France; how therefore could it be due to the subjects who had cut off his head? Freedom was a great name, but a poor *casus belli* unless it were your own that was menaced. Events which had occurred were to be considered done with. They left no legacies. Britain the ancient enemy, France the ancient friend, must be treated on a bare equality. Hatred of Britain was a vague and unreal sentiment. If encouraged to the length that it was allowed to prevent the one nation from entering into relations with the other for their mutual advantage, there could be no folly too impossible for mankind. To remain on bad terms with Britain by choice, and from a general dislike that eluded definition both as to its nature and its object (for no man was altogether certain whether it was directed against the king, the government, or the people), was a paradox that filled his clear mind and humane spirit with immeasurable contempt.

In Hamilton's opinion the honour of his nation was in no way engaged to support the arms of France. So far as honour entered into the discussion it was at a wholly different point. He was deeply concerned that the United States should hold their head high among nations, scrupulously observing the sanctity of their engagements even towards the subjects of those with whom they were at war. The doctrine of repudiation of debts, whether public or private, towards which Jefferson had a kindly indulgence, was to Hamilton the most destructive and abominable of all policies, striking at the roots not only of respect among nations, but of stability of government and preservation of the Union.

When it was suggested by the Democratic faction that Britain might be brought to terms by a policy of whole-sale confiscation of the debts due by American citizens and the American government to her subjects, Hamilton did not trim his phrases to the popular tune. " Serious ' as the evil of war has appeared, at the present stage of ' our affairs, the manner in which it was to be apprehended ' it might be carried on was still more formidable, in my ' eyes, than the thing itself. It was to be feared that, in ' the fermentation of certain wild opinions, those wise, just, ' and temperate maxims, which will for ever constitute the ' true security and felicity of a State, would be overruled ; ' that a war upon credit, eventually upon property, and upon ' the general principles of public order, might aggravate and ' embitter the ordinary calamities of foreign war. The con- ' fiscation of debts due to the enemy might have been the ' first step of this destructive process. From one violation ' of justice to another the passage is easy. Invasions of ' right, still more fatal to credit, might have followed ; and

' this, by extinguishing the resources which that could have
' afforded, might have paved the way to more comprehensive
' and more enormous depredations for a substitute. Terrible
' examples were before us, and there were too many not
' sufficiently remote from a disposition to admire and imitate
' them." [1]

The interests of the States, in Hamilton's view, were not
in Europe, but only in America. With the future of that
continent their destiny was bound up; but whether Europe
should succeed in erasing the name of France from the
map, or France in subduing the whole of Europe, mattered
not one pin's head; and all the loose talk about gratitude
and freedom added not a single drachm to the weight of
the argument. The signal advantage of the American
Republic over all other nations lay in its position, which
enabled it, if only it could keep a cool head, to hold itself
aloof from European broils. Distribution, conquest and
annexation of territory mattered nothing to the United
States, save in the continents of America. Alliances were
to be avoided except in so far as they might serve to keep
American soil free from the menace of European rivalries.

To maintain such an attitude against the honest excitement of your fellow-countrymen is at no time an easy or a
pleasant task. Washington lost his popularity. Hamilton
became an object of execration. Jay was burned a hundred
times in effigy. The remote approval of history is a poor
substitute for the affectionate clamour of your fellow-towns-
men when you emerge bowing gratefully upon a balcony.
To practical fellows like Jefferson a preference for the
former reward appeared a kind of idiotcy. The successful
politician is ever something of a sentimentalist; an astute
sharer in the joys, sorrows and emotions of the people,
even in those which are least profound and permanent;

[1] *Works*, v. p. 406.

and he is not, therefore, to be damned as insincere. But the wise statesman must ever be prepared to accept loneliness for a bride and to cultivate fortitude upon a rock.

Here, as in all Hamilton's public acts, the dominant note is the wise and faithful stewardship of the estate. The stumbling-blocks of popular perversity, muddled thought and imaginary duties were what he set himself to remove. If only his countrymen could be made to realise their true place in the world of nations, their few simple and obvious interests as a people, if the rule of conduct in external affairs could be but once practised with courage and consistency in the tender infancy of the Republic, and made to sustain itself in the teeth of popular clamour—could these things be achieved on one conspicuous occasion, he had the foresight to understand that it would take some man greatly his own superior in force to break away from the tradition that would thus have been created. In a democracy the thing done successfully against the outcry of the people, when it comes in after times to be judged by its results and approved by the wisdom of men whose heads have in the meanwhile grown cool, is like timber in the wind-swept spaces, gnarled and twisted into a prodigious strength.

The principle of aloofness, having been successfully upheld and extended by Washington and Hamilton during the fever of the French Revolution, came in later years, by a singular perversity, to be associated with the name of the least dignified, and one of the most active, of Hamilton's enemies. To any one who has read the scurrilous invective poured out on both men from 1793 to 1797 ; to any one who has realised the eagerness with which Jefferson, Monroe, and their followers endeavoured to destroy all confidence in the characters of the President and the Secretary of the Treasury, it must appear one of the strangest of historical ironies that a lineal descendant of the policy of Washington and Hamilton should now be cherished by posterity under the name of the *Monroe Doctrine*. The compelling force of a precedent boldly established by brave men in times of difficulty is a truly marvellous phenomenon. The spectacle of Monroe, the defeated but undiscouraged assailant of Hamilton's private honour and public policy, roaring most nobly to all the ages out of the stolen skin of the 'Little Lion,' is possibly the crowning triumph of a great idea.

The *Monroe Doctrine* is an unfortunate phrase, suggestive of a pedant, mildly obstinate, carrying a scroll of sheep-skin formulas under his arm. A doctrine, as we understand it, is a prim challenge to argument; a thing open to doubt and controversy, about which endless logic may be chopped, hairs split, and tempers lost, until fashion finds another object.

The *Monroe Doctrine* is, in fact, the very opposite of all this. It is not a challenge, but a very simple warning. Nothing less arguable was ever made, and among its many virtues this is not the least. Deceived by its title, eminent men, on various occasions, have assumed or denied it to be a part of international law. But it has no nearer kin-ship to that branch of human study than to astronomy or tactics. It is in no sense a lawyer's business, but only a statesman's. It amounts to a plain declaration that for certain objects, which are well understood, the United States are prepared to spend the substance and the lives of their citizens until they are victorious or ruined. If another nation chooses to dispute these pretensions it has a perfect right to do so. There is no legality in them that makes that power which refuses to conform a moral outcast. The sanction is not in the conscience of mankind, but in the strong arm of a formidable people. If a time should come when the United States are unable to enforce the observance, or are unwilling to incur the risk and inconvenience of an appeal to arms, they will call in vain to a general congress of the world to support the *Monroe Doctrine*.

The greatness of this idea lies in its simplicity. Instead of higgling and niggling like a small shopkeeper over contiguous house property, afraid to state his object plainly from a fear of abandoning the advantages of obscurity, delaying the accomplishment of his ambitions, destroying confidence, engendering mischief and suspicion at each successive step, one nation has had the sense and courage to declare its intentions clearly and to attach the penalty of war to their infringement. Instead of weakening its position by this procedure, it has enjoyed an immunity from attack that even its great resources and remote position are inadequate to explain. The frank method of a declaration, which is the rule of great business dealings, has so far at any rate proved itself superior to the elaborate duplicity and concealment that European diplomacy has inherited from the Middle Ages.

In establishing this extraordinary method Hamilton had the chief share. The instinct of Washington was his main support, but the part played by the President was rather that of disciple than of master. The clear perception was Hamilton's. The initiative and the defence were also his. There is some sense in the Democratic sneer that the Secretary of the Treasury led Congress, cabinet and chief executive officer of the Republic by the nose. Nonsense begins when it is pretended that any of these three followed him blindly, from personal loyalty or interest, or in indolence. Men did not follow Hamilton blindly. He lacked this quality of greatness; possibly he despised it. His appeal was not limited to the reason of mankind, but it was always through the reason that he made his approaches. In his writings there are many excellent phrases, but they are the cap and plume of the argument, not the main matter of it. His power of reducing the 'forts of folly' lay not in his phrases or eloquence, but in his exhaustive discussion of the theme. The progress of his argument was like that of an army which burns, consumes and devastates every particle of sustenance in the enemy's country, overcoming resistance by the destruction of supplies.

The Declaration of Neutrality was the first position gained. It was a bold step considering the temper of the time and the fact that there was disunion, bordering close on treachery, even in the cabinet. In addition to the outcry it provoked, as a document deemed to be unsympathetic and unfriendly to France, there was the further awkward fact that it involved action. The whole procedure of the eloquent, smiling, fire-raising Genêt was illegal. The minister plenipotentiary of a foreign power had to be restrained, always a delicate and ticklish business; but when a good half or more of the citizens, inspired in a subterranean fashion by their own Secretary of State for Foreign Affairs, were shouting for him enthusiastically, it became a situation of extreme complexity.

Hamilton's method of defending the policy on which Washington and he were united was characteristic of the man and of the nation of his paternal origin. He did precisely what a good English solicitor will always forbid his client upon any consideration to undertake—he trusted to reason and wrote long letters. To trust to the luck of the law and put nothing upon paper that can be avoided is no doubt the safer rule for ordinary men. But Hamilton was not an ordinary man, and he entertained an almost fanatical belief in the efficacy of practical arguments, of reason as distinguished from logic, for persuading an excited democracy to abandon the pursuit of folly.

Nature had not endowed him with wit or humour, so that

he escaped without danger the pitfalls of a mistimed vivacity that have swallowed up so many brilliant controversialists. His writings have a most dangerous quality, for it is all but impossible to read them without being dragged to his conclusions. If Jefferson could have included them in an *index expurgatorius*, he would certainly have risked the imputation of tyranny for the sake of the result. This being impossible, he laid his hand upon the very worst device that could have been contrived: he put up inferior men to answer them.[1] The inferior men got terribly mauled and knocked about, and people with Jeffersonian sympathies, reading, we may suppose, innocently and for the sake of the fun, gradually found themselves in the opposite camp.

The letters of *Pacificus*[2] were aimed at a popular illusion. The plea of gratitude to France was analysed, in a spirit neither hostile nor cynical, but generous and practical; and out of the discussion, as with Hamilton is invariably the case, out of the examination of the particular facts under observation, he arrives at general principles of rich wisdom and wide obligation. To say that he had a lawyer's mind might be misunderstood if the statement were made without qualification. No man was ever more free from the tyranny of legal pedantry or a slavish adherence to forms and formulas; but he was urged on by his nature to that perpetual quest after the governing principle in every new situation and set of circumstances which is the mark of the greatest lawyers.

Pacificus found an unexpected ally in Genêt, who, having in the first instance tickled sentimental unreason with much success, ended by treading on its toes. Neutrality was established in a position unassailable by sympathy with France;

---

[1] *History*, v. p. 340.

[2] *Works*, iv. pp. 460-482. See particularly numbers IV., V. and VI., which seem to reach the high-water mark of political controversy.

but it remained to secure neutrality against attacks inspired by a blind hatred of Britain.

It is probable that, from the point of view of the United States, Hamilton would have made a better treaty, but Jay succeeded in making a sufficiently good one. The differences were removed and substantial advantages were obtained by the Americans. Jay accordingly was burned in effigy, and the infamy of Washington and the Senate in confirming the agreement was denounced under Democratic inspiration in terms that had hardly been exceeded in regard to the treachery of Arnold.

Hamilton, now no longer in office, came to the defence of the government, the treaty, and of Jay. *Camillus* is a tremendously long document, consisting of nearly forty letters that would have occupied not less than a hundred columns of the *Times*.[1] The process of conquest by exhaustion is carried so far that one marvels at the heroic qualities of the generation that was wooed in such a fashion. Few people will read *Camillus* to-day from cover to cover. Those who achieve it, while not ceasing to marvel at the popular taste in 1795, will derive much comfort even from the discussions of Vatel, Bynkershoeck, Puffendorf, Grotius and other classical writers upon the Law of Nations. For the casual reader, interested in the difficult problem of how nations, whose interest it is to be friends, may adjust their differences without loss of dignity, the seven letters which commence the series are still as full of life and meaning as on the day when they were written. Of all Hamilton's writings we should put them in the highest place. There is in them a noble spirit of vigorous wisdom. They have a practical quality which is not sordid, a sympathy and consideration for the feelings of the other nation which is far

---

[1] *Works*, v. p. 189 *et seq.* Eight of these letters were written by Rufus King.

removed from weakness. Even in his onslaught upon the factions and the mischief-makers he is magnanimous. His contempt is terrible, because it is entirely without malice. Looking beyond the persons of his opponents, he pours out a measureless scorn upon government by weak men and vague words; upon the policy of drift, which possesses neither the courage to foresee results nor the energy to prepare for them; upon those people, arguing interminably to delay action, who grudged every sacrifice whether its object were peace or war, who denounced with the same cantankerous hostility all preparations as aggressive, and all concessions as cowardice.

There are two documents of pre-eminent fame in the early history of the United States — the *Declaration of Independence* and Washington's *Farewell Address.* The former was written by Jefferson, while in his thirty-third year,[1] to embody the ideas and aspirations of Congress on the eve of the struggle for independence. The latter was written by Hamilton twenty years later[2] to convey the counsels of the first President to the nation on his retirement from public life. The two papers invite a comparison at several points.

To the cold reader of to-day, who owes no duty of gratitude or reverence in either case, the comparison is to the disadvantage of the earlier document. We are inclined to rate it lower than it deserves, because of the somewhat faded fashion of its rhetorical bedizenments. We lament its lack of restraint, and suspect unreality lurking under a wealth of phrases that have come to be somewhat discredited as currency. It occurs to us, looking back upon the event, that the occasion was one when the simplest words would have served best. We are affected by certain flourishes unpleasantly, as by things misplaced and somewhat gaudy

[1] Summer of 1776.　　　　[2] 1796.　Æt. 39.

We breathe an atmosphere of travesty and burlesque. The ready writer, from an artistic standpoint, is rarely the best spokesman when stern citizens are preparing to go out to battle for the idea of liberty. The proclamations of Generals Botha and Delarey have an accent of dignity which is lacking in the flowing smoothness of Dr. Leyds.

If we are to view this *Declaration* fairly on its merits, we must put on one side both the enthusiasm with which it has been regarded ever since by the American nation, and that derisive contempt with which the brilliant reviewer is apt to welcome the appearance of a new poet. The enthusiastic judgment combines a natural gratitude to the man with the pride of a very remarkable achievement. We are stirred by it as we are apt to be stirred by the contemplation of a monument, good, bad, or indifferent, which has been erected on a famous battlefield. The derisive judgment is equally inadequate, for the cool test of reason cannot be applied to a purely dramatic incident.

Jefferson was constitutionally incapable of writing for posterity. When he attempted it with the greatest care, as in his *Anas* and *Autobiography*, he made the most conspicuous failure. The more he tried for it, the worse was the result, the more contrary to his desires and intentions. But to catch the emotions of the moment and express them in words that made men shout as they read them was his peculiar gift. Even if the *Declaration of Independence* lacks every quality of permanence, and remains a famous piece of writing merely because it is associated inseparably with a great event, that criticism does not affect its virtue for the purpose it was designed to accomplish. It has the essential quality of great oratory, for it blew upon the smouldering embers in the hearts of the men to whom it was addressed until they burst into flame. It proclaimed the justice of the cause, held up an ideal of

A.D.
1793–1797
Æt. 36-40

conduct, inspired hope and courage; and these were the supreme needs of the moment. A still greater man might have achieved this, and at the same time something more. The *Declaration* is no mine of political wisdom, no model of literary excellence; but the thing it did was of far higher importance than the thing it has failed to do.

The *Farewell Address* being less dramatic in its occasion afforded fewer opportunities to the spirit of oratory. It is the testament of a man who, having served his country for five-and-forty years in war and peace, felt that his work was done, his strength for contest spent, his rest well earned. There were no personal or party ends to serve. To a vain man there might have been a temptation to chronicle his services. A lover of applause might have yielded to the desire to part company with a universal benediction—a good word for every one, so that his enemies might unite with his friends in praise of the departing hero. These were the obvious snares. But Washington was not the man to fall into either trap; and had there been a danger, he was saved from it by his choice of a clerk.

The *Farewell Address* is a stern document. Duty is its keynote; not complacency or smooth words. Most men who have read it will be inclined to name the *Farewell Address* as among the noblest public statements that men have made. About his own services Washington says little, except to plead, with every appearance of sincerity, his fallibility, and to justify his retirement, not on grounds of eminent success, but of prolonged labour. He utters three solemn warnings:— against any weakening of the Union; against the growth of party spirit; and against foreign entanglements. As to the second his words have been unheeded; not from a lack of reverence in his countrymen, but from the nature of the case. The authors of the *Farewell Address* desired an excellence incompatible with the form of government that had been deliberately chosen. A Democracy that is not governed by parties, parties that are not affected by the spirit of faction, are things yet undiscovered. But for the rest they have been justified in their countrymen, whether we judge the result by the test of sacrifices, or by the test of success.

To attempt a separation of Washington and Hamilton in the authorship of the *Farewell Address* would be a futile and invidious task. In their political aims no two men were ever more nearly at one. Privately, there would appear to have been a certain barrier of formality. The difference in age, the temperament of the President, the deliberate effort on the part of Hamilton to surround the highest office with respect and stateliness, are enough to explain it. But in public affairs the unanimity was a perfection that leaves us amazed. That Hamilton's extraordinary intellect may have influenced his chief is more than likely; but in every serious emergency the instinct of the two men pointed out the same course. The special function of Hamilton was to set forth the reasons on which the policy was founded, and to discover the means for carrying it into execution. The spirit of the *Address* belongs equally to both. It was the message of Hamilton and Washington together to the people of the Republic.

But what gives this statement a universal value, and places it permanently in the literature of the world, is the mind of Hamilton, and not the character of Washington. It is no disparagement to the fame of one who was a great soldier and a wise ruler to deny him a further reward to which he himself would never have laid a claim. Had Washington written his *Farewell Address* without assistance from any quarter, it is incredible that it would not have been a memorable document, full of noble counsel, high dignity and sincere patriotism; but what makes its im-

BOOK V

THE POLITICIANS

CHAPTER I

The End of an Epoch

A.D.
1795–1797
Æt. 38-40

HAMILTON retired from Washington's cabinet on the last day of January 1795. He had been in office for upwards of five years. He remained in power for six years longer. To the end of Washington's term (March 1797) he was the chief counsellor and the strongest supporter of the President and his government. The letters of *Camillus* and the *Farewell Address* were only the most conspicuous of his many public labours; and it is the fact that his private industry, of which we get a glimpse in his voluminous correspondence, was of an even more arduous character.

The confidence with which his great chief sought his assistance during this stormy period, the deference paid him by the newly constituted cabinet, his successors in office, the admiration and allegiance of the whole Federalist party, might have compensated for the bitterness and abuse of the Democrats had the question uppermost in his mind been the personal one. But this with him was never the case, not from virtue so much as from temperament. The permanence of the works of his hands was ever more precious to him than his own prosperity and reputation. The growing power of the opposition seemed to him to be a menace against the institutions of the Republic. The faithfulness and good opinion of his friends, although grateful to him in a personal sense, did not provide an adequate security against the dangers which he dreaded.

He still continued after Washington's retirement to be the most powerful influence in political affairs until the end of the presidency of John Adams. But during these four years the conditions and their issue were less fortunate. With the new head of the State he was united by their common hatred of anarchy; but in their personal relations all was discord and intolerance. Hamilton, said Adams, speaking bitterly of his own term of office, was all the time "the commander-in-chief of the House of Representatives, 'of the Senate, of the heads of Department, of General 'Washington, and last, and least, if you will, of the President 'of the United States!" It cannot be a pleasant position for any man to preside over a cabinet which reposes its confidence, and takes its inspiration, if not actually its orders, from an outsider—from a lawyer in New York engaged, but unfortunately not absorbed, in the labours of an enormous practice.

The motives of Hamilton's resignation were mainly private. He had spent all his savings. The official salary of the Secretary of the Treasury was, even in those days, an impossible pittance for a man without private means. He was deeply in debt, not through an inability to manage his affairs, but because he had given his time and energies to his country instead of to the pursuit of his own fortune. No suspicion of miscalculation or incompetence attaches to him. Had rich admirers been willing to endow him, and had he been willing to accept their alms, it is probable, from his conduct in the matter of his actual savings, he would have employed the funds shrewdly. The chance, A.D. 1795–1797 Æt. 38-40 however, did not come his way. Political admiration at the end of the eighteenth century had not yet learned to write large cheques. He was in debt, and had no mind to die in debt. He was acutely conscious that his public work had entailed a sacrifice not merely of his own ease, but of the interests of his family. The last nine years of his life were devoted to the honourable but undramatic end of discharging his debts and providing for his children.

On the political side the motive of his retirement is probably clearer to the world to-day than it was to Hamilton himself at the time. He was the man of an epoch, and the epoch was ended. On the ground which the Revolution had cleared the plan of a nation had been marked out, the foundations had been trenched and laid, the fabric had begun to rise. The main work he had set himself with Washington to do was done. The States were independent. They were united. They were financially sound. They were started upon a wise and dignified course of policy with regard to other nations. They were at peace when all the European continent was plunged in war.

For the permanency of human institutions two things are necessary: a clear idea consistent within itself, and a living and vigorous tradition. Thought alone is not enough to entitle a man to the fame of a constructive statesman. It must be converted into action. To him, therefore, who not only thinks, but proves the thought capable of serving his purpose, is the power present and to come. His institutions, like an estate, pass to future generations under a beneficent mortmain.

Of Hamilton's main ideas only that concerned with commercial policy was left unachieved. Political conditions would have rendered it a long and most difficult task. His private circumstances made even an effort towards it impossible. Moreover, he foresaw clearly that if only the fabric of the Union held together, his plans for industries and manufactures would inevitably be adopted, sooner or later, by his successors. For until they were carried into practice a blank would remain in the general scheme of policy, so obvious that it could not be overlooked.

He may not have been fully conscious at the period of his retirement that he had been the chief factor in one of those rare, great works of statesmanship that stand out from the mass of merely useful accomplishment like a mountain island in mid-ocean. For although he had a soaring ambition, he lacked the power of standing back and regarding his times and his own actions therein in a spirit of detachment. The golden, dramatic imagination which has been so rich a recompense to some great men and to many mountebanks, was wanting in his composition. He may not have foreseen, and in all likelihood did not endeavour to foresee, his place in history; but as a true descendant of two shrewd and well-judging races, the Huguenot and the Lowland Scot, he did not nourish his fancy on illusions. He was fully aware at the age of forty, when most men are entering upon their careers, that the greatest work he could ever hope to do was done, and lay behind him. In comparison with what had been accomplished, the present was a time of little problems and wearisome details, of party triumphs and personal ambitions. His energy continued, but the zest was gone out of public life. After having slain giants, only a philosopher could return contentedly to the herding of sheep.

There is a tragical element in these last nine years quite apart from the circumstances of his death. He undervalued what had been done. He feared that the institutions he had been unable to strengthen according to his judgment, would fail to stand the stress of events. His public papers maintain a discreet and statesmanlike reserve upon this dangerous topic, but his private correspondence and his recorded conversations leave us in no doubt as to his opinions.

In addition to the original disintegrating force of State Rights, a fresh and, to his eyes, a terrible danger had arisen in the shape of Democracy. These two forces his great rival Thomas Jefferson had compacted into a party which was growing rapidly in popularity and power, and threatened very soon to seize upon the government. It must be admitted by his strongest admirers that he misjudged these dangers, and overrated the destructive power of both forces. If Hamilton, who saw so far and so wide, did not see these things as men see them to-day, it is not after all very wonderful; for he was bound to judge both pleas as they were presented by their advocates, and to weigh to some extent the characters of their advocates.

The case for State Rights was in the hands of the Democratic party. The chief argument was an appeal to mean motives and dangerous jealousies, which rallied to its support all those who hated the constitution. The true virtues of the State Rights doctrine were hidden as closely from Jefferson as from Hamilton. The zeal of the one, the opposition of the other, were equally grounded upon a misconception of its nature. It was the same with Democracy. The sturdiest upholder of the institution turns with disgust from the records of those years when blatancy and disordered emotions are its representatives. If we were called upon to judge democracy solely upon the manifestations of French and American opinion during the period of the Revolution, we should not hesitate any more than Hamilton did to condemn it utterly.

The growing confidence of the people in Jefferson's inspiration seemed to Hamilton to be proof of his forebodings.

Men have always been apt to take this view of any popular inclination towards a political opponent. But after all, it is the tradition which drives, and the politician who has to draw the coach along. Hamilton, fearful for the safety of his institutions, did not take this comfortable view of the matter. The predilection for Jefferson showed a lack of power in the people to discriminate between leaders who saw into the realities of things, and those others who saw only the shadows that phrases cast upon the wall. From a long and bitter conflict he knew Jefferson to be neither wise nor brave. He knew him to be incapable of looking at the facts. He knew him to be entirely lacking in executive ability, and he assumed as a matter of course, though wrongly as things turned out, that the first need in the President of the United States was that he should be a man of action.

But even allowing for so much of error in his calculations, it cannot be pretended that Hamilton's vision of the dangers to the Union which seemed to lie in State Rights was altogether an illusion, or anything resembling an illusion. More than half a century later one of the bloodiest wars in history, lasting over a period of four years, grimly justified his presage of disaster. All that can be urged against his judgment is that he thought the peril to be more imminent than was actually the case. But even this is doubtful. It is impossible to avoid the feeling, as we read the history of those sixty years, that it was a freak of fortune, good-luck or ill-luck, which postponed the struggle to the presidency of Lincoln. The outbreak might have occurred as naturally under Jefferson or Monroe, Jackson or Harrison.

As regards Democracy, Hamilton must be judged to have been even more in the wrong; for he believed anarchy to be its necessary issue. The spectacle of France had disturbed the compass of his mind, as it disturbed also the judgments of all his great contemporaries; of Fox no less than of Burke, of Washington as much as Jefferson. To one set of thinkers there seemed to be a promise of the millennium, to the other a certainty of the inferno. From the tumults and massacres of Paris, Hamilton argued, without proper allowance either for race or tradition, and without a clear perception of the essential difference between the two cases. Democracy in France, where alone it had been indulged in its purity, had led to inconceivable political folly, to the destruction of order, to wholesale murder and finally to despotism. To his mind this seemed to be a natural and even an inevitable sequence. He did not penetrate the disguises in which the supreme needs and the passionate desires of the two peoples were enveloped. Had he so penetrated he must have distinguished between the two cases and endured less anxiety.

It is of all political events the most improbable that a strong nation will allow its institutions, even in their green youth, to be overset by any merely imaginary grievance. A ferment may be caused by words and phrases that have no practical meaning, but with average good fortune things will settle before it comes to serious action. That a number of agitators and journals depicted Washington as a bloodthirsty tyrant and an oppressor of liberty did not constitute any real menace to the Union. That the citizens of New York and Philadelphia banqueted, and mangled pigs, and shouted French phrases, and wore tricolour ribbons, and sang the Marseillaise Hymn, did not prove them to be impregnated with the spirit of the September massacres. The whole manifestation was a mere fashion, and when we review it calmly at a distance, the most we feel inclined to say of anything having so little real importance is that it was an ugly fashion entirely unsuited to the wearers and their conditions.

A.D.
1795–1797
Æт. 38-40
The obstruction to his plans explains much of Hamilton's antipathy to Democracy, but under what other form of government a man gifted and circumstanced like himself might have been sure of faring better he would probably have been puzzled to explain. Certainly not under a despotism, or a limited monarchy, or under such a republic as he had desired to set up. But finding difficulties in his way at every fresh effort to improve the prosperity of his country, he laid the charge of placing them there at the door of a malicious Democracy, without considering that all men at all times, and under every variety of political institution, have fared as he did, and few of them so fortunately. We feel with him in his chagrin, but we quarrel with his indictment. The far-sighted, swift-thinking reformer, the builder of states and maker of constitutions, may as well lay his account at starting with much mortification. That the people, the force without which all his efforts must fall to the ground, will not understand and cannot keep pace; that on many occasions they prefer the catch-penny tags of his ill-wishers to his own well-reasoned advocacy; that base words often soothe their vanity or allure their selfishness, while truth boldly spoken grates upon their ears and fills their hearts with resentment,—all these things are no good reason for a profound distrust.

During the whole of this period Hamilton was over-wrought, worked almost to death, and assailed with the most malignant calumnies. His courage never flagged. His wisdom in great things remained as clear as ever. But he saw everything black; not only his enemies, but even the people and the future of the nation. It is to his credit that he should have kept the outward form of his faith as firmly as he did. With few exceptions, his public documents give no evidence of distrust. Their appeal is founded always upon reason and directed by high motives. Cynicism is entirely absent. But although we admire the fortitude of his conduct, we are conscious of the presence in him of a spirit that would have made future victory impossible.

Making every allowance for the circumstances, we must judge him to have been of too impatient a temper ever to have held the position of a great party leader in a democracy settled to its round of humdrum business. His true place, and the place which he so gloriously filled, was at the beginning. His fit task, his joy and his triumph, were in dragging order out of chaos, while ordinary men stood about him dazed and confounded by the hugeness of an unexampled crisis. He lacked astuteness and natural cunning. He lacked also sympathy and tact. He treated men severely upon their merits, which is fatal, and failed conspicuously when he attempted to secure the adhesion of important mediocrities, who are at all times vain and usually self-interested. When a compliment would have served his purpose admirably, he gave a reason and left his audience cold. He failed in the management of the rank and file of his party, and he failed no less with popular opinion. He never allowed it to have its head; never waited till a favourable opportunity offered for guiding it as he wished it to go. In small things, as in great ones, if the people were in his judgment wrong, he fought against them. He could not, like Jefferson, stand aside until the storm had passed. This is magnificent but it is not the art of governing a Democracy. He was, in fact, a great statesman, but a poor politician under the conditions that had been imposed. In spite of all his defects he had qualities which, under the British system of parliamentary government, would probably have altered the face of affairs. But under the system of Cabinet responsibility which had been adopted in the United States, what he lacked was fatal and what he possessed was of little value when once the first great struggle was concluded.

CHAPTER II

James Monroe

SHORTLY before Christmas 1792 an incident occurred of which at the time only a vague rumour was bruited in political circles. Had all the five gentlemen concerned in it kept to their words, given as gentlemen (as four of them did), it is improbable the world would ever have known Hamilton in the full strength of his character. To the chief actor it was in all likelihood the severest trial of his life. It was squalid, sensational and undignified. The private life of the Secretary of the Treasury was thrown open, like the house of some notorious bankrupt, when the bills are up and the auctioneer rattles his hammer, to a crowd of vulgar gazers and curious gossips. It is clear that to Hamilton the mere fact that the world was to be admitted to an inspection of his personal affairs was odious and repugnant. The intrusion was what chiefly mattered. That men busied themselves in pronouncing moral verdicts, condemning vice and jeering at the predicament of the sinner, was doubtless an odious aggravation, but it was subordinate. Had the crowd pushed their way in to admire his private virtues and gloat over the spectacle of his domestic affections, it would have been almost as intolerable. For he had never traded, like other statesmen then and since, upon his private virtues. The Scots character at its best, both gentle and simple, abhors such invasions with an intensity that has its equal perhaps only among the Jews. He was a servant of the nation, and as regarded the performance of his public duties any charges, the most malevolent, the most trivial, or the most absurd, he was bound to answer patiently and at length. It was a part of his duty. To have alleged his personal honour as a reason for not answering a political opponent would have struck him as admitting the world to a familiarity which his pride forbade. The world had no right to concern itself with him save as a steward; and for every detail of his stewardship he was at all times fully prepared to answer.

But this plan, whereby a man endeavours to keep his two lives apart—his private life in one watertight compartment, his public in another—has always been difficult in democracies, even in the earliest democracies of which we have records. It requires a vigilance, a correctness of behaviour, a perpetual concern and circumspection even about trifles—good as well as bad, wise as well as foolish—that is seldom found in conjunction with the exuberant temperament of genius. Moreover, it was easier to escape the personalities of Aristophanes, the penetrating curiosity of Athenian scandalmongers, than the rectitudinous inquisition that is enjoyed under the freedom of the press. In private life Hamilton was not always vigilant, not seldom incorrect, and with regard to precautions against assassins, of life or character, he viewed them impatiently, as Cæsar did, considering that immunity was not worth the purchase at such a price.

Accordingly he did not, any more than Cæsar, secure immunity; and the price he had afterwards to give for redemption would have staggered a poorer spirit into bankruptcy. For not only had he to pay dearly in derision, in offence to his pride, in the loss of the good opinion of many good men; but also in the distress and humiliation of a wife whom, in spite of his errant disposition, he loved and cared for, as more respectable characters occasionally do not, from the beginning of their courtship to the end of his days.

In the summer of 1791 Hamilton had drifted into an intrigue with a woman of the name of Reynolds, who professed to him that she had been deserted by her husband. The husband in due course, being a sort of stage husband, appeared upon the scene. At first he attempted the bully; afterwards became lachrymose and pathetic; talked of his ruined happiness and home. Finally, on receipt of a thousand dollars, paid in two instalments, he was consoled; and throughout the remainder of the first act played the part of a zealous and cheerful pandar. Letters passed between the three persons concerned, which Hamilton (vigilant in this particular) filed and docketed. The necessities of Reynolds, induced, as it is hardly necessary to state, by undeserved misfortunes, recurred at short intervals, and Hamilton parted with a considerable sum, in small amounts, in exchange for formal receipts.

The second act began towards the end of 1792, when Hamilton's own department, the Treasury, in the ordinary routine of its public duty, and apparently without the cognisance of its chief, proceeded to the prosecution and conviction of Reynolds and a confederate called Clingman, for subornation of perjury in a case of fraud. Political influence was brought to bear on behalf of the felons; but Hamilton refused to interfere, and they were ultimately released, upon terms which the officials of the Treasury, in whose jurisdiction the matter lay, considered to be regular and advantageous to the public service. When they came out of prison Clingman communicated with Muhlenberg, the Democratic Speaker of the House of Representatives, informing him that his friend and fellow-prisoner, Reynolds, possessed documents that would 'hang the Secretary to the Treasury'; that Hamilton had frequently supplied him (Reynolds) with money for the purpose of speculating in the funds on their joint behalf, their operations being based

A.D.
1792–1797
Æt. 35-40

upon Hamilton's internal knowledge. Muhlenberg hastened
to share these joyful tidings with two members of his party
—with Venables and Monroe, afterwards famous as the
godfather, if not actually as the maker, of the 'doctrine.'
These three highly respectable politicians proceeded to hold
interviews with the two gaol-birds and Mrs. Reynolds, who
now came upon the stage in her true colours. The game
of blackmail was up. There might be advantages, pecuniary and otherwise, in a new policy: at any rate there were
the pleasures of revenge.

The three worthy congressmen eagerly studied the documents offered for their inspection, and being carried away
by excitement, did not stop to ponder over the improba-
bilities. That a minister of finance, accustomed to think in
millions, should have doled out, never more than five
hundred, usually only thirty or forty dollars at a time,
to accomplish his crooked ends, roused no suspicions. They
gravely considered the propriety of going hot-foot to President Washington with their mare's nest; but by good
fortune for themselves and ill fortune for Hamilton, they
prudently decided to ask, in the first place, for an explanation of the damning evidence.

The first scene of act the third was laid at Hamilton's
office in the Treasury, where the three gentlemen were
begged to be seated, and proceeded to open the matter of
their visit. The event may be described in Hamilton's own
words. "Muhlenberg introduced the subject by observing
' to me that they *had discovered a very improper connection*
' between me and a Mr. Reynolds; extremely hurt by this
' mode of introduction, I arrested the progress of the discourse
' by giving way to very strong expressions of indignation.
' The gentlemen explained, telling me in substance that I had
' misapprehended them; that they did not take the fact for
' established; that their meaning was to apprise me that,

A.D.
1792–1797
Æt. 35-40

' unsought by them, information had been given them of an
' improper pecuniary connection between Mr. Reynolds and
' myself; that they had thought it their duty to pursue it,
' and had become possessed of some documents of a sus-
' picious complexion; that they had contemplated laying the
' matter before the President, but before they did this they
' thought it right to apprise me of the affair, and to afford an
' opportunity of explanation; declaring at the same time that
' their agency in the matter was influenced solely by a ⁀se
' of public duty and by no motive of personal ill-will. I ⁀
' memory be correct, the notes from me in a disguised h⁀
' (i.e. to Reynolds) were now shown to me, and without ⁀
' moment's hesitation I acknowledged to be mine.

' I replied that the affair was now put upon a different
' footing—that I had always stood ready to meet fair inquiry
' with frank communication—that it happened, in the present
' instance, to be in my power by written documents to remove
' all doubts as to the real nature of the business, and fully to
' convince that nothing of the kind imputed to me did in fact
' exist. The same evening at my house was by mutual
' consent appointed for an explanation." [1]

Hamilton engaged his friend Wolcott to be present at this
interview. The letters and other documents were taken
from their pigeonhole, and the reading of them commenced.
" One or more of the gentlemen (i.e. Venables and Muhlenberg)
' were struck with so much conviction, before I had gotten
' through the communication, that they delicately urged me
' to discontinue it as unnecessary. I insisted upon going
' through the whole, and did so. The result was a full and
' unequivocal acknowledgment on the part of the three
' gentlemen of perfect satisfaction with the explanation, and
' expressions of regret at the trouble and embarrassment
' which had been occasioned to me. Mr. Muhlenberg and

[1] *Works*, vii. pp. 398, 399.

'Mr. Venables, in particular, manifested a degree of sensibility 'on the occasion. Mr. Monroe was more cold, but entirely 'explicit." [1]

Following upon this, memoranda were made, letters were exchanged, documents were copied. No shred of doubt was permitted to remain by any of the persons concerned that Hamilton's statements were fully accepted by them, and entirely proved by the evidence which he had submitted to their examination. It was further agreed that all notes, copies and originals, should be retained by the gentlemen themselves, and not allowed to come into the possession of the blackmailing trio, or of any others who might misuse them. The undertaking was carefully observed by all except Monroe.

After the interview at Hamilton's house, Monroe "had 'another interview with Clingman, who declared Hamilton's 'explanation to be a fabrication, originally made up between 'Hamilton and Reynolds to cover their real transactions; 'and all this rascally stuff Monroe embodied in still another 'memorandum," [2] which, however, he does not appear to have communicated to either of his colleagues; certainly not to either Hamilton or Wolcott. He then consigned all the papers to 'a respectable character in Virginia,' in whose custody (if indeed he were anything but a pigeon-hole in Monroe's desk) they remained—until they were wanted.

The fourth act took place after an interval of more than four years. The mine was laid in 1792; it was not exploded till 1797. Hamilton had left office, but was still the leader of the Federalist party. Monroe had been minister in Paris, and had conducted himself with so great a fatuity, that Washington was forced to recall him. He was an object of derision and attack to the Federalists. Hamilton's influence with the President and the public

[1] *Works*, vii. pp. 399, 400.   [2] *Works* (Senator Lodge's footnote), vii. p. 370.

had been used with his accustomed energy and frankness to bring about the recall of the scatter-brained diplomatist. The time therefore for firing the mine was clearly indicated by the finger of destiny. Monroe did not hesitate. 'The respectable character in Virginia' handed over the documents to one Callender, the editor of an annual publication avowedly in the interest of the Democratic party, called the *History of the United States.* In the volume published early in 1797, which covered the events of the previous year, the charge of corruption was revived against Hamilton, and was based upon the subsequent memorandum of Monroe. There was a little bungling. The editor did not profess to be 'influenced *solely* by a sense of public duty,' but naïvely pleaded the further justification that the Federalist party were assailing the reputation of the good and valuable man Monroe.

The choice of the instrument of defamation is worthy of notice. Callender was a drunken and profligate rascal. His slanders against Washington were as copious and malignant as those against Hamilton himself. Nevertheless he was in the counsels and confidence of the Democratic party; for the excellent reason that he did them vigorous service in bespattering their enemies with mud. He enjoyed the special protection of Jefferson, who befriended him in various ways and was not backward to aid him with money. This, it may be heartily admitted, he had fairly earned. When he was prosecuted for sedition in May 1800, we find Monroe still his upholder, denouncing the prosecution, and suggesting that the executive should employ counsel to defend him. But in June 1801, and for ever afterwards, he is a 'serpent,' and deserving of a serpent's doom. The explanation of this change in sentiment was that Callender, an artist in calumny, had in the meantime turned his attention to the private life of his former patron Jefferson, where he had discovered materials for the exercise of his talents.

The fifth act was short, and sharp, and full of dramatic movement. Hamilton wrote at once to the three gentlemen—his opponents—asking them for an explanation. Muhlenberg and Venables replied, clearly and definitely: first, that they never had had copies of the documents in their possession, and consequently had no responsibility for the publication, which they regretted and deplored as a breach of an honourable understanding; secondly, that they had always adhered to the opinion expressed by them at the conclusion of the interview in December 1792, viz.—" that ' they were perfectly satisfied with the explanation Hamilton ' had then given, and that there was nothing in the transac- ' tion which ought to affect his character as a public officer, ' or lessen the public confidence in his integrity." [1]

In a joint letter written with Muhlenberg, Monroe thinks " proper to observe that . . . we had no agency in, or know- ' ledge of, the publication of these papers, till they ap- ' peared " [2] in Callender's volume—a statement which places too great a strain upon human credulity. That Monroe alone had the documents which Callender made use of; that Monroe alleged that he had entrusted them 'to a respectable character in Virginia,' whom he did not produce; and that they turned up precisely when they were wanted in order to blacken the character of a man who was leading an attack on Monroe—all these things were sufficiently clear, and the world has never hesitated to draw the obvious conclusion.

Monroe, whose writings are ever tuned to a bleating note, now entered into a separate correspondence with Hamilton. So far from taking the open line of his colleagues with regard to the original interview, he ambiguously hints

[1] *Works*, vii. pp. 400, 450.   [2] *Ibid*. vii. p. 456.

that he has always entertained suspicions, and impudently goes on to state that he will preserve an open mind upon Hamilton's guilt or innocence of the corruption alleged, until Hamilton has laid his explanation before the public. "Whether the imputations against you as to speculation 'are well or ill founded," he proceeds sanctimoniously, "depends upon the facts and circumstances which appear 'against you upon your defence." [1]

It was always dangerous to provoke Hamilton to make a defence, for, as we have seen, he had the gift of the counter-stroke. He continued to conduct the correspondence for a few weeks longer; accused Monroe of being 'actuated by motives towards me malignant and dishonourable'; [2] and informed him that he intended to publish the whole of the documents, along with the present correspondence and a full explanation. Monroe shuffled and blustered. If Hamilton wished to fight, he was ready to oblige him. Hamilton replied courteously that he had no intention of challenging Monroe, but if that gentleman should feel himself aggrieved by the publication of documents in which he was to be pilloried as 'malignant and dishonourable,' Hamilton would be delighted to name his friend. But Monroe explained that he had no such intention.

This is the story. The accusation in Callender's publication was corruption. It was alleged that Hamilton had entered into a conspiracy with Reynolds to speculate upon his knowledge of the government's intentions. The public was ignorant of all the rest.

Three courses were open: to ignore the charge; to deny it; or to tell the whole story. The first was tantamount to an admission. The second could never have ended the matter. The third needed a steadiness of nerve that Monroe and his partner might be excused for believing to be beyond

[1] *Works*, vii. p. 466.   [2] *Ibid.* vii. p. 473.

the reach of human nature. It is clear they calculated upon the second, and relied upon an elaborate and protracted duel of rejoinders and surrejoinders, rebutters and surrebutters, in which they would have enjoyed an infinite advantage, seeing that Hamilton would all the time have been fighting with one hand tied behind his back. He would never, so they may have argued, be man enough, or fool enough, to admit his connection with Mrs. Reynolds, and to publish the squalid documents that alone could clear his reputation. One cannot find fault with their conclusion, which was probably based upon a careful self-analysis. But what might have been the rule for Monroe and Callender was not the rule for Hamilton.

Hamilton elected to tell the whole story; to publish every document in his possession, and to expound the situation, the motives of the parties, and the dangers to the community and to public life arising out of such methods, in that vehement and copious manner which he was famed for pursuing at the bar. He 'exhausted' the case. When he had made an end, there was nothing more to be said. The statement is without a reservation, and yet it is never familiar. He shirks nothing, nor seeks for any shelter against the opinion of the world. His sole aim is to set his honesty in discharge of his public duty beyond attack. A single departure from the strictest rule of simplicity, a single disingenuous excuse or sentimental quaver, would have made the statement odious. Temptations to an eternal loss of dignity lay on every side, but he had only one concern: to clear his honour. No one has yet been found bold enough to challenge the completeness of the vindication.[1]

[1] On the whole matter we are content with the terse verdict of Senator Lodge: "The character which suffers most in the business is that of 'Monroe. On him rests a dark stain of dishonour, of slippery evasion and 'of mean revenge, which has never been wiped out, and which apparently 'can never be lightened or diminished."— *Works* (Senator Lodge's footnote), vii. p. 371.

CHAPTER III

John Adams

A.D.
1797–1800
Æt. 40-43
THE result of the election of 1796 was to make John Adams President of the United States. The Federalists thereby scored a success in the first party contest, but the narrow majority of three votes by which Jefferson, the Democratic candidate, was defeated made it apparent that his partisans were gaining ground.

John Adams has been described by Franklin as "always ' an honest man, often a wise one, but sometimes and in some ' things absolutely out of his senses." [1] Anger was usually the cause of his madness, and while the fit lasted his activity was only equalled by his blindness. Some characters, having been associated with great events, have a way of passing, by mere longevity, from the second rank, to which by nature they belong, into the first rank in the estimation of their fellow-citizens. They become popular institutions. The dramatic virtue of a date has done much to embalm Adams's memory and exalt his reputation. He died on the 4th of July 1826—the anniversary of the Declaration of Independence—and, by an amazing coincidence, on the same day a few hours before him died Thomas Jefferson—both at a great age.

Adams had a pleasant face—plump, self-satisfied, and honourable. In his sayings and writings there is a humorous, sardonic, pompous quality; a dogmatism that suggests a man posing as stupider and more prejudiced than it was actually his nature to be. In the many quarrels and contests of his long life he showed always a very great pugnacity, a very bad judgment and a very hot temper. He

---

[1] *History,* ii. p. 486.

was a strong personal force in the Revolution; but when he had the chance of showing himself a statesman he came to disaster. Judged merely as a politician he was even worse than Hamilton himself.

As it takes two people to make a quarrel, so it takes two conflicting personalities to smash a party. Hamilton without Adams, or Adams without Hamilton, would in all likelihood have kept the Federalists together in a formidable minority. But Hamilton's contempt was excessive, and the jealousy of Adams was grotesque. A party is required by nature to be united. Disunited, it is a kind of disease in the body politic, good for nobody and nothing, not even for its opponents. A party with a single leader, even if he is a bad one, will do more good not only for itself but in the world, than one fighting under the standards of two leaders who cannot co-operate. The disastrous administration of Adams split the Federalists in two, and the party which had made the constitution and had set it to work passed gradually and ignominiously to meaner and meaner things, and finally out of existence.

John Adams's grievance against Hamilton was mainly a personal one. He had no quarrel with his politics, but he suspected him of an overweening ambition. He resented the deference paid to him by his own supporters and even by his own government, and he hated the superiority of his mind. At the first election of a President it was the desire of all men that Washington should be called to fill the post; but according to the clumsy system of choice the candidate who received the second largest number of votes cast for the Presidency became Vice-President. Two candidates, therefore, had to be nominated, and as it was necessary to secure Washington's election it was agreed, on Hamilton's suggestion, that while all voters should give their first vote to Washington, a certain number should throw away their second vote lest by an accident Adams might have been elected. It was a perfectly legitimate device in view of the inconvenience of the system, but Adams took it very much amiss.

When it came to Adams himself being a candidate for the Presidency, Hamilton omitted to take the same precautions, and Adams's wrath was even greater. Our sympathies are with Adams, although logic is against him. If the device was unwarrantable to elect General Washington, it was equally so in his own case. But Hamilton's position was both unfair and unwise. For Adams was the party candidate, and the duty of a party is to support its candidate with loyalty. Hamilton said frankly that he would have preferred it had Thomas Pinckney, the second Federalist nominee (intended for the Vice-Presidency), secured the first position. To leave things in such a position of uncertainty was to reduce party organisation to an absurdity. It would hardly have been more unreasonable if, on the eve of battle, one of the armies was undecided which of two generals it would follow, and left the point to be settled by the issue of the contest.[1]

The result of this half-hearted co-operation was what might have been expected. Federalists who favoured Adams threw away their votes for Pinckney, admirers of Pinckney threw away their votes for Adams. Adams was elected by the narrow majority of three, while Pinckney was defeated by nine votes by Jefferson. It is an undignified episode, and shows very plainly that Hamilton had failed to grasp the rudimentary conditions of government by parties. Indeed, it is clear he hated parties as much as he loved ideas; and the fact that he believed a Republic which rested upon popular suffrage could be conducted on any other system is

[1] Much, however, may be said for Hamilton's course of action, v. Morse's *Hamilton*, ii. pp. 224-27.

A.D.
1797–1800
Æt. 40-43

proof that he did not fully realise the nature of the institutions he had been the means of creating.

A few months later a fresh disagreement arose between the crowned and the uncrowned leaders, and on this occasion the blame lies wholly at the door of the President. The affections and hatreds between nations stand, as Washington had warned his countrymen, upon no basis except pure fantasy. An ounce of real interest, a foolish insult, a single blundering act, is sufficient to banish the whole cloud-cuckoo-town of the sentimentalist like mist before a morning breeze. The same citizens who had with so great difficulty been preserved from a war with Britain as the allies of France in 1793, were with equal fervour clamouring in 1798 for a war with France as the allies of Britain. The Republic of the West had been affronted in the persons of their envoys, whom the Republic of the Seine had treated with contumely.

The nation made ready for war. General Washington was called out of his retirement to become commander-in-chief. He made his own conditions: the first that he should not give his services until the army took the field; the second that Hamilton, Charles Pinckney and Knox should be immediately appointed as his generals. The order of nomination marked the respective rank. He made it clear that he meant to place upon Hamilton's shoulders the burden of chief command, and all the responsibilities of organisation, until hostilities had actually commenced. Adams assented; but when the commissions were made out and signed it was found that Knox had been placed before Hamilton. Washington protested and tendered his resignation. Before this awful threat even Adams in the mad-bull fit was reduced to submission. Hamilton's appointment was ungraciously confirmed after a public exhibition of ill-feeling that destroyed all hope of future concord between the leaders of the Federalist party. The attempt to exclude Hamilton from the command of the army had earned the reprobation not only of Washington and all the leading Federalists, but also of the great majority of the party. It was the first of a series of great blunders which Adams committed during his term of office under the influence of uncontrollable rage. While it began the fatal split among his own supporters, it also shook the confidence of the country in his judgment. For, strange as it may appear, enemies as well as friends, Democrats as well as Federalists, desired that Hamilton should be appointed. In a national emergency safety was the supreme object, and it was felt upon all sides that the chief power should be in the hands of the man who had given the clearest proofs of executive ability.

Hamilton desired peace for his country. War with any nation was to be avoided if possible; but he was not blind to certain advantages of a war with France, which might compensate in some measure for the evils and disturbance. No war with France could take place except at sea, and the British navy kept the ships of the Directory too well employed to give them much leisure for remote activity. On the other hand, Spain was the ally of France, so that war with one meant war with both. The Spaniards held Louisiana and the Floridas, and possessed inconvenient conflicting rights with regard to the navigation of the Mississippi. The object, therefore, of any war would necessarily be the acquisition of these territories and the settlement of these disputes for ever. The United States, given that war was inevitable, had much to gain by it and hardly anything to lose, providing they acted promptly and with a clear aim.

It is probable that Hamilton also saw other advantages in a war, advantages in the matter of internal order and the strengthening of the executive. But the idea that he desired it either from his hatred of France, or because he had ambitions of a Napoleonic career, is not to be entertained seriously. As to the first, not even Bismarck himself was less influenced by his personal antipathies in questions of foreign policy. As to the second, his whole history is a contradiction of it. No man whose object is personal glory will sacrifice his popularity to his opinions, and this was Hamilton's constant habit. At no great crisis of his life do we ever find him engaged in considering whether a certain course of action will or will not conduce to his personal aggrandisement. He belonged to the class of men with whom the accomplishment of their objects is the most powerful motive. In the pursuit of renown he hardly rose above the average of public characters, but his desire for achievement was a passion.

In the end there was no war. It was possible to avoid it with dignity. Adams chose to give dignity away with the bargain. It is beyond doubt that he caught at peace in order to prevent Hamilton from obtaining credit. His action was too inconsistent and precipitate to be explained on any other hypothesis. As at the beginning he had disregarded the calmer counsels of his cabinet in the heat of his indignation against France, so in the end he ignored them in scrambling helter-skelter for peace at any price. This was the second of the series of great blunders by which the ruin of the Federalist party was accomplished.

Hamilton's discharge of military duties during this period of doubtful negotiations was marked by his usual inability to turn out flimsy work. His measures of organisation were effective for their immediate purpose, and possessed in addition the same quality of permanence that is the distinction of his political achievements—the quality of the Roman road-makers who laid for the purposes of a single march a causeway that centuries could not destroy. Wherever Hamilton had been at work his successors found their task reduced, a body of coherent principles, a consistent plan that was capable of service long after the object for which it had been undertaken had been attained or forgotten.

CHAPTER IV

The Victory of Jefferson

IT is not wonderful that a party rent by such internal disagreements was in a poor position to face a contest with its opponents. The attempt to exclude Hamilton from command of the army, and the disgraceful conduct of the negotiations with France, were followed shortly afterwards by a third blunder. Adams, seeing everything red, and unable to tolerate the respect entertained for Washington and Hamilton by M'Henry, Pickering, and Wolcott, dismissed these gentlemen from his Cabinet on the very eve of the Presidential election. Apart from schism, however, the Federalists had lost heavily in public esteem. The blunders of Adams were of a large variety and wide extent. His administration carried things with a very high hand against their opponents. Their Sedition and Alien Acts, passed by a Congress heated by hostility to France beyond the temperature at which wise legislation is likely to be distilled, gave to Jefferson, quietly waiting and watching, the opportunity he needed.

These measures were oppressive, panic-stricken and unwise. They were contrary to the spirit of reasonable liberty, and not beyond suspicion of infringing the constitution. Jefferson seized upon the advantage with his instinctive sagacity. The ears of men were yearning for the old tunes, and he gave them loud and brazen in his best manner: State Rights and the Rights of Man; liberty, equality, and the rest of the phrases, formulas, maxims and war-cries of the golden age of paper constitutions and philosophic revolutions.   He blundered, say critics zealous for his reputation, with pos- terity.   He went far beyond the mark, alienating and distressing good men who would otherwise have ranged themselves on his side.   His object was to create an atmo- sphere favourable to his candidature, and it cannot be denied that he succeeded.   His methods excite more ad- miration for his skill than respect for his frankness.   With characteristic cowardice he concealed his authorship of the most incendiary of his electioneering addresses.   The *Ken- tucky Resolutions* [1] were transmitted to the legislators who brought them forward upon the solemn assurance that his name should not be disclosed.   The kernel of this violent document was a proposition which, if approved, would have been fatal to the Union.   Each state, he announced, had an equal and inalienable right to judge for itself whether or not any act of the central government constituted an infrac- tion of the constitution.   If a state arrived at the conclusion that the constitution had been infringed, nullification of the Act of Union was the proper remedy.   Even for the persons to whom this draft was forwarded its purport appeared too formidable, and it was found necessary to water down certain expressions.   The *Kentucky Resolutions*, according to one admiring biographer, were a wicked act of passion amounting to a precedent and authority for the War of Secession.[2]   But to judge in this fashion is to miss the real point of the matter.   To the true Jefferson, the great planner of electoral victories, the skilful manœuvrer, the brilliant foreseer of popular opinion for twelve months ahead, what did it matter if a few wise and good men were alienated ?   What did he know or care about Wars of

[1] Ford's *Jefferson*, vii. pp. 289-309.   [2] Morse's *Jefferson*, p. 194.

Secession? Jefferson at his greatest is entirely unconcerned
with posterity and its opinion of him. The art in which he
excelled was not the art of governing, but the art of sitting
in the highest place of popular favour. As an artist he was
inspired when he drew the *Kentucky Resolutions*. Their
wild extravagance gave to the extremists of his party precisely what they wanted. The opportunity was one for a
noisy orchestra. A subdued melody would have missed the
mood, and, while it might possibly have earned the respect
of future generations, would have awakened but little
enthusiasm at the time. The man who chooses the right
means to an end will always compel a certain degree of
admiration. The aim of Jefferson was to be President of the
United States at the election following, and the plan of his
campaign was admirably calculated to serve this purpose.

The election which fell at the end of 1800 was contested more keenly and upon clearer lines than its predecessor. Party organisation had advanced by great strides
during the four years of John Adams's presidency. The
campaign began in early spring, with the election of the
state legislatures in whose hands lay the choice of the
presidential electors. Pennsylvania was the first great
Federalist defeat. Short of miracles, the result would be
decided by the voting in New York state, where Hamilton,
conscious of the great issues, was leading his party against
a powerful Democratic combination. His defeat was the
work of Aaron Burr.

Burr was a consummate party organiser in a constituency
compact and small enough to be brought into actual touch
with his remarkable personality. By a truly marvellous
exercise of tact he laid for the few necessary months the
jealousies and discords of the Clinton and the Livingston
groups, and united them in firm co-operation with his own.
He devised a new weapon in party warfare, an elaborate

organisation of ward committees and canvassers, placing his trust in machinery rather than in ideals. New conditions make new tactics. The leader whose pride disdains to adapt the old drill-book to the facts before him is usually out-manœuvred. Hamilton followed the plan which had so well served him in the past,—reason and argument, pamphlets and speeches, vigorous, convincing, dignified, and in the grand manner. Burr in his unconspicuous fashion worked quietly at his lists, interviewed multitudes of unimportant men, pleasing every one by his tactful compliments, his ready counsel, his unassuming courtesy and good manners. He was not fighting for any cause, but merely for victory. Opinions and convictions were never allowed to embarrass the contest or endanger its result. A negative was much safer. The overthrow of those evil-minded Federalists, hankering after monarchy, distrusting the people, tampering with the constitution, filling the air with their noisy dis-cords, was a stronger 'ticket' than any positive propaganda. Burr's party was but newly healed of its wounds, and an outbreak of disunion was a constant menace. He viewed these conditions calmly as a wirepuller, without prejudice and without enthusiasm, and judged the highest wisdom to lie in keeping the minds of his supporters fixed upon the iniquity of their opponents, and not allowing them to stray into premature speculations upon the various uses to which a Democratic victory might be turned.

The unfortunate Burr stands in American history like some figure of straw, at whose riddled reputation every aspirant for a virtuous renown lets off his pistol. He is a sort of universal cockshy for all good men; a kind of scapegoat for democratic institutions. Doubtless he was a rascal who deserved all he got; but he is less distinguished from other politicians by the pre-eminence of his rascality than by the attainment of his deserts. He was certainly a wirepuller, a

A.D. 1800
ÆT. 43

successful practitioner of petty intrigue (if it be desired to call things by unpleasant names); but in our flight of indignation it may profitably be remembered that the methods of working an election which he employed, and which to a large extent he discovered, have been adopted by every country to which we allow the titles of free and enlightened.

The fact is, obloquy has attached itself so tightly to the name of Burr, that it is customary to abuse him for everything he did during his long and variegated life. Among other things for which he has been attacked are the methods he employed during the New York election, and people who employ no other methods at the present time, in New York and elsewhere, shake their heads over him and call him knave. The sin would appear to lie in his originality, and the plagiarists may escape censure. His methods were hated and denounced by the defeated Federalists mainly because they were new, clever and successful. They were pronounced unworthy; but seeing that they fitted the wants of the situation, and have continued to fit them from that day to this, the charge can only be supported upon the admission that Democracy itself is unworthy.

The sum of his offence in this particular is that he applied a sound, businesslike organisation to the problem of a popular election. In principle, when closely examined. we cannot see that it is open to any grave moral objection. Only in some visionary republic will the citizens ever vote in full force without much management. Ideals alone will serve the purpose only on occasions of exceptional exaltation. As for his practice, there is probably much in it that may be reprehended; much dirt and mire, bribery and promises, sordid expectations and mean appeals to low motives, with drams and libations and other like influences which do not enter into our theory of a perfect State. But allowing so much, it is but reasonable to look at the fashion of the times. In the general drab of morality Burr's historical campaign attracts no remark. It is not even a darker shadow. What is remarkable about the event is that he had discovered a machinery for working the Democracy, and that Hamilton had not.

The Federalist candidates were defeated, and with their defeat a Democrat President became almost a certainty. To Hamilton such a result appeared equivalent to the destruction of all his labours; the overthrow of the constitution, repudiation of the debt, a French alliance, and the reign of the philosophers. He made the double error of believing the windy threats of his opponents, and of underrating the strength of his own work. He had a tendency to exaggerate the dangers to be apprehended from men who spoke loud and vaguely. Jefferson was in reality too indefinite, and Burr too shrewd a thinker, to threaten very seriously any existing institution. An arrest of progress was the main thing to be dreaded, but to Hamilton's imagination nothing less than revolution and civil war seemed imminent. The real ballast of his singular character was the confidence and exuberance of youth. Middle age instead of ripening his judgment warped it.

Foreseeing an enormous disaster, and considering that any measure was justifiable to avoid it, he committed the error of petitioning the Governor to call together the old legislature and give the choice of presidential electors to districts.[1] By this means, instead of a solid Democratic vote there would be something less formidable—a division, at all events; possibly a neutrality. For this suggestion, had it been made before and not after the election, there was much to be said. On a former occasion it had even been advocated by Burr himself; but in the particular cir-

[1] *Works*, x. pp. 371-74.

cumstances it was a blunder of the first order, and the proposal was rightly rejected by Governor Jay.

After the New York election a great party leader would have seen clearly that the only chance of defeating the Democrats lay in closing up the ranks. Absolute solidarity was the first essential. Accidents and dissensions among the enemy, of which signs were not altogether wanting, might conceivably have prevented disaster. But Hamilton was not a great party leader, and in the particular circumstances his distrust of Adams ran away with him. It has been assumed, entirely contrary to the facts, that Hamilton, like the President, was actuated by personal pique. The assumption is a natural one, for there was a long account unsettled between them. The last item was an act of stupid insolence that undoubtedly estopped the President from all legitimate complaint and absolved Hamilton of all personal allegiance.[1] It is quite conceivable that Adams's course of fatuous jealousy may have warped Hamilton's judgment of his character; but it is also clear that his action during the elections was not due to any desire to wipe out old scores. Indeed, it may be said truly that on no single occasion during his public career did Hamilton ever allow his political course to be influenced by a spirit of revenge. The sequel to this very election is one of the most conspicuous examples of his restraint. The issue was not a question between individuals; and in all the United States no man realised this fact more clearly than Hamilton himself. It is therefore difficult to explain why he should have prepared a document, written in his usual cogent and convincing style, the main purpose of which was to expound the errors of John Adams, and to lay the blame of the dissensions in the Federalist party at his door. His reasoning and his array of facts were irresistible; but they entirely quarrelled with the conclusion

[1] Lodge's *Hamilton*, pp. 230-31.

of his address, in which he advised that the Federalist party should unite in support of Adams's candidature in spite of everything that had gone before. His first intention appears to have been to publish this manifesto broadcast; but under pressure he reduced the scope of his original design, and the mischievous pamphlet was converted into a confidential communication to the leaders of the party in the various districts of the Union. It is possible that even this folly might have yielded to cooler counsels; but unfortunately, if we may believe tradition, Burr happened to be walking early one morning in the streets of New York when he met the printer's boy carrying the proofs to Hamilton's house. Possessing himself of a copy he proceeded to make the contents of it public, so that the author's original intention was fulfilled.

The indiscretion was much greater than its actual effect. The voting, in spite of the blow to the Federalist party, appears to have been solid. Jefferson and Burr received an equality; between Adams and Pinckney there was only a difference of one.

Then followed a long period of alarm and intrigue. The biographer[1] of Burr represents him as having played the part of a calm and angelic personage, willing to abide by the choice of the people. Biographers of Jefferson, on the other hand, represent Burr as a dangerous and devilish character, ambitious of obtaining the presidency ' by foul means,' and the author of ' a gross betrayal.'

The venue was changed to the House of Representatives, which had to determine which of the two should be President. The choice was therefore in the hands of the routed and distempered Federalists. They believed Burr to be a knave, courteous, amusing, clever, ambitious, and corrupt; but Jefferson they believed to be a successful hypocrite.

[1] Parton.

Things having gone all wrong in the party sense they had grown reckless, and were inclined, like any demoralised and discomfited mob, to let off their pieces in a desperate fashion. It was rather a question with them which of the two candidates they hated least than which would do least harm to the United States. Being entirely beaten and without hope of carrying their own man, they came down to purely social considerations. They knew Burr to have been a distinguished soldier, a very brave man, cynical, brilliant, affectionate, good-humoured, good-mannered, dignified, and most faithful to his personal friends—all these things, but a knave notwithstanding. When the issue was reduced to a question of comradeship they were inclined upon private and personal grounds to prefer the knave to the hypocrite. Their inclination was certainly against the interest of the state, and it is probable that each Federalist was in his heart fully aware of this fact; but he also knew that his opponents of the Democratic faction regarded the election of Jefferson as a matter of supreme importance, and malice urged him to defeat this aspiration.

That Burr intrigued for Federalist support does not appear to be beyond doubt. Even had he done so the fact would hardly justify such grandiose phrases of abuse as 'foul means' and 'gross betrayal,' especially in view of the fact that Jefferson himself gave pledges to his opponents that he would not reverse the chief acts of their policy. The presumption is always against Burr, and therefore it is settled in history that he was open to an offer. While the Federalist party was swithering, the matter was settled by Hamilton. He hated Jefferson as a man and despised him as a statesman. He had no dislike to Burr as a man, but abhorred him as a politician. The idea of this cool, cynical and ambitious adventurer coming into a position where the beloved constitution would lie at his mercy was intolerable. Jefferson

was at least honest in private matters, and in affairs of state A.D. 1801
he had ideals. He would be a weak ruler, but not a rascal. Æt. 44
Moreover, it was clear beyond any doubt that the Democrats
were in a large majority, and that the choice of this party
was in favour of Jefferson. To take advantage of a clumsy
system of election in order to defeat the nomination of the
victorious party appeared to Hamilton to be bad politics.
In great matters, though not in little ones, he kept his head.
Contrary to the irresponsible opinion of his party he urged
the claims of Jefferson. All his great influence was exerted
against Burr, and in the end, against the predilection of his
own supporters, his great rival was chosen President of the
United States.

With the administration of Jefferson Hamilton had no
relations and no influence. He continued to be the chief
mind of the broken and dispirited Federalist party; the
most prominent figure, the most active and industrious
inspirer, exercising great power by his private correspondence and personal influence. But he was no longer in any
sense a director of the policy of his country. He lived long
enough to be reassured as to the permanency of his own
work, to be ashamed possibly of his misgivings, and to
realise the enormous potency of a tradition. The Union
stood. The financial policy which had been so bitterly re-
viled was maintained. The foreign relations were dominated
by the principles of the *Farewell Address*. The doctrine
of the 'implied powers' was stretched, the authority of the
executive was magnified, even beyond his most daring
anticipations, and with his full approval, by the purchase
of Louisiana. It seemed as if Hamilton's opponents were
hypnotised by his institutions. They might protest eloquently, but they were nevertheless subdued. Escape became
impossible. The tradition was everywhere victorious.

CHAPTER V

Aaron Burr

A.D.
1801–1804
Æt. 44-47
AARON BURR became Vice-President of the United States in March 1801, when, contrary to their inclinations, and under the influence of Hamilton, the Federalists permitted the will of their opponents to prevail, and Jefferson was elected to the highest office. The Vice-President is not an active force in government. He is not even a member of it; but a sort of Queen Bee kept in reserve in a cell in case the acting monarch should die or be killed. His position is one of honour and dignity, but of no executive importance. He presides over the Senate, and in earlier times was held to have a kind of reversionary interest in the Presidency.

It was no post for an active and ambitious man up to the ears in debt, with many enemies and a dubious reputation. The President treated him with something more than coolness. Prior to the New York election Burr had been the recipient of letters from the great man distinguished by the warmth of their well-wishing. Jefferson had written taking ' an opportunity of recalling myself to your memory, and of evidencing my esteem for you.'[1] But Burr the quiet organiser of victory in New York State, and Burr the rival for the Presidency, were two very different individuals. Burr had endangered his election, and had shared his popularity. By a man of a less jealous temperament than Jefferson these incidents might have been held sufficient to cancel all previous obligations.

In January 1804, when the next Presidential election was within sight, Burr, who was certainly never found wanting either in courage or candour, sought an interview with Jefferson with the object of arriving at the President's true

[1] Ford's *Jefferson*, vii. p. 145.

disposition with regard to himself. There was a supposed intention on the part of the Virginia clique (Jefferson, Madison, and Monroe) to keep the reversion of the highest office in their own hands. Vice-President Adams had succeeded to President Washington; Vice-President Jefferson had succeeded to President Adams, but Vice-President Burr was not to be allowed to follow after President Jefferson. In New York State the Democratic party was split in two. The Clintonians, supported by the Livingston faction, had now become the bitter opponents of Burr, and had started a paper of a more than usually calumnious character to destroy nim. They were supposed, and not without something to show for it, to draw encouragement from the President himself. The Federalists, it is true, were somewhat inclined to favour Burr; but more from hatred of Jefferson, the Clintons and the Livingstons, than from any love of Burr. Federalist affections were, however, little to be counted upon; for Hamilton had already shown that on any great issue he could overawe all personal sentiments, and as to Hamilton's opinion of Burr there existed no shadow of a doubt.

In these circumstances Burr came to Jefferson to ask that he would put a stop to the 'use of his name to destroy him.' Burr professed himself willing to retire from the Presidential candidature in order to avoid a party schism, but was averse from taking this step unless it were accompanied by some signal mark of favour 'which would declare to the world that he retired with Jefferson's confidence. The results of the interview were hardly encouraging. Jefferson appears from his own account[1] to have spoken at great length, making nothing clear except that he was not disposed to take the step which Burr desired. We gather, although it does not appear precisely in so many

[1] Ford's *Jefferson*, i. pp. 301-4.

words, that had Jefferson been willing to give a promise of office, Burr would have undertaken to withdraw from the coming contest, to leave the Virginian clique a clear field, and to use his influence in New York and the Northern States in favour of the official candidates. But this price Jefferson was not willing to pay; nor had he much temptation to purchase Burr's adherence, seeing that his own re-election was practically certain.

Finding the President disinclined to grant him any terms, Burr thereupon played his own game boldly and at once. He proceeded to strengthen himself in the Northern States, and as a step in the campaign he stood for the Governorship of New York. For this he has been accused of disloyalty; but then it was his misfortune always to be so accused. It is difficult to say why he should have acted otherwise than he did. The official Democrats were no friends of his. They had ignored him upon all occasions, and had lent their names to damage his reputation with his own constituents. He was not a malicious man. His object was not to cause annoyance or embarrassment to his party, but merely to win their confidence by one of the most practical means known to the human race—to make himself so powerful that he could not be disregarded. The Clinton-Livingston factions do not appear to have had any illusions in favour of Jefferson, but they fought Burr heartily for the good and sufficient reason that they were jealous of his predominance. Consequently the issue was once more in the hands of his opponents the Federalists. Again the rank and file of this party was inclined in his favour. Again Hamilton put forth all his great influence with his adherents against one whom he considered to be a national danger. Again Burr was defeated, and the defeat, situated as he then was, in debt and distrusted by his leaders, meant nothing less than the end of his political ambitions.

The catalogue of injuries that Burr had received at the
hands of his great enemy was a long one. If it is true that Washington took his estimate of Burr from his Secretary of the Treasury, then Hamilton had prevented his appointment to a foreign mission, and had again foiled his application for a high military post in the Adams administration. Hamilton's authority alone had prevented him from receiving the votes of the Federalists, and securing the Presidency of the United States over the head of Jefferson. Finally, Burr had been defeated by the same relentless adversary in his forlorn hope of the Governorship of New York, and the position of greatest power in the Northern States. Hamilton had denounced him in public utterances and private correspondence. The unguarded phrases of his letters had passed into the current vocabulary of the Federalist party. However admirable the result for the fortunes of the nation, this personal antagonism was a thing which could not be overlooked. At each fresh attempt towards the attainment of his ambition Burr found himself headed off by Hamilton.

Hamilton and Burr were born within a year of one another. Both had served with distinction in the war. Both had won a high reputation for military organisation, for leadership of men, and for courage, not only of the spirits, but of the head. Both had served on General Washington's staff, although in Burr's case this association endured only for a few weeks. They had been called to the bar at the same time, and immediately and together they found themselves famous as its leaders. Both were dandies, handsome, dashing and gallant. Both were eager and ambitious, well-read and well-mannered. Both were of the same slight build, and diminutive stature, and essential dignity. Burr had wit and humour, Hamilton gaiety and eloquence. Up to the last they met politely in court and in society, and dined at one another's houses. They were not separated by any personal dislike or constitutional antipathy, nor were they knit together by any natural attraction. Each was intelligent enough to take a pleasure in the conversation and good manners of the other. Their relations were not warm, but they were friendly and tinged with a certain respect. Both hated phrases, and had an eye for reality. The disposition of both was to be men of action, and both followed the law with much distinction, but mainly as a means to a living.

In so much that was alike in their personal qualities and in the circumstances of their lives, one great difference prevented a private intimacy or a political alliance. Hamilton, for all his combativeness, viewed politics as a religion, and never as a game. The ideas of the nation, the Union and the constitution, were sacred ideas, hardly to be spoken of lightly even in jest. He desired power, in order that he might strengthen the state. His energies were concentrated upon his ideas, and only to a small extent upon his career. He is a type of great rarity, a fighting politician who was also a disinterested statesman.

To Burr this view of the matter was foolishness. When he believed men guilty of it, which he did but rarely, he spoke of them with a good-natured scorn. The only serious zest of public life was personal: to win the game, to prevail over arduous things, to prove oneself superior to fortune, and men's favour, and every adversary. His manners were amiable, his instincts predatory. What we have already spoken of as the religion of the hive was the mainspring of Hamilton's politics. Burr was a plunderer of the hive, standing in the same relation to men as Atropos the Death's-head moth to bees. To Hamilton the welfare of the race, the eternity of the city, the divine obligation of the law, were as the Ark of the Covenant. He was a man of the world and he lived in rough times, but he kept this faith till Burr shot him in the heart at Weehawken. His strong nature was a cave of passions of every sort and description over which this ideal ruled like a tyrant. It shook his whole being as men are shaken by avarice, hatred, or love; as wild beasts are stirred by danger to their young. When a man is born in whom the instinct of self-preservation, as in a bee, is habitually and spontaneously dominated by the instinct of the safety of society, we are apt to regard him as an admirable but startling departure from the normal type. If it were possible to conceive of a nation in which such a disposition was the rule with ordinary men, it is clear that at its pleasure it could conquer the earth.

Burr also was much driven by his passions, but they were unusual only in their vigour, not in their direction. In a sense both men loved the hive, but Hamilton loved it because it contained bees, Burr because it contained honey.

It is only fair to judge a man to some extent from his own point of view and by his own standards. If he passes this test with credit, it is something even to the world, and a great deal to himself. Like Hamilton, Burr was conscious of great abilities and of a great influence over men. Neither took the slothful servant for his pattern, but all the endowments which each possessed he put to the most daring use. But, unlike Hamilton, Burr viewed his laborious enterprise as being strictly bounded by the limits and conditions of his time. The future that should begin when his own life ended was nothing to him. It did not stir him even to curiosity, far less to labour, sacrifice, or enthusiasm. What moved Hamilton was something far greater than himself, something which surrounded him on all sides, which had been before he was, which would be for centuries after he walked no longer among men. Hamilton beheld a vision. Burr saw no visions, and such men as did he accounted the victims of superstition. He saw only himself and some private persons whom he loved.

Burr did not underrate his own qualities, and he feared nothing. As a ruler of men, as the head of a great nation, he would be best able to justify the gift of his talents and to make them yield the largest usufruct. But both men and the state were of subordinate importance, and although he probably considered, honestly enough, that his triumph would be a high advantage to both, it would not have altered his resolution had he judged the matter otherwise. Men and the state were the medium in which he worked. They were the lump of marble and he was the sculptor. The supreme end was not their happiness, but his own art. His clear objective, therefore, was the highest place, and his first duty was to arrive.

We are familiar with the spectacle of the man who makes a cult of his own career. We who live in peaceful times, under fixed and powerful traditions, can regard this solemn devotion of a man to himself without anxiety; with interest, amusement, or weariness, according to the gifts of each worshipper. Out of little men it produces prigs, out of great ones buccaneers. Burr was unfortunate in his conditions; he might have had a chance in the British Parliament of those days, but he was too artificial a gamester for the circumstances in which he found himself. He needed, as it were, the prop of highly civilised conventions for his success. His pirate nature was hardly exuberant and direct enough for the rough vigour of a new nation. The example of Napoleon was his misleading. Against the wild forces of the Revolution Burr would have contended in vain with his fine manœuvres and delicate intrigue. His faith in himself was serene and imperturbable, but it never amounted, as in the case of Buonaparte, to fanaticism, and that perhaps is the chief cause of his failure as a buccaneer. For in the supreme events it is not sufficient to be reasonably persuaded; the man who is to succeed must be unreasonably confident.

Burr's minor virtues astound us : his industry, his self-discipline—upon Chesterfield maxims—his dignity unruffled by misfortune or success. He was never arrogant and never abased. Exile, poverty, starvation, deferred hopes and private sorrows, the neglect and contumely of his fellow-countrymen found him still the same—smiling, courteous, considerate for the feelings of those whom he met. He had also an extraordinary courage, daring to undertake, persistent in the carrying out, and patient under failure and adversity. His charm made him a conqueror in all societies, nor was it a thing cultivated merely for his own advantage (though, doubtless, he must have known its utility), but sprang spontaneously from a sympathetic and affectionate nature, from an eager and ever youthful interest in thought and in men. He was wanting in enthusiasm in public life, but he was equally wanting in misanthropy. His enemies prevailed, he suffered great misfortunes ; but he never appears, like the good men Jefferson and Monroe, malicious and revengeful. He could lead men of all ranks—not, like Hamilton, only leaders. He was tolerant of foibles, was not impatient of interested motives, and did not exact homage to inconvenient ideals. He neither 'bored' nor drove, avoided treading on men's toes, dealt quietly and courteously, and until the time was ripe appeared to be quite unambitious of any personal distinction. Possessing such qualities, the puzzle is that he should have failed so completely as he did.

One reason of Burr's failure is that, for all his cleverness, he never arrived at seeing things together. He saw them singly, or in twos and threes, with an admirable perspicacity But his sight was dim and blurred when he tried to grasp in their rough proportions all the multitude of facts that compose a situation. He relied too much on the minor arguments. But beyond this, his nature, sympathetic to individual men, was senseless as regarded popular emotions.

He lacked entirely the intuition of Jefferson for the moods of the constituency. It is true that, like Hamilton and unlike Jefferson, he saw real things and not the shadows of phrases; but he saw them in his cool, analytic brain without perspective. A beetle crossing the window-pane was larger than an elk a hundred yards away.

Hamilton not only saw real things, but he saw them in their true proportions. His spirit was ever seeking for a harmony in them, for a law and a purpose. To Burr's clear but disconnected vision things were altogether purposeless and lawless. The only harmony to be sought for by the wise man was in his own career and not in externals. The levity of human creatures, their meanness, sentimentalism, timidity and distrust, all the veneer that covers patriotism, he understood, and no man better; but he entirely misjudged the strength of the fabric because he made no account of what is to be looked for underneath. Something, which is possibly more of an instinct and less of a virtue than what we understand by patriotism, has to be reckoned with at its proper value when a man is meditating violence against the state.

Hamilton also made the error of underrating this resistance. He saw that Burr despised the strength of the fabric, and would attempt to destroy it by a political revolution; that, failing at the first effort, he would not hesitate to plunge the country into civil war rather than abandon his project. Hamilton feared that society would not stand the strain of civil war. There is no doubt that there was in fact in Burr's mind a design for severing the Northern States from the Union should he have succeeded in carrying them in his favour against Jefferson and the Virginia clique. The attempt was rendered impracticable only by his defeat for the governorship of New York. A few years later (after Hamilton's death) we find him actually engaged in an endeavour to detach the South-Western territories from their allegiance by force and arms, and to found a great empire and a Burr dynasty by the conquest of Mexico. His imagination soared to courts, and constitutions, and a military monarchy. His plans were complete and admirably suited for dealing with the opposition of those contingencies which he foresaw, and of such forces as he had carefully measured. But his foresight was at fault, and his calculations were absurdly out of scale. All his tact and courage were insufficient to make even a respectable failure of this enterprise which inhabits the limbo of historical fiascos. Hamilton must therefore be judged right in his estimate of Burr's intentions. When he denounced him as a Catiline and a Napoleon, and prophesied that he would not hesitate to become a traitor to the constitution, he was not using words of vain exaggeration, as was thought even by many upon his own side. His error consisted in his failure to estimate the futility of such an effort.

Another cause of Burr's non-success was the atmosphere of distrust which even from the beginning of his career enveloped his public reputation. Few men have had more loyal and devoted friends, and few, judged by their fidelity to private friendship, have deserved attachment better. But the distrust of people who were not his intimates followed him from the class-room to the grave. It is difficult to discover sufficient grounds for this opinion, but it is even more difficult to believe it to have been ill-founded. It resembles an instinct of the hive against an enemy of the hive. The grounds which are alleged leave always something to seek. The rumours of pecuniary irregularity lack precision. They were never clearly proven, and sometimes they were disproven. The mere existence of debts does not constitute a man corrupt. The attacks of his opponents were party philippics, less violent, certainly, than the charges which Giles and Jefferson and Monroe directed against Hamilton, but of the same order. The malicious mendacity of his domestic enemies, the democratic cliques of New York, carries even less authority. And yet the fact remains that every one did distrust him, with the exception of his personal friends, not only as a loyal citizen, but also as an honest man.

It is impossible, moreover, to resist the conclusion that Aaron Burr, with all his great and admirable qualities, was in fact a sham. Chesterfieldian maxims are not the best foundation for a real human character. His manner and his pose were magnificent. His attitude in the face of the world was sublime. But we have the feeling all the time that he was acting; that in public affairs his eye was fixed upon the pit and the stalls, or, at any rate, upon the critics, rather than upon the object. He made no vulgar appeal to a mean audience. We feel, indeed, that often his sole audience—pit, stalls and critics—consisted of himself, and he was a severe judge. But it was acting all the same. It was self-conscious-ness and concern about the manner of doing, much more than about the thing to be done. The actual goal was always secondary.

To be a great man of action—statesman or buccaneer—there must be a subordination of self-consciousness to the external aim; a simple, artless, overwhelming passion for attainment. Burr is artistic and artificial; in action always the dandy. His style is admirable. He has the most beautiful manners. He is neat and apt. None of his effort is wasted. But always in great attempts he fails with as much certainty and grace as a Stewart Pretender. It was so at the beginning and at the zenith of his fame; and to his credit be it said, disappointment and sorrow, dishonour and neglect, found him still faultless at the end. The game which he believed himself to be playing he lost. The game which he really played he won. His true object was a kind of fantastic self-discipline, in which pursuit he attained the supremest excellence.

His last years are a strange picture. He continues the rule of his early life—eats little, drinks less, works hard and makes love everlastingly. At the age of seventy-eight he marries a lady of beauty, spirit and fortune, and another lady breaks her heart at the event. Within a few months he is separated, coming under the suspicion of infidelity.

Stories of his wit and pose are without end. 'Was Hamilton a gentleman?' inquired some foreigner with a notebook. The reply is filled with a quiet resentment: ' Sir, *I* met him ! '

But there is always the actor: the actor with the severest standard, but still the actor. He is never content with the effect unless he himself, the hardest of the critics, is satisfied. No external applause will compensate. He was not a great man of action, but he enacted the part of a great man of action to admiration.

Two things about him passed the bounds of acting—his generosity and his affection. He had at all times many creditors, and it cannot be said of him that he was depressed by the weight of his obligations. Strictly he was an immoral citizen, because he flouted the sanctity of contract and gave away upon an impulse what was already hypothecated to others. But at least he did not spend upon himself. The simplicity and industry of his life were exemplary. He gave because he could not resist appeals, because he could not help giving. And he was none of your cold givers, but gave always with sympathy; never the benefactor, but ever the comrade. His charity was of the heart, spontaneous, promiscuous and usually misdirected. It lacked organisation, and possibly did more harm than good. It was emotional and not deliberate, and upon all

2 D

CHAPTER VI

Duel and Death

THE immediate cause of the duel in which Hamilton lost his life was so trivial as not to merit examination—what somebody had written [1] that Hamilton had said to somebody else. The challenge was sent upon that verbal pretext, but as Hamilton well knew, the real occasion was an essential antagonism. When gentlemen of delicacy shot one another on account of a lady, it was usual to feign a disagreement about the claret or a difference over cards. It was a graceful fashion which kept logic, and upon rare occasions even gossip itself, from intermeddling in the question. It would have savoured too much of the melodrama if Burr had sent his challenge on the ground of 'an essential antagonism.' We are inclined to agree with his biographer that, having regard to the conventions of the time, the two men were by circumstances foredoomed to fight. They had been pitted against one another, not on one occasion, but on many. The result had not been a drawn battle, but, with a single exception, a series of defeats. Hamilton had been the vigorous and successful aggressor; Burr, constantly within sight of victory, had been completely discomfited. Few gentlemen have ever sent a friend with a message upon more substantial provocation.

It has been generously assumed that Burr challenged, because he was revengeful and a scoundrel. Much discus-

---

[1] Dr. Cooper, in an electioneering letter, had stated that Hamilton had described Burr as ' a dangerous man, and who ought not to be trusted '; and subsequently, ' I could detail to you a still more despicable opinion which General Hamilton has expressed of Mr. Burr.' (Morse's *Hamilton*, vol. ii. p. 356. For account of duel, etc., see also Parton's *Burr*.)

sion, however, has taken place and many words have been wasted upon the question why Hamilton fought. He was a Christian, enlightened and liberal, a hater and despiser of the institution of duelling. He was a man whose courage was beyond suspicion, whose eminence, services and family circumstances might well have justified a refusal. Why had he not the moral courage to decline the combat? Much censure and some elaborate theories leave us to face the fact that he fought because duelling was an institution and because he was Hamilton. Had Jefferson found himself placed in like circumstances he would undoubtedly have refused, and even by the standards of the day his action would have been considered natural and proper. For Jefferson belonged to the new school. He was a philanthropist and a philosopher. His position and influence with his party would have been enhanced rather than diminished by a refusal to engage.

But with Hamilton it was altogether different. His whole scheme of politics and plan of life rested upon the old fashions. What was bad, foolish, or archaic he accepted with the rest in the fear that by eliminating anything the fabric might be loosened. The idea of his state was an aristocracy, and duelling was somewhat in the nature of a cockade. In his own case he attached little importance to the privilege, but he could not logically deny it to others. He had given the provocation, and it was not for him (so he may well have argued) to refuse his enemy satisfaction. The Federalists as a party shared his opinions. If he had suddenly taken up a humanitarian position when it was a case of avoiding a personal risk, he would undoubtedly have been sustained by many of his friends, but he would with equal certainty have lost caste with a large section of his followers. Had Hamilton found himself in Burr's position there is no doubt that he would not have sought a

in his profession. Though generous, he was no spendthrift.
His plan for the investment of his savings was judicious,[1]
and only an accident put him at a disadvantage. The
man of business who so frames his budget as to provide
for every contingency, whose aim is to shelter his property
from every conceivable risk, will never 'make a spoon or
spoil a horn.' He will never be overtaken by failure,
and he will never achieve success. He will deserve blame,
according to the Gospels. He will receive praise only
from the writers of moral tales. Hamilton acted in this
matter as it is worthy to act. He regarded the few main
probabilities, he disregarded the thousand and one things
that were only possible. The Cæsarian maxim applies to
worldly gear as well as to a man's life. There is a pre-
cautionary price at which it is not worth while to possess it.

Hamilton, it should be remembered, gave the best years
of his life to his country, and took for his services less than
a living wage. He lived before the days of party presenta-
tions and teapots full of sovereigns. Millionaires were scarce
in those times in the United States, and neither political
enthusiasm nor personal gratitude had stirred the prosperous
classes to write cheques in six figures for the endowment of
their champions. Hamilton started upon his career as a
penniless student. He gave much time and effort for
nothing, or for an utterly inadequate stipend. He never
enjoyed the recompense due to his military services ; for
he resigned all his claims in order that he might be free
to serve the army by advocating their cause in Congress.
Neither from the Union nor from the State of New York
did he ever receive any allowance of lands such as was
made to officers of similar rank.[2] No man had ever better
excuse for dying penniless.

In his will, made in anticipation of the duel, he estimates

---

[1] He bought land in the vicinity of New York.   [2] Works, x. p. 479.

the chances of his dying insolvent. "Should it happen
' that there is not enough for the payment of my debts, I
' entreat my dear children, if they or any of them shall ever
' be able, to make up the deficiency. I, without hesitation,
' commit to their delicacy a wish which is dictated by my
' own. Though conscious that I have too far sacrificed the
' interests of my family to public avocations, and on this
' account have the less claim to burthen my children, yet I
' trust in their magnanimity to appreciate, as they ought,
' this my request."[1]

"On the fourth of July Hamilton and Burr met, for the
' last time, at the convivial board. It was at the annual
' banquet of the Society of the Cincinnati, of which Hamilton
' was president and Burr a member. Hamilton was cheer-
' ful, and at times merry. He was urged, as the feast wore
away, to sing the only song he ever sang or knew, the
' famous old ballad of *The Drum.* It was thought afterward
' that he was more reluctant than usual to comply with the
' company's request; but after some delay he said, 'Well,
' you shall have it,' and sang it in his best manner, greatly
' to the delight of the old soldiers by whom he was sur-
' rounded. Burr, on the contrary, was reserved, mingled
' little with the company, and held no intercourse with the
' president. He was never a fluent man, and was generally,
' in the society of men, more a listener than a talker. On
' this occasion his silence was, therefore, the less remarked ;
' yet it was remarked. It was observed, too, that he paid
' no attention to Hamilton's conversation, nor, indeed, looked
' toward him until he struck up his song, when Burr turned
' toward him, and, leaning upon the table, looked at the
' singer till the song was done. The difference in the
' behaviour of the two men was doubtless owing partly to

[1] *Works,* x. pp. 481-82.

'their different positions at the banquet. Hamilton, as the 'master of the feast, was in the eye of every guest, while 'Burr could easily escape particular observation. The object 'of both was, of course, to behave so as not to excite 'inquiry."[1] It is an odd picture, and as it is drawn by Burr's biographer, who had the evidence of persons present to found upon, we may take it as authentic.

The duel was fought on the 11th of July, under the heights of Weehawken, upon a grassy platform overlooking the Hudson River. Hamilton fell mortally wounded at the first fire. There has been much dispute as to his action. Burr and his second maintained that he fired at his opponent and missed. The generally accepted version is that, in accordance with his expressed intention,[2] he did not fire at the word, but that his pistol went off as he was falling. It is certain that he refused to have the hair-spring set. The matter is of little moment. If a moral stigma attaches to duelling under the conditions of that time, it attaches because the man consented to engage. That he held his fire, or let off his pistol in the air, is merely irrelevant chivalry.

Hamilton died on the following day. The world mourned for him with a fervour that is remarkable considering its treatment of him in later years, and the speed with which it proceeded to forget him. It mourned; and then, in order that the emotion might be complete, turned upon Burr and made a scapegoat.

Hamilton came by his death as he had spent his life, in the service of his country. He did not die in a private quarrel. If he had fallen at Yorktown or been killed, as nearly came to pass, by the heavy labours of his office, he would not more certainly have sacrificed himself to the interests of the nation. In attacking Burr at every point

---

[1] Parton's *Burr*. [2] *Works*, x. p. 474.

he was not attacking a man whom he hated, but the most formidable and conspicuous type of a class of men whose ambitions, if unchecked, must in his judgment have led to the ruin of the state. He took the whole circumstances of the case into account. He did not overlook the temper or underrate the courage of his opponent. He knew only too well the dangers of political controversy, for his eldest son, a mere boy, had already been killed in a similar quarrel. He was well aware that his unrelenting efforts to exclude Burr from public life were nearly certain in the end to provoke an appeal to arms, which from his own position and the views of the Federalist party and the people in general it would be impossible for him to decline.

Hamilton, Jefferson and Burr are three distinctive types of public men. Hamilton was a type of the statesman, Jefferson of the sophist, and Burr of the politician. Their enmity was fundamental, and in no sense peculiar to the special period in which they lived, or due to any accidents in their circumstances. The predominant motive of the politicians is ever their own advantage. In the case of Burr this was not only the predominant, but the single motive. His adventures and his fortunes, his great talents and his engaging personality, introduced an element of romance. His defects of character led to failure so complete and ludicrous that there is some temptation to misjudge the main issue, and to think of him as harmless merely because of his futility. But romance and futility were both accidents. His career was perfect in the simplicity of its aims. A man of coarser fibre and stronger will would have been a more dangerous enemy to the Union; but no politician that has ever lived is a truer type of mischievous intention.

Hamilton's public career was a long struggle against the politicians and the sophists. In the green youth of the republic the dangers to be apprehended from the latter were of more account than the attacks of the predatory classes. The early period was one of exaltation. Men were wrought up to a high pitch of emotion. The chief peril was lest they should be misled, not by their personal interests, but by an enthusiasm for shadows. Jefferson's loose and eloquent phrases about liberty, fraternity and the Rights of Man were more likely to wreck the Union, by stripping the government of its powers and by involving the nation in struggles which it was too weak to bear, than the plots and combinations of greedy adventurers. But as the tradition grew, as the Union hardened and became strong through the exercise of its functions, the sophists ceased to be a formidable menace. Their intention, after all, was virtue, not mischief. They were great experts in the use of words, which often did not correspond to facts; and, as they guided their own course of action as they would have guided the policy of the state—to a large extent by words—they were not likely to prevail against settled institutions and a vigilant opposition.

By the date of the election of 1800 danger was to be apprehended from a different quarter. Clearheaded men who had no scruples about using the state for the purpose of their own advancement were much greater evils. The sophists, being to a large extent dupes of their own fancies and slaves of the passing moods of the people, might ultimately fall a prey to the intrigues of adventurers hampered by no concern for the national advantage. For the politicians, if successful, would endeavour to use the sophists for their own ends. But when it was a choice between Jefferson and Burr for the Presidency, Hamilton took a practical view of the conditions and acted without hesitation, although he cannot have been blind to the possibility that the course he adopted might cost him his life.

CHAPTER VII

The Failure of the Democrats

MEASURED by years, Hamilton, like Pitt, his contemporary, died young, at the age of forty-seven. It is difficult to picture him as an old man, for the note of his character was youth. It was said of Pitt that 'he did not grow, he was cast.' At twenty-five he was as good as at forty-five. To a certain extent the same is true of Hamilton, with this difference—that he was cast in the mould of a young man, Pitt in that of an old one. The highest virtue of each was his courage; but Hamilton's courage was eager and impetuous, while the courage of Pitt was remarkable chiefly for its extraordinary endurance. There is in all Hamilton's work—writings and speeches—the intense seriousness of youth. The qualities that made him a great statesman and a terrible combatant were force, lucidity and conviction. His confidence in himself and in his ideas is amazing, amounting almost to fanaticism. It is possible that the Union of the States would, in one way or another, have achieved itself had he been shot at Yorktown instead of Weehawken, for it was in the order of great events; but the speculative historian would be puzzled to supply the deficiency or explain the method.

If we seek for a complete presentment of the man in what he wrote and spoke we shall not find it. He treats his public ceremoniously and with reserve. An excessive gravity is the rule. Anger is the only passion which is permitted to appear; not a beam of humour or a flash of wit. The whole procedure is stately and tense. This also is in accordance with the nature of youth.

Hamilton has left us no records of his private life

principles of conduct and disdains to concern itself with the smaller motives. The reverse of this condition is when a magnanimous nature becomes entangled in controversy with mean minds about mean things, when his pursuit of lofty aims is tripped up by petty obstacles. In such a contest the chief danger lies in the distraction. Each file in the legion of mediocrity invites an easy and separate annihilation. Every knave deserves to be trounced. Every fallacy cries out for exposure. A great mind engaged with a multitude of small enemies must be overwhelmed by sheer weight of numbers when once it loses the weather-gage, and is forced to accept a contest on terms of their choosing. Up to the period of the *Farewell Address* Hamilton had kept the weather-gage, and in the compulsion of events had found a gale favourable to his battle. The struggle for independence, the foundation and defence of the Union, strained his nature to its highest pitch. But with the accomplishment of these objects there was a swift change in the conditions. Gradually national interests tended to become subordinate to those of parties, and party interests in turn to those of persons who discovered a business advantage to be gained by inhabiting, like hermit crabs, the derelict shells of political ideas.

Hamilton feared lest the Constitution might not prove strong enough to stand against the results of this general deterioration. When we remember that the Constitution and the tradition which supported it were for the most part his own handiwork, it is easy to excuse his distrust. He regarded the Union with the tenderness and doubt of an anxious lover, who would seclude his mistress from the society of rakes; confident in her good intentions, but dubious of her fortitude. In reality, neither Jefferson fatuously worshipping phrases, nor Burr with his busy intrigue, had even a far-off chance of playing the successful

Lovelace. The constitution was delicate indeed, but not frail. Neither Burr play-acting the part of Catiline, nor Jefferson dressed in the ribbons of popularity, was a danger worthy of consideration. The lassitude of the times was the result of easy circumstances, and any serious peril would have changed it to a fierce alertness. The state of popular opinion in those years may be compared to some strong beast dozing and blinking in the sun.

It was not so much that the efforts of the Revolution had exhausted statesmanship, as that peace, prosperity and a sense of security induced men to rest comfortably upon what had been already done. It was more because they believed the constitution safe than for any other reason that they had ceased to take politics seriously.

For those men who looked beyond party triumphs to the needs and dangers of the future, State Rights and slavery remained two menacing problems, of which there must be a final settlement before the Union could be secure from internal disaster. Two ways were possible to this end: the slow, constant and increasing pressure of a policy, or the sharp means of civil war. Wise men, who loved their country, prayed for the first, but their prayers were answered adversely by the gods. For a quarter of a century power was in the hands of statesmen who were lacking both in vision and courage, and without these qualities in government it is vain to look for strong and consistent effort towards any national aim. The successors of Washington and Hamilton were astute but timid. They kept an unremitting watch against rivals who might supplant them in the affections of the people, but they were negligent and feeble guards against the dangers which threatened the existence of the state.

Jefferson, Madison and Monroe held office in succession, each for a double term, during the first quarter of the

2 E

nineteenth century. Few rulers in the history of modern democracy ever enjoyed office in greater security, had to face opponents so feeble and distracted, or were fixed with the duty of governing a people in an easier temper. Strong men, with such currents to aid them, would have made much progress; but these had no aim in view. They relied upon the wisdom of the people to inspire as well as judge them. They regarded the people not merely as a tribunal but as an oracle. Great things will never come out of a democracy treated in this obsequious spirit by its governors. Statesmen have to submit themselves in the end humbly to the verdict of the man in the street, but to go to him for advice or for ideas is almost as futile as for a captain of a ship to consult his passengers upon problems of navigation. Jefferson's chief sin is that he substituted the ostentatious patronage of a democracy for the leadership of a people.

These three Presidents denied most vehemently that any Federalist revered the Union more than they, or would have been capable of greater sacrifices had it been in jeopardy. They acknowledged, sorrowfully, that slavery was a great evil in society, and expressed desires to see it removed. But unfortunately their personal sympathies were warmly engaged for the doctrine of State Rights, which was the only internal enemy of the Union; and the interests of their supporters, of their private friends and of their family traditions, were bound up with the institution of slavery. In Jefferson's philosophy of eighteenth century phrases State Rights were applauded; slavery, on the contrary, was utterly condemned. He has left it on record that he disapproved of slavery; but, except in early days when it was convenient to denounce the institution in order to add a count to the indictment of George the Third,[1] he was at considerable pains to conceal his opinions from his

[1] See *Declaration of Independence*.

countrymen.[1] His private practice was in fantastic contrast to his beliefs. His public activities did not advance by one hairsbreadth the sacred cause of liberty which he professed to have at heart. In his political career the humanitarian always walked behind the opportunist when the road was too narrow to admit of the two going arm in arm.

It has been maintained that had the United States been compelled to face the difficulties of a European environment during the first half of the nineteenth century, they must have collapsed or fallen asunder. Except for the fortune of their isolated position, and the immeasurable resources which nature had given them, it is alleged that they could not have made head against the intrigue and open attack of their enemies, and against the discontent and disorder that would thereby have been induced among their citizens. But two things have been left out of notice in this calculation, and if the nation had lacked these two things, it must certainly have gone to pieces, despite the advantages of natural wealth and fortunate position. The first of these is the spirit of the people, upon which no crisis up to the present time has ever called in vain. The second is the great legacy of laws and traditions which it inherited from the first eight years of Federal government; the ideas of the sanctity of the Union, of national probity and of a dignified independence. The spirit of the nation is a great force, but it is one which cannot be always on the alert, and, while it sleeps, the part of noble institutions is to keep watch.

The names of Washington and Hamilton, which we honour together, must be honoured in both; for even

---

[1] When Jefferson's *Notes on Virginia*, previously circulated in manuscript, were printed, he imposed conditions that all 'Strictures on Slavery' should be omitted. *History*, iv. p. 453, also pp. 454 and 455.

the spirit of a people is in large measure a tradition with an origin in the effort and suffering of its great men. Washington and Hamilton governed, and directed the policy of the United States when occasion required it against the opinions of the majority. They incurred much hatred in consequence, which even the memory of their services could not keep within bounds. But this bold and uncompromising disregard of opinion is more akin to the special genius of their country, and to the rôle which it has played in the affairs of the world, than the fine discernment, the smooth and pliant dexterity of Jefferson. A man who never disagrees with his countrymen, and who shrinks from unpopularity as the worst of all evils, can never have a share in moulding the traditions of a virile race, though for a time he may make its fashions. Without paradox, we may truly say that Jefferson, in spite of all his triumphs, missed every opportunity. He takes rank among the men who succeeded only in success, but had nothing to show for it at the end, save only success. He maintained himself in office and floated gloriously upon a kind of vapour. He built no new defences for his country, and those which he received in custody he barely kept in repair.

Every difficulty which could be postponed was left to a future generation. Every awkward question was adroitly shelved. He was an indulgent and courteous physician, who alleviated the symptoms and soothed the nerves, but lacked both the skill to understand the cause and the courage to treat the root of the disease. His legacy was a lexicon of phrases, a dramatic reputation of homespun equality, and a tangle for posterity to unwind.

The making of the United States owes nothing to Jefferson except a few eccentric fashions, often ungraceful and sometimes absurd. The work of Washington and

Hamilton, after a long and dreary interval, passed into worthier hands. Sixty years after the duel at Weehawken the constitution was confirmed. What Hamilton had feared came to pass—a civil war; but what he had given his life for was as the result of it secured. The tremendous cost does not lie at his door. To lay so awful a charge against any man is perhaps beyond justice, but as we read of the complacent beatitude of Jefferson, full of years and adulation, our memory calls up a contrasting scene, in which the action is a great rebellion; in which orators of the South invoke not unfairly the protection of his name; in which brave men go into battle with his phrases on their lips; in which the aim of the whole Confederate party, which does him honour, is to destroy the constitution and to break the Union. It is a common event that when a man is dead his name and authority are misused, his words misinterpreted; but Jefferson has to answer a much graver charge than careless sympathy, or a mere verbal indiscretion. The Union which he professed to venerate was intrusted to his keeping, and fortune put it in his power to render it secure. He failed even to make the attempt.

The state which Alexander Hamilton had planned and inaugurated Abraham Lincoln completed and confirmed. It is natural to contrast these two men, who in all superficial things were most unlike—in circumstances, manners, age, temper and appearance. But in the great matter that concerned each of them most nearly they were at one. In many of their qualities they were alike. In both there was the same instinct for reality and contempt for phrases, the same clear judgment and swift decision. Their eyes saw 'far and wide,' and things appeared to them ever in a splendid and true proportion, rhythmical and harmonious, governed by great laws. In richness of nature they were equals, and equals also in integrity and courage. And in both there was the same rare and consummate mastery of the English tongue, begotten of great thoughts and a fiery sincerity, which not only increases an hundredfold the power of a man in his own day, but continues it as an intimate and living force among generations to whom otherwise he would have been but a remote actor or a great historical shadow.

BOOK VI
CONCLUSION

*On the most elaborate and correct detail of facts, the result seems to be that at no time has the wealth and power of Great Britain been so considerable as it is at this very perilous moment. We have a vast interest to preserve, and we possess great means of preserving it. But it is to be remembered that the artificer may be encumbered by his tools, and that resources may be among impediments. If wealth is the obedient and laborious slave of virtue and of publick honours, then wealth is in its place and has its use. But if this order is changed, and honour is to be sacrificed to the conservation of riches, riches, which have neither eyes nor hands, nor anything truly vital in them, cannot long survive the being of their vivifying powers, their legitimate masters, and their potent protectors. If we command our wealth we shall be rich and free. If our wealth commands us, we are poor indeed.—*BURKE.

BOOK VI

CONCLUSION

CHAPTER I

Some General Remarks

An attempt has been made in the foregoing chapters to give a general view of the events which preceded and followed the formal Union of the States, to describe the two hostile tendencies of political thought during that epoch, and to make a rough estimate of the chief personal forces and antagonisms which were concerned in the result. The intention of the author, so far, has been to regard the career of Alexander Hamilton mainly in its relation to the fortunes of the United States of America.

In the remaining pages the achievements of Hamilton will be considered, very briefly, under a different aspect. The quality of his statesmanship, the nature of that inarticulate desire for union on which he built, the strength and the obstinacy of those difficulties which he encountered at every turn, are subjects of universal interest. He is no local hero, but one whose work and greatness have a meaning for the whole world; and for the British race at the present time they have a special and intimate concern.

Among many things that appear to be widely different when we contrast the circumstances of America in the years preceding the convention of Philadelphia with those of our own empire as it stands to-day, at least one thing is the same. In both cases we find the same widespread consciousness of an issue that must be faced before the world has grown much older, that cannot be put off indefinitely by dilatory prudence or sentimental make-believe. The consequences of this issue are so tremendous that even the most reckless partisan is willing at times to treat it with a grave attention. In both cases there is the same vague but impatient yearning for some bold, constructive efforts towards a solution, and on the other hand the same clear and cogent arguments of destruction are brought to bear against every plan which the wit of man has yet been able to devise.

Before proceeding to a consideration of these topics, the author desires to offer a few remarks upon the scope and intention of his work. It may reasonably be urged that reflections of such a character would have figured more suitably in a preface; but for various reasons which it is unnecessary to set forth, it has been judged better to reserve them to a later stage.

The author is fully aware of his many disqualifications for the task which he has undertaken. It is not merely upon the literary side that he is ready to admit the inadequacy of his equipment. Faults arising from this cause might have been easily pardoned. But he is conscious also of a deficiency in knowledge of American political conditions as they exist to-day. Without something more than book-learning the spirit and atmosphere of the United States at the end of the nineteenth and the beginning of the twentieth century cannot be completely understood. A writer, ignorant of these things, lacking the freedom and confidence which an intimacy with American politics alone can give, is debarred from following Hamilton's great ideas into modern times. Although he is dimly aware that morals could be drawn, principles established, and forecasts clinched, he is shut out from the attempt. The few references to later events are therefore of a general character, and are concerned only with facts too notorious for dispute.

It may reasonably be asked why, if the author was conscious of such hampering limitations, he had ever the temerity to undertake the task. His answer is that he undertook it because he was unable to discover any account of Hamilton's career which satisfied his curiosity. In making this statement he denies any intention to depreciate the many learned and diligent American authors who have discoursed upon the topic. He readily admits his debt to their industry, but at the same time he has to acknowledge that their efforts have not met his requirements. Their view of the man and his epoch is in every case too 'American.' It is natural that this should be the case, and it would be the height of absurdity to utter any complaint. But there is room for an estimate arrived at by a different method. To Englishmen the achievements of Hamilton may not mean precisely the same thing as they do to citizens of the United States, but, unless this essay has entirely missed its mark, it will hardly be contended that they mean anything less. Our kinsmen do not hesitate to claim a share in the heritage of our literature, and in fairness, therefore, we may claim some part and interest in their statesmen. The work of Hamilton's life was the solution of problems which we have not yet found any means to solve. That, for us, is the chief interest of his career. Admitting frankly and fully that what he achieved is no precedent to govern our actions, his example is inspiring. We may draw morals from his fortitude and find encouragement in his success. And here and there, as we read his words upon the events and difficulties of a bygone age, the darkness and perplexity of the situation in which we find ourselves is lit up with sudden, luminous flashes which pierce to the four corners of the canopy.

It is probable that fault may also be found with the proportions of this essay. Complaint may be made that certain matters have been forced into an undue prominence, while others which ought to have been dealt with at length have been slurred over in a few paragraphs or sentences. The space devoted to an account of the war will be cited under the first head, and under the second the omission of any substantial discussion of the constitution. But having regard to the author's intention, the war was a matter of capital importance, the terms of the constitution were not. Consequently, although the attempt to describe the course of the dreary and protracted struggle for independence was surrounded with obvious dangers for one who has had no experience in military affairs, it was necessary to make it. The war is the key to the whole situation. If the hazards and difficulties which attended Washington's campaigns are not fully realised, those which attended the acceptance of a formal union and the making of a real one must be entirely missed. The disasters arising out of disunion were apparent from the very beginning of the contest with Britain. In a sense the two struggles—for independence and for union— originated at the same moment, were retarded by the same obstacles, and were achieved by the same spirit, and to a large extent by the same men.

But the constitution occupies a different place. Its terms and provisions are matters of a subordinate interest. Had they been better suited than they were to the needs of the situation, the labours of the early administrations might have been less arduous, but the final result could hardly have proved very different. Or if the constitution had been a much less efficient instrument than it was in fact, the energy and courage of Washington and Hamilton would in

all likelihood have found some means of making it serve
their purpose. The constitution has now been on trial for
upwards of a century, and it can hardly be imagined that
any reflective citizen of the United States would seriously
propose it as a model for another nation which found itself
faced by a similar emergency. Its weakness in certain
directions has been constantly made clear, while in others
its very strength seems to be a danger no less formidable.
Its power for resistance to all reforms, sane or insane, is a
lesson even more of what should be avoided than of what
should be copied. The British constitution is a thing by itself,
and stands outside comparison. But the Canadian constitution is comparable, and as a model it is immensely superior.
Its makers had profited by the experience of others. Its
strength is strongest where the strain is greatest—at the
heart. Sovereignty is firmly established. The majesty of
the law is acknowledged without question from one end
of the Dominion to the other. The characteristics of
Canada are order and freedom. No man fears either that
he will call in vain upon justice, or that the development of
the estate will be hampered by a misplaced strength or an
inelastic charter. The constitution of Canada was made in
1867—eighty years after the convention of Philadelphia—
and the debt which it owes to the efforts and example of our
kinsmen is immeasurable.

It is not, therefore, the precise terms, or even the principles of the American constitution, which move our admiration; but the great facts that the Americans made a
constitution sufficient for their purpose, that they set it to
work, and in a few years built round it an upholding tradition which has stood the fiercest trials. They had no
precedents to guide them. Republican institutions were in
discredit. Obstacles and difficulties existed upon every
hand. And yet men had the wisdom to plan and the

courage to succeed in their attempt. These are the matters to which it has been the object of this essay to call attention.

This book is neither a history nor a biography, but merely an essay upon the character and achievements of a man who, in the author's opinion, was the chief figure in a series of striking events. It has been written, frankly, from the standpoint of Hamilton. The aim has been to make it an honest account; but the aim has not been to make it an impartial account. A staid, unbiased narration of the career of a great man of action, who lived in stirring times, and engaged in controversies of an exceptional fierceness, might have a certain value; but it would never give any true picture of the man or measure of his work. The value of this quality or of that effort cannot be shown by submitting it to the alien standard of some cold arbiter, but only in relation to the divine unity of the character of the man himself. The diatribe of an enemy is preferable, for it has at least a dramatic consistency and the merit of a caricature. Our endeavour, therefore, has been to show Hamilton as he saw himself, and to judge him as he would have judged himself.

But it is not to be denied that there are disadvantages of a serious nature attaching to such a method. One of the best biographical essays that ever was written is Froude's *Julius Cæsar*, but no man in search of a true, positive estimate of Cicero or Pompey would accept it as final. It is necessary to consider not only the limitations of space, but the mood of the reader. To hustle him about from pillar to post, to make him regard characters and events in one chapter from the standpoint of the statesman, in the next from that of the sophist, in the next again from that of the politician, would be to irritate and weary him into an utter confusion. In accepting the dramatic necessities of the situation, we have to realise the impossibility of doing full justice to the rest of mankind. The friends of Hamilton are dwarfed and obscured by the central figure. His opponents are less in shadow, but they appear under a negative aspect. They assume a great importance only when they offend. Our attention is concentrated upon their inconvenient angles, and with the best will in the world, it is impossible to construct a complete and positive likeness upon such evidence. And yet it is impossible to avoid this injustice. In considering any period of history from the standpoint of a great man of action, we are certain—contemptuously certain—of the value of his enemies. We read what they have said, striving to give just attention, but their words have the hollow resonance of an echo.

Indeed, in proportion as an opponent of the man, whose mood and standpoint we have accepted, has ideas of his own, it becomes harder to realise him positively and truly. It is much easier to deal generously with the fighting qualities of an enemy than with the motives which induced him to fight. It is much easier, therefore to draw a picture of Burr than of Jefferson; for in the case of Burr it was only his personal ambition which entered into the conflict, while in the case of Jefferson it was not only his personal ambition, but probably to quite as great an extent his political ideas and sympathies.

And there is this further consideration, that even impartial history is apt to be unfair to the opposition, when the matter under discussion is a series of events upon which the world has already formed a favourable and final judgment. Between the founder of a state and the eccentric human creature, stuffed with an honest conceit, who denounces the great idea on some ground of particular injustice, there is not that tremendous moral gulf which the dramatic brush of history has painted. The good congressmen who formed the opinion that Washington was a poor soldier, who intrigued against him at the height of his difficulties, who stinted his supplies and obstructed his endeavours; the loyal opposition who were quite ready to deal with Pitt and Wellington as malefactors, and hailed any victory of the French with far greater joy than a feat of British arms,— all these were fairly honest people in their way, and not so very different, merely as human units, from their opponents. But history is mainly concerned with other things than the psychology of human units, and leaves the study of it to novelists and poets. If a man has chosen to play a part upon the larger stage, and by ill-luck or a natural propensity has chosen the wrong part, he is damned beyond redemption. History will not waste her time in finding an excuse for him merely because he was a good father, a faithful husband, or a punctual discharger of his debts. Development is a rough force, and if any man has obstructed it, he may not expect to be remembered kindly or with honour by posterity.

CHAPTER II

Whig or Tory?

UNTIL the Federalist party was formed Hamilton described himself as a Whig; and although, like Burke, he considered that the French Revolution could claim no affinity with his political faith, it is probable that he would have maintained himself to be a true Whig to the end of his days.

Even in the flux of politics it is possible to attach a certain general meaning to the party labels. If, at the particular moment, there is often a confusion which obscures the underlying principles, at the end of each epoch things settle down and become clearer. If the terms Whig and Tory stand for any essential differences in human thought, if they are anything better than mere rosettes or favours, Hamilton was not a Whig, but a Tory. It must be added that he was a Tory of the type which great Tory statesmen have beheld in their dreams, but have rarely, if ever, attained to under the conditions of party government His achievements began before government by parties had got to work. Although the greater part of his public life was spent in a bitter contest, hand to hand, the system of faction was not fully accepted as an institution until his retirement. Whether he could have kept his political faith so consistently in later days is open to doubt. What is certain about his actual career is that his ideal never wore a mask or suffered any kind of compromise.

The fact that Hamilton called himself a Whig does not count for much one way or the other. All men who engaged in the rebellion assumed the same title, partly for the reason that the Whig party in Britain was notoriously in sympathy with their demands, their methods and even with their arms; but partly also from the belief that their own revolution was founded upon the 'glorious' principles of 1688. But when the war was ended, when the interest shifted from a struggle with external enemies to problems of a different order, when the chief questions which demanded consideration were those concerned with a settled and permanent foundation, the inadequacy of the Whig cockade became apparent. The Federalists and the Democrats might dispute about their rights in the political tradition, but it is clear that the latter had the juster claim.

The names Whig and Tory are not used here with any partisan intention. The controversy is ancient, and the descriptions themselves are nearly obsolete. The former title, indeed, has almost turned into a term of general abuse.

2 F

It is not intended to claim the shelter of Hamilton's great authority for all the preposterous propaganda which at various times, under the pressure of opportunism or by the misfortune of blindness, have been temporarily associated with Toryism. But if we pierce to the core of those principles which have been devoutly held by the noblest spirits in the opposing parties, we must recognise an essential difference and antagonism.

Hamilton's love for his country was always greater than his love for his countrymen. The emotional side of his nature was stirred by the idea of a nation, rather than by the interests or sufferings of the various masses or classes of which every nation is composed. He was humane, but he was never the philanthropist. At the sight of disorder and injustice he was not swept away by a passionate impatience, but viewed the nature of the evils with a relentless scrutiny. Against the doctrine that some alleviation must immediately be discovered, he was usually found in opposition. His enemies alleged, untruthfully, that his heart was incapable of a generous impulse. What they meant was that he was incapable of acting upon the spur of the moment under no guidance save that of his emotions. His aim was always a complete and permanent cure. He distrusted palliatives and temporary expedients. He would not put forward a remedy for any particular trouble until he had convinced himself that the means proposed would work in harmony with the general principles of his policy.

Hamilton's idea of statesmanship was the faithful stewardship of the estate. His duty was to guard the estate, and, at the same time, to develop its resources. He viewed mankind and natural riches as material to be used, with the greatest possible energy and with the least possible waste, for the attainment of national independence, power and permanency. A means to this end was certainly the pros-

perity of the people, but the end itself was the existence of
a nation.   The emotional spring or motive of his endeavours
was not a passionate love or pity for his fellow-creatures, but
an overwhelming sense of duty towards his Creator, whose
providence had appointed him to the stewardship.   This
attitude may justly be described as beneficent; but, beyond
doubt, it is not the attitude of the philanthropist or of the
eighteenth-century Whig.

His foreign policy was dominated by the same principle.
The nation had been given into his hands, and the task of
keeping it secure was one sufficient for his powers.   What
happened to other nations was the care and concern of other
stewards.   He had private sympathies with France and
Frenchmen, and to a considerably less extent with England
and Englishmen; but these feelings were never allowed to
interfere with the performance of what he considered to be
his duty as a steward.   He judged that the task to which
the Almighty had appointed him was, not to put the whole
world right, but to keep his own country safe.   The view of
the philanthropist is widely different.   During the ferment
of the French Revolution the steadfast refusal of Hamilton
to consider anything but the wellbeing of his own nation
was freely judged to be inhuman.   The Whig spirit condemned him as a cold and selfish schemer.   His enemies
had abundant excuse for their attacks, since they believed
sincerely that an opportunity had offered itself of changing
the whole order of human institutions for the great advantage of the race.   Hamilton profoundly disbelieved in this
opinion, and held unmoved upon his course.

The final test of Toryism, according to some critics, is the
belief in Divine Right.   "The divine right of kings," Disraeli
wrote, "may have been a plea for feeble tyrants, but the
'divine right of government is the keystone of human pro-
'gress."   Hamilton believed in the divine right of government

with his whole heart. The right to enforce order and to compel men to live justly, he derived, not from the interests of the people, but from the ordinances of God. The forms of government without an upholding tradition were useless phrases. That the leaders of men should trim their sails to popularity was in his view a fatal abdication. Human society was something nobler than a mere convenience, a nation something greater than the sum of its subjects. One of the duties of the state was the wellbeing of its citizens, but the whole duty of every citizen was the wellbeing of the state.

The reason of Hamilton's increasing honour is the endurance of his handiwork. The constitution, after more than a century of stress and rough weather, is stronger than it was at the beginning. The public credit is still based upon the foundations which he laid. Foreign relations continue to be governed by the principles which he sacrificed popularity to uphold. The growth of population and prosperity which he foresaw has come to pass. Men did not choose to follow the guidance of his sane and moderate maxims for the regulation of commerce, but at any rate they lived and did their work under the shelter of those institutions which he had the chief share in moulding. He prevailed upon his fellowcountrymen to make a trial of union, and by the audacity of his procedure he filled a written charter with the spirit of life. He left things better than he found them; firm institutions to replace a quarrelsome anarchy; a wide cooperation instead of an insensate independence; a proud nation and a noble tradition where there had been but an angry strife between 'thirteen jarring states.' If a statesman has achieved these things, his lovers may view with equanimity his failure in all meaner contests.

Anything which has stood—a tradition of conduct or the fabric of an empire—compels our admiration with little regard for our personal interest or national pride. A true instinct of mankind insists on homage to those great spirits who have built enduring monuments. The mere permanence is proof of a certain magnanimity in the author. Our imagination working backwards to the confusion of the particular time discovers in each case the same group of qualities— a true judgment, without which the work must have crumbled in a few seasons; fortitude which overcame the doubts of men and difficulties of the material; a grim patience that refused to abandon hope even in the blank spaces of dull stagnation and dreary vigilance. If an institution has stood, we assume that it must in some way or another be harmonious with the divine purpose of the world.

American union, order and good husbandry of the estate make so strong a vision, the memory of enmity and defeat is by comparison so faint a shadow, that no competition is possible between them. In our tribute, therefore, to Washington and Hamilton, nothing is kept back. And even in the case of Germany, which is more recent, our admiration for the great minister who, with so great odds against him, crowned his sovereign and his policy of union in the Hall of Mirrors is not hindered by any conflict of national aims. The reason is not difficult to find. These men, in their various ways, did the work which, when once it is done, the world readily acknowledges to be the greatest. They subdued the forces of disunion, and reduced the most jealous and reluctant interests to a serviceable harmony.

Hamilton discovered, as others before and since have also discovered, that there are two opposite forces to be reckoned with when it is a question of drawing together a loose federation into a nation or an empire: the centrifugal and the centripetal, the forces of disunion and union.

Local sympathies, as well as the interest of mediocrity, are strongly enlisted on the side of the former. They are in favour of flying apart, of the independence of sections, of devolution and separation. They pretend to be satisfied with some sentimental phrase as a bond of union. Anticipating, in the case of any change, a future all in black, they grow impatient as their imaginations conjure up a picture of the apathy, ignorance and incompetence of a strong central government. Running through everything is a tendency on the part of individuals who are unhopeful or unambitious of distinction on the greater stage to cling to and magnify their offices under a number of smaller sovereignties.

On the other hand, in the minds of the people at large, unconcerned with any thought of posts or privileges, when they judge the matter disinterestedly in a cool hour, the idea of union—the centripetal idea—is ever predominant. The instinct of civilisation, seeking security and justice, is towards co-operation. But it is a vague and inarticulate instinct, easy to overcome by sophistry, or by appeals to prejudice, vanity and discontent. The issue of the contest between these two forces is never a foregone conclusion. Among Americans, at the end of the eighteenth century, the centripetal was victorious. In the British empire, at the beginning of the twentieth, the result is still hanging on the balance.

CHAPTER III

Union and its Difficulties

IN the United States, from the *Declaration of Independence* onwards for twelve years until the constitution was accepted, the sentiment in favour of union in the abstract was practically universal. No man dared get up boldly and proclaim himself an advocate of disintegration. But disputes began so soon as it came to a definition of terms. The end was willed sincerely enough, but not the means to it. In popular debate every plan put forward was riddled with objections. The British people, at any rate, need have little difficulty in understanding such a situation, since for many years they have been living in a similar one. The ordinary man in a serious mood has no hesitation in preferring a firm union to an uncertain union or to disintegration. His view is that ours would be a better empire if it were a real empire; if all its countries were bound inseparably together, sharing their burdens, aiming at a development of the whole, offering the swift opposition of a united government and coherent institutions to every threat of foreign aggression. He would be happier in his mind if he were certain that we were one people as much in times of peace, as at those rare moments of high emotion which are the result of danger, grief, or victory. Such is the natural mood of his mind. He is vague, but altogether sincere. It is not his business to think things out; and the foundations of his belief are therefore easily unsettled by the first fluent person who, having put instinct contemptuously on one side, does his thinking on the squares of a draught-board.

This universal, timid adhesion to the principle of union was the material out of which Washington and Hamilton sought to create a strong nation. The widespread distrust of all means calculated to secure this end was the force which had to be subdued. As in the case of Moses and Aaron, plagues came to their aid; but the achievement of union grew each year more difficult owing to the continuance of disunion. Every inconvenience, distress and disaster was adroitly charged by the opponents of union, not, as they should have been, against the condition of impotence which prevailed, but against the folly, or arrogance, or selfishness, or fraud of each neighbour state. The spirit of criticism among the thirteen separate sovereignties was by this means fanned into prejudice, and prejudice into enmity. When any state for a moment seemed to be favourable to a closer union, its motives were immediately impugned. It was suggested that it sought a mean profit by diminishing the natural advantages of its rivals. New York, rejoicing in a harbour and a judicious tariff, bled its less fortunate neighbours at its leisure, resented as a matter of honour any alteration of so lucrative a system, and made its fiscal independence a condition in every scheme of union. Any suggestion to the contrary was resented as the gospel of spoliation.

The case of New York was no exception. The whole atmosphere was charged with the imputation of mean motives, selfish interests and sordid considerations. Charges and counter-charges of narrowness, provincialism and a lack of generosity were freely bandied about. Certain states, it was alleged, had failed to make a fair contribution to the expenses of the war. Certain others would not bear their proper burden in the cost of government. Some were oblivious to the dangers of foreign aggression, and viewed with apathy the injuries which might thereby accrue to their fellow-members of the confederacy. Some, again, called out for treaties to secure their commerce, but found their reasonable demands obstructed by states which had no interest in trade.

The contemplation of our neighbours' shortcomings is not the likeliest road to union. Hamilton denounced the tendency. Washington dealt with it in the grand manner, looking over its head and affecting to ignore it. To our own ears there is a curious familiarity in the phrases. Narrowness, provincialism, the shirking of burdens, an indifference to the wider issues, are trite enough accusations in our own morning newspapers. There is something startling in the echo of history describing a struggle which took place more than a century ago.

Before we bandy reproaches of this kind it is well to realise that there are dangers in doing so. If the charges were entirely true, which they never are, it would be only a degree less criminal to put them forward. We may be sure that they will speedily beget counter-charges, and we may also be sure that there is another side to our own estimate of our own virtues. The average Briton is convinced that he understands his own character and is the victim of no illusions in regard to it. He sees himself in the looking-glass of his mind a free-handed, hot-tempered, magnanimous fellow; businesslike, incorrigibly tenacious, and entirely free from pedantry, except with regard to the strict interpretation of his own promises. He is, of course, aware that foreign nations affect at times to hold a different opinion; but he believes them to be insincere, or charitably excuses them on the plea of envy, ignorance, or ill-temper.

He is proud of his colonies, but in the ordinary way he does not read their newspapers. If he did, he would be shocked and surprised to find that not only the friends of disintegration, but honest, impatient persons who still cling to the idea of a united empire, regard his character under a different aspect. To a considerable section of the Australian people he is held up weekly as a hypocritical usurer, a grasping mortgagee, eternally preaching sermons about thrift and integrity with the object of securing the punctual payment of interest which is due to him. Even his name suffers the indignity of an addition meant to be unflattering: he is not plain 'John Bull,' but 'John Bull-Cohen.' To many of his South African kinsmen he figured, before the war and possibly to some extent still, as a timid and vacillating professor, arguing ever in phrases and contemptuously ignorant of the facts. In Canada there are many who consider him to be of weak intellect, capable of being 'bluffed' into any sacrifice providing it is at the expense of his friends and not of himself. If John Bull were to go into retreat with a bundle of such criticisms, and were to study them patiently until he came to an understanding of the element of truth there is in each unfavourable picture, he might be less ready to endure the superior and often pharisaical commentaries with which certain newspapers and politicians in his own island are prone to improve every occasion. Finding his own motives misunderstood by the captious sections of colonial opinion, he might coolly consider if perchance the cause of the misunderstanding is not to be found in utterances which he has warmly applauded. Criticism which is not meant to improve a man, but to hurt his feelings and disturb his peace, rarely fails to attain its object. He is less likely to strive after self-improvement than to engage in recrimination, and once this dangerous game begins, the enemies of union, of whom there are many in these kingdoms and throughout the empire, have an easy task in feeding the flame with fresh fuel.

The worst difficulties of Washington and Hamilton were of this class. In their case, however, matters were both more confused and more acute than in our own. There were thirteen critics and thirteen subjects for criticism, and no state was ignorant of the unflattering opinions held of it by its neighbours. It is not hard therefore to sympathise with the wrath of Washington and Hamilton against the mischief-makers. From a frequent contemplation of our own imperfections much good may ensue. From the vigorous analysis and setting forth of the imperfections of persons with whom we wish to make a solemn compact, the method is without merit, and malice is ever on the watch to profit by the evil it creates.

The maker of empire wisely and deliberately miscalculates. He ignores and shuts out from view a thousand plausible arguments and undeniable facts, not because he is without reverence for truth, but because the arguments and facts are useless for his purpose and therefore irrelevant. The complaints of one state against another, even when they were just, Washington viewed as bad building material for the edifice he had it in his mind to construct, and having come to this judgment, he put them quietly aside as often as they came under his hand.

Allowing the case of the United States to be no precedent for our guidance, it must not therefore be assumed that their difficulties were less formidable than our own. Indeed, in many matters of high importance the contrary was the fact. There is no such ill-feeling between the states which compose the British Empire to-day as that which existed between New York or Massachusetts and the respective neighbours of each. There is also a pride which is very serviceable; a pride not merely in the vague idea of an empire which covers all, but a more intimate, keen and particular pride which is taken in the achievements of each member of the empire by all the rest. Had Hamilton been equally fortunate in his conditions, there would have been less distinction in his achievement. It is no exaggeration to say that the hatred of state against state blazed out at various times between 1783 and 1788 with a fury which certainly was never surpassed by the popular feeling against Britain. War was actually threatened, and within an ace of being declared, between members of the confederacy; and not war merely for the sake of State Rights and to prevent the Union, but in order to avenge what were felt to be burning injuries.

In the matter of remoteness from one another and from any common centre, the thirteen states were at an immense disadvantage as compared with ourselves. Whether we consider the time necessary for the transmission of news or for the conveyance of citizens from one point to another; whether we calculate by the danger of the journey or by its relative cost, the conditions upon which Americans had the courage to undertake a union were miserably inferior to our own. We are inclined to think and talk as if telegraphy and railroads had been then invented, and tend unconsciously to compare the case of a new country to-day, where these means of development form part of any reasonable forecast, with that of America at the end of the eighteenth century, where they were not so much as dreamed of.

In 1787 Boston was as far removed from Philadelphia merely in time as New York is to-day from London; South Carolina as remote as Cape Town. Measured in certainty, comfort, or safety of travel, Boston and South Carolina were far further removed from the common centre. Relatively to the standard of wealth, the expense of such journeys was much greater. The remotest dependencies of Great Britain are more accessible to-day than were then the states to north and south along the Atlantic Coast, without reckoning the ironbound separation of the east from the settlements in the Mississippi valley. Bad roads, rivers without bridges or ferries, roving Indians, and democrats who combined principle with plunder in their warfare against men who dared to travel in their own coaches, created an isolation which it is difficult now even to imagine.

But the great inferiority of the Union was in communications. The thought or decision which within a day is now flashed to every main outpost of the British Empire would have taken weeks or months to penetrate into the chief cities of the union. A swift understanding between the states was entirely out of the question. Simultaneous feeling or utterance could not exist. And yet, in spite of this tremendous disadvantage, Americans ventured boldly upon an experiment which has succeeded. The country which at the same moment of time is capable of being stirred by the same impulse throughout its length and breadth, is surely wanting in faith and resolution if it puts forward the plea of miles as an obstacle to union.

CHAPTER IV

Nationality and Empire

THERE is an essential difference between the problem which Hamilton set himself to solve and that which we have to consider at the present time. His aim was to make a nation : our aim is to make an empire. The word 'empire' figures constantly in his writings, but the meaning which he attaches to it is merely that of a vast extent of territory. It is a synonym for a great nation in contrast with a small one. The force of nationality did not enter into his calculations, or if he considered it at all, his object was to nip the idea in the bud. The principle of separate nationality was the enemy of his policy, and he sought by every means in his power to destroy it.

In our case any scheme of empire which should ignore the force of nationalities is predestined to ruin. But it was different with Hamilton. His aim was practicable, and in a great measure, though not altogether, he achieved it. He did not love the states. Their meanness and vanity, in his judgment, had completely overlaid their virtues. He was ruthless to their plea of separate sovereignty, and equally contemptuous of their sentiment for local traditions. His one aim was strong government, for he had suffered much from a weak one. We view the problem with different eyes. Local tradition has a certain degree of sanctity. The principle of nationality is welcomed, not only because it is inevitable, but for the further reason that in the huge body of an empire it is the only means to preserve vitality. If we would we cannot put it on one side, and if we could no one but an academic architect in pasteboard would regard it in the light of an advantage. Nationality is a bugbear and a stumbling-block to the impatient reformer; to the rhetorical man of feeling it is an end in itself; but to the statesman who has the skill to use it, it is possibly a way to the widest and the firmest union the world has ever known.

The one thing which is harder to deal with in our own case than in that of the Americans is nationality. The long growth and establishment of the states, which must be parties to the intended union, are at the same time our hardest problem and our strongest hope. Between the *Declaration of Independence* and the Convention of Philadelphia there was an interval of only twelve years: between the War of Independence and the present time a period of a century and a quarter has elapsed. Hamilton had to deal with saplings that could be pleached and trained. Our task is with older and tougher timber. If the British Colonies possess a less definite sovereignty than the thirteen states, they are much more certainly independent nations. Indifference, faint-heartedness and the obscure vision of our ministers, working in alliance with the estranging seas and the long lapse of time, have built up, during the nineteenth century, a proud and almost a ferocious self-reliance.

The difficulty arising out of the maturity of the timber is the creation of the nineteenth century. That period of time, if we may personify it, was used to think and speak with much complacency of its achievements in the matter of colonial policy. It was firmly persuaded that the main characteristics of this policy were a lofty wisdom and a serene generosity, and that the success of its administration was no less conspicuous than the virtue of its methods.

The new century is like a young heir, confident that he can do better with the estate. Bringing a fresh mind to bear, he jumps to the conclusion that things have been wofully mismanaged and ill-developed, and kept back and under in a thousand ways. Filled with eager projects of improvement he is apt to be irreverent towards the ideas of his predecessor; but it is better that he should be irreverent than a sluggard, content to let everything alone, loving his ease, and well satisfied with his income. It is less important that he should be respectful than that he should be bold; and in a young heir the two qualities are seldom found together.

It is difficult to withhold our sympathy from the impatient thinkers of the new school who demand contemptuously to have the wisdom of the colonial policy of Britain from Grey to Gladstone explained to them. The Radical party alone, during this period, appears to have been possessed firmly by any ideal—the ideal of Bright, which aimed at sending out strong sons into the world, encouraging them to be self-reliant, wishing them as soon as possible to become independent, and hoping sincerely they might turn out a credit to the family.

But this, it is hardly necessary to say, was not the Whig ideal, if indeed the existence of an ideal is not inconsistent with the just conception of a modern Whig. The Whigs, who entertained a timid preference for union in the abstract, were terrified by the least murmur of discontent or threat of separation. In a manner at once lavish and ungracious, grudging yet hasty, they gave away concessions which, by

in while they lasted. At best their wisdom was but negative. It is wise to know what you yourself are unable to do; but it is rash always to assume that the thing is therefore impossible. In this limited sense alone was British colonial policy at all worthy of praise. Being afraid, at least it had the wisdom not to try to appear brave, or to attempt the heroic in anything.

As a result of the wisdom of Whigs and Tories during the nineteenth century our self-governing colonies are independent nations in all but name; or perhaps it would be more true to say, in all but their loyalty to the idea of a united empire, which is in no sense the work either of Whigs or Tories but of destiny. The situation is vastly more complex than that of the American States, and being more complex it demands a simpler solution.

CHAPTER V

Commerce under Two Aspects

HAMILTON is remarkable among statesmen for the wide extent of his endeavours, and fortunate in having left behind him enough work—done, half done, and attempted —to make us certain of the vision which possessed his mind. A commercial system was an important part of his plan of national policy.

He held no brief for manufactures, merchanting, or agriculture. His aim was a balance, and his idea of the duty of the state was to regulate a just and proportionate development all along the line. He was no advocate of protection for the benefit of any trade or interest unless the advantage of the community as a whole appeared to him to be involved in such a course. If it be true that the tendency of modern American legislation has been to consider the prosperity of certain classes as an end in itself, and to ignore the equal and concurrent development of other branches of industry, his name cannot be invoked. The goal of his policy was a nation supplying the whole of its own needs, which should be independent of foreign countries for its means of subsistence and even for its luxuries. The aim may be open to attack on various grounds; but in view of the variety of soil and climate which is covered by the United States, it cannot be set aside on the ground that it was impracticable. Nor can it be argued against him that individual effort would have been adequate to the task, or that there was any hope of accomplishing it without the intervention of the state.

Like Adam Smith, Hamilton was keenly alive to the advantage of the double bargain. Assuming that in any exchange both parties as a rule are benefited, he considered that it was an advantage to any country if both parties were citizens of that country. If a grower of wheat required a pair of boots, it was better if he bought them from an American cobbler than from a German, for then the profits on both transactions remained in the States.

The wealth of a nation, according to his philosophy, could never be gauged merely by an addition of the private fortunes of its inhabitants. It was necessary to regard the manner in which their capital was employed and invested. From the statesman's point of view a man who had a million sterling fixed in foreign securities, of one kind or another, was a much less valuable asset in computing the wealth of the nation than one who was employing the same sum, or even an immensely smaller sum, in mills or farms in his own country. Even if the income of the former citizen were greater in amount, he was still immeasurably inferior in the imperial balance-sheet. The wealth of a community is to be reckoned mainly by the sums which are fixed within its own borders, giving employment to its own workers.

The wealth of individuals, in so far as it is placed abroad, is of little value except to the individual investor and to the fortunate country which he is assisting to develop. The manner of the investment is the all-important question for the statesman whose unit is the nation he is called upon to govern. The mere amount of it is irrelevant. To the economist, on the other hand, who regards the whole world as the unit, and not any single country, the manner is of subordinate interest; the chief object is the amount.

The belief that commerce between nations is a safeguard of peace has had a remarkable influence upon the policy of Britain. The proposition cannot stand historical scrutiny. Commerce has no more to do with peace than it has with war; or perhaps it would be juster to say that in its nature it has much to do with both. So long as the relations of two men or of two nations can be kept mainly to the interchange of goods of one class against goods of another class, commerce is akin to peace, and is a strong influence in maintaining it between the two parties. But when this relation alters, and from being seller and buyer they become rival sellers, it is akin to war. The former of these cases, the peaceful relation of buyers and sellers, held good in the main when Britain first accepted free-trade as a practical rule of statesmanship. We supplied the world with manufactures, and received in return raw materials and food. The wealth of Britain was for the moment admirably served by the new arrangement. Ideas of national development were then unfashionable. Any imperial system, or plan of regulating commerce in order to promote political strength, seemed, in the warmth and effulgence of a sudden prosperity, to be a rude device of antiquated error and more savage times. The policy of Britain from the beginning of the sixteenth to the middle of the nineteenth century was suddenly and somewhat too hastily discovered to have been a colossal error. No authority could save it from derision. No practice, however successful, in Britain or elsewhere, was deemed worthy of respectful consideration.

As years have rolled slowly by, the aspect of things has insensibly undergone a change. The growth of the imperial idea throughout the world, the consolidation of races, hitherto held loosely together by treaties or traditions, have become an articulate ambition. The utility of commerce as a means of binding together, strengthening and developing each separate empire against the world outside it, has gradually come to be accepted everywhere save in our own two islands. The other states which are united under the British crown have unanimously rejected our economic creed, and have used the force of commerce in order to make nations, since it had been despised and discarded for the purpose of making an empire.

Concern for the maximum prosperity of mankind as a whole has ceased to colour with the faintest tinge the policies of nations. The ideal which for a brief time men entertained when the Crystal Palace was set up in Hyde Park, an ideal of national boundaries crumbling into anachronisms, of armies and fleets melting into legend, under the influence of a tepid fraternity and the interchange of commodities, is now everywhere abandoned. It is useless any longer to pretend that commerce with free-trade as her handmaiden can act as a peacemaker when confronted with a universal array of deliberate, vigilant and self-conscious systems. Trade, and all that appertains to it, is recognised by intelligent rulers to be the most powerful instrument of empire. It is restricted indeed, but most lovingly cherished. If it cannot make a full boast of freedom, at least it is prosperous, and to such a degree that many people are in doubt whether under the economic as well as under the political aspect there is not an advantage in restraints on liberty.

In a comparatively short space of time a great change has come over the appearance of international affairs. Before the end of the nineteenth century the greater part of mankind had returned to the views of earlier epochs. The peaceful tendency of commerce is now less triumphantly insisted upon. To foreign competition, rightly or wrongly, are attributed the phenomena of mills standing idle, and a large number of millions of our population on the verge, as it is alleged, of starvation. The explanation may conceivably be erroneous. Not foreign competition, but some accident or folly may be the true cause; but the fact still remains as we have stated it, that commerce appears to the average Englishman of to-day to be less akin to peace than it did to his radiant ancestors in the sixties and seventies. Its accent is no longer friendship, and if it is not actually hostility, it has moved a long way in that direction.

Owing to the growth of the imperial idea on the one hand, and to the rivalry of commerce on the other, the firmest rule of business among private men has risen into a great political importance. The merchant or manufacturer cannot afford to buy in the cheapest market if the cheapest market happens to be the shop of a rival trader. He does not hesitate to put temptation on one side, and to buy at a dearer rate from some independent source, selling for the time being at the meagrest profit rather than strengthen the hands of a competitor. No trader is ignorant of the folly of increasing his rivals' output, enabling him thereby to cheapen still further the cost of his goods by swelling the scale of his operations.

The practice of the individual merchant is not an infallible guide to the statesman who undertakes the regulation of commerce, but it is at least as valuable as the speculations of the student who proceeds upon the single motive of clear-sighted acquisitiveness. In the particular instance, and granting, what it is impossible to deny, the existence of a strong and jealous national objective in other nations, the analogy of the trader appears to apply. Viewing the matter from the political standpoint, taking the nation, and not the world, as the unit whose strength and security it is the business of the statesman to consider, the trade relations of two independent countries stand upon an entirely different basis from those of allied states or of a mother country and her colonies.

Trade relations between the states of the Union in 1787, between the German principalities before 1870, between the various dominions of the British crown to-day, were and are desirable without a single reservation. The danger of strengthening a rival does not enter into the consideration. The empire being the unit in each of these cases, the states, principalities and dominions have a common object—to increase the strength and prosperity of the whole. The policy of free intercourse is obviously sound. Its accomplishment is by comparison more easy. Its results have a reasonable prospect of permanency.

But in dealings with foreign nations, even if we ourselves are exempt from all jealousy and suspicion, and are content to treat the national object as a foolish fetish, the other party to the bargain is animated by a wholly different ambition. For while he is anxious to arrive at any arrangement which may assist the prosperity of his industrial classes, he has at the same time the second and predominant motive to increase the strength of his nation, relatively to the strength of other nations. The joint prosperity of the people of Great Britain and Canada may be fairly assumed to be the object of any wise statesman in either country; but the joint prosperity of Great Britain and Germany is not, as the world is now constituted, nearly so important a consideration as the relative superiority in riches and power of the one empire over the other. Each party is eager to conclude a favourable arrangement for commercial purposes, but will always keep an eye upon the political aim, and be jealous of strengthening the sinews of a rival, or of jeopardising his own empire as an independent, self-contained and self-sufficing unit.

It would be no less absurd than unjust to hold the conclusions of the classical economists up to a cheap scorn. Viewed in a proper relation to public affairs, their labours have been of inestimable value. The quarrel, indeed, is rarely with the men themselves, but with their impatient and shallow misreaders who are unable to discriminate between the principles of a science and the maxims of an art. These disciples insist upon applying the cold conclusions of a study whose matter is the wealth of the world, as if they were practical rules for the government of each particular country. They judge action and test policies in the spirit of some nervous reader of a manual on chemistry who, having ascertained that arsenic is a poison, would therefore refuse to take it as a drug.

In putting forward a plea for the respectful consideration of Hamilton's commercial policy, it is necessary to admit that he is in disagreement with the text-books. The national aim was everything in his philosophy. He had not lived long enough to see political economy uplifted into a religion. He took the science for what it was worth, grateful for what he could get out of it. Orthodoxy and heterodoxy in his day were terms of no meaning in this connection. When it served his purpose he made use of the science, but he would have viewed with astonishment any pretensions in it to dictate a course of political action.

It has happened, rather unfortunately perhaps, that free-trade, which was a conclusion of the economists, has come to be a question between political parties. What is apt to be forgotten is that the doctrine of *laisser faire*, or the devil-take-the-hindmost, was equally an article of their faith in the days of orthodoxy's greatest splendour and authority. Political economy was as confident with regard to free-contract as with regard to free-trade. Socialists have made inroads upon the former doctrine, and no political partisan, however respectful to the early writers, is prepared to take up the position of Cobden in this matter. State regulation, which he denounced and deplored, is become the rule. The fanatics for free-trade have now to bend the knee to the Baal of factory acts and land purchase. Is the one contention truer than the other? From the principles of the classical economists it is certain that the one ensues as inevitably as the other. Logically the one is impossible without the support of the other. And for the purpose of governing a people to their best advantage the one is as unimportant as the other. Both are doomed to be overridden by a wise opportunism which, finding itself face to face with a hotchpotch of human affairs, has to make the best way it can out of the difficulty.

CHAPTER VI

Sovereignty

SOVEREIGNTY is an essential condition of union. The authority of the Continental Congress during and after the War of Independence was not sovereignty. This body had a great nominal dignity. The roll of its functions was sonorous and imposing; but there was no reality, for it lacked the power to enforce its decrees. Compliance depended upon the pleasure of the separate states. Although charged with the conduct of the war, it could levy no taxes.

Although congress was entitled to make treaties, the states could refuse to carry out the terms; nor had they any scruples in exercising their power. Congress could raise foreign loans so long as foreign creditors misunderstood the situation, but was without the means of discharging the debt or collecting the interest. At every turn it was checked and humiliated, till in the end it became a pure farce. Its attitude towards the states was that of a man, hat in hand, recommending, advising, imploring, and usually, after the war had ended, speaking to deaf ears. Without sovereignty, union is merely a figure of speech. The union of hearts, the tie of kinship, a common sentiment, were put forward, then as now, as something more potent than any formal bond. These were the phrases of diffidence, dreading a new departure, or of malice, veiled under a thin civility. From the statesman's point of view they were merely words. So far as they corresponded with any genuine belief, they were but the raw materials of union, and not union itself; a quarry, not a house.

In this important matter of sovereignty we are somewhat further on the way than the Americans in 1787. Our aspiration towards the essential is acknowledged by our affection for the person and office of the King, and to a certain extent by the dignified pre-eminence of the British Cabinet. Popular opinion throughout the empire is not outraged by the idea of monarchy, or even by the thought of a strong central power. But the case with which Hamilton had to deal was very different. Not merely kingship, but any force in government was classed without discrimination under the head of tyranny. Tyranny was even alleged to be a danger inherent in all central power, whether the functions were exercised by one or many; whether the one or many took by inheritance, or were chosen by the broadest democratic suffrage; whether the sovereign authority were elected for life or for a single year. This dread of tyranny was the great fixed idea of the times, and the chief difficulty of the Federalist party was how to overcome it. At every turn we meet with the blind and disheartening argument that mere strength in government is identical with tyranny. Not only on the hustings, but in the speeches and letters of serious men, the question is constantly raised why the states, having but recently concluded a long and ruinous war to get rid of a foreign tyrant, should create and set up a domestic one in its stead. It is argued, with a dreary iteration, that the powers which the British Parliament sought to exercise would be no less odious and intolerable if exercised by a parliament elected by American citizens.

When, however, we come to inquire closely into this matter of sovereignty, we are amazed to find how strong a likeness there is between the States of America before the Union and the British Empire at the present day. The difference lies in the dispositions of the two peoples, not in their political circumstances. In spite of our aspiration towards sovereignty (so strong and universal as almost to amount to a belief that somewhere in the empire a clear sovereignty does actually exist), in spite also of the fact that we are haunted by no fixed idea which confounds strong government with tyranny, we are victims of the same disease. There is no sovereignty. Everything hangs on sentiment, influence and management. In the Three Kingdoms sovereignty so far has not been impaired; but outside these islands it is a very different matter. The theory of the empire seems hardly to have moved a step forward since the War of Independence. Now, as then, the King accepts the advice of the Prime Minister of Great Britain and Ireland. The Prime Ministers of his other dominions have no direct access to his confidence, and he is precluded from acting upon their direction unless with the approval of the British Cabinet. Under the guidance of a dignified committee which meets in Downing Street, he conducts the whole foreign policy of the empire, declares war, or makes peace, or signs treaties whereof the consequences may affect the remotest regions of his realm. Under the same guidance he assents to or rejects the legislation of the self-governing colonies, approves the acts of the Indian Viceroy, and the measures devised by his Colonial Minister for the good government of the crown colonies and territories.

The theory, indeed, of sovereignty is complete and without a flaw, but it is also startling if we view it from a democratic standpoint. The imperial sovereignty which is exercised in the name of the King actually resides in the British Prime Minister, a gentleman who holds his office at the pleasure of the majority of the British House of Commons. Therefore, in the ultimate appeal, a majority of British voters is the supreme power in the empire. One democracy—for the time being the most numerous—holds a sovereignty, not merely over those portions of the King's dominions where, as in the case of India, the form of government is frankly autocratic, but over other democracies whom we think of and who think of themselves as self-governing.

It has been the subject of much discussion whether or not a democracy is capable of exercising the functions of a despot over subject races, and the matter is not yet at rest even with the example of India before our eyes. But what has never been questioned since the War of Independence is that a democracy pretending to a sovereignty over other democracies is either a phantom or the most intolerable of all oppressions.

In regard to the foreign affairs of the empire, sovereignty appears to best advantage. But even here, when carefully examined, its tenure is precarious, its warrant, in reason if not at law, is dubious. The true meaning of the situation is no less painful than it is plain. The most powerful member of a loose confederacy is content to defend her fellow-members from foreign attack for so long as they are willing to acquiesce in her policy. Those whom she so protects are on their part content to acquiesce in her policy, to risk a considerable danger, to forgo their share in an honourable authority, for the solitary advantage of the evasion of a pecuniary burden, if we believe the mischief-makers, or from a loyal confidence in the imperial intention, if we believe our own instincts. But what is clear equally to the optimist and the cynic is that the other states will cease to acquiesce at the moment when our foreign policy has the appearance of being in serious conflict with their interests or their honour. The equilibrium is so unstable that no argument upon tradition can persuade us it has any of the elements of safety. Even with fine weather it is only a miracle that maintains it, and under rain or storm there must be a shifting of the balance that can have no issue but disintegration.

Leaving foreign affairs upon one side, we are equally dismayed by the lack of any efficient check, not merely upon colonial legislation, but also upon purely British legislation. This want may imperil the very existence of the union if there is no power equal to the task of restraint or co-ordination; no courage equal to the exercise of such power; no judgment capable of directing the courage. And such is unfortunately the case. On British legislation there is not even a formal veto, while the veto upon colonial legislation is scrupulously preserved only because it is hardly ever exercised. Even if a colony desired to institute polygamy or slavery, or to practise repudiation, it would be a matter of the utmost delicacy to defeat its

intention. For the exercise of the only veto which exists
is, in plain words, the tyranny of one parliament over
another—of one democracy over another.

The theory of the British constitution is, as it stands,
clearly intolerable, except in disuse. The powers which are
imagined to exist in it would never stand the strain of being
put in force. The exercise of the legal right of veto would
provoke greater and more just resentment than if the matter
lay in the sole discretion of the King. The consequences
being so obvious, we have declined upon a timid make-
believe, and for the sake of peace and goodwill have laid
sovereignty upon the shelf, regardless of the fact that
sovereignty is the very essence of union.

If the government of Great Britain and Ireland, which
we term somewhat grandiosely the Imperial Parliament,
desires anything to be done which requires colonial co-
operation, it must go like the old Continental Congress,
hat in hand, arguing, persuading, cajoling and entreating.
By a fine tradition it has the full dignity of sovereignty; but
in reality it is as impotent as the Continental Congress, and
only less ridiculous because it has learned from experience
the timid wisdom not to court rebuffs.

Our real reliance is upon the sentimental quality of each
great emergency to produce a dramatic co-operation. But
it is wise to remember that in a dramatic impulse, though
there is *élan*, there is not and cannot be much staying-
power. The tie of affection or kinship is the raw material
of union, not union itself. '*Influence*,' said Washington,
'*is not government*.' A power which we refuse to influence
we shall hardly grant to sentiment. The union we complacently acknowledge is a mere shadow—not a political
fact, but a poetical fancy. It has the health of an invalid
who is free from pain so long as he will lie still in one
position. Such is its present frailty, that in a protracted

struggle of varying fortune, it must almost inevitably fall asunder.

The hope and strength of our great empire are in popular government, but the hope will be disappointed and the strength will fail if the need of a true sovereignty be overlooked. Sovereignty can never be secure while it rests upon a confusion of legal formulas and brittle sympathies; but only when it has been founded boldly upon the free and deliberate choice of the citizens of the empire.

CHAPTER VII

The Duties of Empire

MANY ways have been tried to the millennium, but experience has shown that no short cut leads there. There was the way of Rousseau, obliterating boundaries and distinctions by an appeal direct to the heart of humanity; a great aim, that failed because it ignored the things which are Cæsar's. There was the way in more recent times of what has been called the Manchester School, among whose teachers John Bright was incomparably the noblest spirit. As we look back upon the period between 1850 and 1880, we are conscious of his moral force gradually increasing year by year, until finally, having converted not only the rank and file, but the leaders themselves, it came to dominate the policy of the whole Liberal party. The cause of his supremacy does not lie in any argument, but in a quiet dogmatism and the intense faith of a lofty and disinterested character. Almost alone among statesmen he had the courage to be a visionary. He sought peace in a world of many independent states, small or moderate in size, and he viewed commerce in rose-colour as a bond of amity. This way has also failed, partly for the reason that commerce is not any nearer kinsman of peace than it is of war; partly also because, despite his sympathies with the North in the war of Secession, Bright was blind to the centripetal instinct, and negligent of the eternal ambition of great races.

Rousseau saw a short path across a few green fields. Bright's road was somewhat longer, but it was well beaten highway and easy travelling. We have followed it now for two generations with a virtuous fortitude, but if we pause to look around us at the landmarks of the region, their appearance and position are disconcerting. Either they have shifted or else we ourselves have wandered circuitously; for the goal is more remote than when we started upon our journey.

Another way to the millennium has advocates who at least are not open to the reproach of coming to us with their hands full of alluring promises that are to be immediately fulfilled. Their goal is so far off that it can hardly enter into the calculations of any practical man who chooses the road. Only visionaries are confident that the peace of the world can be attained as the result of a balance among a few gigantic empires. But following the analogy of commerce, there is much to be said for their aspiration. Negotiation is always swifter, adjustment easier and less damaging, when the principals are few and great, than when arrangements have to be concluded between a multitude of small and jealous men. All the personal obstacles to a good settlement are much reduced. The main issues become clearer, and interest asserts a greater influence than umbrage. It is therefore not impossible to believe that if there were only a few great empires in the world, a permanent peace might more easily be attained by the methods of wise and reasonable concession, than in the present welter of the competing interests and fantastic pride of innumerable disproportioned principalities.

It has been already stated that the union of the American States is not put forward as a model for the union of the British empire. Pericles' advice to the Athenians may well be borne in mind. "Our state does not enter enviously into ' a comparison with the laws and systems of others. We do ' not imitate them; but rather we provide them with an ' example." If there be a boast in these sentences, it is desirable to remember that there is also a warning. We, who have the right to speak no less proudly, have need to beware of the same danger. As the American States found their own way to union; as the German States followed an entirely different road and arrived at the same goal —so must we look at the facts of our own case and beware of landmarks that are apt to mislead the traveller by a treacherous resemblance. The real usefulness of these instances is less in showing precedents that are safe to follow, than in disclosing to us the true nature of union, which is sovereignty, and its inexorable condition, which is sacrifice.

Any political arrangement in which powers are withheld, or granted upon terms, or are subject to revision at the will of any member of the confederacy, is not a real union, but only an alliance. It is lacking both in stability and permanence; for the assent of the parties to the contract may at any moment be withdrawn. The test of union is the utter sovereignty of the central government, which must be free and able to act directly upon, and to touch, without the favour of any intermediary, the humblest of its citizens in the remotest corner of its dominions. Its subjects are not states but people; and according to the tradition of our race, this power can only be secure and beyond question if the government be the choice of the whole people. Judged by this test, the British empire at the present time is not a political fact, but only a phrase, an influence, or a sentiment. As in the case of the states before the Convention of

Philadelphia, there are in our case abundant materials out of which union may be built; but the same materials, unless they are used with courage and intelligence to this end, may as readily be turned to the opposite purpose, and out of the very virtues of our people a fatal independence may be irrevocably assured.

In the matter of sacrifice there is equally no escape. There is no way round. The separate states must be ready to incur it no less than individual men. Legislatures must be prepared to part with some of their authority, statesmen with much of their consequence, the people themselves, for the moment at any rate, with things which are dear to them. The aim and hope of this sacrifice is an immeasurably greater benefit at some later time. It may happen, as in the case of the American Union, that the advantage will be gained by our own generation; but for a proud nation this is of little moment if our children shall have reason to acknowledge that their fathers were good citizens. But sacrifice, whether of blood, or labour, or dignity, or riches, is the price of a secure union, and it is impossible to escape the payment. America and Germany have paid it, and there is no discordant voice among us in acknowledging their virtue. Japan also has paid it with a splendour of contempt for the present, and of hope in the future, that proves youth to be a quality which the oldest nation may renew. Britain has already paid much on account; but in order that what we inherit from our fathers may be secured to our children, we are bound to fix our eyes, not upon our private advantage, not even upon the immediate prosperity of any particular state, but upon the ultimate strength and happiness of the whole Union of the Empire.

It is well to grasp clearly the conditions of union and to consider, before we make the attempt, what are the main difficulties to be surmounted. But having made our survey, having coolly appraised all the risks and hardships, it is not open to us to make a choice. The right of decision, whether we shall remain where we are or go forward on a bold adventure, is not in our hands. We are confronted, not by alternatives of policy, but by a plain, inexorable duty. We may choose indeed, but not as a merchant chooses between courses which promise a greater or a less gain. Our case is that of a brigade which, receiving orders to assault and capture a position, has a choice only between obedience and dishonour.

With us, as with Hamilton, the single principle which rules over everything is the faithful stewardship of the estate. The plea of prudence will not avail us if we dig in the ground and hide away the talent. While we may readily grant that no task of a like difficulty has ever yet called upon any nation to undertake it, we may also consider that a successful achievement would leave the works of every age far behind it. The knowledge that so great a thing has never yet been done in the history of the world is in itself a reason to the British race for cheerfully attempting it.

When we contemplate the nature of the opportunity 'in all its dimensions of length, breadth, height, and depth,' we tremble at the possibility that it should be missed. The mere numbers of our own people, scattered throughout the empire at the present time, are no measure of our responsibility. The duty of stewardship looks further ahead, at a population that may be, at homesteads that are not yet built, fields that are still unbroken. Few men would wish to shirk the burden of our inheritance, but the confusion is apt to overwhelm our understandings and misguide our efforts. We allow ourselves perhaps to be too much oppressed by the maxim that charity begins at home. We are discouraged when we contemplate the base and huddled poverty of our great cities, and are too ready to turn with impatience upon a teacher who reminds us sternly that this hideous problem is only a part of the cares of empire. It is not the mere weight or number of the burdens that renders them intolerable, but quite as often faults of balance and adjustment. It is easy to pass from pity to despair at the sight of black squalor and hungry discontent if we insist upon regarding these alone. But if the mind's eye be allowed to range 'far and wide' over the field of duty we shall see things in a truer proportion, and may discover that a double load is easier to carry than a single one. If we are responsible for all the misery which is packed in our great towns, we are no less responsible for those wide, unpeopled tracts where fresh winds blow. If England is full of cities where life is sorrowful, where clothing, food and shelter—even air and the light of the sun—are hard to come by, it may be worth a thought whether the true remedy is not to be found in the acceptance of the whole imperial burden, in the development of an inheritance where men and women of our race can live and children be born to them, where the soil is rich with the promise of plenty, and the climate stern enough to keep the vigour of our manhood.

But even if the remedy for social disorders were not to be found in the performance of the imperial duty, that duty remains unaltered. As we sit quietly at home reading the names of places on Mercator's Projection, it is natural to be proud of our ancestors who served under Burleigh or the Pitts. The results of their indomitable efforts lie around us on every side. In the west there is a great Dominion, in the south a great Commonwealth, in the east a great Empire. From Table Mountain to the delta of the Nile there is a chain of states, territories, protectorates, and spheres stretching out on either hand from the Indian Ocean to the Atlantic. There are islands all the world over, some as

large as European states, and strong places in every sea
and on every coast. Our obligation to the sixteenth and
eighteenth centuries is not cancelled or diminished because
the nineteenth, wearied by a struggle that was nearly
fatal, fell asleep, and awoke again to find itself in a hum
of material prosperity which it mistook during fifty years
for the millennium. We are still burdened with the honour
of the stewardship. The nature of our duty has changed,
but the duty itself is plain. The estate is of such vast
extent that it is hard to think of a boundary which it would
be desirable to set farther out, or of a corner that needs to
be rounded off. The period of acquisition may be said to
have ended. The new task is to make a worthy use.

The question which now presses for an answer is—what
can we make of all this? Can we make more if we stand
fast by the ideal of John Bright; if each part goes its own
way, thinking merely of its own immediate advantage, doing
only the duty which lies nearest to its hand, keeping a kind
heart and a smiling face for all men, but for its kinsmen no
more than for strangers? Can we still approve the ideal of
sturdy sons whose destiny is independence?

This solution has been deliberately rejected, not because it
is too arduous, but rather because it is too easy. It does not
cover the whole field of duty. It misses the special meaning
of an opportunity which has offered itself to us alone among
all nations whose history has been preserved. During the
past thirty years a new light has been thrown upon our
affairs. The whole view has changed. Political duties
appear in a different proportion. Independence, bustling
and shouldering its way along, is no longer accepted as the
worthiest aim for each separate member of the union. The
idea of a joint stewardship is gradually imposing itself upon
every earnest mind. The goal is a wide co-operation whose
consequences are fervently believed to be an unexampled

order, prosperity and strength. As the thoughts of the people have become clearer, statesmen have grown less diffident, and not in one state or in one party, but in every state and in all parties, there is a stir and murmur of life. The desire for union is suddenly discovered to be deeply implanted in our hearts. Men are prepared for sacrifices, if only the leaders would understand, and will hardly be satisfied that their object has been attained unless they are called upon for sacrifices. Confidence in the old policy of disintegration is utterly destroyed. Nor will people believe that the new policy of union is to be achieved without an effort. They are suspicious of advice which assures them that true safety is to be found by drifting with the easiest currents. Their minds are fully possessed by the greatness of the endeavour, and they have judged rightly that the difficulties which attend it must be in proportion. A problem of this magnitude, in their opinion, cannot be solved without guidance of the forces. The industrious cupidity of distracted individuals, the energies, ambitions and rivalries of particular states can never carry them to their goal.

The final question with us, as with Hamilton, is how we may convert a voluntary league of states, terminable upon a breath, into a firm union. It is useless to regret what has been done or left undone during the past century; but it is not altogether profitless to consider in what position we might have found ourselves to-day had British policy during that period proceeded on the centripetal instead of on the centrifugal principle.

Few will be found to deny that the empire in such case might already have become a strong political fact; that we might have retained within our own boundaries a vast population which is now lost to us; that the resources of our rapidly accumulating wealth, instead of being lent out to strangers, might have been employed in the development of our own estate, benefiting us not merely in usury, but in the use. For the currents of investment, no less than those of emigration, are capable of being controlled and diverted by an intelligent policy, pursuing a steady and consistent aim.

So much is granted by many who will grant no more. True, they say, we might have had a stronger empire, but we should have attained it by the sacrifice of what is of still higher value. The whole might have gained much, but the parts would have lost more. The spirit of freedom and self-reliance would have been discouraged. The growth of material prosperity might have been arrested.

Granting the sincerity of this doctrine, it is hard to understand how it comes to be held. If we accept it we are compelled also to believe that the malcontents of New York were in the right, and that their own state, and probably the remaining twelve as well, would have thriven better in disunion than bound together. So far as the plea may be tested by arithmetic, it resolves itself into an absurdity; while if we judge it by our sentiments, or by those instincts under whose guidance we go about our daily business, we have to do violence, in accepting it, to every principle upon which we are wont to act in our private affairs. It is no less opposed to all the lessons of individual experience than to those of political history.

"But," it will be said, "in the eagerness of your argument 'the principle of nationality has been overlooked. The 'American Union succeeded because it made a single nation. 'If British Union is to succeed we also must make a single 'nation. An empire which admitted nationality would be 'no true union, and an empire which crushed nationality 'would be intolerable." An empire, according to this theory, is either a ruthless tyranny or an empty abstraction.

Those timid minds who dread the extinction of the national spirit, while they maintain it to be incompatible with a firm union, are apt to ignore the facts which lie nearest to them. The union of Scotland with England has lasted for three centuries if we count from the accession of King James the Sixth; for two centuries if we reckon from the Act of Union. Yet Scotland retains, as England also retains, every characteristic of a proud and self-reliant nation. The national life of Scotland is the growth of a thousand years. For more than ten centuries Scots kings have ruled and Scots pride has remained unbroken. If we were in search of a type to illustrate the meaning of the word 'nation,' we should turn to Scotland. Her nationality is no abstraction, but a tingling reality; a living organism, and not a mere legend of the poets. She has all the stern virtues of a nation and all the fantastic punctilios. The love and fidelity of her children, scattered in the four quarters of the world, are proofs which stand fast against the scorner. Her valour, her arrogance, her belief in her own destiny have not been quenched by the free citizenship of a wider empire. Her traditions have suffered no wound or injury in a loyal co-operation. With the example of Scotland before us it is wise to have confidence. The meaning of Empire to a free people is not a stunting and overshadowing growth, but a proud and willing subordination. Its aim is the security of a great inheritance, and while it will augment the resources and the power of every member of the union, it will also touch each separate state and private citizen with a firmer courage and a finer dignity.

APPENDIX I

JAMES HAMILTON, the father of Alexander Hamilton, was the fourth of eight sons of Alexander Hamilton of Grange, in Ayrshire, by Elizabeth, eldest daughter of Sir Robert Pollock of that Ilk. Alexander Hamilton of Grange was in direct descent from Walter de Hamilton, the second son of Sir David de Hamilton, Dominus de Cadyow, the common ancestor of the elder branches of this famous house, head of the family, and a person of great consideration during the reign of King David II. (He is mentioned as one of the Magnates Scotiæ at a meeting of the Estates held at Scone, 27th March 1371.) The Hamiltons of Cambuskeith received their first grant from King Robert III., *inter* 1390 *et* 1406. To Cambuskeith were added the lands of Grange, as appears from a charter dated 7th May 1588. ARMS: *gules*, a lion rampant *argent*, betwixt three cinquefoils *ermine*. *Crest*: an oak-tree proper. *Motto*: "Viridis et fructifera."—*Memoirs of the House of Hamilton*, John Anderson, 1825, pp. 254-257.

APPENDIX II

CHRONOLOGICAL TABLE

Date.	Age of Hamilton.	Event.
1756		Seven Years' War begins.
1757		[Jan. 11] Alexander Hamilton born
1758	1	
1759	2	Fall of French power in Canada (Quebec taken).
1760	3	Accession of George III.
		Fall of French power in India.
1761	4	Resignation of Pitt the elder.
1762	5	Lord Bute's ministry.
1763	6	Seven Years' War ends (Treaty of Paris).
1764	7	
1765	8	American Stamp Act passed—resistance of the colonies.
		Lord Rockingham's ministry.
1766	9	Stamp Act repealed—Chatham's ministry.
1767	10	American imports taxed.
1768	11	Duke of Grafton's ministry.
1769	12	A. H. apprenticed to Nicholas Cruger.
		Boston occupied by British troops.
1770	13	Lord North's ministry.
		American import duties removed except on tea.
1771	14	
1772	15	[Oct.] A. H. arrives in New York.
1773	16	[Autumn] A. H. enters at King's College (Columbia).
		[Dec.] Boston Tea Riots.
1774	17	[July] A. H. speaks at Meeting in the Fields.
		Continental Congress meets at Philadelphia.

Date.	Age of Hamilton.	Event.

1774   17   [Dec.] A. H. pamphlet, 'Full Vindication.'
Repressive measures passed against American colonies.

1775   18   [Feb.] A. H. pamphlet, 'The Farmer Refuted.'
[April] Skirmish of Lexington.
Americans besiege Boston.
[June] Battle of Bunker Hill.
Washington appointed Commander-in-chief.
A. H. pamphlet, 'Remarks on the Quebec Bill.'
A. H. joins 'Hearts of Oak' Volunteers.
[Dec.] Failure of American attack on Quebec.

1776   19   British evacuate Boston.
[March] A. H. appointed captain of New York company of artillery.
[July 4] Declaration of Independence.
[Aug.] Washington defeated at Brooklyn.
[Dec.] Washington victorious at Trenton and Princeton.
Adam Smith's *Wealth of Nations.*

1777   20   [March] A. H. appointed A.D.C. and Military Secretary to Commander-in-chief with rank of Lieutenant-Colonel.
[Sept.] Washington defeated at the Brandywine and [Oct.] Germantown.
[Oct.] Burgoyne surrenders to Gates at Saratoga.
Conway Cabal begins.

1778   21   Americans enter into alliance with France and Spain.
[May] Death of Chatham.

1779   22   Siege of Gibraltar begins.
[Sept.] French and American attack on Savannah repulsed.

1780   23   [May] British capture Charleston.
A. H.'s first memorandum to Morris on establishment of National Bank.
[July] French reinforcements arrive.
[Sept.] Americans defeated at Camden.
Treachery of Benedict Arnold.
[Dec.] A. H. marries Miss Betsy Schuyler.

Date.	Age of Hamilton.	Event.
1781	24	A. H.'s second memorandum to Morris on establishment of National Bank.
		A. H. resigns Military Secretaryship.
		Second French fleet sails for America.
		Dissensions in American army.
		A. H. begins 'The Continentalist.'
		[Oct.] Surrender of Cornwallis at Yorktown.
		A. H. captures 1st Redoubt.
1782	25	A. H. appointed receiver of Continental Taxes for New York State.
		A. H. elected to Congress.
		A. H. called to the Bar.
		Victories of Rodney.
1783	26	[Jan.] Preliminaries of Peace arranged.
		[Dec.] Pitt the younger's ministry.
1784	27	Americans begin to violate terms of the Treaty of Peace.
1785	28	Conference on waterways at Mount Vernon.
		Paper money.
		Civil war (Shays's Rebellion).
1786	29	Convention of Annapolis.
		A. H. represents New York at Convention.
1787	30	Convention of Philadelphia.
1788	31	Convention of New York state at Poughkeepsie.
		Ratification of constitution by majority of states.
1789	32	Washington elected President.
		[May] Opening of States-General.
		[July] Fall of the Bastille.
		[Sept.] A. H. Secretary of the Treasury.
		[Dec.] Jefferson appointed Secretary of State.
1790	33	A. H. reports on Public Credit.
		A. H.'s Financial Policy accepted.
		Burke's 'Reflections on the French Revolution.'
1791	34	A. H.'s plan for National Bank accepted.
		[June] The flight to Varennes.
		British Minister (Hammond) arrives in U.S.
		American Minister (Pinckney) arrives in England.
		Jefferson's and Madison's opposition to A. H.

Date.	Age of Hamilton.	Event.
1792	35	Washington re-elected President.
		The French Republic proclaimed.
		[April] France declares war on Austria.
		[Sept.] Battle of Valmy.
		[Nov.] Battle of Jemappes.
1793	36	[Jan.] Execution of Louis XVI.
		France declares war on Britain and Holland.
		Washington issues 'Declaration of Neutrality.'
		A. H. writes letters of 'Pacificus.'
		Genêt (Minister of France) arrives at Charleston.
		Genêt attacks Washington's administration.
		[Dec. 31] Jefferson resigns.
1794	37	Jay goes to Britain to negotiate treaty.
		[July] Robespierre beheaded.
		Whisky Rebellion.
1795	38	A. H. resigns Secretaryship of the Treasury.
		Jay's Treaty with Great Britain.
		[Oct.] Napoleon fires on Paris mob.
		[Nov.] The Directory.
1796	39	Napoleon's campaign in Italy.
		A. H. writes letters of 'Camillus.'
		A. H. drafts Washington's 'Farewell Address.
1797	40	John Adams elected President.
		[Feb.] Battle of Cape St. Vincent.
		[Oct.] Battle of Camperdown.
1798	41	U.S. prepare for war against France.
		Washington nominated Commander-in-chief.
		A. H. second in command.
		[Aug.] Battle of the Nile.
1799	42	Napoleon First Consul.
		[Dec.] Death of Washington.
1800	43	Presidential Election Tie.
		[June] Battle of Marengo.
		American Treaty with France.
1801	44	Jefferson becomes President and Aaron Burr Vice-President.
		Pitt resigns.
1802	45	[March] Treaty of Amiens.

Date.	Age of Hamilton.	Event.
1803	46	U.S. purchase Louisiana from France.
		[May] Britain declares war on France.
1804	47	[May] Napoleon Emperor.
		[July 11] A. H. killed in a duel with Aaron Burr.
		Pitt's second ministry.

INDEX